SCANDAL

Scandal

The Sexual Politics
of the British Constitution

❧   ❧   ❧

Anna Clark

PRINCETON UNIVERSITY PRESS

Princeton and Oxford

Copyright © 2004 by Princeton University Press
Published by Princeton University Press, 41 William Street, Princeton,
New Jersey 08540
In the United Kingdom: Princeton University Press, 3 Market Place,
Woodstock, Oxfordshire OX20 1SY
All Rights Reserved

Second printing, and first paperback printing, 2006
Paperback ISBN-13: 978-0-691-12601-2
Paperback ISBN-10: 0-691-12601-1

THE LIBRARY OF CONGRESS HAS CATALOGED THE CLOTH EDITION OF
THIS BOOK AS FOLLOWS

Clark, Anna.
Scandal : the sexual politics of the British constitution / Anna Clark.
p.   cm.
Includes bibliographical references and index.
ISBN 0-691-11501-X (acid-free paper)
1. Great Britain—Politics and government—18th century.   2. Sex—Political aspects—
Great Britain—History—18th century.   3. Sex—Political aspects—Great Britain—History—19th century.   4. Political corruption—Great Britain—History—18th century.
5. Political corruption—Great Britain—History—19th century.   6. Great Britain—Politics and government—19th century.   7. Scandals—Great Britain—History—18th century.
8. Scandals—Great Britain—History—19th century.
9. Great Britain—Constitutional history.   I. Title.
DA480 .C567 2003
320.941'082'09033—dc21   2003043349

British Library Cataloging-in-Publication Data is available

This book has been composed in Minion and Bodoni Poster

Printed on acid-free paper. ∞

pup.princeton.edu

Printed in the United States of America

3   5   7   9   10   8   6   4   2

TO ANNE CARTER

CONTENTS

ILLUSTRATIONS

ACKNOWLEDGMENTS

For permission to reproduce illustrations, I would like to thank the British Museum, the Huntington Library, the Public Record Office, and the University of Minnesota. I am grateful to the University of North Carolina at Charlotte, the Huntington Library, and, above all, the University of Minnesota for generously funding the research on which this book is based, and the Humanities Institute of the University of Edinburgh for providing office space and collegiality in the summer of 1998.

Seminar and lecture audiences at the University of North Carolina at Charlotte, the Atlanta Labor History seminar, the University of North Texas, the University of North Carolina at Chapel Hill, the University of Tennessee, the Institute for Historical Research, Warwick University, the University of Essex, Purdue University, the University of Missouri, the University of Wisconsin, and the University of Minnesota have all made helpful suggestions for different chapters. I would like to express my gratitude to Dror Wahrman, Marilyn Morris, Judith Bennett, Melinda Zook, John Bohstedt, Suzanne Desan, Ted Koditschek, Ian Fletcher, Catherine Hall, and Leonore Davidoff for inviting me to speak and for their useful comments on my chapters. At the University of Minnesota, I have derived intellectual sustenance from discussing my work with many of my colleagues, especially M. J. Maynes, Eric Weitz, Thomas Wolfe, John Watkins, Andy Elfenbein, and Juliette Cherbuliez, and from presenting my work to the Center for Advanced Feminist Studies, the Comparative Women's History Workshop, and the Theorizing Early Modern Sovereignty and the Engendering Politics groups of the Humanities Institute.

Many archivists and librarians helped in this work, especially Carol Urness, former Curator of the Bell Library, and Donald Clay Johnson, Curator, Ames Library of South Asia, both at the University of Minnesota; Elizabeth Dunn at the Duke University Library Special Collections; the librarians and photo staff of the Huntington Library; at the British Library, the staff of the manuscripts department and the India Office Library; and archivists at Somerset, Norfolk and Norwich, Kent, Hertfordshire, and Dorset Record Offices.

The three readers for Princeton University Press improved the book enormously with their critiques. James Epstein brought his expertise on radicalism and the constitution, Cynthia Herrup her own insights into seventeenth-century scandal, and an anonymous third reader crucial suggestions for background in eighteenth-century literature and definitions of scandal. At Princeton University Press, Brigitta van Rheinberg's editing clarified and enlivened the book and helped move it away from historiographical obscurity.

I am very grateful to John Watkins, Andy Elfenbein, and Ted Koditschek for reading my penultimate draft thoroughly and making many helpful suggestions. Lisa Disch, Kirsten Fischer, Jean O'Brien, Juliette Cherbuliez, and Jennifer Pierce critiqued several chapters and brought insights from their different disciplines. John Smail was very helpful to this project in its early stages. Marilyn Morris and Clare Midgeley read early drafts of some chapters and provided useful comments. P. J. Marshall kindly read an early version of chapter 4 and corrected many (although I am sure not all) errors concerning the eighteenth-century British empire in India. Jane Rendall, Eliga Gould, Andy Elfenbein, Marilyn Morris, Jim Tracy, and Elaine Tyler May sent me their forthcoming or unpublished work. My mother, Sylvia Clark, proofread the final manuscript. Dena Leiter helped me clarify the introduction. I am grateful for the hospitality and support of Alison Oram, and Chris Dymkowksi and Pauline Gooderson in England. My family continues to be supportive of my work.

Above all, Anne Carter has read many versions of most chapters and improved the book and my life with her humor, intelligence, and love. The book is dedicated to her with my gratitude.

ABBREVIATIONS

BL   British Library

BMC   *Catalogue of Personal and Political Satires Preserved in the Department of Prints and Drawings in the British Museum.* 11 vols. London: British Museum, 1952.

EIC   East India Company

PRO   Public Record Office

SCANDAL

Introduction

In 1813, George, the prince regent of England, tried to prevent his wife, Caroline, from seeing their daughter, Charlotte. George hated Caroline, a buxom, flamboyant, gregarious German princess he had been betrothed to sight unseen. They separated a year after the wedding, a few months after Charlotte was born. Not content with banishing Caroline from the court, George had his ministers investigate her for adultery in 1806. This so-called Delicate Investigation cleared Caroline of adultery but rebuked her for unsuitable behavior for a princess, such as sitting on a couch with another man. But George himself had long been notorious for lavishing taxpayers' money on mistresses, palaces, gambling, horse racing, and banquets. In 1811, he took on more serious responsibilities as regent when his father, George III, finally lapsed into permanent dementia.

The prince regent persisted in his vendetta against his wife and daughter. In 1813, when their daughter Charlotte was seventeen, she began demanding more freedom, supported by her mother. In response, George tried to reopen the investigation into Caroline to prove her an unfit mother. He confined Charlotte to a lodge on the outskirts of Windsor, visited only by her grandmother once a week. Undeterred, Charlotte escaped from Windsor to be with her mother.[1] Crowds cheered the royal princess and jeered at the king. Opposition politicians supported Caroline and Charlotte in Parliament, and public meetings applauded the princesses and denounced the regent.

Today, we often lament that such minor affairs become huge scandals, contaminating the public world of politics with private lives. Sex scandals seem trivial and prurient, unworthy of the attention they excite, in contrast to financial or political scandals, which involve crucial public issues. But this book will concentrate on sex scandals in order to argue for their significance. Scandals force us to question the division between the public and the private. This distinction, of course, is one of the foundations of modern political thought, but as feminists have long demonstrated, it is a shaky one.[2] Sex scandals could become symbols for larger political concerns.

Finally, these scandals could have an impact on politics by triggering political mobilization around these issues.

Sex scandals sustain the public's interest because they reflect a society fissured by disagreements over sexual morality. To incite scandal, after all, is to behave in a scandalous manner, inappropriate to one's social role. But in the eighteenth century, sexual morality was confusing and changing.[3] Old ideas that viewed women as insatiably sexual coexisted with new doctrines of female passionlessness.[4] Many religious people believed in the values of chastity, temperance, and self-control. Others squandered their fortunes on gambling, and took mistresses or lovers as a matter of course. While scandal stereotyped such behavior as characteristic of high society, it cut across class lines: some middle-class people, and many laboring people, formed common-law marriages and drank heavily. Scandal erupted because people could not agree on sexual morality. For some, Caroline behaved just like other aristocratic women by entertaining men alone; for others, this proved her immorality.

Scandals also focused on the question of privacy. In the eighteenth century, the very idea of privacy was fairly new. Many religious people believed that private virtues were the foundation of public life: they believed a good citizen must be a good husband and father. But George's supporters claimed that his private life was irrelevant, that he had a right to private pleasures while enjoying the respect of his public office as regent. This flagrant example of the double standard also exposes the inequity at the heart of the supposed division between public and private. The prince regent flaunted his mistresses but viciously violated the privacy of two women: Caroline and Charlotte. He wanted to seclude his wife and daughter in the home, while he enjoyed public life. Women were to remain in private but had no right to privacy: Caroline's every friendship was investigated. Caroline, however, boldly challenged the double standard.

Rumors and gossip circulate all the time behind the scenes, but they mutate into scandals only when an instigator seizes (or invents) a secret and brings it to the public's attention. The secret becomes a scandal when it triggers a widespread public controversy. This book is concerned with those sex scandals that became intertwined with the politics of the day, when rumors about a political figure's personal life contributed to wider debates. Sometimes scandalous rumors helped to fuel a larger political campaign, but sometimes the scandal itself sparked off a political firestorm. Why do some scandals take off and profoundly affect politics, while other scandalous rumors fail to persuade public opinion? The answer has to do with the instigator's ability to sustain his or her credibility, to use the scandal to symbolize wider political causes and mobilize public opinion.

Scandals raise the question of what politics is really about. Is it a matter of politicians contending for individual or party advancement out of their own ambition, stirring up public excitement with emotion? Or is it a matter of principles, ideals, and policy? Political entrepreneurs can use scandal as a political weapon in their own careers.[5] Instigators of scandal reveal—or invent—sexual secrets at a particular moment, distracting attention from other issues or linking scandals with their own political agendas. In 1813, politician Henry Brougham, who opposed the Tory government, brought Caroline's case before the public in order to gain advantage for his own Whig party. Scandals often seem to exemplify the worst of trivial, sordid, opportunistic politics.

Critics often wish that politics was an idealized realm where rational people discuss important issues; some have envisioned the eighteenth century as such a time, when bewigged gentlemen sat in coffeehouses calmly expounding on political philosophy and members of Parliament spoke with erudition and dignity.[6] In fact, the eighteenth-century political world was just as squalid as our own. Politicians hurled venomous insults at each other, laughed at their enemies, and collapsed in tears on the floor of Parliament; radicals spread scurrilous rumors, and mobs rioted in the streets.

Yet scandal did not necessarily corrupt eighteenth-century politics with trivial issues; in fact, scandal opened up politics by revealing corruption and by making political debate accessible to a wider audience. Scandals can serve as a bridge from one version of politics to another; for instance, opportunistic rumors can inspire interest in larger political causes. Scandal sometimes fuels the democratic process, drawing people into politics, whereas arid, abstract discussions might keep them out.

The instigators of scandal can expose a politician or public figure as motivated not by lofty ideals but by sordid private concerns. In the early nineteenth century, the ruler was supposed to use his influence for the public good, not his personal interest. Reformers portrayed the prince regent as a hypocrite for persecuting his wife for adultery while he demanded that the government grant lucrative offices to the relatives of his mistresses. In doing so, they critiqued the entire system of influence and patronage. How could the monarch's patronage be seen as legitimate if he was secretly controlled by those who manipulated his sexual desires?

Sex scandals can communicate political issues to people usually uninterested in politics because, unlike complicated and hard-to-follow financial scandals, they can be told through familiar stories of broken hearts, broken families, broken marriages.[7] For instance, by confining his daughter to a remote lodge, Prince George resembled the tyrannical fathers of gothic novels. These stories can also provide symbols for larger political issues. When George began his quarrel with his daughter, many Britons already blamed him for political corruption and high taxes. Reformers claimed that he treated his daughter just as badly as he treated his people; they celebrated Caroline and Charlotte in order to denigrate the prince.

Radicals and conservatives tended to use sex to symbolize wider political issues in somewhat different ways. Radicals equated the ruler's excessive lust and unbridled, unconstitutional power. They feared his private interests and family quarrels would contaminate the public good of the state. Scandalous satires and caricatures also undercut the respect and awe surrounding the monarch; for instance, caricatures depicted the prince regent as a corpulent, half-drunk, blubbery creature unable to focus on affairs of state.[8] For conservatives, sexual affairs threatened to disorder the hierarchy of family, society, and state. For instance, supporters of the prince regent equated Caroline's defiance of her husband with radical challenges to the throne. They caricatured her as a blowzy prostitute all too friendly with the servants.

Scandals had their greatest impact when activists were able to link personal problems with larger political issues and to mobilize public opinion in protest. For instance, people met in London, and indeed all over the country, to write addresses supporting Caroline. The radicals linked Caroline's fate to the persistent problems of corruption, which fattened the rich at a time when the poor suffered under the hardship of war.[9] The freeholders of Middlesex blamed the treatment of Caroline and Charlotte on the "defective state of representation." They opposed "the detestable oligarchy of Great Britain, united in one impenetrable Phalanx, against the Cause of her Royal Mother, [and] . . . the abused People of England."[10] By meeting together in support of a royal princess, they could also discuss the cause of parliamentary reform and criticize the war against Napoleon.

British politicians feared such mobilization. After all, British critics had argued that decadence and immorality contributed to the French Revolution. They had heard of the scandals over Marie Antoinette's lovers and knew that their own ruling elite was vulnerable. Historians have demonstrated that over the course of the eighteenth century, scandals undermined the legitimacy of the French monarchy. Enlightenment writers blamed female political influence for corruption at court and alleged that sexual whims and personal connections determined policy and patronage.[11] As the French Revolution loomed, a flood of private scandals served to discredit the aristocracy in the eyes of the public.[12] Obscene pamphlets stripped the monarchy of its sacred aura by portraying the king, queen, and aristocracy in an amazing variety of sexual combinations. Lynn Hunt has argued that the very violence and obscenity of these scandalous works made it possible for the revolutionaries to execute the king.[13]

Scandals also played a significant role in eighteenth- and early nineteenth-century British politics. Of course, the British avoided revolution in the late eighteenth century. Several historians assert that Britain did not fall prey to revolution at that time because it enjoyed a conservative consensus.[14] This book, in contrast, will argue that British society was racked by conflict over how it was to be governed. Scandals in Britain illuminated a central debate of eighteenth-century politics: Should the personal influence of royals and aristocrats determine politics, or should public opinion and the public good shape political action?

On one hand, the idea of the public good shaped the structure of the British government in the eighteenth century. Britain became a strong state through creating efficient institutions such as a powerful navy and a bureaucracy that raised considerable revenue to fund it.[15] Parliament maintained its legitimacy by claiming to represent the people. After 1688, the king was a constitutional monarch who shared his power with Parliament.

Yet personal and familial relationships still structured politics, both literally and metaphorically, which is why scandal was so important. The king retained much patronage power and could choose his own ministers. An aristocratic oligarchy controlled Parliament through family connections and personal influence. The monarchy and aristocracy claimed that when they bestowed patronage, they rewarded merit and knit society together. Indeed, many historians argue that deference upheld the hierarchy of eighteenth-century society.[16]

Eighteenth-century reformers asserted that family dynasties should have nothing to do with politics. Government, they argued, should operate not through personal influence and patronage but on the basis of transparency, reason, merit, purity, and virtue.[17] The very strength of Britain's parliamentary ideal and state bureaucracy made the continuation of patronage and influence more outrageous because it undermined the efficiency of the government. They wanted to open up Parliament so that members would not be chosen because they married into a great family, obtained the favor of a noble lord's mistress, or bribed the voters. If reformers could claim that lust, rather than benevolence, motivated a monarch's patronage, they could undercut his credibility—or perhaps even the whole system.

More specifically, the scandals with which this book is concerned raised several important constitutional issues. According to traditional ideas, the constitution was balanced between king, lords, and commons. But the constitution was partially unwritten, and it could be debated. Three issues persisted in the eighteenth century: the role of the monarch, the role of Parliament, and the role of the people and public opinion.

The monarchy was always particularly vulnerable to sex scandals because it required the legitimate procreation of heirs through royal marriages. Monarchs also stressed their personal character by using images of the king as father to justify their power. In the seventeenth century, the Stuart dynasty used patriarchal thought to legitimate its claims to absolute rule, buttressed by the theories of Robert Filmer.[18] But personal scandals could undermine the image of the king as a stern patriarch—and the philosophy of absolutism that lay behind it. For instance, rumors circulated that James I bestowed patronage on his male favorite, Buckingham, because he desired him, not because he was meritorious.[19] Sexual scandal played a role in destroying the reign of James II in 1688, when rumors circulated that his Catholic heir was an imposter smuggled into the queen's bed in a warming pan. This scandal contributed to the larger issues of religious conflict, royal sovereignty, and parliamentary power.[20] After the Glorious Revolution of 1688, in which James II was forced to flee, Britain became a constitutional monarchy.[21] No longer could a monarch easily use the image of king as father to justify absolute power, especially after John Locke refuted Filmer's theories: a king was not a father, he argued, and his subjects were not children but citizens who had a right to consent to their government.

In the eighteenth century, the monarch was supposed to rule in partnership with Parliament, following the law and the public good rather than his own personal inclinations. When George III revived the image of the king as a good father, he wanted to be seen not as an authoritarian, absolutist father but as a nurturing parent.[22] However, radicals used scandal to portray the king as an oriental despot, undercutting the image of the king as father. The theme of oriental despotism linked scandalous images to a political critique. The early eighteenth-century French philosopher Charles Montesquieu articulated this theory by claiming that oriental despots acted on their passions instead of ruling according to law. This theory outrageously generalized about Asian rulers and contributed to Britain's imperial quest. Montesquieu held up Britain as an ideal constitutional monarchy, in contrast to the horrors of despotism.[23] But Britons also feared that such despotism could infect their own polity. Radicals used sexual scandals to allege that British monarchs, such as George IV, were becoming oriental despots, for instance, when he tried to use Parliament to divorce his wife and when he wielded his power without regard to law. As we shall see, as regent, George fueled the flames of this accusation by building an oriental palace by the sea in Brighton, where he reveled in luxury with his mistresses.

Montesquieu also argued that female political influence could undermine the stability of a state. He wrote that female courtiers enjoyed freedom in European monarchies, but they also had too much power; men had to curry their personal favor in order to get ahead. Female influence therefore undermined the distinction between the public good and private interests. In oriental despotisms, alleged Montesquieu, women were enslaved, but the despot also enslaved himself to lust, spending all his time with his concubines and ruling the government from within his seraglio. As a result, the intrigues of harem women could contaminate the state. Montesquieu warned that European monarchs could become despots, especially if they allowed too much influence to female courtiers.[24] Radicals took up this theme, claiming that the king's mistresses exerted excessive political power. In 1816, for instance, a tract claimed that a "female courtier . . . of an intriguing disposition" influenced the prince regent to push through "many measures which were obnoxious to the people."[25] It was always easy to discredit a politician by claiming he was controlled by a woman, since female political influence never seemed quite legitimate, especially if it was motivated by sex.

The theme of illicit sexual influence could be used to symbolize Parliament's struggle with the monarch. Although the king had the right to choose his own ministers, Parliament might resist his power if he selected a man whom Parliament did not support.[26] The king's opponents could undercut the legitimacy of his ministers by spreading scandalous rumors that they were appointed because of "backstairs influence," "secret influence," or—worst of all—"petticoat influence." As we shall see in chapter 2, radical politician John Wilkes claimed that the king's mother compelled her son to choose her lover Lord Bute as prime minister.

Aristocratic dominance over Parliament could also incite scandal. The general term "aristocracy" included both the nobility and the gentry, accurately reflecting their status as the governing elite.[27] For the aristocracy, the "family" meant the dynasty, which transmitted fortunes, land, and political power.[28] These great families used their wealth and influence to create networks of loyal followers and kin, all defined as part of their dynastic interest. Because family, social, and personal connections were so important, some aristocratic women could exercise political influence through patronage and relationships with powerful men. The peerage (the nobility) controlled the House of Lords, but the House of Commons was supposed to represent the people who elected it. In fact, the landed aristocracy chose many members of the House of Commons. In local areas, they earned the deference of voters through philanthropy and patronage. Aristocratic ladies played an important role in maintaining good relations with constituencies.[29]

Aristocratic dominance coexisted with a strong tradition of electoral independence. In some urban constituencies the electorate represented a cross section of the population, ranging from laborers and artisans to wealthy farmers and merchants. But only 17.9 percent of adult men could vote in the late eighteenth century, most voters had to meet some property qualification, and the lack of a secret ballot left them vulnerable to pressure by landlords and employers.[30] If voters did not defer to great families, candidates could attempt to coerce them with bribery and threats. Voters expressed their resentment at the aristocracy's personal influence by generating insulting rumors during elections (and, of course, rival candidates took full advantage of such scandals). For instance, voters sometimes expressed hostility toward the "petticoat influence" of the ladies who participated in elections.

Scandals inspired debates over the nature and composition of public opinion. Members of Parliament often expressed the traditional constitutional view that the House of Commons was the only legitimate representative of the people.[31] Once they had chosen their representatives, the people did not have the official right to associate or even to discuss political ideas; Parliament could even imprison those who criticized it. Despite this conservative opinion, throughout the eighteenth century, politicians had to recognize that wider public opinion was a significant force. If Parliament did not respond to a scandal by investigating and clearing up corruption, public opinion could claim that it was not serving the public good, and that the people needed to provide an alternative to Parliament to compel political change.

Of course, given the lack of polls, it is impossible to measure accurately shifts in public opinion in the eighteenth century, but the press from that time can give some insight. Scores of newspapers in London and the provinces circulated political news and social gossip as well as reports of commerce and trade, reaching mainly the middle and upper classes. Britons avidly read and debated the latest newspapers and pamphlets in coffeehouses. Caricatures were especially important to scandal because they ridiculed politicians and used sexual and other kinds of symbolism to refer to larger political issues. Middle- and upper-class Britons collected these prints to paste on their walls or compile in albums, to amuse party guests; ruder caricatures decorated privy walls. Laboring people could gaze at caricatures in shop windows; printers produced satirical ballads for them, and after 1800, caricatures began to reach the poor.[32]

The government did not precensor publications, but it, as well as opposition parties, often tried to manipulate public opinion by subsidizing newspaper publishers and pamphleteers. Politicians could pay to have scandals embarrassing their enemies inserted into newspapers—or suppress scandals with bribes. The government, however, also exercised its power to prosecute publishers for printing libel, sedition, and blasphemy. But many newspapers remained independent.[33] Scandal, especially sexual scandal, could overcome government efforts at censorship or manipulation. Newspapers needed to publish accounts of such scandals or lose circulation, and by persecuting sexual rumors the government spread such embarrassing gossip. Censorship became its own scandal. When newspapers defeated censorship, they expanded freedom of the press.

Who had the right to participate in public opinion? This question was hotly contested, especially from the 1760s onwards. For conservatives, legitimate public opinion would include the nobility, gentry, the very wealthy, and the clerics and intellectuals who associated with them.[34] But the middling sort—hardworking tradesmen, professionals, farmers, and merchants—felt they had the right to express their opinions by voting if they had the franchise, and by demonstrating if they did not. Until the 1790s, they did not often articulate their identity as "middle-class," as a coherent group who deserved rights, but they expressed hostility to the aristocracy.[35] Early in the eighteenth century, middle-class shopkeepers, merchants, and professionals viewed themselves as virtuous, religious, hardworking, sober, and chaste, in contrast to an aristocracy they saw as corrupt, decadent, lazy, and effeminate. Novels such as Samuel Richardson's *Clarissa* encouraged this view by telling the story of a wicked aristocratic libertine who kidnapped and raped a virtuous, middle-class young woman. Of course, middle-class young men were just as likely as their aristocratic peers to engage in libertine behavior.[36] Yet a gentlemen could use family connections and prestige to escape the consequences of his actions, whereas middle-class men relied on their reputations to gain credit. Middle-class men became frustrated when they found their way to advancement blocked, despite hard work and education, when aristocratic gentlemen could leapfrog over them due to family influence and patronage. Critics often declared that the political virtue of the nation resided in the independent middle class. The aristocratic elites in part held on to power because they acknowledged the validity of middle-class values, protected middle-class property, and encouraged commerce, as Paul Langford notes.[37] Scandals could break apart this tenuous aristocratic connection with the middle class.

Scandals could overcome political apathy and trigger widespread public meetings to demand change. After all, scandals had a long-lasting impact on politics only if they resulted in the organization and mobilization of public opinion to pressure Parliament. And during this period, people of the middling sort (often together with the more independent, less wealthy gentry) began to organize themselves into associations that gave them an alternative power base to Parliament and local aristocratic control.[38] These associations provided the tinder that scandal could spark into mobilizing public opinion.

Most of the scandals to be described here did not inspire laboring people to organize. Laboring people tended to be more concerned with issues such as food prices, press gangs, enclosure, and wages than with the personal peccadilloes of the great.[39] However, by the end of the story—when George became king and Caroline tried to claim her throne—radical working-class activists linked their political oppression with the queen's marital woes.[40]

The study of scandals can also give us insight into the role of women in the political public. Some historians have asserted that women gained an increasing place in the public sphere in the eighteenth century.[41] Indeed, some elite eighteenth-century women published novels and poetry, a few became successful playwrights, and many enjoyed access to the burgeoning world of public entertainments in the flourishing cities. Some aristocratic women exerted personal political clout through their family and social connections. For those who accepted the aristocratic system of patronage, their clout was perfectly acceptable. But radicals who rejected the system of patronage could raise the cry "petticoat influence" against them. Portraying influential ladies as corrupt and power hungry, they linked traditional ideas of women as insatiably sexual with the fear of female political power. Of course, critics vastly exaggerated female political influence in order to undercut their real targets: the king's power, a political party, or even the aristocracy in general. As an alternative to petticoat influence, some women could exercise intellectual influence instead. By the later eighteenth century, some women claimed the right to participate in politics as reasonable beings acting in the public good. Others wished to replace aristocratic petticoat influence with female domestic influence. However, scandals were often directed at any women who took a political role or displayed personal autonomy.

Masculinity was also an important issue in eighteenth-century scandals.[42] Masculinity, for instance, often symbolized power and authority. However, as conceptions of proper authority changed, so did the masculine images of power: Was the proper man the father, the soldier, the citizen? Radicals could challenge the image of the king as father by celebrating the independent man, whose love of women, wine, and song proved his love of liberty. But conservatives stirred up scandal against libertines, portraying them as irresponsible scoundrels who attacked the stability of family and state. Three different ways of thinking in the late eighteenth century generated competing understandings of masculinity and femininity, the public and the private, therefore influencing the different ways people reacted to scandal. One of the most influential political philosophies of the eighteenth century was classical republicanism. Not to be confused with the American political party, these thinkers idealized the ancient Roman republic.[43] As in Rome, they believed that citizens must focus on the public good and actively participate in politics, instead of allowing the monarch to control them. They emulated the *virtù* of the ancient Roman citizen. While related to our modern notion of "virtue," *virtù* derived from *vir*, or masculinity, similar to virility, and connoted strength, courage, and aggression, the virtues of a soldier.[44] Classical republicans celebrated the masculinity of independent radicals who defied the court. Conversely, they accused their enemies of "effeminacy," one of the most common political insults of the eighteenth century. Effeminacy generally connoted self-indulgence in luxury and unmanly behavior. The effeminate man might be accused of associating too much with women, having too many mistresses—and/or engaging in sex with men, which eighteenth-century people termed "sodomy."[45] This self-indulgence, it was feared, could lead to corruption. During the 1750s, effeminacy was also commonly linked with the French influence over the aristocracy and fear of French power.[46] Scandals about homoerotic behavior therefore acquired a wider political meaning.

For classical republicans, scandal resulted when private vices contaminated the public world. Emulating the ancient Roman republic, they believed that citizens must sacrifice their private family interests for the public good.[47] They worried that the private interests of aristocratic personal connections and family-based patronage could corrupt the political world.[48] For them, the public was the realm where disinterested, rational, virtuous men should serve the common good, joining together as equals; the private was the family and sexual relations, governed by hierarchy, emotion, and personal interests.[49] Sexuality tended to represent private, selfish desires that blurred the boundaries between public and private. However, while criticizing the great noble families that dominated court politics, classical republicans believed that independent country gentlemen should lead society, regarding tradesmen and the laboring poor, let alone women, as incapable of political reason.

A competing eighteenth-century philosophy—that of sensibility—focused on the individual's introspection, emotion, and empathy with others,

instead of virile competition.[50] For those influenced by sensibility, scandals proved that the public world of politics was irredeemably tainted and that the basis of morality lay in the private world of the family. The philosophy of sensibility was expressed not in political strife but in novels and poetry. In the tales of sensibility, a sensitive, moral hero would become disillusioned by the corrupt world of politics and retreat to his country seat, where he could serve the public good through philanthropy. People influenced by this philosophy discussed literature and ideas in their genteel salons, but they found politics contaminating. For them, the ideal man was not the belligerent soldier but the domesticated father. The literature of sensibility also developed an alternative ideal of femininity to "petticoat influence": the refined, pure lady who listened intelligently in the salons and penned poetry in her boudoir. However, if women entered politics, they could be scorned as unfeminine.[51]

By the late eighteenth century, the increasing influence of Evangelical religion built upon the ideas of sensibility but intensified its moral message. Evangelicalism was the religion of the heart: searching for an authentic, soulful spirituality, yearning after salvation, experiencing intense anxiety about sin, going out to convert new souls.[52] Some Evangelicals remained within the state Church of England, but others became Dissenters, such as Methodists or Baptists. At first, most Evangelicals focused on spirituality and stayed out of politics; the "world" seemed distracting from union with God. By the late eighteenth century, Evangelicals started to enter politics through the humanitarian movement. In the 1790s, they feared that recurring scandals about the sexual behavior of the aristocracy and royal princes would undermine the social order. They used these scandals to insist that Britain's elite must reform itself, must bring the values of the private world of the family into the public world of politics.

SCANDAL AND EIGHTEENTH-CENTURY POLITICS

Throughout the eighteenth century, scandals erupted concerning the role of the monarchy, the aristocracy, and public opinion, but until 1763 they failed to pose a serious threat to the political order. How and why were scandals contained in the first part of the eighteenth century, and what changed?

Until George III, eighteenth-century monarchs—Anne, George I, and George II—were relatively weak. This weakness could lead to scandal if they were perceived as controlled by their favorites. For instance, Queen Anne caused a scandal when she rejected her favorite, Sarah, Duchess of Marlborough, a prominent Whig, for Abigail Masham, who was more identified with the Tories.[53] Politicians subsidized scurrilous literature which insinuated that Abigail Masham serviced the queen sexually as lady of the bedchamber.[54] The Tory Mary Delariviere Manley novelized the scandal, using "sexual depravity and licentiousness" to "reflect and underscore the political corruption and dishonesty in the public sphere."[55] However, this scandal involved competition over patronage rather than larger constitutional issues.

When Queen Anne died without an heir, Parliament rejected the Stuart descendants of James II; instead, it turned to the Hanoverian dynasty, a line of Protestants from a small German princely state descended from James I. By choosing an alternative to the Stuart dynasty, Parliament also implicitly turned away from the absolute hereditary right of the monarchy and asserted its ultimate authority to choose a dynasty. As a result, it set a precedent for overseeing the private lives of princes.

Tension remained between the view of the two political parties, the Whigs and the Tories, over the philosophy of the monarchy. The Tories celebrated "church and king"—the established Church of England—and the absolute right of hereditary monarchy, while the Whigs took credit for the Glorious Revolution, stressed the power of Parliament, and allowed somewhat more tolerance for the Dissenters. To be sure, they were not like present-day political parties; instead, they functioned as factions, motivated by the search for patronage as much as or more than principle.

One of the great scandals of the eighteenth century, the South Sea bubble, tainted the regime of the first Hanoverian, George I. The bubble originated when the South Sea Company bought shares of the national debt, expecting to pay for it with vast profits from trade with Chile and Peru. The company parlayed these expectations into a pyramid scheme, aided by bribes to royal ministers and the king's mistresses, and propagandists such as Jonathan Swift and Daniel Defoe.[56] When the bubble burst, an outcry over corruption erupted; the fickle luck of the stock market was often portrayed as Fortuna, a seductive yet capricious woman.[57]

Robert Walpole stepped in to contain the scandal. Becoming one of the first politicians to function as prime minister, he took charge of the government in 1721 to cover up corruption, restore the financial stability of the nation, and enable the king to control the Commons. Because George I and then George II were both German, oriented more toward their native Hanover than toward England, Walpole found them easy to manipulate. The influence of the king's mistresses and the favor of George II's queen, Caroline of Anspach, helped Walpole control the monarchs he served.[58]

The press tried to spread scandal about Walpole's court politics. Henry Fielding, the novelist, satirized the alliance of Walpole and Queen Caroline as the "Devil Henpecked," the title of his play.[59] Poets imitated the Roman poet Juvenal to attack Lord Hervey, a courtier, as a sodomite or hermaphrodite, implying he sexually submitted to the minister.[60] But Walpole successfully repressed these scandals. He imposed strict censorship on the theater in 1737 and tried to restrict and bribe the press, paying off male journalists by offering them government offices. Although several female journalists had made their living by spreading political sex scandals in the early eighteenth century, the number of female journalists declined as they lost the outlet of party political writing and could not take advantage of government patronage.[61] Female journalists were denounced as "shameless scribblers" of "libelous memoirs" who as women should not be capable "of such malice or impudence."[62] By the 1740s and 1750s, political journalism and rhetoric deteriorated into squabbles among politicians and squalid attacks on individuals, rather than debates over principle.[63]

Walpole modified the character of Parliament by repressing party conflict. He allowed only the Whigs into the government, keeping them dependent on his favor.[64] The Whigs neglected their principles, becoming an oligarchy, a tightly knit network of men "bound to one another by countless ties of family relationship and mutual obligation." They married off their daughters to each other for political advantage and dispensed patronage in offices to solidify support.[65] Walpole emphasized the idea that the monarch (and his ministers) and the great families of Parliament could be trusted to look after the public good of the nation—but the people should have no voice.[66]

The frequency of elections was reduced and the franchise tightened.[67] Over the course of the century, the percentage of the adult male population who could vote declined from 23.9 percent in 1715 to 14.4 percent in 1831.[68] Urban voters expressed their resentment at "private family interests" and corrupt parliamentary politics. But the opposition generally did not call for an expansion of the franchise. Dominated by independent country gentlemen, they failed to organize a deep base among the middling sort of people. The oligarchies deployed their powers of patronage, deference, and repression to reassert their control in provincial towns and London.[69]

By the late 1730s and 1740s, however, the idea of patriotism caused trouble for the government. Patriotism meant support for the British empire, Protestantism, commerce, and property. Some country gentlemen began to ally themselves with merchants and traders to demand an expansion of empire and victories for British power. They stirred up scandal by accusing the government of incompetence in fighting wars that were necessary for Britain's strength and commercial interests. Public opinion rallied around Admiral Edward Vernon, who defied an incompetent superior, and General John Byng, whom the government falsely accused of malfeasance. Men such as Vernon became militaristic, patriotic, manly heroes whom voters could celebrate while reviling the corrupt, effeminate courtiers of the government. Populist aristocratic candidates could command the votes of those laboring men who enjoyed the franchise and stir up crowds to apply political pressure. The notion of the brave hero defying the effeminate aristocrat deployed a notion of masculine independence that cut across class, as historian Kathleen Wilson observes.[70]

These scandals failed to have a lasting impact for several reasons. The issues they raised could be resolved if the government restored the hero of the scandal, like Admiral Vernon, to his proper place or if justice was served. In elections, charismatic aristocratic leaders could gain popular support against the government without promising any real structural change that would enable more men to vote.

The government distracted attention from these scandals by manipulating the language of patriotism for its own ends. By the 1750s, the prime minister, William Pitt, the elder led Britain to imperial triumphs in the Seven Years' War, gaining popular support for the government.[71] Antiaristocratic protest could be displaced onto anti-French xenophobia.[72] As Linda Colley has brilliantly observed, the government believed that the people should have no voice, but in order to keep power it had to respect the influence of public opinion by stirring up the principle of patriotism.[73] She and other historians assert that this patriotic consensus enabled the government to maintain aristocratic, royal, and clerical domination through the eighteenth century, and even strengthened it after 1760.[74] I will argue, however, that the 1760s was a political turning point.

1763–1821

From the 1760s onward, a series of scandals began to erode the patriotic consensus. Whereas earlier challenges to the royal and aristocratic dominance were limited in scope, late eighteenth-century radicals and reformers sometimes used scandals to demand profound changes in the constitution and the political order. Radicals defined patriotism as loving one's country but opposing the government.[75] The 1760s therefore represented a significant transition in British politics, raising new constitutional issues concerning the monarchy, political parties, parliamentary reform, the press, empire, and the role of women in politics.

The power of the king became controversial, since the new king, George III, took a more active role. He dismissed the Whig oligarchy and exercised his right to choose his own prime minister in 1763. In 1783, he pressured Parliament to dismiss an incumbent ministry he disliked. These actions stirred up constitutional debate about royal power.

Party politics revived. Deprived of office, the Whigs began to function as an opposition party and to some extent resuscitated their principles. They resented the king's imposition of a prime minister unpopular in Parliament. The Whigs were still composed of shifting factions tied together by both personal and dynastic loyalty, but its radical wing tended to emphasize the power of Parliament and resent the prerogatives of the Crown. Yet they were not egalitarian democrats: they regarded the aristocratic Whig dynasties as the natural representatives of the people. The intensification of party conflict, however, meant that more elections were contested, and more voters could express their opinions.

Radicals went far beyond the Whigs to challenge directly the traditional notion that Parliament was the only legitimate forum for public opinion. They used scandal to savagely criticize both the monarchy and Parliament. As a result, the number of newspapers and their circulation expanded exponentially; the number of caricatures exploded, and they became much more defiant and scornful of politicians and royalty.[76] Censorship was often defeated as an unconstitutional infringement on the liberties of the subject.[77] These scandals also helped initiate huge reform movements and waves of associations demanding parliamentary reform from the 1770s onward. These movements went beyond earlier eighteenth-century criticisms of corruption to demand an expansion of the franchise.[78]

As politics opened up, the role of women began to be questioned. On one hand, radicals often used the image of petticoat influence to attack aristocratic corruption. On the other, more women began writing histories and feminist tracts and even organizing themselves into debating societies. Although a few women had written feminist tracts earlier in the century, the role of women became the subject of widespread discussion only in the 1780s and 1790s. But people debated whether the problem was women's rights or women's influence.

The celebration of empire also became controversial. The American war led some to question the equation of the empire with patriotism; for them, patriotism meant defending the Americans against an oppressive government. As Britain expanded its empire into India, critics used scandal to crit-

icize imperial abuse and exploitation. As a result, imperial ideology needed
to be revamped.

This book explores these themes through a series of scandals. Chapter 2
contrasts radical and conservative uses of sexual scandal as a political
weapon. It tells the story of John Wilkes, a radical politician who attacked
George III's constitutional right to appoint his ministers. Wilkes claimed
that sexually voracious women and submissive sodomites controlled the
court. The government turned the weapon of scandal against Wilkes by
prosecuting him for publishing pornography and expelling him from Parliament. For conservatives, Wilkes's sexual libertinism symbolized the
threat his political challenge posed to the hierarchy of British society.
Wilkes equated his libertinism with political liberty and defended his right
to behave as he wished in private. But he failed to defend the right to privacy of his former ally, renowned historian Catherine Macaulay.

Chapter 3 uses scandal to illuminate debates about women in electoral
politics. Recent works have claimed that aristocratic women enjoyed increasing influence over politics in the eighteenth century, most notably
Georgiana, the dazzling duchess of Devonshire. However, this chapter will
argue that the influence of such women over elections did not advance the
interests of women as a whole, only the interests of dynastic aristocratic
power. Furthermore, political influence could be a burden for aristocratic
women, as is apparent from the tragic story of the countess of Strathmore,
whose husband used her family's clout to win an election, but then savagely
abused her to seize her fortune. Other women articulated alternatives to
aristocratic female influence: women of the debating societies began discussing the possibility that women could vote in elections and serve in offices for the public good, not for their family's interests.

Chapter 4 explores how gendered rhetoric reflected different philosophies of empire through the attempt by Edmund Burke to impeach Warren
Hastings, governor-general of Bengal. In an attempt to appeal to a wider
humanitarian public, Burke tried to stir up scandal by alleging that Hastings was responsible for the abuse of Indian princesses. Some see Burke as
a critic of imperialism, but by portraying India as passive and feminine, he
created new justifications for empire. This chapter will also examine why
Burke's scandal spectacularly failed. Although we now think of Burke as the
dignified founding father of conservatism, many contemporaries ridiculed
him as opportunistic and unbalanced, prone to overheated rhetoric and
unfounded accusations.

Chapter 5 shows how scandals about private life acquired a new political
significance in the era of the French Revolution. Scandals about Marie

Antoinette and the British aristocracy undermined the basis for royal and noble dominance. In response, conservatives tried different techniques to redeem the aristocracy. While Edmund Burke defended Marie Antoinette against scandal and bolstered the aristocracy, moralist Hannah More warned the aristocracy to become true Christians or risk losing their rule.

In chapter 6, I will show that female intellectuals such as Mary Wollstonecraft and Hannah More developed very different alternatives to aristocratic petticoat influence: women's rights, or female moral influence. But both become the subject of scandal. This chapter will ask why scandal squelched Wollstonecraft's feminist ideas whereas Hannah More could overcome scandal.

The problem of petticoat influence did not disappear. In chapter 7, I recount the Mary Anne Clarke affair, which exposed the problem of corruption in government patronage. Clarke was the mistress of the duke of York, the king's son and commander in chief of the army. When officers bribed her, he would promote them. After this became public, an investigation revealed that offices were bought and sold not only in the army but also in Parliament and the East India Company. The affair discredited aristocratic patronage, revived the parliamentary reform movement, and impelled the government to begin to clean up corruption.

In chapter 8, I continue this theme by revisiting the Queen Caroline affair, which changed the relationship of the monarchy to public opinion. While historians have looked at this scandal from the point of view of gender and class politics, the constitutional issues it raises have been neglected. In 1820, George IV, notorious for his own adultery, used the House of Lords to attempt to divorce his wife. Even his own ministers thought that he was abusing the constitutional power of the monarch for his own petty, vindictive, personal purposes. This huge controversy generated a debate over the proper role of the monarch: Should he be defended as a symbol of the traditional order of church, king, and empire? Or was his status contingent on his virtue and his service to the people?

Sexual scandals, therefore, can illuminate some of the major themes in eighteenth-century historiography and help change our view of the century. Public opinion was not a unified force united around the empire, but diverse and divided. Conflict, not consensus, characterized the long eighteenth century.

❧   ❧   ❧

Wilkes, Sexuality, and Liberty:
How Scandal Transforms Politics

In 1763, rumors circulated that George III's mother had instructed him to appoint her lover, the Scottish Lord Bute, as his prime minister. The rumors of their love affair were ridiculous—both parties were elderly and notoriously staid—but the gossip spread from the court to the streets.[1] Overnight, papers were plastered on London walls with the slogan "No Petticoat Government, No Scotch favorite."[2]

John Wilkes assiduously spread the scandal about the king's mother—known as the princess dowager—and Bute. But his own morals were open to question. A flamboyant, witty libertine, Wilkes seduced scores of women despite his squinting, ugly face. He also penned pornography, mistreated his wife, and caroused with prostitutes. Why did Wilkes denigrate the morality of the prime minister when he himself was so vulnerable to scandal?

Wilkes spread sexual innuendos with a serious intent. He used these rumors to critique the king's constitutional power, drawing upon the analysis of radical historian Catherine Macaulay. In response, the government turned scandal against him, prosecuting him for blasphemy and sedition, citing his obscene *Essay on Woman*. However, the government's tactic failed to discredit Wilkes. Instead, he stirred up a huge movement for parliamentary reform, raising the constitutional issue of the relation of public opinion to Parliament.

In the resulting battle to win over public opinion, conservatives and radicals used scandal as a weapon against each other, in the process revealing highly contested understandings of the place of the public and private in politics. Wilkes asserted that his private life had nothing to do with his political service. But Wilkes spread scandal about Catherine Macaulay's private life. By contrasting the ability of Wilkes and Macaulay to manipulate and defeat scandal, we shall see how radical definitions of privacy failed to protect women.

WILKES VERSUS THE KING

Wilkes's life reflected the tension between politics as a struggle for interest and politics as principle. His contemporaries debated whether he was just an opportunistic politician, using dirty tricks to revenge himself against his enemies, or an idealistic leader who sacrificed himself for liberty. On one hand, Wilkes was an outsider influenced by Enlightenment ideals. A commoner lacking aristocratic connections, his father was a wealthy distiller and his mother a Dissenter, meaning she did not subscribe to the established church. They could not send the young John to be educated at Oxford, which excluded Dissenters, so they dispatched him across the channel to the university at Leiden. There, he met figures such as the atheist Baron d'Holbach, who exposed him to radical Enlightenment values.

On the other hand, Wilkes used his fortune and his wit to gain entrée into aristocratic culture. During his education, he made useful contacts among aristocratic types, such as Charles Townsend, of the political family, and Thomas Potter, dissolute son of the archbishop of Canterbury. At Sir Francis Dashwood's Medmenham Abbey, Wilkes cavorted with his brother "monks," wittily exchanging obscene Latin bons mots and mocking religion with phallic rituals. He probably wrote the *Essay on Woman* there together with Thomas Potter.[3] Wilkes scorned romantic love: he had been married off to an older woman for her fortune, and, not surprisingly, the marriage failed. They separated, and he allowed her only £200 a year out of her former estate.[4]

At first, Wilkes's outrageous libertinism and Enlightenment sensibility did not interfere with political ambitions. One could play by the rules of the game in public and ridicule them in private. As another famous libertine, Lord Chesterfield, advised his son in his influential published letters, a gentleman should please others by being civil, affable, polished, and polite—but deceive and dissimulate to get his way, especially with women.[5] This polished masculinity also suited the patron-client relationship, which is how Parliament and the court worked at that time. Temple, his patron, teased Wilkes about his amorous adventures with Mrs.—— of Soho on "the flowery paths of Venus" but also expected deference: Wilkes wrote to him, "I am my own man, and Lord Temple's."[6]

Wilkes hoped that these public and private connections would help him obtain a lucrative political office. He entered formal politics by using his wife's fortune to win over the voters of Aylesbury with thousands of pounds. In Parliament, he followed William Pitt, leader of the "patriots" of the 1750s who celebrated imperial conquests and mercantile interests. Pitt directed the Seven Years' War, which opened new avenues for commerce and spread Britain's glory throughout the globe. Britain won many territories in India and the Americas from Spain and France. But it was also an expensive war, and when the new king George III hesitated at extending it, Pitt resigned from office in 1761. Wilkes therefore lost an important patron who could have obtained him an office through personal influence. But Wilkes was not content to wait in the wings; instead, he became a political entrepreneur, beginning his periodical the *North Briton* in 1762 to challenge government policies. And scandal became his political capital.

THE MONARCHY AND THE CONSTITUTION

George III had decided to change the rules of the game of politics. He rejected the Whig oligarchy, which had dominated through dynastic ties and patronage. Instead, he declared that he would choose his ministers for their virtue rather than their connections. George III wished to be a "patriot king," personally ruling according to the good of the country. He trusted Bute because his mother, the princess dowager, had earlier chosen the cultured, moralistic Bute as his tutor.[7] It did not matter that Parliament thought Bute was haughty and incompetent: the king believed he had the constitutional right to choose his own prime minister over the objections of Parliament. He dismissed the Whigs from office and replaced them with Bute's chosen followers.

Aghast at losing their decades-old monopoly of government and its patronage, the Whigs believed they had a hereditary right to government offices because their ancestors had defended the constitution in the Glorious Revolution. The Whigs also accused the king of trying to claim too much personal power. The king might be able to choose his ministers, they admitted, but he should follow the feeling of the country, rather than his own personal inclination, to select someone respected and influential in Parliament.[8] According to the dominant interpretation of the constitution, the king was right, but the constitution was largely unwritten, and the Whigs could find valid alternative constitutional arguments. But they tended to exaggerate the alleged conspiracy behind Bute's appointment.[9] Eventually, Bute resigned under all this pressure in April 1763, but long after, the Whigs claimed Bute exerted a "secret influence" behind the scenes.

In the *North Briton*, Wilkes translated these constitutional debates into satirical, allegorical narratives. He revived the old story of Queen Isabella, the mother of Edward III, who brought her lover Mortimer into power with disastrous results. Wilkes used this story to warn of the dangers of the influence of a "mother, actuated by strong passions, and influenced by an insolent minister." He editorialized, "O may Britain never see such a day again! when power acquired by profligacy may lord it over this realm; when the feeble pretensions of a *court minion* may require the prostitution of royalty for their support."[10] Wilkes also evoked the attacks on Queen Anne and her favorite, Abigail Masham, and on Queen Caroline, through whom Walpole allegedly ruled the nation in the reign of George II.[11] He capitalized on anti-Scottish bigotry to denounce Bute and ridicule the many Scottish courtiers and government servants, descending to the crudest insults by claiming that Scottish women were unattractive since they never washed.[12] And of course, some thought that Wilkes was simply motivated by sour grapes, since Bute's ministry would not grant him a patronage office. Wilkes's satire, however, communicated a more substantial critique of the king's constitutional claims than that put forth by the Whigs.

Historian Catherine Macaulay provided the theoretical and historical ammunition for the Wilkesite cause in her multivolume *History of England*, which began to be published in 1763. The republican Macaulay argued that the seventeenth-century Stuarts became tyrants when they asserted despotic powers and allowed their selfish, personal interests to overcome the good of the nation. While Macaulay noted that "it is not the business of an historian to dwell upon, or even expose, those imperfections and vices which have no influence on the public weal," she believed that the personal lives of monarchs were relevant when they interfered with the public good. To prove her point, Macaulay recounted tales of the pernicious influence of the male and female favorites of monarchs. She denounced royal women's meddling into politics, such as Henrietta Maria, Queen Mother to Charles II, who returned from French exile "in hopes of having the same influence in the cabinet which she had in the late king's time."[13] Although Macaulay came from a political family—her brother, Alderman John Sawbridge, was an ally of Wilkes—she did not wish to, nor could she, enter the political fray directly. She led a salon of radical republican intellectuals who held themselves apart from conventional politics.[14] Macaulay's tone was lofty and her volumes expensive. However, she very much influenced Wilkes, who attended her salon—and who transformed her constitutional analysis into popular language that could reach much larger audiences.[15]

Wilkes used satire to undercut the king's control over patronage. The king's supporters portrayed him as the "fountain of honor," who rewarded the accomplished few who served the nation. By depicting Bute as gaining his position through sexual favors, obscene images reflected in a fun-house

FIGURE 1   *The Scotch Broom Stick and the Female Besom* (1763), BMC 3852.
© The British Museum. Scottish courtiers look up at the princess, astride on a
broom, and Lord Bute, with a stick and a boot (for Bute). A male courtier on the
right, looking up the princess's skirts with a telescope, says, "I see the road to Preferment, 'tis well fenc'd and water'd," and the courtier next to him says, "There's the
road, thro bushy park." The princess says, "Here's a besom for you, the rusian bear
is not more carnivorous" than she (referring to Catherine the Great), and Lord Bute
says, "Come lassie let's make the most of the game for I am strong in hand, and we
are above the Vulgar."

mirror the king's contention that he wished to appoint his ministers on the
basis of virtue. According to Wilkes, this personal influence was completely
illegitimate, the most crass and corrupt exchange of sexual favors for selfish
political purposes. One caricature, by Wilkes's friend the Marquis Townsend, depicted the princess sitting on a zebra (she really kept a zebra in her
park), dispensing favors to Scots.[16] In another caricature, *The Scotch Broom
Stick* (figure 1), a crowd of Scotch courtiers gaze up at the princess dowager
(the king's mother) and Lord Bute, the prime minister.[17] One courtier looks
up under the princess's skirts and comments, "I see the road to Preferment;
'tis well fenced and water'd," and another points the same way, adding,
"There's the road, thro bushy park"—a pun that alluded to the royal
"Bushey Park" and the princess's genitals. In part, this caricature expresses

resentment at the Scots who came down to London and gained offices in the British government, allegedly displacing Englishmen. But it also undercut the notion that patronage could be obtained through personal favors—especially women's favors—rather than merit.

Wilkes also attacked the idea that George III was like a father, who should be trusted to look after his people. George III's supporters claimed that as a good father chose his servants, the king had the right to select the ministers he respected for their virtue.[18] To refute this argument, Wilkes and Macaulay revived the seventeenth-century theories of John Locke, who declared that citizens did not have to obey the king like children obeyed their father; instead, they had the right to resist an unjust ruler.[19] Popular imagery portrayed George III not as an awe-inspiring father but as a child attached to his mother's leading strings. When he rode through the London streets on his way to visit his mother, the mob asked if he were going to suck.[20]

By insinuating that the princess dowager had an affair with the Scottish Bute, Wilkes and his supporters implied that Stuart blood contaminated the Hanoverian dynasty, bringing the danger of Stuart tyranny. Wilkes's virulent anti-Scottish rhetoric, therefore, was not only an appeal to xenophobic British nationalism but also an attack on what he saw as the danger of Stuart absolutism. Wilkes also undercut the general principle of hereditary succession and aristocracy, repudiating what he called the "Tory" notion that "there is a divine, hereditary and indefeasible right in any family . . . that *Englishmen* were all born to be slaves to a few persons, who happen either by accident to possess a larger fortune, or by his own lewdness and debauchery, or by the wicked mean arts of a father or grandfather, to worm themselves into an estate." To be sure, he defended the virtues of the Whig families who made the revolution and the Hanoverian dynasty, counterposing them with the hereditary vice of tyranny in the Stuart line.[21] He even insinuated that Lord Bute had infected the princess dowager with venereal disease (i.e., a "reigning disorder"), adding "any person who can make out a *hereditary* right to this disease, treated gratis."[22] It was important for Wilkes to use satirical, even obscene, language to make these points. Satirical narratives disrupted lines of inheritance: caricatures portrayed the queen as sexually corrupt, as bodily degenerate, and the king as ill conceived, perhaps illegitimate.[23]

The theory of oriental despotism gave a theoretical substance to these satires. According to Montesquieu, a despot rules according to his own personal inclinations and even lusts, without regard for the law.[24] As Catherine Macaulay explained it, not only oriental despots but also monarchs could fall prey to this problem: "Now, the designs of an individual being commonly to gratify his own lusts and private advantages, and those lusts and private advantages being ever incompatible with the good of the public, it leads him [the monarch] to employ those villains, whose abilities are equal only to cunning, and proper only to the destruction of the commonweal."[25] Although monarchs ruled according to law, personal influence—especially the influence of aristocratic women and royal mistresses—could always undermine the probity of the court and lead to despotism.[26]

Wilkes's satires, and the other myriad songs, caricatures, and satires circulating in London, translated the theory of oriental despotism into graphic images. First, these satires mocked the monarch's phallic power. The king displayed his power by carrying the regalia of office, including his scepter, when he spoke at the opening of Parliament. But in these satires, the scepter became a phallus, an emblem of lust rather than sovereignty. For instance, a popular song, "The Staff of Gisbal" (figure 2), depicted the Scottish Bute holding a phallic rod. It declared that neither the "Cherokee King, or Nabob of Bengal / Can boast such a Staff as the Staff of Gisbal [Bute]," insinuating that Bute's thirst for power exceeded that of such "savage" or oriental despots. As Rachel Weil comments on earlier pornography about Charles II, phallic imagery suggests both that a ruler will become a tyrant, unbounded by the rule of law, and that his power was uncertain and undisciplined.[27] This song also hinted that the power illegitimately lay in the hands of Bute, rather than the legitimate sovereign, George III. In his secret *Essay on Woman*, Wilkes took the metaphor even further, mocking Bute by comparing his penis to that of a giant "Jack Ass" who tried to sleep with a princess. He also satirized Bute's pretensions to moral superiority:

Then in the scale of various Pricks, 'tis plain,
Godlike erect, BUTE stands the foremost Man.[28]

The phallus became a floating, insecure signifier of power that could be claimed by anyone, rather than an emblem of power firmly attached to a patriarchal dynasty. Another caricature (figure 3) depicts the princess as a phallic woman: she carries a huge boot (Bute = boot) on her back and grasps the phallic spur that projects in front of her. A flagpole also protrudes out of her loins, held by Bute, who pops out of the boot.[29] If a woman could seize phallic power, perhaps it was an uncertain source of political potency.

Second, these satires expressed the theory that women would influence a despot to rule according to his personal inclinations rather than the law. For instance, the song "The Staff of Gisbal" goes on to allege that Madame de Pompadour, reviled for her political influence, envied the staff as more

THE

STAFF of GISBAL:

An Hyperborean SONG,

Translated from the Fragments of OSSIAN, the Son of FINGAL.

By a YOUNG LADY.

" *Arma virumque cano.*" VIRGIL.

N. B.   This SONG is a suitable Companion to the Book of GISBAL.

I.

YE frolickfome Laffes in Country and City,
    Attend for a while to a frolickfome Ditty !
Thou Spirit of OSSIAN, great Son of FINGAL,
Affift me to fing of the STAFF of Gisbal !
                    Derry down, &c.

II.

When this notable Chief of the HEBRONITES Land
Before BATHSHEBA ftood, with his STAFF in his Hand,
The Damfels around her cry'd out, one and all,
" What a *wonderful* STAFF is the STAFF of GISBAL"!
                    Derry down, &c.

III.

From the Days of old ADAM there has not been found,
Thro' the World's ample Circuit, a STAFF fo renown'd :
Not the CHEROKEE KING, or NABOB of BENGAL,
Can boaft fuch a STAFF as the STAFF of GISBAL.
                    Derry down, &c.

IV.

If Madame Pompadour had this Prodigy feen,
She'd have own'd it was fit for the Ufe of a Queen ;
And that LOUIS LE GRAND, with his BATON ROYAL,
Was lefs *magnifique* than the STAFF of GISBAL.
                    Derry down, &c.

V.

Of fuch exquifite Virtue this STAFF is poffeft,
It will kindle Emotions of Love in your Breaft :
For a proof of this Truth, I appeal to them all,
Who have ever beheld the fam'd STAFF of GISBAL.
                    Derry down, &c.

VI.

No STAFF ever made of *Gold, Silver,* or *Wood,*
Could compare with this Compound of pure *Flefh* and *Blood* :
A STAFF fo upright, I may venture to call,
A STAFF for a PRINCESS — this STAFF of GISBAL.
                    Derry down, &c.

VII.

Entomb'd with his Fathers when GISBAL lies rotten,
Though worn to a *Stump*, it fhall ne'er be forgotten :
As a *Trophy* we'll bear it to WESTMINSTER HALL,
And hang up the *Remains* of the STAFF of GISBAL.
                    Derry down, &c.

VIII.

If Critics fhould cenfure, or Witlings fhould laugh,
And fay " furely Mifs ftands in Need of a STAFF,"
I defy the moft fwaggering Blade of them all,
To produce fuch a STAFF as the STAFF of GISBAL.
                    Derry down, &c.

LONDON: Printed for the AUTHOR, and Sold by the Bookfellers and Print-fellers. 1762
Gisbal publ. July 1762.   [Price Six Pence.]

FIGURE 2   "The Staff of Gisbal" (1762), BMC 3848. © The British Museum. Gisbal stands for Lord Bute. He carries his staff of office in a symbolic position, and is
dressed in plaid to signify Scottishness.

FIGURE 3   *Provision for the Scotch Convent*, in *The British Anecdote to Caledonian Poison* (London, 1763), vol. 2, p. 49. Reproduced by permission of the Huntington Library.

magnificent than Louis's "baton royal," associating Bute with French absolutism. Wilkes emulated the underground French literature that had begun
to link Louis XV's sexual promiscuity with despotic power and the illegitimate influence of his mistresses; in the *North Briton*, Wilkes declared that it
is "ruinous to the state and public interest, where the despotism of a favorite
minister has been acquired, and maintained by female partiality."[30] Of
course, like George III, the new king of France, Louis XVI, "identified with
sexual monogamy and royal justice, embodied paternalism in the new
style." Nonetheless, the underground literature ridiculed him as impotent
and unable to control his luxury-loving wife.[31] Satires that displaced a king's
authority onto his mother or mistress were using the technique of metonymy, in which an item associated with or next to a subject is used to represent it, for instance, a scepter for monarchy or, more threateningly, a king's
mother, wife, or mistress. When writers and caricaturists used this trope,
they evoked anxiety by displacing the ruler's legitimate sovereignty onto a
woman, who was not supposed to have power.[32]

Wilkes and his supporters portrayed the princess dowager's power over her
son as excessive, illicit, and monstrous. For instance, the poem *The Group* depicted the princess as a "tygress . . . her game, devouring, ruin, all her roar."[33] In
the play *The Three Conjurors*, modeled on *Macbeth*, the princess dowager is
Hecate, who whisks "MacBoot" off to safety on her broomstick.[34] In *The Scotch
Broom Stick* caricature (see figure 1), the princess rides a broom backward to
present herself to Bute's pole; a powerful figure, like a witch, a devouring
vagina dentata, she declares, "The russian bear is not more carnivorous I love
power as well as she." The Russian bear, of course, was Catherine the Great,
known for her lovers—and her absolute reign. The princess was thus compared to a witch and a beast, both images of uncontrolled, illicit, sexual power.

Wilkes himself did not hate women in general—indeed, he seems to
have loved too many of them—but his supporters exaggerated hostility toward royal female influence into a generalized misogyny.[35] A 1766 poem reviling the vices of the court proclaimed, "Hell and confusion what a life is
here, / When men thus truckle, women domineer!"[36] Another spurious *Essay on Woman*, one often thought to be the real version, baldly declared,
"Woman is the Foe of Man" and aimed to "trace the mighty errors of her
mind."

> In Men we various ruling passions find,
> In Women—two alone divide the mind;
> Those only fixed, they first or last, obey,
> The love of pleasure, and the love of sway.[37]

Crowd

The graphic nature of these images helped Wilkes spread the scandal to the street and harness the power of the crowd. When the government tried to have the common hangman burn the *North Briton* in public, the people extinguished the flames with mud. Wilkes's plebeian male supporters linked "the struggle for the breeches" in their own marriages to the princess dowager's alleged illicit power.[38] Crowds drew upon the iconography of rough music, a popular ritual punishing women who dominated their husbands, by parading around the city with boots and petticoats on poles. A song for Wilkes's birthday, sung at clubs around the city, compared the plight of the king, ruled by his mother, to that of henpecked husbands:

> Though by Petticoat Rule many a Man's made a Fool,
> In subordinate stations of Life;
> Yet 'tis sure a Strange Thing that a British born K——
> Should be noodled by M[inister]r and W[hor]e.[39]

A French or German king, the song implied, might be dominated by women, like Louis XV and Madame de Pompadour, but a manly British king should not be so weak.

The crowds made the situation dangerous for the government. How could it respond to scandal without fueling its flames? According to Horace Walpole, the government intended to seize Wilkes for the insult to the princess dowager, but "on reflection it was not thought advisable to enter on the discussion of such a subject at Westminster Hall"; they feared that Wilkes would not respect "decorum" but would further ridicule royalty in his defense.[40] Satire made censorship difficult because its authors could excuse sedition as humor, and prosecuting grotesque sexual rumors about royalty only served to publicize them. But outrage turned into action when Wilkes criticized the king's speech at the opening of Parliament in the famous Number 45 of his *North Briton*. Criticizing the Treaty of Paris, which had ended the Seven Years' War, he lamented that the "honor of the crown" was "sunk even to prostitution" through the machinations of the king's ministers, who did not deserve such office. Although in this context Wilkes used "prostitution" as a political metaphor, not in a literal sense, he no doubt intended to convey a sexual innuendo, and the king took this as a personal insult.

Wilkes's authorship of the *North Briton* was officially anonymous, and after all, he was only one of many circulating these rumors. But he was the most persuasive, and the most dangerous. Egged on by George III, the government issued a general warrant against Wilkes for seditious and treasonable libel.[41] Under this warrant, which specified no person or suspicious item, it sent constables to search his home, where they seized his private papers, including jovial letters to his patron, Lord Temple, joking about their sexual adventures, and a friendly yet obscene satire on Lord Sandwich.[42] As soon as they found him, they imprisoned the man himself in the Tower. However, by arresting Wilkes, the government made its own actions into a scandal.

Wilkes used the occasion to raise the constitutional question of the right to freedom of speech. Wilkes argued that members of the Parliament had a right to criticize the king's speech, since it was actually written by the chief minister and expressed his policies. The king should not be able to impose a minister on Parliament. Furthermore, as a member of Parliament, he claimed, he had the right of freedom of speech and immunity from arrest. Chief Justice Pratt agreed with the latter point and freed Wilkes on the latter ground.

Unfazed, Wilkes republished the *North Briton* and, while he was at the press, ran off a few copies of his pornographic *Essay on Woman*.[43] The *Essay* romped through ridiculously erudite puns celebrating the joys of sex between men and women—and denigrating sex between men. Above all, it proclaimed, "Fucking's the End and cause of human State, / And man must fuck, or God will not create." But the *Essay* also satirized political and religious targets with a more serious intent.[44] Wilkes felt it was his duty to use obscenity against the king and clerical authority because, according to one theory, European monarchs became theocratic despots when they regarded any criticisms of themselves as blasphemy.[45] The *Essay* implied that Bishop George Stone had a sexual affair with George Sackville, who had earlier been charged with cowardice and was long rumored to be a "sodomite."[46]

Unfortunately for Wilkes, a printer's assistant wrapped his sandwich with the discarded proofs. As the assistant ate his lunch with a friend, they idly looked at the greasy paper and found the verses equating Bute's penis with that of a jackass.[47] The printers conveyed this news to their friend the Reverend J. Kidgell—according to Walpole, a "dainty priggish parson"— who passed it on to the authorities.[48] The government had found the excuse it had been looking for to discredit Wilkes. A Middlesex jury indicted Wilkes for publishing the *Essay on Woman* and the *North Briton*.

The government hoped that by prosecuting Wilkes for blasphemy as well as sedition, it could use scandal to turn the people against him. The government could therefore separate Wilkes from the parliamentary opposition, defuse his constitutional challenge, and discredit him in the eyes of public opinion. No doubt many found Wilkes's scurrilous language to be distasteful and the news of his obscene pornography deeply shocking.

Kidgell denounced Wilkes's *Essay on Woman* in his own pamphlet: "If Blasphemies . . . are to be forced upon the PUBLICK with Impunity; farewell dear LIBERTY for ever! No Kingdom under the Sun will be so sincerely to be pitied as Great Britain, when the Laws of her Country shall become a Prey to Libertines, and (O Grief of Griefs!) the RELIGION of it to infidels."[49] In Parliament, even his former allies, such as Pitt, hurried to denigrate Wilkes as a blasphemous libertine who deserved no support as an individual.

In denouncing Wilkes as a libertine, however, the government faced several problems in its management of the scandal. First, it faced the chronic problem that by exposing Wilkes's libertinism it incited prurient interest. To avoid this problem, it suppressed any publication of the *Essay* itself, but this left people wondering what all the fuss was about. The government had even tried to dissuade Kidgell from publishing his own pamphlet about the *Essay on Woman*.[50] After all, this pamphlet only incited further interest in the *Essay*, as Kidgell's indignant extracts and paraphrases made himself seem ridiculous and the *Essay* more enticing. He warned readers that "the Prophaneness throughout the whole Work is of a shocking, new, and wonderful Invention," and excited interest in the notorious comparison of Lord Bute to a jackass by adding, "In another of his horrid Elucidations, the natural Abilities of the Ass are made the Subject of his unclean Description, the blameless SCRIPTURE being still hawled in [*sic*] to be responsible."[51] Second, by prosecuting Wilkes because he was a libertine, the government laid itself open to charges of hypocrisy. George III claimed he chose his ministers on the basis of virtue, but several were known to keep mistresses. Most notoriously, Lord Sandwich, a notorious libertine and gambler (he gave his name to the sandwich, which enabled one to eat and gamble at the same time) and a denizen of Medmenham Abbey, read aloud excerpts from the *Essay* in the House of Commons and pronounced himself shocked, just shocked, at its contents.[52]

Wilkes and his supporters defended him through counterattack. They portrayed government prosecution of Wilkes as a distraction from attacks on liberties of the subject and from the aristocratic vices of sodomy and corruption.[53] Of course, the real *Essay* could not be found, so several faux versions were published to capitalize on Wilkes's notoriety. One poem implied that while Wilkes was prosecuted for enjoying "natural" female charms, sodomy was the pleasure of the court. The anonymous author of this essay introduced himself as one "who, from his earliest infancy, ever detested the remotest hints of any Back-shot collusion." He went on to depict the Olympian court laughing at the British mortals worrying about private fornication "when proud Oppression stares men in the face."[54]

By raising the issue of sodomy, Wilkes appealed to the baser prejudices of the London populace. By the eighteenth century, the image of a man who desired other men as a "sodomite," cowardly and effeminate, began to be established. Sodomy was punishable by death, but men sexually interested in men managed to find each other in certain pubs and parks, occasionally establishing a nascent subculture.[55] Earlier in the century, moral vigilance crusaders had formed themselves into associations to cleanse the London streets of "sodomites" and prostitutes.[56] London crowds were all too accustomed to amuse themselves by stoning men accused of sodomy in the pillory. A 1763 broadsheet, for instance, ridiculed a "sodomite" as effeminate and encouraged crowds to pelt him; indeed, he died from the abuse.[57] Some Enlightenment thinkers ridiculed such prejudices, arguing that the law should ignore "sodomites," since nature would solve the problem. But Wilkes and his close friend the poet Charles Churchill were notably obsessed with the issue, unlike one of his friends, who advised him not to worry about "unnatural pleasures," for they pale in comparison with the joys of heterosexual love.[58]

Campaigns against sodomy often had political connotations. Earlier attacks on "sodomites" could come from a conservative perspective, portraying them as unnatural criminals who disturbed and dissolved the proper hierarchical social order, or as patriarchs who dramatically failed in their responsibilities.[59] But Wilkes and Churchill linked sodomy with political oppression. Men seeking sex with other men, Churchill claimed in his poem *The Times*, plied their trade

in public at our very doors
And take the bread from much more honest Whores.
Those who are mean high Paramours secure,
And the rich guilty screen the guilty poor.[60]

Wilkes also drew on works equating sodomy with courtly favoritism. For instance, Catherine Macaulay revealed the lubricious correspondence between James I and his male favorite, Buckingham, to buttress her argument that kings all too often followed their own personal whims: "His friendship, not to give it the name of vice, was directed by so puerile a fancy, and so absurd a caprice, that the objects of it were ever contemptible. . . . he valued no person for any endowments that could not be made subservient to his pleasures or his interest, and thus he rarely advanced a man of real worth to preferment."[61]

The classical republican attack on "effeminacy" gave Wilkes's satire a vocabulary. Courtiers were often scorned as "effeminate" because they resembled women, loved women too much, submitted to the king, or allowed themselves to be corrupted by luxury. The Latin prose and poetry that inspired this language explicitly linked effeminacy to passive sodomy. The Roman poet Juvenal especially inspired Wilkes and Churchill.[62] Juvenal portrayed courtiers as effeminate creatures who submitted to passive homosexual acts to gain the favor of the great; the poet used words such as *molles* and *cineadus*, which meant men who took the passive role in sex with other men. The Romans' sexual system was not based on exclusive heterosexuality and homosexuality but on the sexual dominance of the male citizen over boys, servants, foreigners, slaves, or women. To take the passive role, for a Roman citizen, was to submit, to lose manhood, to show cowardice, even to lose citizenship.[63] Conversely, for a man to dominate another sexually was an unfair exertion of power. Wilkes's supporters emulated this association of sodomy with effeminate submission to attack courtiers, although they did not, unlike the Romans, accept active "sodomites" as manly. Apparently George Onslow swore that "if the House of Lords were to commit s[odom]y on the House of Commons, the Commons would vote it no breach of privilege" when the House supinely allowed the Lords to persecute Wilkes.[64] An anonymous author praised Wilkes for fighting against the "stream of courtiers . . . the French fop . . . in pink and silver dressed" and compared Bute to a "S——d——mite" for taking revenge behind the scenes: "Thou stabb'st behind, afraid to face, and fight."[65]

Of course, Wilkes and his friends could be seen as fops. After all, they were unmarried (or, in Wilkes's case, separated), flamboyant, libertines themselves. When Churchill began profiting from his poetry, he abandoned his status as a parson, discarding his "dignified black . . . clerical garb . . . in favor of the famous blue coat with metal buttons, a gold-laced hat, and ruffles."[66] Similarly, another foppish clerical friend, John Horne, left one suit each of scarlet and gold, white and silver, blue and silver, flowered silk, black silk, and black velvet with Wilkes in Paris.[67] But Wilkes and his friends combined their epicurean lifestyle and fashionable clothes with a belligerent masculinity; Wilkes twice proved his own political manhood by dueling.[68] They defied constituted authority, debonairly flourishing their lace cuffs and brandishing their swords with equal panache.[69] They enjoyed luxury but abhorred courtly deceit and dissimulation, contrasting their open bravery with the courtiers who curried favor with corrupt superiors.[70] The fop could be a libertine who regarded himself as above "the vulgar herd . . . and therefore not subject to moral censure."[71]

Yet Wilkes moved beyond the independent, elitist masculinity of classical republicans, who believed that only independent, propertied gentlemen should actively participate in politics as citizens. He stirred up crowds on London streets to demonstrate in his favor, explicitly appealing to the "middling and inferior sorts of people."[72]

THE PEOPLE AND THE CONSTITUTION

Wilkes therefore raised another constitutional issue: the place of the people in politics. He declared that the principle that the "People" have a right to "intermeddle in government" is "the voice of Locke, the voice of our laws, the voice of reason."[73] Wilkes equated his woes with those of the people, portraying himself as a hero who defended freedom of speech and the privacy of the subject. The general warrants used against him infringed the liberty of the subject as guaranteed in the Bill of Rights. Any government that overturned these rights brought back Stuart tyranny. Not only members of Parliament, he claimed, but "the middling and inferior sorts of people" needed protection from general warrants that authorized the seizure of persons and invasions of houses.[74] He linked his experience to oppression faced by apple growers in the West of England. Needing new sources of revenue, the government imposed a tax on cider mills, but to enforce it, the unpopular excise service ransacked homes and farms as its agents searched for illicit mills.[75]

Parliament deprived Wilkes of his political base by stripping him of his seat and outlawing him for blasphemy and sedition. He seemed to be finished as a political figure, expelled from the game of politics. Unable to draw on Pitt's or Lord Temple's patronage, his periodical censored, Wilkes fled to Paris. He spent several years exiled in France and traveling in Italy, losing his fortune—and enjoying himself with his sensuous but rather temperamental Italian mistress. When he returned in 1768, he was imprisoned as an outlaw for evading his earlier conviction for blasphemy and sedition and had to spend two years in the King's Bench Prison.

Wilkes used his popular support among the people, however, to defy Parliament, directing his cause from prison. He began to play the game of politics in a different way, refusing offers from supporters to obtain a pocket borough for him or help him bribe once again the electors of Aylesbury.[76] Instead, he determined to win an election in London, using the techniques of mass campaigning and political organization. His supporters efficiently canvassed voters and brought them to the polls.[77] Wilkes successfully fought, and won, election as member of Parliament from Middlesex, but Parliament expelled him as an outlaw for his earlier conviction on *The Es-*

say on Woman and the *North Briton.* These elections caused great turmoil, as supporters and opponents battled in the streets, and crowds gathered outside the King's Bench where Wilkes was imprisoned (in luxurious surroundings). When troops fired on the Wilkesite crowds, killing eleven Londoners, Wilkes's support only intensified. Nonplussed, he mounted another successful election campaign in 1769, but Parliament again refused to seat him because he was a convicted blasphemer and seditious libeler. Instead, it gave the seat to his vanquished rival, Colonel Luttrell, even though Luttrell got fewer votes. The government and Parliament were acting as if they, rather than the voters, should decide elections.

These actions sparked off an intense constitutional debate. The traditional view, held by the king as well as the Whigs, was that Parliament was the only legitimate representative of the people. Edmund Burke and the opposition faction, the Rockingham Whigs, continued to insist that Parliament defended the people against the king's usurping prerogative, and in turn, the people should trust Parliament to look after them.[78] A "Real Whig" asserted that Parliament was the only place where politics could be debated, for it was composed of the "flower of the gentry" rather than the dregs of the people, such as coffeehouse politicians.[79] But Catherine Macaulay refuted the Whig argument, showing that the real problem was the overweaning prerogative of Parliament, which did not really represent the people.[80] Wilkes wrote that "the Rights of the People are not what the Commons have ceded to them, but what they have reserved to themselves"; conversely, the Commons owed its privileges to the "People's gift."[81]

Wilkes's support ran deep; it included some gentlemen worried at the constitutional implications of the government's persecution, and many urban middle-class people and even laboring people. For instance, a print titled *Political Electricity* depicted an "electrical chain" linking all the woes of Britain: Bute's tyranny, the new minister Grafton's vices, declining trade, troops firing on "a few old women and boys" who gathered outside the King's Bench where Wilkes was imprisoned, and a mob of country women and children "starving for bread."[82] As it happens, 1768 was a time of intense industrial unrest. Although Wilkes did not incite the strikes and riots of weavers and coal heavers, his defiance of established authority seemed to inspire them. The weavers proclaimed their own "Independent and Bold Defiance."[83]

Even some women supported Wilkes, despite the misogyny of so many of his followers. In Newcastle, it was reported, "The women interest themselves in his favor, and are as zealous as the men, but not so outrageous."[84] Satirists depicted ladies "no more languishingly" drooping in bed, but eagerly reading newspapers and debating Wilkes's defense.[85] Female advocates of Wilkes often sent him tokens of their regard, such as a turkey or a pair of "nett ruffles."[86] But opponents used this female sentiment to discredit his cause as silly.[87] In the Middlesex election, a broadsheet ridiculed women's support for Wilkes with double entendres about the member for Middle Sex.[88] The conservative Samuel Johnson pontificated that the "madness has spread through all ranks and both sexes; women and children have clamored for Mr. Wilkes; honest simplicity has been cheated into fury, and only the wise have escaped infection."[89]

Women, however, could play only a marginal role in Wilkesite politics because Wilkes's masculinity was the basis of his political mobilization. Wilkes capitalized on the traditions of male bonding to create a form of political organization that could defy Parliament.[90] Wilkesite political organization was based on fraternal bonds, which despite his elite connections could cut across the vertical levels of society. Wilkes himself belonged to several clubs, as Brewer notes, ranging from the Freemasons to the Bucks, popular with young rakes. In Birmingham, for instance, tradesmen met in the Red Lion tavern,

> Where social pleasure never met reproof,
> Where joys convivial crown the festive board,
> And every son of LIBERTY'S A LORD
> Where laughter-loving friends a thousand ways
> Provoke to wit, or chaunt their roundelays.[91]

Wilkes's libertinism reassured, rather than repelled, men accustomed to heavy drinking in their clubs and pubs and at elections. To be sure, politicians had long bribed voters with free-flowing beer. But for Wilkes, heavy-drinking male bonding should be a sign of independence, not slavish submission. In one caricature of a drunken election scene, Wilkes lifts a bumper with one hand and scornfully refuses a bribe with another.[92] A bacchanalian frenzy erupted when one Burke, a Wilkesite, was elected in Wendover: "All the pipes were broken at the same instant; in a few minutes the Room was cleared of Smoke and full of Liberty. Wilkes and Liberty, Burke and Wilkes, Freedom and Wendover. Empty Bottles, Broken Glasses, Rivers of Wine, Baths of Brandy, Chairs overturned . . . others in rising from their knees fell under the Table, there to lie till the light of the day should be sober enough to lift them."[93]

Newspapers also expanded the political public by the late 1760s, increasing exponentially in number and circulation. Wilkes played a central role in helping them become more free from censorship, for instance, through the

Printers' Case of 1771, which allowed newspapers to print parliamentary debates.[94] But his scandalmongering also boosted circulation, which freed newspapers from reliance on government subsidies. The Wilkesite *Middlesex Journal*, for instance, combined gossip with ultraradical critique.[95]

For some commentators past and present, such crude language and personal invective contaminated political discourse, which should have been conducted on a more rational, impersonal tone.[96] But Wilkes defended himself from his contemporaries, even friends, who rebuked him for the "indelicacy" of his language. He declared to one correspondent that he needed to "forget the lessons imbibed" from "French philosophers and ancient thinkers" or "I should be undone as tribune of the *people*."[97] The personal politics of these campaigns can be seen in another light. The politics of scandal signaled the expansion of the political public.

PUBLIC AND PRIVATE?

Both the government and the radicals used personal images and scandalous rumors to discredit their opponents, celebrate their heroes, and convey constitutional arguments. Each side attacked its opponent's private life, but the government and the radicals espoused dramatically different views of the relationship between the public and the private.

The government side tended to equate public and private virtue. It opposed the notion that the people had any place in politics, advising the common people to stay out of the public world and instead mind their families' private businesses, trusting the king and his ministers to look after them as a good father. For instance, one pamphlet alleged that men, women, and children of the common people neglected their work because they were obsessed with politics; fathers criticized ministers, careless of "the fidelity of their own wives, the chastity of their daughters, their sons, or their own honor or virtue."[98] Yet by appealing to voters against Wilkes, the government acknowledged the power of public opinion in electoral campaigns.

Government supporters equated Wilkes's sexual debauchery with his political disorderliness and claimed that if he succeeded, all order in the family would decay. To undercut Wilkes's popularity with religious city burghers, opponents portrayed him as a blasphemer and a bad husband.[99] They reminded voters that he married his wife for money and then abandoned her.[100] A letter mocked the Wilkesite slogan "Wilkes and Liberty" to urge his supporters to "restore him to your suffrages to debauch your wives and daughters, and prove to all the abettors of profaneness and immorality, that the voice of the mob is the voice of the devil." Government advocates claimed that Wilkes was a servant of the devil, and if his cause won, "the church lands shall become the possessions of my priests, and the temples be converted to public use, and formed into brothels for performing the rites of obscenity and lewdness."[101] Opponents alleged that if Wilkes could defy the Crown, he could also overturn family order: "modern patriotism," sniffed one newspaper writer, means that "children [are] taught to be disaffected from their lawful governors."[102]

Conservatives contrasted Wilkes's libertinism with the king's image as a gentle father.[103] One pamphlet admonished the people to hail George III "as your most indulgent father, a father that takes a pride in maintaining the liberties of people." They must trust the king's choice of ministers, since "so good a father cannot mean the ruin of his children."[104] George III had "proved himself a dutiful son, a tender husband, an affectionate father, a kind master, a faithful friend, [who] may naturally be supposed to possess the qualities of a good King."[105] By evoking the image of the king as father, George III's supporters did not necessarily mean to resurrect Filmer's patriarchal argument for absolute royal authority. In the eighteenth-century context, the king was supposed to be a gentle father who nurtured rather than dominated his people.[106]

These arguments failed to convince Wilkes's supporters, who were angry at the king for refusing to accept their petitions of grievances. Minor official Philip Francis reported, "The King has been most abominably insulted in returning from the House. I never saw such a concourse of people, nor such outrageous behavior."[107]

To oppose the image of king as good father, Wilkes and his proponents began to argue against the power of scandal they themselves had incited. Only public service mattered, they argued; the king's private paternal virtue was irrelevant. They followed Locke's argument that the authority of the king did not derive from his authority as a father. "Junius," Philip Francis's very secret pseudonym, recounted this theory in greatest detail in his highly influential letters to newspapers. Recounting the abuses of the court, he asked the king, "Is it any answer to your people, that among your domestics You are good-humored,—that to one lady You are faithful;—that to your children You are indulgent?" These private virtues did not matter because they did not benefit society as a whole. As he declared, "The Kingdom swarms with such numbers of felonious robbers of private character and virtue, that no honest or good man is safe."[108]

Newspaper commentators echoed Junius by refuting the notion that the king was a father to his people. A good king should not enshrine himself in his palace "in domestic Felicity with his beloved Queen, and beauteous Progeny," wrote the pseudonymous Camilla, when his minions invaded the homes of his people and imprisoned fathers of poor families. In order to be a good father of his people, he must defend them from oppression.[109] "A Whig" pointed out that a king who defended the liberty of his subjects could safely "indulge his passions in private"; in contrast, a "less able Prince may be a saint in domestic life," but if personal views guided his conduct, "he can never govern Great Britain with ease."[110]

This theme could be extended in an even more radical direction. Another writer, reviving the civil war moniker "Lilburne," asserted that the true parents of the Commons were the people, not the king. In fact, he argued, the king should be retired to enjoy his family, and "the people will be suffered to enjoy their liberty." Implicitly threatening a revival of the scaffold, Lilburne called for a true reformation of Parliament to represent the people.[111] "Poplicola" went even further: kings are "not the friends and fathers of their people, as is sometimes romantically expressed, but their enemies and devourers."[112] The *Whisperer* extended this trope to a radical Lockean republicanism: "The K—— ought to remember, that his family came to the crown of these kingdoms by one revolution, and that it is possible they may lose it by another." If the people's rights were invaded, the social contract of the constitution was dissolved and they had a right to dismiss incumbent power.[113]

Even though Junius asserted that only public service mattered, he also viciously exposed the private lives of the king's ministers. He reviled the duke of Grafton, the prime minister and king's favorite, for flaunting his mistress Nancy Parsons and marrying "a near relation of one who has debauched his wife."[114] How could Junius justify these attacks? He argued that the private vices of ministers became a public concern if personal connections, heredity, or favor led to political power. For Junius, public virtue meant republicanism, the "general attachment to the common weal, distinct from any partial attachment to persons or families." When the king appointed unintelligent and corrupt aristocrats such as Lord Sandwich and Francis Dashwood because of his personal favor, "ministers are no longer the public servants of the state, but the private domestics of the Sovereign."[115] Junius also pointed out the hypocrisy of the king in celebrating virtue while appointing Lord Sandwich, the notorious gambler, to high offices.[116] By stressing the vices that ran in aristocratic families such as those of Grafton, Bedford, and Luttrell, Junius countered the traditional view that virtue was an aristocratic inheritance. In a world ruled by heredity, royalty, and personal connections, power followed blood lines—but illicit sex could contaminate its legitimacy.

The scandalmongering also continued the earlier Wilkesite theme that the princess dowager controlled politics, depicting her as a malignant force who was responsible for "the shameful and deplorable Condition of this Country."[117] *The Political Songster* compared her to Madame de Pompadour and lamented that "Female Pride shall hold the Land / In humble subjection."[118] The obsessive concern with the alleged influence of the princess dowager illustrated, in concrete images, Burke's more abstract theory of "secret influence," that a secret conspiracy unconstitutionally controlled the king.[119]

Radicals also accused other English noblewomen of intriguing like Madame Dubarry in France.[120] John Almon, Wilkes's ally, claimed that Martha Ray, Lord Sandwich's mistress, acted as intermediary for the sale of offices in the Admiralty.[121] Although the charges were disproved, many other rumors circulated about female political influence at this time, as part of the general denunciation of female adultery.[122] One newspaper commentator explicitly warned that "when such notorious prostitution of honor and political virtue, continues to infect the *majority* of the men of rank in the senate . . . little hopes can be entertained, that the present depravity and indelicacy of the ladies, will effectually be reformed."[123] And this theme intensified the misogyny of the Wilkesite movement. When "Junia" wrote to Junius protesting at his scandalmongering, he condescendingly replied, "I should be glad to furnish her with [a topic] more fit for a Lady to handle [than politics], and better suited to the natural Dexterity of her Sex."[124] A caricature depicted a woman as half beautiful lady, half skeleton, and proclaimed, "Who tries to lose the liberty of Britons—Woman!"[125]

Yet Junius argued that while men such as Wilkes indulged in private vices, they were irrelevant to his public service.[126] Many commentators asserted that Wilkes's bad moral character was beside the point when one considered his heroism in defending constitutional liberties.[127] Joseph Towers declared, "There is a degree of public virtue, which may be sufficient to cancel many private vices."[128] His marital troubles, argued one letter writer, were his private business.[129] Catherine Macaulay believed that Wilkes's *Essay on Woman* was "between God and his own conscience" and sent him money to help pay his debts.[130]

Going beyond the defense of Wilkes as a person, his supporters argued that the citizen's right to privacy should not depend on his virtue. One letter writer asserted that it did not matter that Wilkes had "no public or private virtue"; the government had endangered the liberty of the subject by using a general warrant and by seizing Wilkes's papers. If citizens did not defend Wilkes, the government would invade their privacy as well.[131] An

anonymous letter proclaimed, "What is practic'd against Wilkes (a sad debauched dog that used his wife ill 'tis true) may be practiced against us."[132]
A letter in the *Public Advertiser* claimed that by persecuting Wilkes for blasphemy, the government was just trying to distract attention from its attacks
on the liberties of the subject; after all, any gentleman making a joke, or
writing a comedy, could be attacked on the same grounds.[133]

Wilkes and his supporters asserted the privacy of thoughts against governmental intrusion. Wilkes defended the *Essay* as "an idle poem" and declared, "In my own closet I had the right to examine, and even try by the
keen edge of ridicule, any opinions I pleas'd." He added, "Only a *Stuart*
could make the refinement in tyranny of ransacking and robbing the recesses of closets and studies in order to convert *private amusements* into
state crimes."[134] One commentator feared that if the government could enter
a home and seize private papers, personal secrets (such as adulterous affairs) as well as confidential commercial documents could be published, endangering family harmony and business success.[135] The *Whisperer* boldly asserted that a magistrate had no more "right to direct the private behavior of
men" or "to model people's speculations," than he had to regulate their
dreams.[136]

Of course, Wilkes was a political entrepreneur, not a consistent philosopher. At the same time as Wilkes insisted on his own privacy, his supporters
attacked his enemies' private lives in the Middlesex election. His Middlesex
constituency included many Dissenting and Anglican merchants and
tradesmen who espoused a much more strict standard of morality. To gar-
ner their support, Wilkes's supporters portrayed his opponent, Colonel
Luttrell, as a notorious roué who seduced and abandoned the young Arabella Bolton. One pamphlet told that Bolton was the daughter of a gardener
who worked for the Moreton family. When Luttrell visited them, she caught
his eye, but she resisted his advances. Undeterred, he drugged and violated
her with the help of a procuress after the manner of Lovelace and Clarissa.
A gentleman, claimed the pamphlet, would have been "overcome with remorse" and tried to compensate her, but Luttrell "spurned upon all the laws
of nature, honor and humanity."[137] The Arabella Bolton affair represents an
early use in popular politics of the melodramatic metaphor of the seduced
maiden abandoned and betrayed by the wicked aristocrat. For instance, the
Wilkes' Jest Book referred to her as "The Forsaken Maid."[138] In contrast, argued some of Wilkes's supporters, Wilkes was an honorable libertine: "He
never did . . . invade, either by force or by fraud, the honor of any maid or
matron: so that even his pleasures have been regulated by the strictest max-
ims of honor."[139]

By portraying Luttrell as a rapist, Wilkes's supporters reminded voters of Lord Baltimore, who allegedly raped and abducted a Dissenting milliner, Sarah Woodcock. Acquitted in 1768, Lord Baltimore was identified with the government, especially Lord Sandwich. After he took a grand tour to Constantinople, his enemies called him the Bashaw of Maryland,[140] and accused him of forming his own seraglio back in England.[141] Wilkesites therefore linked Lord Baltimore and Colonel Luttrell—and, by extension, the government—to theories of oriental despotism, equating sexual indulgence and excessive power. The Lord Baltimore and Luttrell affairs also acquired class connotations. Sarah Woodcock become an emblem of the virtue of the Dissenting middle classes of London preyed upon by a vicious aristocracy.[142] The Wilkesite attack on Luttrell's immorality may have been effective: in the Middlesex elections of 1768–69, clergymen and substantial traders were reluctant to vote for Luttrell.[143]

By 1771, however, Wilkes's attempt to portray himself as a "new man" faltered and failed to persuade public opinion. His limitations as a political entrepreneur became apparent. Wilkes saw himself as the champion of liberty and genuinely sacrificed his fortune and career for the cause. But he also flaunted his vices as if he did not have to obey conventional moral codes. He used the Middlesex sheriff's coach to visit his mistress, who lived in the same neighborhood as his mother; Mrs. Wilkes protested that he should use more discretion.[144] Wilkes also alienated one of his supporters, a city alderman, by seducing his wife.[145]

Wilkes's ego became even more of a problem. He was genuinely committed to liberty, but he reveled in his status as hero—and antihero. For instance, he wrote to his friend Jean Baptiste Suard, flush with his own popularity, "England is now a demon-o-cracy—Who is the *demon*? Wilkes."[146] Wilkes failed to see that the cause he had sparked transcended his own status as hero. "Poplicola" "pointed out, "It is not the *sound* of Wilkes, that we are to follow, but the *cause* of Liberty."[147] "Chaerephon" scorned Wilkes's pretension to be a patriot, asking, "Shall we find his thoughts center in any thing but the convivial pleasures of the dinner?"[148] No longer could reforming organizations be based on informal associations of libertine gentlemen: a critic of Wilkes noted that his only supporters were "a little knot of *jolly* fellows" at Appleby's Tavern.[149] Indeed, the founders of the Bill of Rights Society, which granted Wilkes funds to pay the debts he incurred while serving liberty, were outraged when he squandered the money on wine, women, and song.[150] Tradesmen could forgive an amorous dalliance, but unpaid debts endangered the survival of their businesses. Wilkes became more and more egotistical and disputatious, insisting that all the funds raised be paid to him rather than shared with other defenders of the cause. Rumors began to circulate that Wilkes bilked charities of their funds. Wilkes failed to recognize that these associations were founded for the public good, not his own private gratification.

As a result, Junius's assertion that only public service mattered, not private vices, came under attack from both the right and the left. Some radical political commentators asserted that private vices and public virtues could no longer be separated.[151] One writer insisted, "Who errs in *private*, never can act well."[152] "John Bull" warned his fellow citizens, "For the Sake of our Religion, our Laws, of our Country, and of your Families," beware of Wilkes, who "was guilty of every sort of Profligacy and Debauchery."[153] Some radical commentators celebrated fatherhood and family life as the basis for political action. "Prognostic" advised the "merchant and the mechanic" to "let the company of their wives, and the instruction of their families, take up more of their time than tavern," but all should struggle to "preserve their liberties from the least violation."[154] Wilkes's flamboyant libertine masculinity seemed too aristocratic for the tradesmen and merchants of London, accustomed to guarding their reputations and credit with a more sober, self-restrained manhood.

Conservative and radical opponents of Wilkes gained fresh ammunition from a new scandal in 1771 that enabled them to equate radicalism with gender transgression. The Reverend John Horne, a former close friend and ally of Wilkes, accused him of complicity in a gambling scandal: large sums had been bet on the question of whether or not the Chevalier d'Eon was a man or a woman.[155]

D'Eon, a renegade French diplomat, had long been seen as an ally of Wilkes. He had earlier inspired his own scandal when he refused to return secret diplomatic papers to France in 1763. The French government, concerned, since the papers contained plans for a possible French invasion of England, threatened to kidnap d'Eon. As a result, radicals equated d'Eon with Wilkes, both facing persecution from oppressive governments, and the two men eventually struck up a friendship. A rather slight and foppish man, d'Eon tried to prove his masculinity by offering to duel any critic. But by 1771, he seems to have started circulating the rumor that he was a woman in disguise, perhaps as an effort to escape persecution by the French government.[156] He still went about in public dressed as a man, and refused to confirm or deny the rumors. As a result, frenzied betting erupted over his sex. After all, this was an age in which gentlemen would place large sums on cockroach races. D'Eon become a metaphor for deceit and sexual ambiguity. Like Wilkes, he claimed to be a radical hero, but he deceived the people as to his true nature. In June 1771, a caricature entitled "The Female Freemason" publicized these rumors still further, implying that Wilkes, like d'Eon, was just another popular fraud like Mary Toft, who claimed to have given birth to rabbits.[157]

Conservative forces seized upon the opportunity to link Wilkes and d'Eon for overturning the natural order of society altogether. The caricature *The Rape of Miss d'Eon from France to England* played on d'Eon's ambiguous gender to discredit Wilkes's pursuit of "liberty" as "the Madness of the Time."[158] Similarly, the *Public Advertiser* mockingly proposed the erection of a new Magdalen Institution across from Bedlam, where insane "Patriots" could be confined to shelter the rest of the community from the annoyance of their "wild Ravings." "Mademoiselle d'Eon is to be necessary Woman . . . Jack Wilkes is to be Turnkey, and Mr. Catherine Macaulay Keeper of the Patriots."[159]

To distract public attention from the d'Eon controversy, Wilkes revived his earlier scandals about courtly sodomy. The King had pardoned a Captain Jones for committing sodomy on a thirteen-year-old boy (the boy's age did not enter the controversy). During his election for Lord Mayor in September 1772, Wilkes made this a campaign issue, alleging that the pardon demonstrated once again the immorality of the court.[160] Crowds sang obscene verses about the king and Jones, and theatres complained their audiences had disappeared, too preoccupied with debating the matter.[161]

The Captain Jones case illuminates contemporary attitudes toward homosexuality as well as the political uses of antisodomy rhetoric, revealing that late eighteenth-century people shared a stereotype of the sodomite as cowardly, effeminate, and only interested in sex with men.[162] Captain Jones's defenders declared that he had shown no signs of this "vice," implying he did not have the requisite personality.[163] To excuse the pardon the *St. James Chronicle* praised Jones's "conduct at the siege of the Havannah, where he gave such proofs of courage and bravery, as are seldom to be found in a mind debased by vice and effeminacy."[164] Several "women of the town" eagerly attested that they could personally attest to Jones's virility.[165] Newspaper writers alleged that in the privy council, some noblemen argued that "the greatest Men among [the Greeks and Romans] were known to practice [sodomy] with impunity."[166]

The enemies of Captain Jones, who far outnumbered his defenders, seized this opportunity to link sodomy to a variety of social and political ills.[167] One correspondent to the *Morning Chronicle* declared, "When murder and unnatural lust cease to be capital crimes in the eyes of the supreme magistrate, the state is sunk into the last degree of political depravity."[168] "A

determined Englishman" compared the court of George III to that of James
I "as much in favoritism as in despotism."[169] Another letter, clearly inspired
by the controversy, denounced the custom of sending young gentlemen on
a European tour because "they are ... sometimes infected with the most unnatural and detestable of all vices, and generally import with them a fond-
ness for arbitrary principles of government, and an antipathy to the free
constitution of this kingdom."[170] A squib from "Effendi Vizier" also linked
the scandal to oriental despotism, referring to George III as Jorjie Caliph,
who ruled over the "Court of S[odo]m."[171] Another said Jones received a
pardon only because he was a "Ministerial Tool's Tool."[172] The whole scandal threatened to damage the king's reputation for "conjugal and paternal
virtues."[173] It reached as far as Newcastle, where radical preacher James
Murray equated the court of George III with that of the biblical Moab, corrupted by adultery and sodomy while the people suffered.[174]

Wilkes used the Jones issue for his wider campaign for reform of the
harsh criminal code of Britain.[175] Wilkes, as an alderman, asked why the
king should pardon a crime of "black and flagitious nature" when many
"inferior crimes" must be punished by death.[176] One outraged letter writer
stated that "the punishment of the criminal" seems to "be magnified or diminished according to the station he holds in life, or the prostituted friends
he boasts of at Court."[177]

Wilkes's automatic recourse to homophobia reveals the shallowness of
his defense of private life. He was unable to carry out fully the logic of his
Lockean separation of the public and private; he might have equally argued
(as did one of the correspondents in the Jones case) that "sodomy" was a
private act that did not need to be persecuted under the criminal justice system, since it, like his own libertine behavior, was condemned mainly by the
church.[178] Furthermore, by contrasting sodomy, despotism, and foreign vice
with the virtues of the freeborn Englishman and his constitution, Wilkesites based political rights not on reason but on nationality and masculinity. Wilkes's belief that only public service counted, that personal life was a
private matter, really meant that only heterosexual men had the right to do
whatever they wanted in private.

WOMEN IN PUBLIC AND PRIVATE

John Wilkes never applied his analysis of public oppression to private life,
but some of his female correspondents did. A lady named "CB" sought his
assistance after she refused the husband her father chose for her, and fell

into poverty after her family and friends rejected her.[179] A female "friend to liberty" acknowledged that "politicks [*sic*] is a science not allowed a proper study for Women," but she insisted that "he who is a slave abroad is the greatest tyrant at home."[180] Charlotte Forman, a penurious journalist and translator, regarded marriage as a potential "exchange [of] Liberty for Slavery" and avoided it. Forman commented that "wretched Woman" is "doomed . . . to be subjected to her Husband" or "to lead a solitary lonesome life, and sink gradually into oblivion."[181] These women all wrote to Wilkes in private, but one, the pseudonymous Mary Seymour Montague, publicly refuted Wilkes's *Essay on Woman* in her own *An Original Essay on Woman*.[182] Seymour Montague criticized traditional marriage, asking,

Why Lordly Males are authorized to rule,
And Female Wit sometimes obeys a Fool.

She defended women from the misogyny of Wilkes's supporters, pointing out, "The Libertine thinks all Women lascivious, because he has reduced one or two to Prostitution."[183]

Yet Catherine Macaulay, Wilkes's greatest female ally, did not apply her political analysis of oppression to women's condition in the 1760s and 1770s. Instead, she tried to transcend her sex by writing as a public intellectual. Even she could not escape the misogyny of her time: despite her importance to Wilkes's cause, he ultimately turned a scandal about her private life against her.

Ironically, if Catherine Macaulay had been a man, she might have had a career like that of Wilkes. Like him, she was a wealthy London commoner influenced by Enlightenment principles who enjoyed pleasure and parties. Although her accomplishments gave her an austere, masculine image, she wore rouge, played cards, and gave fashionable parties that began at midnight and ended at three. An "attentive affectionate wife and mother," she believed that "ice cream strengthened and braced the stomach."[184] Of course, as a woman, Macaulay could not attend university, whether Oxford or abroad, so she had to teach herself and rely on other intellectuals. After her husband's death, she intensified her scholarly pursuits and began to keep her radical salon. When the intellectual Elizabeth Carter encountered her at a rout, she was awed by this "fine fashionable well-dressed lady, whose train was longer than anyone else's train," but even more impressed by her ability to discourse on "Spartan laws, Roman politics, [and] the philosophy of Epicurus."[185]

Macaulay fit into the classical republican tradition of masculine virtù by sacrificing her private interests for a public cause. Forgiving Wilkes for a debt, she wrote, "The only object of my ambition and the honest aim of my life is that I may die with the pleasing consciousness of having . . . always acted with the part of a good Citizen."[186] As a woman without a vote, landed property, or aristocratic connections, she could not engage in electoral politics. So she contributed to the radical cause with her constitutional analysis, her courage, and her history. Macaulay's focus on analyzing public life prevented her from developing an overtly feminist analysis of women's rights until her *Letters on Education* of 1790, which will be discussed in chapter 6. In 1767, she even argued that "to prevent aristocratic accumulation of property" females should not enjoy inheritance rights, although of course their education should be funded.[187] As we have seen, she criticized the influence of royal women in the Stuart dynasties.

At the same time, in her *History of England*, she balanced her criticisms of female political influence with praise for female heroines.[188] She told the story of Lady Rachel Russell, who defended her home against the Tories, and mentioned the female petition supporting Lilbourn on freedom of conscience.[189] In two instances, she implicitly criticized the plight of women in marriage. First, she sympathized with the "mortifying" fate of Charles II's queen, "unite[d] in the indissoluble bonds of matrimony with a profligate rake."[190] Second, she criticized Mary for allowing William to supplant her as a monarch: "Though Mary was very well acquainted with the churlish ambition of her husband, yet, in this point, she was in a great measure influenced by notions she had conceived of conjugal fidelity and domestic subordination." As a result of her belief in the "blind rule of an indiscriminate obedience," William acquired too much power.[191] Here Macaulay came close to applying her analysis of tyrannical power in public to the woes of marriage, but her concern remained public politics, not private oppression.

Macaulay's critics believed that as a woman she should not claim a public voice. Indeed, her political opponents denounced her as "masculine," "factious," and "licentious."[192] Undeterred, she wrote, "The invidious censures which may ensue from striking into a path of literature rarely trodden by my sex, will not permit a selfish consideration to keep me mute in the service of liberty and virtue."[193] When she wrote her *Observations* in 1770, she insisted on speaking for the public good despite the "long and malevolent persecution" she had endured for writing her history.[194]

A few women saw her as a pioneer who proved female abilities. An unpublished poem from 1763 hailed her for challenging the notion that women were made only for men's delight. Macaulay was a "genius" who "bids even Lordly man himself to be free," showing "woman fitter both to Rule and Write."[195] Mary Seymour Montague praised her as one of a group of learned women, including the classics scholar Elizabeth Carter, the novelist Frances Sheridan, and the playwright Susanna Centlivre.[196] When Macaulay lamented that so few other women espoused the cause of freedom, her female correspondents assured her that indeed she would find learned, radical women if she looked beyond London high society to Dissenting women in the provinces, or farther afield to France and Boston. In response, she began corresponding with American, Quaker, and French women, who praised her learning and courage.[197]

Male radicals applauded Macaulay for sacrificing her private happiness to write histories in the people's cause.[198] But they tended to see her as an exceptional, masculine woman, much like Athena sprung from the head of Zeus. The masculinity of this exceptional woman could be contrasted with the effeminacy of men afraid to defy the king.[199] Macaulay became an icon of political virtue. For instance, in the radical satire "The Marriage of Junius to Miss Laetitia Liberty," Macaulay joins the bridal procession as "the Character of Freedom," while Wilkes is surrounded by forty-five gentlemen.[200]

Like Wilkes, Macaulay allowed herself to become the embodiment of liberty—but also set herself up as an idol to be destroyed by scandal. She had shared a house in Bath for several years with the rather elderly Dr. Wilson, who was also Wilkes's ally. They both sympathized with republicanism and loved learning, and Dr. Wilson adopted her daughter. Macaulay disregarded the gossip about their relationship and insisted that it was platonic, a meeting of minds. Dr. Wilson practically worshiped Macaulay for her learning and her radicalism. In return, she allowed him to mount an elaborate ceremony lauding her accomplishments on her birthday in 1777. He presented odes to her that declared, "With dauntless freedom by one matchless Maid, / Britannia's glory through the world displayed." They went on to proclaim,

> In her fair pages *Spartan* virtue shines;
> With *Roman* valor glow her nervous lines . . .
> Go on, my Fair! till low beneath thy feet
> Oppression bends, and Freedom reigns complete . . .
> And *Public Virtue* to thy Mem'ry raise
> A Column of imperishable praise.[201]

Dr. Wilson also literally placed her on a pedestal, erecting a statue of her in the garden of Saint Stephens Church, London. He placed a rather odd inscription on the side, which declared,

> Once in every age I could wish such a woman to appear,
> As a proof that genius is not confined to sex;

But at the same time—you will pardon me—
We want no more than one Mrs. Macaulay.

Catherine Macaulay could be lauded as exceptional, but he did not wish her to inspire all women. However, the parishioners of Saint Stephens objected to the statue, especially since Macaulay stood for republican principles.[202]

Perched on a pedestal, Macaulay was easily knocked down. The scandal came the next year when at the age of forty-six, she married William Graham, her doctor's twenty-one-year-old brother.[203] Although all she had done was marry for love, a hail of ridicule immediately descended upon her. For critics, this evidence of female sexual self-assertion erased her eminence as a historian and thinker.[204] A satirical farce, performed on a main London stage, portrayed Macaulay as a "rich widow" who "attempts to extort money from her several admirers."[205] A poem called "The Female Patriot" alleged that she betrayed Dr. Wilson, who had enthroned her at Bath, "where the numerous band of Poets, Patriots, Puppies, Pimps, presented their respective homages to this extraordinary idol in the most humble posture, and with the most flattering tone of adulation." Since Dr. Wilson, according to the poet, could not satisfy her, Macaulay married the younger man out of lust; overcome with desire, she threw her historical papers in the flames to worship her handsome young husband. According to the poem, she abandoned her principles for love:

> Lo! Catherine thus with am'rous fetters bound
> In magick thraldom did the God surround;
> In vain, Liberty, I feld to thee,
> Alas! M——c——y was no longer free.[206]

Another poem asked why

> She!—who to all the World beside
> Has blazon'd forth the monstrous Pride
> Of *Kings*, can she crouch mute
> Beneath a Husband's Yoke, whose Nod
> Is Law, whose Will's a ruling God
> That will not brook Dispute?[207]

To be sure, a reply asserted the rights of widows to marry again.[208] But for most critics Macaulay had lost credibility merely by revealing herself to be a human being, not a goddess of liberty.

Wilkes spread scurrilous rumors about her, most hypocritically, given his long series of mistresses. He wrote to a friend, "Ten thousand particulars are now told of the female historian's insolence [and] capriciousness." Wilkes claimed that even Macaulay's own letters showed her to be a "most abandoned prostitute, and a swindler."[209] However, in these allegedly indecent letters to Dr. Wilson, Macaulay just praised Dr. Graham for curing her various stomach ailments.[210]

News of Macaulay's marriage overshadowed the publication of the new volume of her *History*, which addressed the eighteenth century up to her own time, sharply criticizing Parliament, the Whigs, and the Tories.[211] Macaulay continued to publish volumes of her history, as well as a thoughtful theological pamphlet. But she did not publish another political pamphlet until 1790, when she penned a reply to Burke. Instead, she turned away from contemporary English politics and focused on her correspondents in America and France, who still lauded her service for liberty.

Macaulay could not openly defend herself from scandal. No doubt she thought that her private life should be no business of the public, only her public service to the cause. But the scandal she faced revealed that for women, the distinction between public and private was illusory. She had chosen the genre of narrative history, based on her belief in facts, truths, and disinterested discourse, and she found it impossible to descend to the rough-and-tumble world of the daily press. Her marriage had deprived her of her political ally Dr. Wilson, and her far-flung female correspondents could not defend her in the press or in the clubs and pubs of London. Macaulay, unlike Wilkes, was a lone individual without a movement to help her recover from scandal. Once her female body was revealed, her words would not be taken as evidence, only her sex.

Mary Seymour Montague, in contrast to Macaulay, believed that women must publicly refute misogyny and band together in defense. She envisioned an intellectual retreat, much like that of Sarah Scott in *Millenium Hall*, where women could

> Expand each Foliage of the searching Mind,
> Which free by Birth, dull Custom has confin'd
> To chase fair Science in the Fields of Light,
> And win from Prejudice each stolen right.[212]

Seymour Montague dedicated her poem to the "Female Coterie," "Ye fair, who met each other to improve, / And vulgar Codes of Prejudice remove." The "Female Coterie" may have been the female club formed by some "distinguished ladies" in 1769; but despite their own reputation for virtue, they were mercilessly reviled as improper, and the king and queen seriously disapproved.[213] One newspaper correspondent, nonetheless, in 1771 suggested that "ladies" should form their own coffee room, since "their conversation has often been productive of many salutary methods, for private and public good, and in an age where liberty is so much the reigning topic of conversation, why may they not have the liberty of assembling together, without incurring censure from the public?" Outside of the political system, he thought, women might be able to overcome political animosities and divisions.[214] Indeed, as shall be described in the next chapter, the opening up of politics inspired by the Wilkesite movement led to the creation of debating societies where men and women could mingle—or even where women could assemble and discuss public issues together. The "Female Coterie" may have evolved into the gambling clubs run by elite aristocratic ladies, who also used them as political salons.

CONCLUSION

John Wilkes was able to take the constitutional issue of the king's power, which Catherine Macaulay raised in her sober tomes, and communicate it to the streets through crude satires and graphic images. He helped open the political world beyond the closed circles of Parliament and the court to wider numbers of middling and laboring men. Even if the increased newspaper circulation of the time was based on the appeal of personal scandal, the resulting profits gave the press more independence from the government. His court cases established lasting constitutional protections for the liberty of the subject and freedom of speech. Wilkes significantly moved radical politics beyond earlier attacks on corruption by refusing to indulge in anti-Catholic rhetoric and by advocating universal manhood suffrage when he finally took his seat in Parliament in 1776.

Wilkes defended himself from the scandal of *The Essay on Woman* by asserting that only a man's public service mattered, not his private life. This theme became an important Whig weapon against the paternal justification for monarchy and a defense against incursions on private rights of individual conscience. Wilkes linked a man's right to participate in public politics and his right to conduct his private life as he chose, equating liberty with libertinism. While classical republicans saw the ideal citizen as the propertied householder, Wilkes called for a much more democratic notion of manliness that reached from elite gentlemen like himself through the middling sort and laborers. But Wilkes violated his own principles about privacy by accusing Luttrell of being a seducer, and exploiting the fear of sodomy as an electoral issue. He thus helped to solidify the emerging stereotypes of men who sexually desired other men as effeminate, cowardly sodomites. By gossiping about Catherine Macaulay, Wilkes made clear that for him, the right to privacy did not extend to women; rather, it was the right for a man to do whatever he wanted to women in private. Her public service in providing constitutional and historical ammunition to the Wilkesites mattered little when her private reputation could be smeared.

Wilkes himself could not escape the personal politics of scandal. Although he portrayed himself as a libertine for the cause of liberty, his constituencies demanded a more virtuous and controlled private life. By the late 1770s, he seemed to be just another ambitious politician, seeking City of London offices in order to pay off his debts. In 1782, he switched from the opposition to support of the king. Wilkes could not disentangle his own status as hero, or his libertine lifestyle, from the larger cause of political change.

The controversy over the American war more or less eclipsed sexual scandals about individual politicians. Sexual scandal did not disappear in the late 1770s, but it became less central to politics. In part, this was because the issue of secret feminine (or effeminate) influence over the king faded when the princess dowager died in 1772. The biggest political scandal of the late 1770s, the threatened court-martial of Admiral Keppel, concerned the conduct of the American war rather than sexual malfeasance.[215] To be sure, gendered images appeared in the rhetoric of the American war, as government supporters portrayed the Americans as ungrateful children who betrayed their mother. But the Americans asserted that they were not children, but men, and that family metaphors had nothing to do with politics.[216] The issue was not so much the personal politics of the court, but the constitutional questions of Parliament and empire.

By the late 1770s, the movement Wilkes inspired had successfully transcended its origins to focus on the larger cause of parliamentary reform. Associations and debating societies created new forms of political organization and discussion beyond parliamentary politics. By focusing on liberty and reason, they even made it possible for a few women to assert their right to participate in the political process, as we shall see in the next chapter. But the issue of petticoat influence reappeared when the constitutional questions of king and Parliament revived in the early 1780s.

❧ ❧ ❧

CHAPTER THREE

Influence or Independence:
Women and Elections, 1777–1788

In 1784, Georgiana, Duchess of Devonshire, swept through the muddy streets of Westminster, her silk gowns dazzling the local shoemakers and butchers. A flirtatious leader of fashion, she was canvassing for the Whig candidate Charles James Fox, a known libertine. Their activities sparked a scandal; caricatures mocked her as a drunken harridan and him as a gambler. Yet Fox triumphed in Westminster and credited the duchess with his victory. In contrast, Mary, Countess of Strathmore, a wealthy and intellectual heiress, found no power in politics. After impulsively marrying adventurer Andrew Robinson Bowes, she helped him win election as Foxite Whig member of Parliament for Newcastle; but in return, he savagely beat her behind the scenes.

The lives of these two aristocratic women can illuminate debates on women's place in the late eighteenth century. Some historians argue that the duchess overcame this scandal to set a precedent for women's advance into politics.[1] New research has brilliantly uncovered extensive evidence of eighteenth-century female aristocrats' participation in politics, but we must ask whether all women, or just aristocratic ladies, benefited from this trend.[2] Furthermore, women's role in politics needs to be understood in the context of larger contemporary debates about the constitution, for the scandals about women in elections were directed just as much against aristocratic power as against female participation in politics.

These debates centered on the question of influence versus independence. The aristocracy and the Crown controlled most elections through their influence. Many contemporaries believed that this aristocratic influence was legitimate and that the people should defer to the great families at the pinnacle of society. Because elite women's political activity derived from this influence, it did not cause scandal for most of the century.[3] Even the Whigs, who criticized the Crown, believed that aristocratic dynasties should lead politics. But eighteenth-century voters also upheld a tradition of independence, declaring that they should vote for the candidate who would uphold the people's interest.

As political entrepreneurs, the Whigs Charles James Fox and Andrew Robinson Bowes appealed to independent voters as champions of the Commons against the Crown. Like Wilkes, they equated masculine libertinism with liberty. But radicals claimed that the Commons was not truly independent because it was controlled by aristocratic dynasties, not the people. Radicals criticized the activities of aristocratic women such as the duchess of Devonshire and the countess of Strathmore in order to denigrate aristocratic power. Some radical moralists even argued that the libertine masculinity of Fox and Bowes could lead to corruption. Electoral scandals could therefore express constitutional debates in vivid terms, even as they exploited personal politics.

INFLUENCE OR INDEPENDENCE

The political power of aristocratic women derived from the system of influence. Aristocratic dynasties could control parliamentary elections directly or through more subtle techniques.[4] Often, the great families of a constituency settled among themselves who would stand, so there was no need for a contested election. Aristocratic patrons nominated members for 30 percent of the 658 seats in the House of Commons, and the number rose over the course of the eighteenth century. In these constituencies, electorates were typically small and dependent on a patron.[5] A few aristocratic women could inherit their dynasty's control over a constituency, such as Lady Irwin, who nominated two members of Parliament for Horsham, and Mrs. Allanson, who could select two for Ripon.[6]

In constituencies where elections were contested, great families had to use their influence. What did this influence mean? In part, voters traditionally deferred to the dynasties that had controlled their areas for generations. Families earned this deference by doing them favors and spreading charity. During elections, the great families had to canvass, pressure, and entertain voters and mount elaborate campaigns complete with broadsheets and banners.[7] Elite women played a crucial role in this process: they could bestow patronage indirectly; they often controlled livings for clergymen; and they set up schools for poor children and established workshops to employ laborers. Great ladies had to open their houses to entertain influential voters, call upon their wives, and even canvass in the streets.[8]

Aristocratic families also exerted influence by direct material means, granting benefits and threatening to withdraw them if voters did not comply with their wishes. Given the lack of a secret ballot, landlords could instruct their tenants how to vote, employers could threaten to fire workers who failed to follow their partisan wishes, and philanthropists could tell the parents of schoolchildren whom to favor.[9] If elite women owned land, they could tell their tenants how to vote. For instance, Anne Damer, the noted sculptor, wrote to Mr. Grenville, "As a *true Old Whig* I should have been most ready to give my votes, had I any to dispose of . . . but the fact is that . . . not an acre have I."[10] Of course, voters sometimes defied landlords, employers, and philanthropists, but more often such pressure could determine the outcome of elections.[11]

Candidates had to appeal to public opinion by making speeches to electoral clubs, inserting letters and columns in newspapers, and distributing squibs, ballads, and broadsheets supporting their cause. Both men and women could contribute squibs and songs, even if they did not vote. Of course, these publications had to be paid for, which was another reason that elections were so expensive. The combination of the personal politics of aristocratic influence and the need to appeal to public opinion also meant that scandalous rumors about candidates could become weapons in electoral campaigns.

In the tradition of independence, many voters asserted their right as freeborn English men to enjoy the franchise and to instruct their members of Parliament. While county voters had to have some property, in borough constituencies (often more urban), the franchise was sometimes fairly evenly distributed through the social structure, ranging from workmen, to shopkeepers, to professionals and gentlemen. In such areas, electorates were too large to bribe.[12] Enfranchised men organized themselves into clubs to negotiate with candidates and celebrated their victories by carousing with bumpers of beer. Both enfranchised and unenfranchised men became part of the larger political nation by signing petitions to Parliament and the king.[13] Everyone, even women, could participate in elections by joining the crowds celebrating the triumphant candidate. Yet electoral independence was associated with a virile masculinity that usually excluded women.[14] Plebeian women could cheer in the streets and parade in electoral processions, but they could not join electoral clubs or vote.[15]

Was this independence compatible with aristocratic influence? Overall, voters largely accepted aristocratic influence, some historians argue, paying proper due to the status of wealth, title, and tradition. To portray eighteenth-century electoral politics as corrupt would be anachronistic, they argue, judging the past by the standards of the present.[16] For instance, although these historians admit that candidates sometimes bribed voters, they suggest that bribery was rare and ineffective.[17]

Voters found it difficult to assert their independence successfully.[18] Over the course of the eighteenth century, the electorate declined as a percentage of the adult male population, from 23.9 percent in 1715 to 14.4 percent in 1831.[19] Many large towns, notably new industrial areas such as Manchester, did not have the right to elect a member of Parliament at all. It is not anachronistic to portray eighteenth-century electoral politics as corrupt because many contemporaries denounced the bribery and corruption they saw all around them.[20] Voters protested when employers sacked workers who voted the wrong way.[21] What conservatives saw as deference, philanthropy, and patronage, radicals saw as illicit influence. How could voters exercise independence if their jobs or tenancies depended on how they cast their ballots?

Radicals sometimes linked feminine influence with this corruption. They claimed that noble families had their female relatives campaign to get around the constitutional proscription against peers interfering in elections to the House of Commons.[22] To avoid prosecution for bribing male voters directly, radicals alleged that candidates' agents chinked gold into the hands of voters' wives.[23] In the play *The Country Election*, the crooked agent Quirk advises his cronies, "Don't forget to tip an old woman's tongue with gold." Following his advice, the candidate passed a guinea to one voter's wife with an openmouthed kiss.[24]

From the 1760s onward, the revival of party politics added a third element to the tension between aristocratic influence and independence. Once George III dismissed the Whigs, they went into opposition, and as a result, Whigs and the government party more frequently and hotly contested elections. But neither the Whigs nor government supporters functioned as parties in the modern political sense; rather, they were shifting factions tied together by personal loyalties and patronage. Whig leaders could turn from opposing to supporting the government. Members of Parliament tended to follow wealthy, charismatic, or powerful leaders, whatever their principles. Because parties were based on personal loyalties and shifting factions, scandal could erupt over the personal lives of political leaders.

The social and family connections behind parties also provided new ways for elite women to participate in politics. Great ladies wore ribbons and adopted fashions in the colors of their parties, turning theater and social events into displays of political loyalty. In London, aristocratic women controlled high society, organizing balls and even gambling clubs. In the provinces, great families competed through party politics. In the novel *The*

General Election, the heroine remarked, "In the country, a lady is nothing, if she is not a politician," and claimed that ladies of the opposite party hissed at her from their carriage.[25] But party conflict could also shift the terrain of politics away from traditional aristocratic interests: Mrs. Osborn, sister of a member of Parliament, lamented the more competitive politics of the 1760s, when the radical and parliamentary oppositions, and upstart merchants and "nabobs," wealthy East India Company officers, challenged the traditional stable landed interests: "Even the very ladies are changed in dress and behavior" as they canvassed in campaigns.[26] While canvassing for members of one's own family might be a traditional obligation for an aristocratic lady, canvassing for a party might seem scandalous.

Despite the importance of personality and faction, some differences of principle could be distinguished between the parties, chiefly focusing on the right of the king to choose his minister, and the relationship of Parliament and the people. Their different philosophies could also be expressed in competing images of the family. However, when parties tried to use the rhetoric of family values, they became vulnerable to scandal.

Government supporters were often conservatives who tended to celebrate the divine, indefeasible right of the monarchy. They defended the king's right to choose his own minister and denounced the existence of the Whig party as scandalous, motivated by selfish factionalism rather than the interests of the country at large. Sometimes known as the Tories (especially later in the century), they celebrated an ordered, deferential society with the monarch at its apex and the family as its base. They promised to defend the Church of England against Dissenters and praised England's ordered, pious, hierarchical society.[27] While these conservatives believed that the people should acquiesce to the government rather than asserting their independence, they also knew that they had to appeal to a wider public. By emphasizing family virtue, among other issues, they attracted many Dissenters and provincial middle-class people, broadening the government's base in public opinion. The government appealed to them by portraying the king as a good father.

One faction of the Whigs, known as the Rockingham Whigs and in the 1780s led by Charles James Fox and Edmund Burke, developed a set of principles that opposed the government position and rationalized the existence of their party. Edmund Burke transformed Wilkes's scandalous insinuations about the princess dowager's influence into a wider constitutional critique of an alleged double cabinet of advisers to the king. While the actual existence of this double cabinet has been seen as a "heated fancy" of Burke's imagination, Burke used such fantastic images as metaphors for his constitutional points.[28] For Burke, royal influence was based on private likings and secret favors and was unaccountable to Parliament; he feared that its exercise would transform the constitutional monarchy into a "despotism" with overweening power.[29] He argued that the Whig party was constitutional and necessary because it would counterbalance the king's power, protect the liberties of the people, and act on principles of public virtue. This party would also do a better job of managing public opinion and preventing the disorders that disrupted the nation in the Wilkesite era. However, the Rockingham Whigs stressed the rights of Parliament more than the rights of the people. After Parliament overturned Wilkes's election at Middlesex in 1771, Charles James Fox proclaimed, "I pay no regard whatever to the voice of the people . . . their business is to choose us; it is ours . . . to maintain the independence of Parliament."[30] Fox soon became more friendly to reformers, but his priority was always the Commons' struggle against the Crown. Burke criticized Parliament for overturning Wilkes's election, but he opposed efforts to extend the franchise.[31]

Burke believed that parties could exert legitimate influence based on public virtue and openness. By using the image of the family to explain his idea of party, he justified the continuance of aristocratic influence. He declared that "commonwealths are made of families, free commonwealths of parties also," defining the family here in its broadest sense as a hereditary noble dynasty, including distant relatives and followers. Burke believed that the Whig dynasties exemplified "hereditary virtue" because their ancestors had defended liberty in the Glorious Revolution of 1688.[32] "Natural regards and ties of blood" strengthened party loyalty and connections. The Crown should not have a monopoly on patronage; instead, a member of Parliament should be able to bestow offices on "children, brothers, or kindred" or the "children of mayors" in his own constituency. This patronage would be legitimate because it would be open and public, and because it would strengthen the power of the Commons and the party against the Crown.[33] To be sure, Burke also believed politics should be based on "friendship, virtue and independence."[34] But he defined friendship as the patronage that enabled him to gain office, virtue as the aristocratic heritage of 1688, and independence as the possession of landed property.

Radicals and reformers believed that aristocratic family interest should be kept separate from politics, and they distrusted Parliament and the party system. Catherine Macaulay's constitutional analysis aided their cause. In her reply to Burke's pamphlet, Macaulay discerned what Burke really meant by family: the Whigs wished to extend patronage to their families and followers. She warned that however much they claimed to defend liberty, the

Whigs were just another "aristocratic faction and party, founded and supported by the corrupt principle of self-interest."[35] During 1688–89, she argued, the Whigs gained the confidence of the people as guardians of their rights, and by 1770 claimed to defend them against "the undermining and irresistible hydra, court influence," but in fact, the real danger lay in "the more terrifying, yet less formidable monster," the prerogative of Parliament. At the same time, she portrayed the Tories as enemies to democracy and idol worshipers because they defended the indefeasible right of the Crown.[36] Radicals sometimes illustrated Macaulay's elevated and abstract argument by using images of aristocratic ladies to epitomize corrupt aristocratic influence.

Radicals and reformers challenged the notion that Parliament was the only legitimate representative of public opinion and refuted the organization of parties on the basis of influence, personal connections, and dynastic ties. They did not think voters could exert true independence in the current electoral system. As a debater declared, "It is a fact universally felt, that undue influence robs the great body of the people of their political rights, by the smooth medium of bribing their wants and passions."[37] Instead, they believed the people should organize themselves outside of Parliament on the basis of principle, individual rights, and open discussion of ideas. By 1779, the Association movement for parliamentary reform demanded an end to corruption and the expansion of the franchise. Inspired by the American war, it wanted to fundamentally transform politics.

The Association movement illustrates the mixed potential of radicalism for women. On one hand, its adherents continued to associate independence with masculinity, contrasting the luxuriousness, corruption, and effeminacy of the court and the aristocracy with the "manly" virtues of the freeborn English man.[38] But the Association movement differed within itself over who was to enjoy this right. The country gentlemen of its dominant Yorkshire wing still believed that only property-holding men qualified as voters; they were more interested in purifying Parliament than in expanding democracy. Middle-class men sometimes linked the right to vote with the right to command and serve in militias, challenging the association of the aristocracy with military leadership and the right to lead politics. In doing so, they linked militarism, masculinity, and the vote. On the other hand, some elements of the Association movement began to redefine citizenship in ways that might be applied to women. The Society for Constitutional Information believed that the political nation should include not only voters but also those left out of the electoral system.[39] The Reverend Thomas Northcote supported the idea that the vote was a birthright of humanity, not a traditional custom or a privilege of Britons.[40] Another author wrote that "social virtue and knowledge . . . is the best, and only necessary qualification" for the vote.[41] According to that notion of virtue, some might consider women eminently qualified.

A new way for women to participate in politics emerged, based on independent thought rather than the influence of aristocratic ladies. While the Association movement did not permit women to join, it both grew out of and stimulated a vast expansion of debating societies, some of which did admit women.[42] Unlike the heavy-drinking, ultramasculine Wilkesite clubs and pubs, the debating societies were more genteel, based on witty and rational interchange. They appealed to a wide variety of people—as long as they could pay the modest admission fee. The Westminster Forum, for instance, was "Frequented by people of different classes / Old dons and young smarts, old dames and young lasses."[43] A few mixed societies allowed women to speak, but most women found it too difficult to debate in public, experiencing the "natural timidity of those who have but lately assumed their rights and privileges."[44] So they formed their own female societies.[45] The leaders of La Belle Assemblée began by reassuring audiences that "the Ladies, knowing nothing of the affairs of state, do not interfere with them."[46] They soon became more bold. While aristocratic ladies derived their influence from their wealth and dynastic position, the debating society women applied the Association movement's emphasis on public service and independence to themselves. For instance, in 1781, La Belle Assemblée asked "whether it would not be for the benefit of this Country, if Females had a Voice in the Elections of Representatives, and were eligible to sit in Parliament, as well as the men?" Between 1780 and 1788, the societies debated five times whether women should vote and hold office.[47] However, debaters sometimes argued that women were still too vulnerable to courtly influence to be trusted with the vote.[48] Commentators often ridiculed the female debaters and derided their presence in public as improper.[49]

Charles James Fox and his Whigs tried to appeal to the wider public of the debating societies and the Association movement. But his vacillating political opinions became a central issue in electoral scandals. In the late 1770s, Fox attacked what he saw as the king's excessive influence and opposed his policies in the American war. By 1780, Fox even flirted with the radical Westminster wing of the Association movement. Together, they denounced Lord North, a conservative Whig who served the king as prime minister and masterminded his war policy. In elections in 1777 and 1780, the Foxites appealed to those inspired by Wilkes and the Association movement to assert the independence of the people against the Crown.

But Fox was an ambitious politician who wanted political office and knew that only the traditional intrigue of political influence could help him attain it. He saw his chance in 1782 when the government fell after the debacle of the American war. As the leader of the third-largest opposition group in Parliament, he formed a coalition to force the king to accept his ministry. Distrusting Shelburne, the leader of one of the other Whig factions, he decided to form a coalition with Lord North, his former enemy. The king reluctantly accepted this strange alliance, but he hated Fox. Fox used his power to pass an East India bill through the House of Commons, which would have given him control over the policy and patronage of India. His opponents, distrusting Fox's motives after he allied with the antireform Lord North, feared he would use this patronage to control future elections. The king and his supporters also claimed that the bill would undermine the power of the Crown.[50] (For more on this bill, see chapter 4.) The king pressured members of the House of Lords to veto the bill, with the implicit threat that they would lose royal patronage if they did not.[51] As a result, Fox had to resign from the government, and the king chose the young William Pitt as his prime minister. Once again, as with Bute, the king asserted his right to choose his minister, whatever the Commons thought.

In the 1784 election, Fox unsuccessfully attempted to regain his majority in the House of Commons. Fox presented himself as a champion of the people and Parliament against the overweening crown. But could he persuade radicals and reformers disappointed at his coalition? Pitt tried to appeal to wider public opinion as well, adroitly addressing moralistic provincials by celebrating the king as a good father; he also promised reform. As a result, politics became intensely personalized, divided between Foxites and Pittites.[52]

Given the personal nature of politics and the attack on corruption, it is not surprising that the masculinity and femininity of political figures became a flash point in these conflicts. Discussion of elections in 1777, 1780, and 1784 in Newcastle, Westminster, and Norwich will help address the question of whether voters accepted the aristocratic dominance of politics and whether they succeeded in asserting their independence.

NEWCASTLE AND THE COUNTESS OF STRATHMORE

In 1780, Andrew Stoney Bowes won a seat in Parliament, representing the bustling northern city of Newcastle. He campaigned for the cause of liberty, like Wilkes celebrating his libertine reputation as a free and easy, independent man.[53] But how independent could Bowes be if he relied on the dynastic connections of his wife, the countess of Strathmore? The countess campaigned for her husband, alluring voters with her sparkling diamonds and her generous philanthropy. Did her activities help advance the wider cause of women in politics?

The story of Mary Ellen Bowes, the countess of Strathmore, illustrates the complicated hurdles eighteenth-century women faced when they advanced into public life. At first glance, she had every advantage: beauty, wealth, and intelligence. A friend of bluestockings such as the Shakespeare scholar Mrs. Elizabeth Montagu, the countess knew several languages, botanized extensively, and wrote poetry and at least one play.[54] Her father, George Bowes, bestowed upon her the fortune he had amassed in the coal mining industry. In a typical match of new money and old titles, she married the earl of Strathmore, who combined her name with his to found the Bowes-Lyon dynasty. Her distant descendant, Elizabeth Bowes-Lyon, married George VI and gave birth to Elizabeth II, becoming England's beloved queen mother. But Mary Ellen Bowes's life was much less happy than that of her descendant. Her first husband, the earl of Strathmore, scorned her erudition and prohibited her friendship with Mrs. Montagu. Although she bore five children to Strathmore in six years, she also took several lovers. After Strathmore died, she felt free to stretch her wings and explore her botanical interests. She also consented to marry her lover George Grey, who had returned from India with a fortune. Preparing for this marriage, she signed a separate settlement that prevented future husbands from controlling her fortune. But her wealth and learning could not protect her from sexual insult—and the vagaries of her own heart.[55]

The widowed countess soon fell prey to the newspapers' appetite for high-society gossip. The *Morning Post*'s scurrilous editor, "Parson" Bate, filled his columns with stories of her flirtations. But Grey refused to defend his fiancée's honor by challenging Bate to a duel. Andrew Robinson Stoney, a notorious Irish fortune hunter, ostentatiously took up the gauntlet and fought Parson Bate himself. His wounds aroused Mary Ellen's sympathy; he won her heart, and her hand. Overcome by his chivalrous act, she agreed to marry him, and he agreed to take her surname, becoming Andrew Robinson Bowes. However, both parties entered the marriage lacking crucial information. She failed to notice that Stoney's wounds were suspiciously slight; he and Bate had probably staged the duel to capture her affections.[56] He did not know that he would not have access to her vast property. Of course Bowes soon found out and began physically and mentally torturing her so that she would give him control over her fortune.[57]

Lacking access to the countess's full wealth, Bowes was still able to profit from her political connections. In 1777, he unsuccessfully ran for Parliament in Newcastle, capitalizing on the countess's holdings there and the heritage of her father, who served as a member of Parliament for nearby Durham.[58] Amazingly, Bowes's dubious character did not become an issue in 1777, even though he had thrown his previous wife, a local heiress, down the stairs at a public meeting, and everyone knew he kept mistresses and cheated at cards.[59] Instead, voters focused on the tensions between great families, local elites, and Newcastle tradesmen.

Local members of Parliament tried to draw upon traditional deference while appealing to the voters' independence.[60] For instance, George Bowes, the father-in-law, was known as a champion of independence who erected a golden statue of Liberty in his gardens. George Bowes was a good example of the newer commercial and industrial interests who rose into the aristocratic elite by marrying into titled families and entering Parliament. The former Newcastle member of Parliament, Sir Walter Blackett, had identified himself as a Patriot who supported the elder William Pitt, darling of the people in the 1750s and 1760s. But radicals felt betrayed when Blackett turned away from the Patriot cause to the court and sided with the local Newcastle elite against working men. When Sir Walter died, his nephew Sir John Trevelyan hoped to fill his place as a member of Parliament, assuming that voters would defer to this dynastic succession.

Many Newcastle voters, especially the artisans who enjoyed the franchise as freemen of the city, prized independence above deference. A "Free Burgess" advised voters to disdain "to be transferred like slaves, goods, and chattels" from Sir Walter to his nephew and, instead, "manfully to maintain our own independence."[61] Many Newcastle voters had sided with Wilkes in 1768–70, and apparently even the women were becoming vociferous in his support.[62] Reformers often expressed resentment at aristocrats who failed to support the interests of commerce and the needs of poor and middling class people. For instance, James Murray, a radical Dissenting preacher, criticized the local gentlemen for building an assembly room where they could celebrate "the ceremonies of Bacchus" instead of rebuilding the bridge over the River Tyne, which would have aided industry.[63] He denounced the royal court for taxing the people in order to pay their whores.[64]

These radicals needed a candidate with the means to stand against Sir John Trevelyan; they chose Bowes, hoping he could defeat the local oligarchy.[65] Bowes opposed the administration and promised to obey his constituents' instructions. He lauded the independence of the electors, "the honest Indignation which has marked your Opposition to a most shameful and arbitrary System."[66] Bowes appealed to plebeian voters who liked aristocratic leaders for embodying the principle of manly freedom: the freedom to proclaim political independence, and the freedom to carouse and drink.[67] As a tavern song declared, Bowes's "sprightly wit has made him fit / To speak his mind so free."[68] To be sure, he was the first to laugh at his own jokes, and his long nose bobbed up and down as he talked.[69] But his good looks, military experience, quick wit, and bold principles won over many men. He not only supported Wilkesite principles but also emulated Wilkes's libertine persona, appealing to the "Bucks, Bloods, and Beaux" of Newcastle.[70] Even the moralistic preacher James Murray supported Bowes in 1777, perhaps hoping that his independence would outweigh his libertinism.[71]

Yet Bowes also drew upon traditional dynastic elements, asking for voters to choose "in the interest of one of the most popular, best, and respectable families in the north of England."[72] Lady Strathmore's support ensured that "many persons of respectability" favored him. At Bowes's later trial, witnesses testified that "Lady Strathmore interested herself very much in Mr. Bowes's interest, when he stood candidate for Newcastle, though she advised him against it; but he dressed her in diamonds, and did every thing to allure her."[73]

The countess performed her duties as a traditional political wife, which enabled Bowes to draw upon the persuasive power of patronage, deference, and philanthropy. She opened up her great house of Gibside to the people on her birthday and roasted an ox to distribute to the poor people of the town. A song by "Felicia" praised Bowes and his "generous" wife, calling on the citizens to "Come see Bowes, and my Lady / Who makes all Newcastle young ones gay."[74] Newspapers reported that she gave money to charities such as the lying-in hospital and also sponsored a performance of two plays, *The Word to the Wise* and *The Padlock*.[75] Of course, the newspaper report about the plays may have been a satirical squib, for these titles were rather too appropriate for an abused wife. In fact, during the very election campaign, Bowes beat the countess so severely she became partially deaf. As her maid testified, she "saw the torn hat which belonged to her Lady, and also saw her Lady with a black eye. Her Lady appeared dejected, and to have no will of her own."[76] As the countess later wrote, "I was constantly in such terror and confusion from the Blows, threats, curses, and ill language I had recently received . . . that I was, for some time rendered incapable of hearing or replying to what people said even in common conversations."[77] But in 1777, the Newcastle public seemed not to know or care about this abuse.

Instead, femininity became emblematic of corruption. Bowes's opponents portrayed the countess's campaigning as an example of bribery. A

Trevelyan supporter alleged Lady Strathmore invented "a new way of offering bribes"—she sat all day in the window of a public house, occasionally dropping a "trinket or jewel" and rewarding voters who picked them up and returned them.[78] While this story cannot be verified, the countess did offer at least one Newcastle freeman a job in return for his vote. Years later Samuel Haggerston of Newcastle appealed to the countess to fulfill her promise to give him a place in her colliery in exchange for his vote, "knowing that Ladyship belongin to such A good Honourable famley that if ever they promes any thing we all beleved that it would be Granted."[79] But Bowes's opponents also used employment as a political weapon; the mayor allegedly discharged a butcher and other tradesmen for voting for Bowes.[80]

Bowes accused Trevelyan of bribing voters via their wives. Trevelyan's agent had instructed his employee to give money to the wives of voters but had warned him "that the two husbands must not be present when I treated with the wives." Indeed, when a Trevelyan supporter offered to "treat" Mrs. Elliot, she indignantly refused his coins, declaring "her husband, brother and cousin were determined to vote for Mr. Bowes, "the radical candidate."[81] Wives who accepted Trevelyan's coins might have seen the vote as a form of family property, to be traded to the highest bidder.[82] However, husbands legally owned any money their wives received. Bowes was hypocritical to attack Trevelyan for getting at voters through their wives. Like many candidates, he gave funds to support wives of nonresident freemen while their husbands traveled to Newcastle to vote.[83]

Bowes finally succeeded in winning the Newcastle election in 1780, when he stood as a radical candidate supporting Charles James Fox and the Association movement. He declared that "every honest man" must support the movement for parliamentary reform, unless he was "perverted by motives of private interest, or party connection." His supporters hoped that "great *talents and responsibility* will for once overcome the influence of overgrown power and family connections."[84] However, the radicals and reformers split over Bowes's candidacy.[85] One of his opponents in the three-way race, Thomas Delaval, had long supported Wilkes and the Association movement more consistently and vigorously than Bowes. Bowes seems to have triumphed over Delaval with opportunistic tactics. He appealed to the less savory aspects of British radicalism by attacking Catholics and, at last minute, allied himself with the more conservative candidate, Ridley.

Increasing evidence revealed that Bowes resorted to bribery. As a result, the radical Dissenting preacher James Murray turned against him.[86] London voters reported that Bowes had been seen visiting Lord North and Mr. Robinson, who was in charge of distributing Treasury funds to win elections for the ministry.[87] In Newcastle, it was widely reported that Bowes ordered some custom house officials to vote for him, claiming that they should have received instructions from the Treasury to do so. When this matter became public, he claimed that all the other candidates tried to obtain votes in such ways.[88] Bowes wrote to a friend in 1780, "Pray use ANY MEANS" to secure Newcastle freemen resident in London to vote for him.[89] Once in Parliament, he voted against Lord Mahon's bill that would prohibit the "treating" of wives of nonresident freemen—an easy way of augmenting voters' rewards.[90]

Fourth, Bowes more openly allied himself with aristocratic, dynastic interests. Following Whig traditions, he again argued that the people should defer to his dynastic Bowes connections; after all, the family had defended the people's liberties against the Crown and local elites. Bowes needed to counter those conservatives who said Bowes was a Johnny-come-lately who only acquired a fortune through a recent marriage. To build upon familial interests legitimately, they argued, a candidate must be a good paternalist landlord with ancient, permanent roots in the community and a good moral character. In response, Bowes declared that as the husband of the countess of Strathmore he was "entitled . . . to avail himself of the hereditary influence which she derives from the merits of her ancestors."[91] His supporters argued that by choosing a lady "of great proficiency in the polished arts and literature," Bowes proved his own merit. Bowes also stressed the great commercial connections of his wife's fortunes, which brought prosperity to Newcastle.[92]

Many radicals, however, objected to the implication that they should vote as the great families instructed, whether they were Whig or government supporters. A "poor burgess" wrote that electors should not have to vote because of family interests: "We may admire the refinement and elegance of a S[trathmore] but we will scarce be brought to consider ourselves, as the hereditary appendages to any estate or family in this or any other neighborhood."[93] Radicals denounced Bowes's support from peers such as Lords Ravensworth and Northumberland as an unconstitutional interference in elections.[94] In ruder language, a song mocked Bowes as proclaiming

> By fortune peculiar a fortune I've got
> But fortune elsewhere, believe I have not
> I'll spend it as won, which cost me no *pain,*
> By *standing a Member, again and again.*[95]

Bowes's character finally became an issue.[96] "Sic Sentio" asked voters, "Is he a person of notoriously immoral conduct? for the welfare of the civil state is always connected with the religious one."[97] Only the female inhabitants of Newcastle, however, publicly protested at Bowes's violent treatment of his wife. In 1780, and again in 1784, squibs signed by women were the only ones that linked Bowes's abuse of his wife with his political dishonesty. A "Lady" published an election song warning voters against Bowes's mendacity and pointing out that he was really "the tool of Ye Lords and ye Dukes." She also equated voters with the countess of Strathmore:

> We have not yet took him for better for worse;
> Alas! she who purchas'd this arm full of woe
> Has a bitter bad bargain—then let us say no.[98]

Apparently Newcastle women were especially active in their "industry" in "ransacking every anecdote of his private life" to discourage votes for him. However, Bowes's supporters in the *Chronicle* depreciated their efforts as "improper."[99]

Bowes lost his seat in 1784. He disappointed the radicals by rarely voting in Parliament. Instead, he supported the unpopular Fox-North coalition in hopes of obtaining an Irish peerage.[100] In the 1784 campaign, Bowes still claimed to celebrate independence, arguing that his constituents had instructed him to vote with Fox; but now they saw Fox as an opportunist and a traitor to the radical cause. Bowes also resurrected anti-Catholic prejudice, but after the Gordon riots of 1780, in which anti-Catholic mobs nearly burned down London, many radicals disliked this theme.

Bowes tried to turn the motif of "petticoat influence" against his chief opponent, Charles Brandling, who hoped to capitalize on the deference owed to his long-established Newcastle family. Bowes's supporters asked, "Is the Representation of Newcastle, the first commercial Borough in this kingdom, a . . . matter of Family Property?"[101] In a remarkably scurrilous and hypocritical broadsheet, Bowes's supporters depicted Brandling as hiding under the petticoats of his wife, the heiress Elizabeth Thompson, who wanted him to pass a seat in Parliament on to their son.[102] In response, a "Lover of Petticoats" assailed Bowes's hypocrisy in riding on his own wife's petticoat, which was "now most terribly *soil'd, maul'd* and *tatter'd* by Mr B——s' ill usage of it."[103] Bowes's own moral character again became an issue. The *Newcastle Chronicle* stated, "The private life of Mr Brandling is marked with the possession of every moral and domestic virtue. Can as much be said of his opponent?"[104] Furthermore, Charles Brandling had more credible radical credentials, having long supported causes such as Wilkes, America, and parliamentary reform.[105]

Voters also may have turned against Bowes because he no longer enjoyed access to governmental patronage and bribes after the fall of the Fox-North coalition. And he failed in his duties as a paternalist landlord, cutting down the timber at Gibside, evicting tenants, cutting wages of mechanics, beating servants, raping maids, and discontinuing traditional charities.[106] Bowes withdrew just before the poll in 1784, his political career finished.

What can this episode tell us about the wider implications of scandal for electoral politics? Bowes's abuse of his wife never became a major electoral scandal; only women seemed to care about this issue. But Newcastle women did not have an organized forum to protest against such abuses, and the countess of Strathmore was isolated from her former influential friends such as Mrs. Montagu, who might have helped her. Above all, the elections of 1777 and 1780 showed that male radicals could celebrate the masculinist Wilkesite heritage of independence and support a vicious wife beater. Bowes's character only became a scandal when he bribed voters and vigorously defended dynastic politics; only then did radicals turn against him. Bowes's career can also address the problem of whether aristocratic influence and voters' independence could be balanced in a viable electoral system. The fact that he seems to have won by dubious means in 1780 indicates the traditional politics of deference and corruption was much more powerful than radical independence. Radicals had hoped that he would support independent principles but found that corruption was a much stronger force than their local organization.

The sad story of the countess of Strathmore can also cast doubt on the argument made by some historians that aristocratic women necessarily enjoyed power through their participation in politics. For the countess, canvassing was an onerous burden rather than a means to power; she merely served as a conduit for dynastic influence. Her story also reveals the extreme vulnerability of women to scandal whatever their dynastic, intellectual, or political resources.

The fear of scandal kept the countess in her abusive marriage. When her mother urged her to leave her violent husband in 1777, the countess feared that a "too malicious World" would not "countenance . . . a Woman's parting from her Husband" unless she endured "a long series of uninterrupted ill-treatment of years."[107] And she did endure such ill-treatment. After he lost the 1784 election, Bowes intensified his already vicious campaign against his wife. He burned her with candles and tried to pierce her tongue with a pen. After she finally escaped and instituted divorce proceedings, he forcibly abducted her in 1786. Bowes bribed a constable to arrest her in London on a false charge, then bundled her into a carriage, which he drove furiously through ice and snow into Yorkshire. He forced her to spend the night in a pigsty and threatened to rape her and stab her with a hot poker. She defied him in the belief that "my sufferings in so just a cause gave me more pride and pleasure, than the first princess in the world."[108] Finally, she escaped and, in a series of trials, had him prosecuted for conspiracy, adultery, and abuse.

Bowes tried to turn scandal against his wife in these trials, appealing to "the great tribunal of the public."[109] He purchased a share in the *Universal Register* (which later became the London *Times*) to put his case.[110] Bowes, who claimed that it was improper for his wife to settle her property away from him, found sympathetic audiences for his argument that married women should not control large estates. After all, this was an era in which the courts imposed more and more limits on married women's ability to control their own fortunes.[111] Bowes also portrayed the countess as a drunken adulteress who needed to be subdued to avoid "petticoat government."[112] He may have paid Gillray to publish two malicious caricatures, one of which depicted the countess as "Lady Termagent Flaybum" who beat her son, and the other of which portrayed her as a Messalina who caroused with squalid washerwomen and venal lovers.[113] Despite these public relations efforts, he was found guilty of abducting Lady Strathmore and confined in King's Bench prison for three years. Many people regarded Bowes as an inhuman monster, a tyrant who abused a cultured lady.[114] But others blamed Lady Strathmore for her own misfortunes. A roman à clef depicted her as coquettish, cruel, and concerned only with clothes and titles, a spoiled rich woman who cheated her husbands by controlling her own fortune.[115]

The Westminster election may tell a different story. Charles James Fox triumphed there in 1784 with the help of the duchess of Devonshire. Westminster was also an area where women formed their own debating societies and asserted their right to participate in politics. Did the duchess of Devonshire, then, fare any better than Lady Strathmore?

THE 1784 WESTMINSTER ELECTION

Georgiana, Duchess of Devonshire, was renowned for her beauty and flamboyant character. Although she wrote a novel, she was not an intellectual like Catherine Macaulay, Elizabeth Montagu, or even the countess of Strathmore.[116] She spoke in an affected family dialect, telling her favorites "love oo" instead of "love you." Married at a young age to the duke of Devonshire, who neglected her for his mistress, she may have been lovers with Fox, and later bore a child to another man. Her chief vice was gambling, at which she lost thousands of pounds. But gambling also gave her a public role in the world of high society. She led fashion, introducing ridiculous high wigs surmounted with ships or birds' nests. To show her support for the patriotic volunteer militia, she adopted a militaristic style with blue jackets and gold buttons. An astute politician, the duchess devoted herself to Whig principles—and her family and personal connections.[117] Her salon provided a venue where the Whig leader Charles James Fox could return from sittings of the House of Commons to refresh himself with thrilling bets on faro, while he touched base with allies and consulted with the duchess on politics. Her mother, Lady Spencer, taught her how to campaign for her family's interest in Northampton with the traditional weapons of great ladies: dazzling displays of hospitality and gracious benevolence.[118]

In the 1784 Westminster election, the duchess used these traditional skills to elicit deference from voters, but she was not just campaigning for her own family interest. She also deployed influence in a different way, winning over voters' hearts and minds with a public relations campaign. A fox's tail in her hat, or a fox-fur muff, symbolized her allegiance to Fox, and the colors of buff and blue in her dress signaled loyalty to the Whigs.[119] For instance, at a performance of the classic Whig drama, Addison's *Cato*, she appeared in battle array of orange and blue cockades with beauty patches on the right cheek, while the Tory duchess of Rutland jeered at Cato and displayed her white and pink cockades and a patched left cheek.[120] She even rode in a balloon decorated with the Whig colors. Together with a phalanx of Whig ladies, the duchess of Devonshire also canvassed in less glamorous locales; she traversed the muddy streets of Westminster to personally persuade artisans to vote. Despite the vicious slanders she faced, Fox triumphed in Westminster, a victory many attributed to the duchess's aid.

To assess whether the duchess of Devonshire advanced women's participation in politics, it is necessary to place the Westminster election in its larger political and constitutional context. Westminster potentially enjoyed much more independence than other constituencies because of its unusually wide electorate. Twelve thousand of its male citizens could vote, including artisans and shopkeepers. This electorate was politically diverse. As Londoners, many of them espoused a tradition of fierce independence. Some voters organized themselves into clubs that supported the Whigs, but others preferred to keep their independence and joined the radical Westminster Association, which advocated manhood suffrage. Other voters supported the government out of conservative inclinations or because they felt they could benefit from doing so. Westminster was not dominated by the influence of a great aristocratic family. However, many tradesmen depended on the royal court's custom. They also enjoyed the commercial patronage of many members of Parliament. Since Westminster was the site of court and government, national issues played an especially important role in its elections.

Three candidates sought two places in the 1784 Westminster election. Charles James Fox, as a Whig, ran against Admiral Hood and Sir Cecil Wray. Hood, a popular naval hero, enjoyed widespread popularity among all groups, so his election was assumed. Wray was a reformer affiliated with the Association movement, but the king, the government, and the prime minister supported him in order to prevent Fox from coming back into power. Fox and Pitt were actually the central characters in this election, and their dispute involved important constitutional issues. Their careers displayed some similarities: each was the scion of a politician father, and each claimed to support some measure of parliamentary reform.[121] Yet their personalities differed dramatically. Meticulously groomed, the young William Pitt was slight and sharp-chinned. Only twenty-three when he became minister, Pitt inherited political clout from his father, William Pitt the elder, who championed the freeborn Briton and British naval triumphs. The younger Pitt's brilliance lay in his ability to marshal a forbidding array of facts and reason. A contemporary described him as "cold and distant in his manners, reserved to excess, and affectedly stately in his deportment."[122] His continence only broke down when it came to drink, but that was normal for a gentleman of his time.[123] This personality enabled him to cleverly combine the traditional politics of patronage with attention to public opinion. Pitt advocated moderate parliamentary reform, thus appealing to radicals, but his close ties to the king and his own rigid personal morality reassured those who feared change. Pitt and his supporters presented him as the epitome of prudent, self-controlled masculinity.

In Pitt's version of the constitution, the king had the right to choose his minister without party interference, and it was legitimate for him to influence Parliament to vote against Fox. The king's supporters, of course, had argued along similar lines when they defended Bute in 1763. However, Pitt also modernized this argument and made it much more sophisticated to win over public opinion. For him, patriotism meant "a disinterested and equal attachment to the just administration of the Laws—to the prosperity of the People—and to the glory of the Sovereign."[124] He promised to support moderate parliamentary reform but argued that the king could best defend the liberties of the people against a parliamentary oligarchy.[125] Drawing on the traditional hostility to political parties, he and many supporters claimed the Whigs' facade of reform hid their true nature as a corrupt faction.[126]

Fox's swarthy complexion and unruly mane of dark hair made him instantly recognizable. He also began his career capitalizing on the heritage of his father, a successful politician who gained a fortune in office through dubious means. But Fox used his eloquence as a weapon, deploying vivid invective, appeals to principle, and astute argument.[127] During the 1770s the younger Fox moved toward radical causes, championing the cause of the Americans and, by 1780, supporting the radical Westminster Association, which called for near-universal manhood suffrage. These allies felt betrayed when he formed his coalition with Lord North. Yet he still claimed to be the champion of the people against the despotic power of the Crown. When the king dismissed him from office and replaced him with Pitt, Fox accused the king of using unconstitutional secret influence by threatening to withdraw his patronage from members of Parliament unless they voted against Fox. Fox depicted the Commons as the defender of the people's liberties and revived Burke's theory of secret influence in the cabinet.[128]

Both sides deployed scandal by using personal attacks to illustrate these constitutional differences. The Foxites depicted the problem of unconstitutional secret influence as Pitt's "backstairs" influence. They explicitly compared Pitt's influence over the king to the princess dowager's supposed secret influence over Bute.[129] Fox, sang his supporters, stood for "the brave and the fair, our rights and our laws," while Pitt represented the "mincing minions" of the court. Another squib attacked "the dapper tribe of boy senators" and "the unmanly runners of the immaculate youth."[130] One of Fox's allies, the playwright Richard Brinsley Sheridan, emulated Wilkes's attack on courtiers by comparing Pitt to James I's male favorite, and possible lover, Buckingham.[131] Another pamphlet brought up Piers Gaveston, the favorite, and rumored lover, of Edward II.[132] Since Pitt never seemed interested in women, his enemies insinuated he must be sexually attracted to men. Fox's supporters insinuated that Pitt was a "woman-hater"—a euphemism for "sodomite"—because he never married or had affairs. By 1785, the satirical poet Peter Pindar circulated rumors about Pitt's friendship with a young man named Steele, with whom he vacationed in Brighton.[133] However, these insinuations tended to be made indirectly and only occasionally, since it was obviously rather dangerous to accuse the prime minister of sodomitical tendencies.[134]

More overtly, Fox's supporters contrasted his virile heterosexuality, his carousing, and his womanizing with Pitt's youth and sexual neutrality. They criticized Pitt for his cold and reserved temperament: "His debauches are without mirth, his conversation without affability, and even his gallantry without *enjouement*."[135] The Foxites therefore revived the Wilkesite celebration of the libertine as defender of the people's liberties. Fox's libertinism was his own appeal, celebrating wine, women, and song. In the words of one ballad,

> Not a wench in the place
> But admires his face
> For a sharp, roguish eye has my sweet Charley O
> . . . The firmest of Patriots is sweet Charley O.[136]

Interestingly, however, Fox modified Wilkes's libertinism away from misogyny; instead of attacking women, he spouted the rhetoric of chivalry, making much of Wray's support for a tax on maidservants, which Fox declared would steal wages from the mouths of hardworking women.[137] The caricature, *Procession to the Hustings after a Successful Canvass* (figure 4), includes all these themes: the rooster and breeches signifying Fox's virile manhood, his political defiance, the petticoat his chivalrous protection of maidservants, and the key, his attack on backstairs influence.

This libertinism, however, could also alienate some voters. Pitt therefore appealed to a broad coalition: those with conservative inclinations would naturally support the government and the king, but more liberal middle-class people, even Dissenters, might respond to an appeal to morality and a promise of reform. The government therefore portrayed Fox and the duchess as libertines whose disorderly personal lives, and inability to control their passions, presaged a dangerous disorder. As in the Middlesex election in 1769, government forces also portrayed the Foxites as undermining order in the family as well as the nation. A father warned voters, "Can you . . . give your support to the high priest of drunkenness, gaming, and every species of debauchery . . . ?"[138] Fox's enemies pointed out that both the duchess of Devonshire and Fox lost thousands of pounds at gambling, as Phyllis Deutsch has shown.[139] Was Fox simply interested in controlling the government to gain the keys of the Treasury and the fountain of patronage? They insinuated that the duchess supported Fox not for noble reasons of principle but out of selfish interest: they alleged she wanted Fox to win so that he could grant patronage to her husband, enabling him to pay off their gambling debts.[140]

Fox's opponents stirred up their worst scandals against the duchess and her female companions. Newspaper columns told ladies that they should not "meddle" with politics and accused them of violating the "common decency" and "dignity" expected from married ladies of quality.[141] Caricatures

FIGURE 4   Thomas Rowlandson, *Procession to the Hustings after a successful Canvass* (1784). Reproduced by permission of the Huntington Library. The breeches bear the inscription "Man of the People," the middle lady carries a sign with a fox and the slogan "And the Rights of the Commons," the third lady carries a petticoat with the slogan "No tax on Maidservants," and a man carries a sign with the slogan "Key of the Backstairs."

mocked the duchess as a "public woman," a euphemism for prostitute, who returned drunk and disheveled from a long evening of kissing butchers for their votes.[142] They rebuked her for gallivanting about Covent Garden while her husband nursed the baby at home: "While her grace is busied in canvassing the Constituents, her domestic husband is employed in the nursery, singing '*Hey my kitten!*' and comfortabl*y rocking the cradle!*" (figure 5).[143] They accused her of trying to wear the breeches, the symbol of male potency and political power. Fox's opponents undermined his manhood by portraying him as controlled by a woman with whom he was allegedly having an affair. Caricatures also associated the duchess with actresses and kept mistresses. For instance, another lady who canvassed for the Whigs was Mary Robinson, known as Perdita, the actress who had affairs with the Prince of Wales and Fox. These caricatures depicted the duchess's political

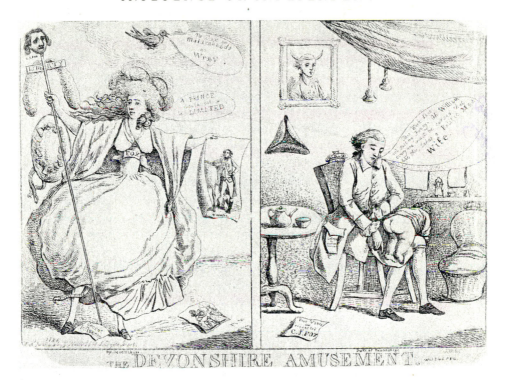

FIGURE 5   *Devonshire Amusement* (1784), BMC 6624. © The British Museum.
The duchess tramples on a sheet with the words "Secret Influence" and says, "A
Prince should not be limited," referring to the Prince of Wales, Fox's ally, who was
in contention with Parliament over his allowance. The duke of Devonshire says,
"This Work does not suit my Fancy. Ah William everyone must be cursed that like
thee, takes a Politic Mad Wife." A sheaf of papers entitled "Letters to a Married
Woman" falls out of his pocket, perhaps referring to his own adultery.

activities as immoral and theatrical, based on mercenary connections
rather than independence and genuine conviction.[144]
Why did the duchess incite so much hostility when other women also
canvassed? Like the duchess, the ladies who canvassed for Fox supported
the Whigs out of family concerns, but they also had their own agendas, like
Frances Ann Crewe, confidante of many politicians, and Anne Damer, the
noted lesbian sculptress.[145] On the other side, the duchess of Rutland led a
phalanx of ladies supporting the government. In part, the duchess of Devonshire faced hostility because she was lobbying publicly for a man linked
to her only by personal and party connections instead of by family ties.[146]
But party politics had enabled both Whig and government ladies to expand

this traditional role to support candidates on the basis of party and principle. In some ways, Fox's enemies singled out the duchess for attack because she was a political entrepreneur, an individual seeking her own influence and fame not only in fashion but also in politics. Her very success made scandal a necessary weapon against her.[147]

The Whig political machine vigorously defended the duchess of Devonshire. Unlike the countess of Strathmore and Catherine Macaulay, she had organized supporters who would issue squibs and caricatures stoutly refuting the calumnies against her. Fox and the Whigs celebrated the aristocratic women who canvassed for them as inspiring exemplars of "Female Patriotism," as in figure 6. In another caricature, Truth and Virtue assist the duchess as she tramples on the prostrate male figure of scandal.[148] Foxites mocked those who would send ladies back to the kitchen instead of allowing them to develop their superior talents.[149] A supporter declared that since ladies "have shown abilities equal to the task of policy and government," British men should support their liberty.[150]

Did the duchess of Devonshire advance the cause of all women in politics? The Foxites ridiculed the less glamorous women canvassing for Wray, describing the campaign of the rotund Mrs. Hobart as the "Court Canvass of Madam Blubber."[151] Although the debating societies had repeatedly raised the issue of the female franchise, the duchess of Devonshire and Fox did not themselves advocate votes or offices for women.[152] The Foxite Whigs praised aristocratic female patriotism, rather than trying to extend women's rights. They did not try to mobilize members of female debating societies or encourage the wives of tradesmen, or female shopkeepers, to join Foxite political clubs.

Supporters of the duchess of Devonshire argued that she and Fox were attacked because they advanced the democratic cause of the people.[153] Indeed, opponents depicted Fox as a demagogue who appealed to drunken tailors and shoemakers.[154] In response, Fox rejected the notion "that *poor* men should not . . . concern themselves about the safety of the constitution!"[155] Foxites lauded the duchess of Devonshire because she "vindicated the independence of the Electors" and "saved them from the arbitrary interference of the Court."[156]

The Foxites, however, believed that the people should trust the old Whig families who had lead the revolution of 1688—like the Cavendishes, the dynasty of the Devonshires—to look after their liberties.[157] In many ways, the Foxites belonged to the tradition of patrician leaders who appealed to both deference and independence. A song praised the duchess of Devonshire as a "protectoress" of the people of Westminster, as in the good old days of Queen Bess's "petticoat government."[158] One poster made Fox's aristocratic

Liberty and Fame introducing Female Patriotism to Britania
— She smiles —
Infused with a Fortitude from Heaven. Vide Shakespears Tempest.

FIGURE 6 *Liberty and Fame introducing Female Patriotism to Britania* [*sic*]
(1784), BMC 6599. Reproduced by permission of the Huntington Library.

appeal all too clear; it was financed by Lord George Gordon, disgraced for
inciting the Gordon riots:

Charles James Fox

Civil and Religious Liberty!

The Ancient Families and the Old Nobility![159]

Many radicals from the Association movement for parliamentary reform distrusted Fox as antidemocratic. Although a few stuck with Fox, most
Westminster radicals supported Sir Cecil Wray, an unequivocal reformer
who had chaired the Society for Constitutional Information.[160] Furthermore, they believed Pitt would be more likely, and more able, to push reform through Parliament. Following Catherine Macaulay, these radicals believed that Parliament, rather than the Crown, was the main danger to the
people's liberties.[161] The unitarian John Jebb distrusted Fox's commitment
to reform after he allied himself with the hated Lord North; Jebb had ad-

mired Fox's abilities, but "his intimacies, his connections, bind him down to other counsels, and the habits of his life have gotten too much hold of him, and ambition is his ruling passion."[162] As one pamphlet reminded voters, Fox was an aristocratic turncoat who had asserted the rights of Parliament against the Wilkesites in 1771. Then, Fox dressed as a fop in the height of fashion, wearing "the red-heeled shoe, the white feather, and the embroidered suit," but as he drew closer to the radicals, he dressed in "a greasy coat and uncombed locks" to "harangue" the debating societies.[163] Fox's plebeian supporters repelled these middle-class radicals who thought that only men with some property could vote independently; they feared that laboring men could be corrupted too easily with a bribe or the promise of a job.

The long-standing hostility against female influence, so apparent in the Wilkesite era, reappeared.[164] The duchess of Devonshire's canvassing scandalized radicals not because she was a woman but because she exerted illicit aristocratic influence, enabling dynastic politics and corruption to persist. They accused her of using bribes to win over artisan voters; in figure 7, the duchess kisses a butcher and slips a purse into his trousers.[165] Whether or not the duchess actually handed over bribes, she could promise tradesmen lucrative custom if they voted for her.

For radicals, these techniques were unacceptable. The Whigs used the language of liberty, they argued, but they were just another "aristocratic faction." One correspondent denounced "the shameful depraved efforts of male and female gentry" to keep their hold over the House of Commons with "threats and corruption" causing their "relations, connections and dependents, to be elected representatives."[166] Reformers wanted plebeian men to participate in politics independently, not swayed by representatives of great aristocratic families. Ridiculing Fox's obsession with "backstairs influence," a commentator asked, "What is the most genuine description of *Secret Influence?* . . . D[uche]sses employing all the fascinating attractions of female beauty, to cause [tradesmen] to vote contrary their judgment." He went on, "As it is held *unconstitutional* and *unlawful* for *Peers* to i*nterfere at elections*, it is equally so for *Peeresses*."[167] Similarly, a pamphleteer accused Fox of acting "with a *secret* and principal eye to private connections . . . for the pitiful gratification of *Family-Compacts!*"[168]

Fox triumphed in Westminster, however, overcoming all this scandal and controversy. The Whigs gave the duchess of Devonshire much of the credit for winning this closely fought election. The voting went on for days, and the tired duchess dragged herself away from a country rest in order to bring more voters to the polls. The scandalous insinuations about her private life simply did not bother plebeian voters, and, as with Wilkes, Fox's libertine character appealed to more voters than it alienated. Pitt was out-

Pd.d by W Humphrey 227 Strand.

FIGURE 7   Thomas Rowlandson, *The Two Patriotic Duchesses on their Canvass, requesting the favor of an early poll* (1784), BMC 6494. Reproduced by permission of the Huntington Library. The duchess of Devonshire kisses a butcher while slipping a purse in his pocket; the duchess of Portland tries to kiss another butcher, who spurns her advances.

raged. He aided the defeated radical candidate, Cecil Wray, in his attempt to have the election overturned on account of corruption.[169] Pitt apparently even threatened to arraign the duchess for bribery. But despite Pitt's stern appearance of integrity, the government also resorted to patronage and bribery in Westminster and elsewhere. Pitt's associate, John Robinson, documented all the government largesse he distributed behind the scenes.[170]

While Fox won in Westminster, Pitt's candidates triumphed in the nation as a whole. But public opinion proved to be more significant than bribery in determining the outcome of the 1784 elections. The Pittites won in boroughs whose electorates were too large to control through bribery and patronage.[171] Pitt cleverly manipulated public opinion. Conservatives, of course, supported him out of monarchical and religious sentiment. But news of the duchess's and Fox's libertine lifestyles also alienated many provincial reforming, Dissenting intellectuals.[172] By supporting moderate parliamentary reform, Pitt also appealed to radicals who distrusted Fox as a factious aristocratic politician and false patriot. Reformers lauded the election as the triumph of the people against the "diabolical views of a designing aristocracy."[173]

Hostility to "petticoat influence" and family dynasties also emerged in at least two provincial 1784 elections. As we have seen, the influence of the countess of Strathmore and the problem of "family compacts" played a part in the 1784 Newcastle election. This issue surfaced in Norfolk as well. Voters in Norwich, the center of that county, had long expressed hostility to "family compacts" of the local aristocratic and mercantile families who dominated their representation in Parliament and in the city.[174] In the 1784 election for Norfolk, the magnate Thomas William Coke campaigned as a Foxite Whig who had supported the Association movement.[175] His wife, Lady Coke, aided her husband's campaign by canvassing and writing to her influential friends at court, just as she had helped Coke with his agricultural experiments, promoted Norfolk manufacturing, and held open houses at Holkam Hall. But opponents used her female influence to discredit the campaign. Associating Coke with Fox, his opponent insinuated that Coke was a libertine too influenced by a woman.[176] They advised voters to select a man who was from a "respected family," not a "slave to party," for "men of bad character and vicious habits in private life, never pursue virtue in public!"[177] Evoking the squibs against the duchess of Devonshire, Wodehouse supporters warned voters against Lady Coke's canvassing:

> Let not beauty vanquish you;
> Form'd to conquer, form'd to please,
> Gaze no more on charms like these;
> From the winning Graces flee,
> Hostile now to Liberty.[178]

A writer named "Belinda" asserted disinterested "female patriotism" against Mrs. Coke's canvassing, which she saw as illicit Whiggish family influence."[179] Of course, these attacks on Lady Coke were somewhat hypocritical, since the wife of Coke's opponent also aided her husband's efforts.[180] But they played a small part, along with the larger issues of revulsion against the Foxites and the controversy over the East India Bill, in forcing Coke to withdraw from the poll. Coke accepted defeat philosophically, but his wife "seemed very much hurt by it."[181]

CONCLUSION

Did the participation of women in elections in the 1780s advance women's role in politics? The duchess of Devonshire herself withdrew from public campaigning, but she continued to exert influence over the Whigs behind the scenes, and other aristocratic women canvassed in Westminster in 1788.[182] But these women did not create a new role for women in public, unless the public was conceived in a very traditional sense as the aristocratic elite. The duchess simply expanded aristocratic women's roles as confidantes, agents, and advisers beyond their traditional service to family connections, to service to a wider party cause. But her impact was short-lived for several reasons. First, canvassing could be just as much a burden as an opportunity for aristocratic women, as the tragic case of the countess of Strathmore demonstrates. Second, aristocratic women canvassing publicly always faced the danger of scandal. In part, this scandal stemmed from the sexual double standard, but it also had political connotations. Conservatives could attack campaigning ladies for undermining social and political subordination, while radicals saw them as emblematic of illicit aristocratic influence. By the early to middle nineteenth century, aristocratic women withdrew from their more public roles under the pressure of the ideology of separate spheres, although they continued to instruct their tenants how to vote and still corresponded with politicians behind the scenes.[183]

The women of the debating societies established a much more important precedent than the duchess of Devonshire, first by associating together and learning to speak in public, and second by raising the question of the female franchise. To be sure, the canvassing ladies repeatedly sparked debates on women's political place in 1784, and in 1788, the female debating society La Belle Assemblée revived, apparently led by Mrs. Hobart, the duchess's rival in the 1784 election.[184] They asked, "Do not the extraordinary abilities of the Ladies in the present age demand Academical honors from the Universities—a right to vote at elections, and to be returned Members of Parliament."[185] Even the mixed Westminster School of Eloquence agreed that ladies deserved "praise, not censure," for interfering in elections. But motions advocating women's political role were often defeated, and the very presence of women in public caused controversy.[186] The *Times* sniffed, "It is a disgrace to the modesty of the sex, to see a woman debating a question among a parcel of idle apprentice boys, at a Sixpenny Assemblage."[187] The precedent the debating women set was not taken up. The female debating societies disappeared after this last efflorescence in 1788, although women occasionally appeared in mixed societies.

What can these scandals tell us about the nature of electoral politics in general? In Newcastle, Norwich, and Westminster, aristocrats ensured their electoral dominance not just by eliciting deference from voters but by corrupting and coercing them, distributing bribes to their wives, or threatening to fire them from jobs. In response, independent voters protested vigorously. However, as voters in Newcastle and Norwich discovered, finding truly independent candidates was difficult. Still dependent on aristocratic candidates to front their campaigns, they faced turncoats and defeat more often than independent triumph.

After 1784, many Britons became increasingly disillusioned with party politics. Some reformers turned against the possibility of extending the franchise to more working people after the anti-Catholic Gordon riots devastated London in 1780. They hoped that Pitt would be able to pass more moderate parliamentary reforms, which could remedy the problems with the system without destabilizing society. But Pitt soon disappointed them, abandoning reform to staunchly support the king in more conservative policies. As a result, many Britons distrusted all politicians, even Pitt, as irredeemably corrupt. After recounting Norwich political gossip to his friend, W. Taswell proclaimed, "But enough of Politicks—an unpleasant subject at best! . . . I seldom hear it introduced without trembling for the good humor and peace of the company."[188]

Commentators contrasted the integrity and "domestic tranquility" of the industrious middle class with the cynical corruption of aristocratic high politics. Depicting the 1784 election as "forty days madness," J. Williams declared that it was better to earn one's money by industry rather than endure the "perpetual slavery" of "dependency on the great."[189] In his famous poem "The Task," William Cowper unfavorably compared the "patriots bursting with heroic rage" he read about in the newspaper with the "female industry" of his relatives, who calmly tended the hissing tea kettle in a cozy domestic scene far removed from the turmoil at Westminster.[190]

Some female intellectuals tried to reverse the association of femininity with corruption by portraying themselves as pure and independent of party interests. Men entered politics out of self-interest and uncontrolled ambition, they argued, whereas women had better judgment, since they could not gain anything from patronage. At La Belle Assemblée, the ladies asserted that "unlike other orators their lamps were not filled with treasury oil," that is, they were not bribed by government money.[191] In 1787, Hannah More claimed the sober, rational conversation of Mrs. Montagu's salon was superior to the sordid world of politics where Edmund Burke wasted his sublime talents.[192] The Evangelical movement, both within and outside of the Church of England, presented an ideal of femininity based on purity, even female moral superiority. A new notion of "female influence" began to emerge, far removed from the corruption of party politics, and instead rooted in domestic life."[193]

By the mid-1780s, Evangelicals began to emerge from their domestic retreats to cleanse what they saw as the moral corruption of the nation. Humanitarianism became an alternative to party politics. Most notably, the antislavery movement erupted as an enormous cause that transcended party divisions.[194] By the time of the French Revolution, some of the most influential propagandists against slavery were conservative female religious writers, drawing upon this notion of moral influence. Female moral influence could be exercised through the pen, not requiring distasteful canvassing in public, and it lacked the taint of electoral corruption by domineering aristocrats. The next three chapters will explore whether the idea of female moral influence was a useful standpoint for women.

When William Cowper perused the newspaper as his female relatives tended the tea kettle, he was reading the speeches about the impeachment of Warren Hastings, the subject of the next chapter. These politicians drew upon humanitarian sentiments to try to reach provincial middle-class readers like him. Edmund Burke even alleged that Cowper's soothing cup of tea was obtained by the tortures of Indian women.[195] Could Burke and his allies succeed in winning back those Britons alienated by deference, party politics, and corruption?

CHAPTER FOUR

Edmund Burke and the Begums of Oudh: Gender, Empire, and Public Opinion

Playwright and politician Richard Brinsley Sheridan opened the 1788 impeachment trial of Warren Hastings, governor-general of India, with a stirring speech. He claimed that Hastings ordered troops to invade the zenana, or women's quarters, of the princesses of Oudh.[1] Hastings knew, Sheridan thundered, "how sacred was the residence of women in India. A threat, therefore, to force that residence, and violate its purity by sending armed men into it, was a species of torture."[2] Sheridan thus implied that Hastings was a vicious violator of Indian womanhood. As the audience wept, Sheridan collapsed on the floor of Westminster Hall, overcome by the power of his own rhetoric.[3]

The fundamental issues of the Warren Hastings trial, however, had nothing to do with sexual violence. The so-called princesses, in Indian terms "begums," were the mother and grandmother of the ruler of Oudh, a large, powerful state northeast of Bengal. Hastings had sent his troops to the begums' zenana to seize treasure he claimed they owed the British. This incident contributed to charges that Hastings was corrupt and cruel, waged unauthorized wars, and extracted excessive revenue.[4] However, the criminality of his actions was unclear. So his enemies, the Whigs Sheridan, Charles James Fox, and Edmund Burke, decided to impeach him for the legally vague "high crimes and misdemeanors" rather than treason or a specific criminal offense. In eighteenth-century Britain, impeachment was a rarely used procedure that enabled Parliament to charge officials with misgovernment.[5] The House of Commons began the process in 1786 by investigating Hastings's actions and bringing the charges of impeachment against him. By 1788, Burke, Sheridan, and Fox—the managers of the prosecution—took the case to the House of Lords, where the peers sat in judgment on him. The lords heard the trial for only a few months at a time, however, so it dragged on for seven long years. They finally acquitted Hastings in 1795.

Each side appealed to public opinion in a different way. At first, Hastings followed the rules of traditional politics, lobbying the court and the East India Company (EIC) on the basis of personal connections and financial interests. Burke, Sheridan, and Fox addressed a wider humanitarian public by using the techniques of scandal to attack abuses in India. They personified the problems of British policy in Warren Hastings; using lurid, sexualized language, they translated the obscure, technical language of Indian policy into compelling metaphors of violation and oppression.[6] At first, their tactics succeeded. Newspapers filled their columns with the debates, pamphlets took sides, letter writers expressed their horror. The trial became a sensation, impelling ladies and gentlemen to queue for long hours for tickets, losing shoes and ribbons in a mad crush to get into Westminster Hall.[7] Why, then, was Hastings acquitted? The answer will show why some scandals succeed and others fail to have an impact.

key

Although the impeachment did not change British policy in India, it provided a forum in which competing philosophies of empire could be aired for the wider British public.[8] Hastings took a pragmatic tack, arguing that as governor-general he needed to use any means necessary to ensure British power and extract revenue from India. Burke and his allies took a more moralistic tone, arguing that the empire should be governed by the principles of the British constitution, with an accountable government that acknowledged the rights of its subjects. However, this chapter will question whether Burke deserves his reputation as a fierce critic of empire.

Both sides had to face the problem of moral relativism as Britain acquired a colony with a vastly different culture than its own.[9] Could the standards of the British constitution be applied to a land so different in religion, culture, and governance? Like today, issues about women's roles could be a flash point in such debates. Hastings knew and respected Indian culture, but he believed that the British should act like Indian rulers, ruthlessly punishing their enemies. It did not matter that the Begums of Oudh were elderly princesses, Hastings thought; regardless of their femininity, they defied British authority and needed to be subdued. Burke believed that the British empire must respect the different cultural traditions of India, and that Hastings's attack on the begums represented an egregious violation of its values of female seclusion.

Images of femininity and effeminacy played an important role in the scandal because the theory of oriental despotism dominated debates over India's governance. Ancient Greeks and Romans had portrayed Eastern rulers as decadent, effeminate, and despotic. In the late seventeenth century, French travelers François Catrou and François Bernier built upon these ancient stereotypes in their accounts of India.[10] Combining the two traditions, Montesquieu depicted oriental despotism as a tyranny of one man who ruled without law, indulging his lust for power and pleasure enforced by fear.[11] To explain how the Muslim Mughals, so few in number, could rule over millions of Hindus, travelers portrayed them as masculine, unrestrained in their cruelty and sensual indulgence, and easily able to dominate the Hindus, who seemed passive, feminine, soft, and born to submission.[12] Furthermore, they claimed that the excessive masculine lust of Muslim rulers could transmute into effeminacy; the third generation of Muslim conquerors lost their warlike spirit when they immured themselves in the delights of the harem.[13] Those critics who took a moralistic approach to empire, such as Burke, emphasized the themes of effeminacy, lust, and cruelty when drawing upon the theory of oriental despotism. Others took a more pragmatic approach, arguing that since the Indians were accustomed to forceful rulers, the British should act as oriental despots themselves.[14]

THE BRITISH IN INDIA

The British presence in India began on the practical grounds of commerce. A royal charter of 1600 bestowed the East India Company with a monopoly over trade with India. The company slowly established commercial relations with the large, powerful, and sophisticated Mughal empire. As that empire began to fragment in the early eighteenth century, the British took advantage of the situation to expand their power. In the Battle of Plassey in 1757, General Robert Clive defeated the nawab (princely governor) of Bengal. As a result of this battle, Clive gained control over Bengal's revenues and put a puppet nawab at the head of its government.[15]

Critics feared that as the British acquired an empire in India, oriental despotism would infect its polity. While many lauded Clive as a hero, others saw him as an oriental despot, accusing him of ruthlessly crushing his opponents with opportunistic military tactics and corrupting Parliament with his wealth.[16] Furthermore, many more British "nabobs," a corruption of "nawab," brought back fortunes from India, flaunted their riches, and purchased seats in Parliament.[17] Moralists feared the British would meet the fate of the Romans, weakened and "effeminized" by Asian luxuries pillaged from their conquests.[18]

Facing these fears, Parliament debated how to govern the new British-controlled domains in India. Although some worried about oriental corruption, others took a more pragmatic perspective.[19] The EIC in London could not control its officers in India, who became embroiled in expensive wars against Indian princes. Falling revenues outraged the stockholders and the government, which hoped to profit from India's vast wealth. Factions competed over who would control the EIC's lucrative patronage. Finally, the Regulating Act of 1773 enabled the company and the British government to together appoint a governor-general and council of Bengal, with authority over all British territories in India. The government promised to crack down on private profiteering, to ensure that the Indian territories would benefit Britain, and to hold EIC servants more accountable.[20]

Warren Hastings, the first governor-general, was very different from the swashbuckling Clive. A practical, pragmatic man, Hastings promised to serve the king by the "acquisition of new resources of wealth and affluence to the British Empire . . . by means which the most wary prudence might allow."[21] Hastings believed in administrative efficiency and the British "ideology of transcendent law and sovereignty," promising to clean up the abuses that had sapped EIC profits and horrified the public.[22] Deeply learned in Indian languages and culture, he found many flaws in the theory of oriental despotism, but he adopted some of its elements.[23] Whereas the theory stereotyped Indians as decadent or effeminate, Hastings knew that Indian princes could be formidable military foes. Furthermore, he refuted the notion that India had no laws and ordered Hindu and Muslim legal codes to be translated and implemented in British-controlled courts.[24] However, Hastings's knowledge of India became a tool for control, for he believed that British administrators could rule most effectively by following Indian traditions of sovereignty.[25] Like the Mughal emperors, he formed alliances with nawabs of nearby states and lavished gifts and loans on them. In turn, he demanded heavy revenues from the nawabs and waged war against those who opposed him.[26] He wrote to colleagues in 1776 that "despotism . . . is the only constitutional mode of Government known among" the Indians and is therefore inevitable.[27]

Despite Hastings's practical and efficient outlook, his tenure always faced controversy. He had to share power with the council of Bengal, several members of which opposed him at every turn. Among them, Philip Francis became his most implacable enemy. Francis was a minor government official who almost certainly anonymously wrote the Junius letters during the Wilkesite controversy; the government may have sent him to India to stop his criticisms. Influenced by Enlightenment principles, Francis planned to reform the British presence in India, but he also intrigued against Hastings to advance his own ambitions. Francis continually accused Hastings of corruption and oppression.[28]

As a result, Hastings had to walk a fine line between emulating the munificence of Mughal traditions and avoiding the appearance of corruption. For instance, when Bahar Ali Khan, the eunuch administrator for the Begums of Oudh, came to visit Hastings in Calcutta, Hastings "sent him a thousand rupees for his entertainment" and put him up in lavish lodgings. When Bahar Ali Khan entered the audience room, he saw that Mrs. Hastings "had placed pearls, worth many a thousand rupees, in a large bowl, and she was throwing the kittens in upon them. They could not climb out for when they tried to stand up, the pearls slipped under their feet." Mrs. Hastings laughed at their struggles, and her cruel ostentation mortified Bahar Ali Khan, who feared that his own gifts—a costly saddle and jewels—would not impress the governor-general. Indeed, Hastings waved away his offerings, sighing that his enemies on the Bengal council would accuse him of receiving bribes.[29]

Hastings also had to reconcile some contradictory ideas about women presented in European views of the East. Well aware of the custom of purdah, or female seclusion, the British assumed that Indian women *should* and *would* be quiet and passive.[30] Yet the British were also familiar with Montesquieu's argument that in oriental despotisms, women's intrigues in the harem could disrupt the polity.[31] Indeed, begums (wives or concubines of Indian princes) often exerted considerable political influence, especially during unstable times such as dynastic struggles over succession.[32] Hastings encountered three such women: Munny Begum and the two Begums of Oudh. Hastings instructed his subordinates to respect Indian female seclusion, but he also treated these begums as political actors who must bend to British will.

Munny Begum, the chief concubine of the Bengal nawab Mir Jaffir, taught Hastings it was dangerous to assume that Indian women would be passive. Mir Jaffir had been the figurehead nawab of Bengal, compliant with British control. Conveniently for the British, when he died, his heir, Mubarak-ud-daulah, was too young to rule on his own, so in 1772 Hastings appointed Munny Begum as guardian and superintendent of the young nawab's household. Hastings selected her rather than a male prince or bureaucrat for two reasons: first, Munny Begum hated Mahommed Reza Khan, a Bengal deputy who resisted British control; second, Hastings believed that as a woman she could not establish a rival power base.[33] However, in some Muslim dynasties, the mother of the heir actually gained considerable political clout by educating the young heir and running his elaborate household.[34]

Hastings's rivals criticized this appointment by pointing out that Munny Begum was not actually Mubarak-ud-daulah's mother; they alleged that she bribed Hastings to gain her position. Indeed, she had granted Hastings several lakhs of rupees (worth several thousand pounds) as an entertainment allowance. The Indian minister Nuncomar also produced letters from Munny Begum offering bribes to Hastings. Munny Begum denied writing the letters, so Hastings had Nuncomar prosecuted for forgery. The trial took place in the supreme court Hastings had established in India, presided over by his ally, Judge Sir Elijah Impey. Using the procedures of English law, Impey found Nuncomar guilty and had him hanged. Hastings's enemies claimed that he allowed a woman, Munny Begum, to rule Bengal, and that he judicially murdered Nuncomar.[35]

Hastings encountered two more formidable begums in Oudh. The nawab of Oudh (Awadh), Shujah-ud-daulah, resisted British influence, but after the British defeated him, they made him into an ally.[36] Hoping Oudh would serve as a buffer state for Bengal, Hastings lent Shujah money and troops to help him defeat rival rulers. With great ferocity, Shujah drove out the Rohillas, an Afghan people who dominated a Hindu population. Known as an aggressive, domineering character, he was accused of raping his defeated rivals' women.[37] But he owed a great deal to his own women; his mother, Sadr un-nisa Begum, influenced him greatly through her wise council, and his wife, the Bahu Begum, helped his war efforts by giving him all her own treasure, down to her nose rings. In gratitude, he entrusted her with the state seals (meaning all state business went through her hands) and sequestered much of his treasure in her zenana.[38] After Shujah died, three factions contended for predominance in Oudh: the Bahu Begum, her son and Shujah's successor, Asof-ud-daulah, and the British.

The Bahu Begum became an even more powerful political figure, as contemporary Indian chroniclers affirmed.[39] She both drew upon the deference due to secluded ladies of ruling families and operated successfully as a power broker. To be sure, confined in the zenana, she had to rule through her eunuchs, including Bahar Ali Khan, who administered her territories and troops. But the Bahu Begum "practically governed" her town of Faizabad. Known for her cleverness and "great administrative ability," she had her own personal army and tax collectors to collect the revenues from her extensive *jagirs*, or landholdings. Under the Mughal system, the ruler granted *jagirs* to his subordinates, which they administered in return for receiving their revenues.[40]

The Bahu Begum exerted so much power because Oudh's new ruler, her son Asof-ud-daulah, lacked his father's aggressive, resolute character. To escape from the begums' influence, Asof moved his court to Lucknow, where he patronized art, music, poetry, and his male favorites. But there his ministers and the British competed over who would control him. The British needed to oversee Oudh's finances, they argued, to ensure payment of Shujah's debts for the Rohilla wars. The British sent one of their officials, Nathaniel Middleton, to function as a Resident at the Oudh court, directing the nawab's affairs through a cadre of military officers. As the expenses of his court exhausted his revenues, and the British kept on demanding payment of his father's debt, Asof believed the begums' treasure could solve his money troubles.[41]

Hastings, Francis, Asof-ud-daulah, and his minister Murteza Khan all claimed that the begums had no right to Shujah's treasure, for under Muslim law widows could inherit only one-eighth of their husbands' estates and enjoyed their land revenues only at the pleasure of the ruling monarch. However, they were arguing from a rigid interpretation of the Muslim code that did not take into account the privileges of wealthy begums, who could receive gifts from their families and husbands as their *jehez* (their own treasure), which they could retain after their husbands' death.[42] Furthermore, the begums were loath to give up the silks and jewels that composed their treasure, for these garments and ornaments symbolized their sovereignty and dynastic heritage.[43]

The Bahu Begum believed that she could manipulate the British for her own ends. Deploying the language of female passivity, she implored Hastings to "exert yourself so effectually in favor of us helpless women" by protecting her from Asof's demands. Hastings agreed, signing a treaty in which the begum gave up some of her treasure in return for protection of her landholdings. But the Bahu Begum also used the language of imperious control: she commanded Hastings to replace one of her enemies with her favored minister; appealing to Hastings's concern with efficiency, she assured him her ministers would collect the revenues, and "whatever sums are due to the English chiefs I will cause to be paid."[44] The Bengal council was appalled that the begums dared interfere with politics, violating their presumptions about Indian female passivity.[45] Philip Francis observed, "I cannot conceive that she has the least Right to interfere in the Nabob's Government; in a Country where Women are not allowed a free Agency in the most trifling domestic Affairs, it seems extraordinary that this Lady should presume to talk of appointing Ministers, and of governing Kingdoms."[46]

In 1781, the begums' quarrel with the British became entangled in a much more serious situation—revolt in Oudh. Hastings illegally sent his favorite, Colonel Hannay, to intensify revenue extraction in Oudh, aggravating its inhabitants, already irritated by the aggressive commercial tactics of English traders.[47] Their discontent intensified when Hastings demanded extraordinary revenues from Cheit Singh, the raja (Hindu ruler) of Benares, a holy city in Oudh. Hastings and Cheit Singh had signed a treaty in which the raja agreed to pay specified revenues for the British, and the British allowed him to rule. When Hastings needed money to pay for a war in South India, he insisted that as an ally, Cheit Singh must pay revenues beyond those specified in the treaty because the wartime circumstances were exceptional. When Cheit Singh refused, Hastings claimed that he violated his treaty with the British.[48] Hastings sent troops to Benares to arrest Cheit Singh, but they faced fierce resistance, and Hastings himself was almost captured. In the process, the troops drove Cheit Singh's mother out of her zenana and pillaged her treasure.[49]

The Bahu Begum supported Cheit Singh against the British "in the most open and violent manner," reported Colonel Hannay, describing the revolt as "a concerted plan for the extirpation of the English."[50] The Bahu Begum, like Cheit Singh, felt that the British had violated their treaty with her. Still demanding repayment of their debt, the British kept pressuring Asof to resume control over her *jagirs*, or landholdings. In reaction, the Bahu Begum began threatening the British. As she wrote to Middleton, the Resident in Oudh, "Should the Country be lost to me, it shall be lost to all. I give you this Intimation—note it." The British Resident did not always believe that the begum dictated such belligerent letters on her own, but a Persian administrator at her court, Faiz-Bakhsh, verified that the letters represented her thoughts; indeed, the Bahu Begum's eunuch administrators and her mother-in-law persuaded her to tone down her missive.[51] Although the begums later denied responsibility for the revolt, most historians agree that they instructed their eunuch administrators to incite the villagers and headmen to revolt against Hannay, and sent money and raised troops to help Cheit Singh fight the British.[52]

The next year, the famous attack on the zenana of the Begums of Oudh took place. Middleton and the nawab Asof sent their troops to seize the begums' treasure, in part, Hastings later claimed, to punish their revolt. The troops occupied Faizabad, but when they entered the begums' zenana to seize the treasure, the two elderly women had already left. Apparently, the begums moved out of their palace and dismissed many of their retainers in an effort to turn the people against the British. In the impeachment debates, Sheridan blamed Hastings's troops for starving the concubines of the Khord Mahal, Shujah's harem, and forcing them to break purdah by fleeing into the town in search of food, but other sources claimed the begums had stopped feeding the women.[53] The British gained control of the situation by imprisoning the begums' top administrators, two eunuchs, shackling and depriving them of opium for some months. As a result, the begums released much of their treasure.

INDIA IN BRITISH POLITICS

Hastings's wars and heavy-handed tactics, meanwhile, caused controversy back in Britain, as his enemy on the Bengal council, Philip Francis, tried to stir up scandal with letters home.[54] Hastings became entangled in the debate over whether Parliament, the Crown, and the EIC would control India's policy and patronage. Trying to increase Parliament's power over the EIC, Charles James Fox and Edmund Burke controlled a committee of the House of Commons which recommended that Hastings be dismissed. But the EIC refused, anxious to assert its autonomy. When Fox came into office in 1783, in coalition with his former enemy the conservative Lord North, he thought he had the power to defeat the EIC. The centerpiece of his administration was the East India bill of 1783, which would have strengthened parliamentary control over India. Under this bill, Parliament would appoint an independent board of commissioners to "superintend all company operations and appointments from Britain." Since Parliament would select the board, it could control imperial policy—and benefit from imperial patronage.[55] What Parliament gained, the king and the EIC would lose.

Fox and his ally Burke addressed several different audiences to pass this bill. To appeal to traditional parliamentary and mercantile interests, Fox and Burke used technical arguments. They claimed their new structure would be more efficient; detailing the exact revenues of the EIC, they argued that its corruption had diminished the potential wealth India could have brought to Britain. Fox and Burke also shaped their rhetoric to appeal to public opinion outside of Parliament in less technical and more emotional terms. To address traditional Whig and radical concerns, they argued that the corruption of the EIC threatened to infect the British polity by giving the Crown too much power. They also drew upon increasingly popular Enlightenment sentiments of humanity to depict Hastings as an unjust and corrupt governor responsible for a terrible famine. Fox portrayed the English in India as rapacious, oppressive, and uncontrolled. To stop their brutality, Parliament must strip the company of its autonomy and patronage. He proclaimed it was an "odious tyranny" when "thirty million of men, gifted by Providence with the ordinary endowments of humanity, should groan under a system of despotism unmatched in all the histories of the world."[56]

Edmund Burke brought moral fervor to this attack. He was a philosopher who had written an influential tract of the sublime and the beautiful; a somewhat pinched, stooped figure, he was instantly identified by his glasses in caricatures.[57] To defend Fox's India bill, Burke asserted the "natural equality of man" and proclaimed that Indians were not barbarians but "a people for ages civilized and cultivated." Burke used the story of Asof-ud-daulah and the Begums of Oudh to appeal to the emotions of his audience. Warren Hastings and his minions, Burke thundered, selected "the pious hand of a son to . . . tear from his mother and grandmother the provision of their age, the maintenance of his brethren, and of all the ancient household of his father."[58] The begums were "bereaved even of their jewels: their toilets, these altars of beauty, were sacrilegiously invaded, and the very ornaments of the sex foully purloined!"[59] However, the "younger members" of Parliament, led by Pitt, laughed at his speech and mocked his sublime rhetoric.[60]

The fact that Burke and Fox had formed a coalition with their former enemy, the conservative Lord North, undermined their credibility in 1783. As noted in the last chapter, their enemies portrayed them as opportunistic party politicians rather than principled moralists. Fox's opponents feared that if his East India bill passed, he would appoint the members of the independent parliamentary board over Indian affairs, command vast Indian patronage, and therefore acquire despotic power.[61] Caricatures mocked Fox as a turbaned oriental despot and Burke as a hypocritical orator whose humanitarian rhetoric thinly veiled an appetite for plunder.[62] The EIC stirred up public opinion by claiming that Fox's bill would destroy its "chartered rights," and that if its rights could be stripped away, all chartered property would become insecure.[63] The House of Commons passed the bill, but the Lords defeated it, due to the king's intervention, and Fox fell from power.

The new prime minister, William Pitt, passed his own East India Act in 1784, which ensured that the Crown rather than Parliament controlled India. The act enabled the Crown to appoint a board of control over the EIC and strengthened the power of a governor accountable to the king. To be sure, Pitt's East India Act remedied many of the abuses of which Burke complained. It aimed to "preserv[e] the Company's wealth" for the good of the nation; it pledged that Britain would forgo further conquests or territorial expansion in India; and it promised that the EIC would not interfere with native customs.[64] Hastings finally resigned and returned to England in 1785. Lord Cornwallis, his replacement as governor of India, instituted fiscal, political, and moral reforms aimed at preventing private trading and corruption.[65] However, as Burke presciently observed, Cornwallis—and the other future governors of India—also acquired "powers totally unlimited."[66] As he and other governors-general defeated Indian princes who opposed them, the empire inexorably expanded.

Determined to press on with the India issue, Burke and Fox focused their attack on Hastings. Impeachment became their new weapon. Under the British constitution, an official could be impeached even if he had resigned. Impeachment brought before justice those who had endangered the good of the government and the people at large; they could be punished by a fine, imprisonment, or even death. But impeachment also enabled Parliament to challenge the crown, often over matters of foreign policy.[67] A party or faction that lost control of the government could still appeal to Parliament to impeach an official on the grounds of misconduct.[68] But the process of impeachment was long and drawn out. First, beginning in 1786, the House of Commons investigated the charges and decided on their validity. The managers of the impeachment included Fox, Burke, and Sheridan. They drew up the articles of the impeachment and, after the House voted to accept them, took the case to the House of Lords. The Lords then functioned as an open court, holding the trial in Westminster Hall. The press reported the whole process, supported by a flood of pamphlets for and against Hastings. As a result, the wider public also sat in judgment on him.

At first Hastings failed to mobilize public opinion effectively for his cause, oblivious to the changing nature of parliamentary politics and the need to appeal to humanitarian sentiment.[69] Hastings employed Major John Scott, a member of Parliament, to stir up support for him with lobbying and pamphlets, but Scott was bumbling and ineffectual, a clumsy and unpersuasive writer.[70] Hastings seemed to regard his main audience as the royal court and the shareholders of the EIC. Even before he arrived from India, his wife curried favor with the king and queen. Mrs. Hastings had long been rumored to be the path to Hastings's patronage, which was probably untrue, but she definitely acquired fabulous diamonds in India, which she loved to display. She lavished gifts of these diamonds on the king and queen. But these traditional means of gaining favor backfired. Critics alleged that Mrs. Hastings was trying to bribe the king and queen to support her husband.[71] After a performer in Covent Garden caused a sensation by swallowing stones, caricatures depicted the king and queen ingesting diamonds into their grotesque craws.[72] As one poem remarked,

Now God save the Queen, while the people I teach,
How the King may grow rich, while the Commons impeach;

Then let Nabobs go plunder, and rob as they will,
And throw in their diamonds, as grist to his mill.[73]

In her *Hastiniad*, Eliza Ryves portrayed Mrs. Hastings pouring diamonds and opals into the queen's lap: "Millions of wealth, the spoils or bribes, / Of ravag'd India's royal tribes."[74]

Throughout the 1780s, Scott and Hastings's other supporters defended him against Fox's and Burke's emotional rhetoric on pragmatic grounds. They argued that the governor-general had administered Bengal efficiently, preserved the empire in India, and increased revenues.[75] Drawing upon the theory of oriental despotism, his supporters claimed that Hastings simply acted as a Mughal ruler would by demanding extraordinary revenues from the begums and Cheit Singh and attacking them when they refused.[76] Hastings's friends portrayed the begums as "intriguing women" who were "incapable of managing [large] property."[77] Other supporters said that as recalcitrant rebels, the begums should be repressed. When his opponents found it hard to believe that elderly begums and eunuchs posed any danger to the British, a defender declared, "It was not the sex, nor the age of the begums that Mr. Hastings was to consider, but the numbers of men that were at their disposal."[78]

Hastings's 1786 defense speech to the Commons also drew upon the theory of oriental despotism to justify violating British treaties with Cheit Singh and the begums: "I know not how we can deny that existence of many *despotic principles* in the Mogul system of Government; but wherever *those* exist, the *powers* of the prince will be every thing, and the *rights* of the subject nothing."[79] This sentence came hours into Hastings's tedious speech, which he droned aloud from a prepared text. In fact, in 1788 Hastings claimed that he had not seen all of the speech before he read it and that his agent Nathaniel Halhed inserted the sentence on oriental despotism. Hastings repudiated the notion that Indian princes ruled without law.[80] But it was too late; the defense of despotism had entered the public record, and Burke used it to portray Hastings himself as an oriental despot.[81]

Burke, Fox, and Sheridan focused on a much larger audience than the court or the EIC: the newspaper-reading public disillusioned by the party politics of 1784.[82] Styling themselves as champions of humanity, they attempted to redeem their party from the stigma of faction and to portray themselves as virtuous friends united to act for the public good.[83] Like Burke, Richard Brinsley Sheridan had long struggled to combine his principles with the search for patronage. Sheridan succeeded in high society—and high politics—after the duchess of Devonshire admired his plays and introduced him to Fox. A charming man whose looks were marred only by a drinker's red nose, the Irish Sheridan sympathized with Wilkes and saw the impeachment as a chance to combine his ideals with his dramatic skill.[84] He called upon members of Parliament to "divest themselves of party prejudice and political feeling, and if on examining facts, truth should appear, our cause is gained."[85] A Stafford constituent praised Sheridan for "saving millions of helpless creatures from the bloody hand of rapine and murder," a task more worthy than claiming "the tinsel of power—The baubles of office."[86]

The election of 1784 had produced a Parliament more independent of ministerial leadership and more willing to consider social issues such as abolition of the slave trade, reform of the criminal laws, prisons, and poor laws, and prohibition of cruel popular sports.[87] Humanitarian advocates also mobilized public opinion outside of Parliament, most notably in anti–slave trade associations, and even the unorganized reading public closely followed humanitarian causes through pamphlets, newspapers, and even novels and poetry.[88] Some viewed both Indians and Africans as victims of European tyranny and inhumanity.[89]

Elite women increasingly contributed to public opinion in the 1780s, attending debating societies and joining in the anti–slave trade agitation. They also attended the impeachment trial itself, where the fashionable world came to see and be seen. Newspapers reported on the fashions at the trial: the ladies attending Burke's famous speech wore "beautiful headdresses, decorated with wreaths of roses, myrtles, jessamine in bloom, and other exquisite and rare hothouse productions."[90] In fact, the impeachment was the only political event extensively covered in the *Ladies Magazine* during the 1780s.[91]

Burke's and Sheridan's speeches drew upon the conventions of "sensibility."[92] Long popular, the novels of sensibility stirred their audiences' tears with heartrending stories of innocent maidens oppressed by evil villains. Antislavery advocates also deployed the methods of sensibility to create sympathy for enslaved Africans.[93] In their speeches, Burke, Sheridan, and their supporters deliberately wished to induce tears in their audiences, often weeping themselves.[94] As Sheridan told Parliament, "They could not behold the workings of the heart, the quivering lips, the trickling tears, the loud and yet tremulous joys of the millions whom their vote of this night would for ever save from the cruelty of corrupted power."[95]

Burke also wrote the articles of impeachment in a style calculated to appeal to this wider audience.[96] The constitutional tradition of impeachment, with its vague definition of "high crimes and misdemeanors," allowed him to do this. As he explained, in impeachments "statesmen who abuse their power . . . are tried . . . not upon the niceties of a narrow [criminal] jurisprudence, but upon the enlarged and solid principles of morality." Burke focused many of the articles of impeachment on female victimization.[97] Article 1 accused Hastings of allowing troops to plunder the castle of Cheit Singh's mother, "contrary to the Practice of civilized Nations, and particularly offensive to the Manners of the East, and the Respect there paid to the Female Sex." Similarly, article 2 declared that Hastings caused "Outrage and Violence offered to the Persons and Properties of . . . the Mother and Grandmother of the present Vizier Asoph ul Dowlah, Nabob of Oude."[98] Article 6 dealt with Nuncomar and Munny Begum.[99]

Burke's tactics did not always succeed. For instance, the House of Commons rejected his proposal to impeach Hastings for the Rohilla wars as well. He and his supporters tried to blame Hastings for Shujah-ud-daulah's excesses against the Rohillas, portraying Shujah as a vicious murderer who "extirpated" the "brave" Rohillas, invaded their zenanas, and tried to violate their young daughters. But Burke's vivid story about the Rohillas foundered on his lack of evidence, and these charges were dropped.[100] To be sure, Burke detailed the main issues of impeachment in the rest of the twenty charges, including corruption, waging illegal wars, and disobeying orders. Above all, Burke accused Hastings of governing through "personal influence" instead of British law and justice—in other words, acting as an oriental despot.[101] Once the House of Commons passed the articles of impeachment, Burke brought them to the House of Lords, which sat in trial on Hastings. His task was to combine an emotive, vivid style, which would appeal to the public, with the evidence and argument to convince the peers.

In 1788, Burke opened the impeachment trial with a vision of India as a "Republic of Princes," with a sophisticated ancient culture. He repudiated Hastings's alleged defense of oriental despotism by pointing out that India enjoyed a long heritage of law codes and benevolent administrations. Burke tried to create empathy for the Indians by portraying India as an idealized English society, with its great aristocratic dynasties, landed squires (the *zemindars*), and grateful peasants.[102] Into this idyll, Burke declared, Hastings stormed, ravaging, exploiting, and ultimately destroying Indian society. Burke accused the EIC and Hastings of disrupting the traditional, hierarchical, dynastic family, which he saw as the basis of Indian society and British life as well.

Burke and Sheridan presented themselves as defending the "rights of man against man's oppression."[103] As a result of this language, some critics have lauded Burke as an exceptional critic of empire.[104] Indeed, Burke and Sheridan seemed to speak in antiracist terms.[105] Defending the revolt of

Cheit Singh, Sheridan asserted that resistance to oppression was "a duty he owes to that common God who where he gives the form of Man whatever may be the complexion—gives also the feeling and the Rights of Men."[106] Writing to Miss Mary Palmer in 1786, Burke claimed he was defending "a set of people, who have none of your Lillies and Roses in their faces, but who are the image of the Great Pattern as well as you. I know what I am doing, whether the white people like it or not."[107] Yet both Burke and Sheridan supported the existence of empire, as long as it was cleansed of corruption and oppression and based on clear legal principles.

Neither Burke nor Sheridan believed that Indian men could enjoy the same rights as British men. Burke argued for a notion of natural rights, by which he meant the right to be governed by laws, to enjoy liberty, to have one's customs, traditions, and inherited privileges respected, but not the right to participate in politics. Sheridan declared that the instinct of liberty was "less active in the Indian than in the Englishman," so someone had to save them.[108] The solution to their oppression was not Indian justice, "the ineffective bauble of an Indian pagod!" but "British justice . . . august and pure."[109]

Burke and Sheridan actually contributed to emergent racial stereotyping and helped rationalize the empire by depicting Indians as powerless creatures who needed to be rescued. Burke and Sheridan emphasized Indian passivity by depicting Indians as feminine victims of Hastings's tyranny.[110] To be sure, they justified Cheit Singh's revolt against Hastings, but their portrayal of the begums carried much greater emotional power for the British. In writing his begums speech, Sheridan had to overcome copious evidence presented to the House of Commons (and preserved in his notes) that the Bahu Begum had helped Cheit Singh's rebellion.[111] To be sure, he skewered Hastings's inconsistent justifications for seizing their treasure, but he failed to present the begums as rational actors responding to British threats.[112] Instead, he presented them as "innocent, defenseless" old women and Hastings as a vicious violator who sacrificed "female dignity and distress to parricide and plunder."

This motif clearly evoked contemporary gothic romance and oriental tales, which added exotic settings, suspense, horror, and violence to the conventions of sensibility.[113] As Burke observed to a friend, Sheridan "has warmed with a sort of love passion for our begums," transforming his speech into an oriental romance.[114] Sheridan also blamed Hastings for the sufferings of the women of the Khord Mahal (Shujah's harem); he claimed the troops blocked food from reaching them, so "driven to despair by famine," they shamefully left the sacred seclusion of the harem to "pour forth in sad procession" before the eyes of the townspeople, only to be "driven back by the soldiery, and beaten with bludgeons to the scene of madness which they had quitted."

As in the gothic novels of the time, both Burke and Sheridan claimed that the villain destroyed families with his lust for power and treasure.[115] Sheridan accused Hastings of coming between the Bahu Begum and her son Asof. Asof owed his life to his mother, Sheridan argued, "for one day, his savage father [Shujah-ud-daulah] in a rage attempting to cut [Asof] down with his scymeter [sic], the Begum rushed between her husband and her son, and saved the latter through the loss of some of her own blood; for she was wounded by the blow that was not aimed at her." This stabbing scene closely resembles those found in gothic novels and dramas, where fathers tragically kill their own children.[116] Then, Sheridan went on, Hastings forced Asof to seize his mother's treasure, breaking the bond between mother and son. Sheridan drew upon universal human sentiments, for filial piety was "the primal bond of society . . . it causes the bosom to glow with reverberated love." While trying to evoke audiences' empathy, he also portrayed the begums as distant and other, arguing that Hastings failed to respect the sacred seclusion of the zenana, so different from the freedom of English women.[117] As in gothic dramas, the heroine could never rescue herself; the heroes Sheridan and Burke stepped in to save the day.[118]

Both Burke and Sheridan also painted a more disturbing picture of India as an emasculated land.[119] When they used the begums to stand for India, they metonymically indicated the lack of masculine sovereignty there, the feminizing of Indian men. While Burke associated the sublime with masculine government, he linked the beautiful with femininity and the family, which needed the protection of the state.[120] Burke described the Hindus as "these people who are the softest in their manners, approaching almost to feminine," who must be allowed to follow their ancient religion and family customs.[121] Of course, it was a cliché to call the Hindus "effeminate." But Burke, and to a lesser extent Sheridan, wished to portray Hindu men as passively feminine rather than threateningly effeminate. "Effeminacy" had rather negative connotations of self-indulgence and "unmanly weakness," qualities Englishmen despised and reviled in the eighteenth century. By describing the Indians as "feminine" rather than effeminate, Burke attempted to evoke a manly protectiveness toward them. Interestingly enough, Burke and Sheridan never brought up the fact that Asof-ud-daulah was sexually interested only in men, even though Sheridan all too eagerly made homophobic insinuations against his political enemy, Pitt. In this instance such invective would have undercut his own case by eroding sympathy for the begums and Asof.[122] To be sure, Burke regarded Muslim men as more war-like; he contrasted the brave, cultured, and honorable Rohillas with the vicious, aggressive Shujah-ud-daulah.[123] But Burke and his allies accused Hastings of effeminizing even Muslim men.

While the theory of oriental despotism alleged that effeminate Indian princes neglected their duties by indulging themselves in the seraglio, Burke and Philip Francis twisted this notion to blame the British for the vices of the Indian princes under their control.[124] As Francis explained, Indian princes "were driven by their oppressions into the inmost recesses of their Zenanas," where they intoxicated themselves with "opium and strong liquors, in order to deaden the sense of the misery . . . the devastation that British rapine had occasioned in their territories."[125] Article 8 of the impeachment accused Hastings of attributing the "distresses of the Country [of Oudh] . . . to the vices of the said Vizier's [Asof-ud-daulah's] own character," when it was Hastings's failure to supervise Oudh properly, and his extortionate demands and corrupt associates, that ruined Oudh.[126]

Following the theory of oriental despotism, Burke also depicted powerful women intriguing from the harem, somewhat contradicting his earlier focus on victimized princesses. For instance, Burke criticized Hastings for giving too much power to a woman, Munny Begum, thus effeminizing the nawab of Bengal. He portrayed Munny Begum as a former prostitute and slave who usurped the government of Bengal with Hastings's help: "a secluded woman in the place of a man of the world . . . a fantastic dancing girl in the place of a grave magistrate . . . administering [Bengal's] justice, presiding over all its remaining power, wealth and influence, exhibiting to the natives of the country their miserable state of degradation, and the miserable dishonor of the English Company."[127] Munny Begum was a *stepmother*, for Burke, "a name of horror in all countries," and not a legitimate representative of a royal family. To Burke, Hastings's appointment of a woman in this position demonstrated most egregiously the English policy of disrupting the dynastic succession of Bengal. To discredit him, Burke portrayed Hastings's motives as "amorous and sentimental"—but mainly a lust for lucre.

Instead of the virtuous paternal ruler, Hastings was portrayed as embodying his power in sensual indulgence and uncontrolled, unrestrained masculinity; his coconspirator, Munny Begum, usurped authority with her evil, feminine sexuality. Both represented raw, new power, untempered by generations of aristocratic tradition. Bengal, therefore, was a land where the social order was inverted, where Hastings, a man of insignificant birth and education, a "bullock contractor," as Burke scornfully termed him, dictated as a tyrant. Hastings's persecution of the Begums of Oudh—representing the landed interests—symbolized this world turned upside down. Burke feared that the striving, aggressive stockjobbing middle classes would overturn the delicate balance between commerce and landholding in British society. His depiction of Hastings as a sexual predator served as a metaphor for Hastings's corrupt business dealings: unrestrained and uncivilized, commerce resembled a rape, unless it was softened by manners, restrained by laws, and subordinate to aristocratic power—just as marriage tamed the power of sexuality.[128]

Burke also modeled his speech after Cicero's attack on Gaius Verres, a Roman provincial governor put on trial for abuses during his rule of Sicily. Cicero feared that Verres's mistreatment of the Sicilians would turn them against the Roman Empire and deprive the empire of its revenues, much as Burke feared that Britain would lose India and its treasures. Like Hastings, Verres was accused of bribery, legal corruption, extortion of revenues, and insulting the religious customs of the Sicilians. By emulating Cicero, Burke could present himself as a dignified Roman statesman; a caricature depicted him in a toga, his rhetoric defending the feminine figures of Britannia and India.[129] But Burke also emulated Cicero's tactic of sexual insult: the Roman also alleged that Verres combined his "irrepressible and unbridled covetousness" with "wanton lust," robbing women of their inheritance, consorting with prostitutes, disrespecting the seclusion of Sicilian ladies, and even raping young women.[130] Cicero thus portrayed Verres as a man whose ambitious masculinity burned out of control in a "frenzy" of power and lust.[131] Burke combined this classical precedent, however, with orientalist motifs.

Burke ratified the orientalist stereotype that Indians combined the worst of masculine and feminine vices. He feared that oriental vices would contaminate the British, who would become enmeshed in the sexual confusion and corruption of the East. According to Burke, "secret and mysterious . . . black men" could easily become despots under the service of corrupt East Indian officials. He described native officials as "reserved and timid, patient and dissembling, . . . disposed to . . . low Intrigues, and the miserable Arts of Subterfuges of Servitude, [rather] than . . . a manly Assertion of their Rights." These racial vices could infect Europeans, Burke worried. By portraying Indians as effeminate and corrupt, Burke undermined the possibility that they could rule themselves.

At the same time, Burke feared that this effeminacy could mutate into the hypermasculinity of Indian despotism, excessive in its lust for power and torture. The problem with Hastings, Burke implied, was that he became too Indian, an oriental despot himself. He described Hastings's crimes in hyperbolic racial terms: "a heart blackened to the very blackest, a heart dyed deep in blackness, a heart corrupted, vitiated, and gangrened to the very core."[132] However, unlike the swashbuckling Clive, the rather sedate and domestic Hastings, sitting plainly dressed in Westminster Hall, was hard to imagine as a vicious villain. To fit Hastings in his overblown rhetoric of evil, Burke equated him with a torturer named Debi Singh.

In the conclusion to his speech, Burke intended to focus on corruption, claiming that Debi Singh bribed Hastings to appoint him as a tax collector in Dinajpur and Rangpur, and then extorted excessively heavy revenues. Discovering evidence that Debi Singh ordered tortures, Burke wrote to Francis, "What an affair . . . it has stuff in it, that will, if anything, work upon the popular Sense. But how to do without making a monstrous and disproportiond [sic] member; I know not."[133] To work upon the popular sense, Burke embellished an explanation of Hastings's oppressive tax system with the language of oriental fantasy. He painted an orgiastic scene of Debi Singh, a "great magician," corrupting young English officials by offering them public prostitutes with names like "Mine of Gold, Pearl of Price, Ruby of Pure Blood." Debi Singh also demanded impossibly high revenues from the landholders of Dinajpur and Rangpur. In response to these tortures, Burke proclaimed, these "patient" people "burst at once into a wild, universal, uproar and unarmed rebellion."[134] In fact, the peasant revolt was highly organized and established an alternative administrative system, but Burke wished to portray the Indians as feminine, childlike, chaotic, and doomed to fail.[135] He emphasized many of the landholders "happened to be women."[136] When they could not pay, Debi Singh sent in his bailiffs without regard for the "sacred treasure" of the seclusion of the zenana. Burke alleged that in search of revenues, Debi Singh also tortured the *ryots*, or peasants, and forced them to watch their virgin daughters and chaste wives be violated in public: "In order that nature might be violated . . . where the remembrances of our infancy and all our tender remembrances are combined, they [Debi Singh's officials] put the nipples of the women into the sharp edges of split bamboos and tore them from their bodies. Grown from ferocity to ferocity, but cruelty to cruelty, they applied burning torches and cruel slow fires— my Lords, I am ashamed to go further."[137] Although, of course, Burke did go further, describing these practices in such lurid detail that the hall was in an uproar and Mrs. Sheridan fainted.

PUBLIC OPINION

At first, Sheridan and Burke's emphasis on female victimization seemed to stir up public opinion successfully. Provincial readers "inveighed with vehemence against [Hastings's] cruelties to the women."[138] Hugh Mulligan, the antislavery writer, denounced Hastings as

> Bloody, remorseless, dead for mercy's strain,
> While bloody virgins weep, and to the Gods complain.[139]

Burke's speech, however, did become a "monstrous and disproportiond member." In his *Philosophical Enquiry*, Burke had justified the thrill of pleasure audiences experienced at violent spectacles, because such horrors also stimulated pity for the sufferers.[140] But by emphasizing the torture and violation of women, Burke also risked creating "a spectacle of pain" that could turn his audience into voyeurs. Indeed, attending public executions was a popular amusement at the time. Humanitarians were trying to abolish pain and torture, making violence a taboo. By solely depicting slaves or Indian peasants as victims of horrific violence, however, humanitarians risked rendering them as powerless creatures who could never help themselves, who needed to be rescued by white people. Furthermore, by making pain taboo, they also turned it into "a source of illicit excitement," appealing to audiences' prurient interests, as Karen Halttunen observes. And this excitement could quickly turn into "revulsion and disgust."[141] Mr. Gillum's satire of Burke's speech reveals how his appeal to humanity could induce contempt: "The brawls of Bramins now invade the ear—A pair of half-starved begums next appear."[142] A caricature satirized Sheridan's speech as consisting of nothing but "begums begums begums."[143]

The eroticism of Burke and Sheridan's oriental fantasies also became all too apparent to their audiences. For instance, to justify the Bahu Begum's influence over her son, Burke claimed that the mother of the Ottoman sultan chose a virgin for her son every night. But the erotic scene he evoked completely erased his point: "The whole Court were in a convulsion of laughter, while the *young ladies* around, behind their fans, were tittering applause. The unfortunate clerk could scarce keep his spectacles on his nose for laughing."[144] (See figure 8, where a caricaturist depicted Burke in an erotic revery.)[145] Satirists ridiculed Sheridan and Burke's implication that Hastings was a rapist. "Simpkin" mockingly declared,

FIGURE 8   *A Reverie of Prince Demetrius Cantemir, Ospidar of Moldavia* (1788),
BMC 7307. © The British Museum. Burke dreams of an elderly mother of a sultan
presenting a virgin to her son, saying, "I have procured another Lamb for my Son."
The sultan sits under a copy of the Koran. Burke sits under a bust of "Mahomet."
The open book quotes from his speech, "I have observed that the greatest degree of
respect is aid to women of quality in the East and that the strongest instances of ma-
ternal affection and filial duty prevail there."

> How licentious, how wicked, how base are the men,
> Who would ravish old women of three score and ten![146]

Another caricature (see figure 9) depicted the impeachment trial as a
"Raree Show," like a crude performance at a fair, featuring Hastings as a
"Prodigious Monster arrived from the East" biting into a voluptuous In-
dian female.[147]

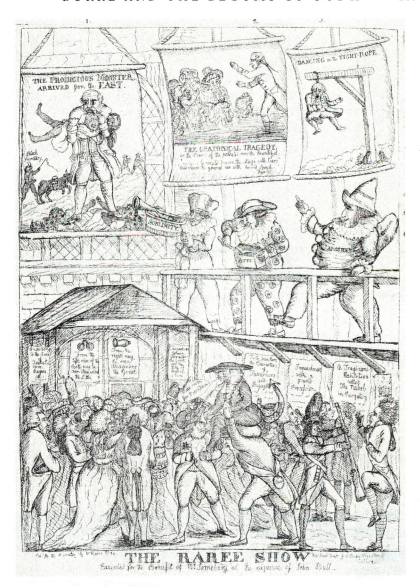

FIGURE 9 William Dent, *The Raree Show* (1788), BMC 7273. © The British Museum. Hastings is the "Prodigious Monster biting a naked Indian woman's breasts. The middle banner depicts Burke orating to an audience, mostly women, who weep so much they almost drown in their tears. The slogan is "The Oratorical Tragedy, or the Power of the pathetic of the beautiful," satirizing Burke on the sublime and the beautiful. Burke, dressed as a clown, blows a trumpet with a banner marked "Sublimity." Sheridan and Fox are also portrayed as clowns. Below, ladies and gentlemen crowd into the trial.

The "Raree Show" also caricatured Fox, Burke, and Sheridan as clowns who performed at a carnival stall. It ridiculed Burke's notion of the sublime by describing the trial as an "Oratorical Tragedy" that proved "the power of the pathetic over the beautiful." Indeed, the commercial theater seemed to be a poor imitation of the drama going on in Westminster Hall, with its fashionable audiences and orientalist fantasies.[148] When Sheridan collapsed at the end of his speech, the satirist Simpkin claimed,

> 'Tis a trick, which *Stage Orators* use in their need,
> The Passions to raise, and the Judgment mislead.[149]

Burke and Sheridan's theatrical rhetoric threatened to transform the House of Lords from "a vast stage of justice . . . awful from its high authority . . . into a theater of pleasure."[150]

Commentators criticized Burke and Sheridan for overstepping the bounds of decorum expected in the House of Lords, where nothing "passionate or exaggerated will be admitted."[151] Simpkin attacked Burke's accent as "the Irishman's Howl," which made "the Stream of his Eloquence muddy and foul."[152] Especially by the waning years of the trial in 1794, Burke faced increasing criticism for his "coarse" invective and "filthy allusions to nature's laxations."[153] In fact, some of Burke's contemporaries thought he was a "little deranged" or at best an "ingenious madman."[154]

The trial also became much like a play whose run went on too long. As the House of Lords heard witnesses for a few months each year, and the years ticked by, the actors seemed to be mouthing the same old tired lines. Audience interest waxed and waned, judging by the fluctuating price of tickets and decreasing number of fashionable peeresses who attended.[155] The actress Mrs. Wells demonstrated her contempt for Burke by mending her stockings as she watched the trial.[156]

The scandal also illuminates the character of public opinion in the late eighteenth century. Audiences judged the impeachment as a trial, not a theatrical performance; they could thrill to the eloquence without being persuaded by it. Even Sheridan's great speech was seen as a wonderful performance that failed to convince reason.[157] Eventually public opinion responded in a fairly rational way to debates, as Susan Staves observes: by assessing evidence, principles, and motives.[158] Burke, Fox, and Sheridan fought to keep ordinary rules of evidence out of the trial, arguing that Parliament was a tribunal that transcended legal regulations, but this proved to be their undoing. By 1788–89, the managers of the impeachment failed to produce convincing, clear-cut evidence for their charges during the examination of witnesses. The begums appeared as rebels against British authority, and it turned out that Hastings was not directly responsible for the oppressions Debi Singh committed; indeed, he punished him.[159] In 1789, for instance, an anonymous spectator noted in his journal of the trial, "It begins to appear that the prosecution is carried on with a malice and rancor on the part of the Managers that is inexcusable that the facts they assert are not at all authenticated and that they do all they can now to mislead."[160] The contradictions of Burke's arguments about women started to become more apparent. For instance, in 1789, the newspaper the *World* asked why Burke and Sheridan excused the influence of the Begums of Oudh but denounced Munny Begum for controlling the reins of power.[161] While Burke and Sheridan drew upon orientalist stereotypes to portray Indian women as either passive victims or intriguing villainesses, contemporary women writers used oriental settings to flirt with cross-cultural romance and obliquely criticize their own culture. They fantasized that under the veil, women could take unaccustomed freedoms.[162]

Burke knew it was important to win women over to his cause, for he believed that twenty thousand women should be included in the four hundred thousand nobility, gentry, wealthy men, and intellectuals who composed the public that mattered.[163] But the women whose opinions are recorded did not simply swoon at Burke's sentimental appeals. Like men, they relied on their rational judgment as well as their own political and economic interests. After all, women could own stock in the EIC.[164] Eliza Ryves satirized the governor-general's alleged corruption in her poem *Hastiniad*, drawing upon her long-standing Whig sympathies to side with Burke and Sheridan.[165] Fanny Burney wrote in her diary that Burke "frequently made me tremble by his strong and horrible representations," but when she recognized that ill will motivated his passion, the violence of his rhetoric recovered her judgment. Attached to the court, perhaps she also favored Hastings for political reasons.[166] The famed learned Lady Elizabeth Montagu followed the trial closely through the letters of her nephew, Baron Rokesby, whose career she patronized; she believed that Hastings's defense of the empire justified his conduct.[167] Hannah More, a conservative philanthropist, also supported Hastings.[168] Elizabeth Hamilton, a Scottish intellectual whose brother served in India, praised Hastings's patronage of Sanskrit scholarship and denounced the "rancorous misrepresentations of envy and malevolence, . . . the florid harangues, and turgid declamations" against him.[169]

Hastings and his government allies also began developing more effective defense techniques that reached a wider audience. They financed the publication of pamphlets and newspapers that satirized the trial. For instance, in 1789 the Treasury subsidized the *World*, hoping that its columnist Simpkin's satire on Burke would deflect inquiries into the EIC. By 1790, all ministerial newspapers made fun of Burke and the Hastings trial. However,

Burke's bombast and lack of evidence also alienated his own supporters. By 1790, the trial had become so unpopular that even Foxite Whig newspapers would not defend it.[170]

Burke's personal attack on Hastings also backfired. As the trial dragged on for years, Burke become the demonic persecutor and Hastings the victim who incited public sympathy. Furthermore, by personifying the oppression of India in the person of Hastings, Burke deflected attention from the question of whether Britain should be in India at all.[171] For instance, when Burke failed in his attempt to pin the blame for Debi Singh's tortures on Hastings, he also lost the chance to point out that the British demand for revenues helped cause the miseries of the Rangpur peasants and incited their revolt. He depicted the system as bad because it was created by an evil man, Hastings, not because the British government would inevitably oppress India.[172] His failure enabled Hastings's supporters to claim that excessive revenue extraction and coercion of peasants were customary practices in Mughal India and therefore acceptable for British agents to use.[173]

Some of Hastings's sympathizers believed the whole system of British government in India was based on unjust conquest, but they argued that Hastings simply carried out the policies mandated by the government and the EIC. If Britain wished to retain its possessions in India, Thomas Erskine argued, it must be prepared to hold them by force: "The unhappy people of India, feeble and effeminate as they are from the softness of their climate, . . . still occasionally start up in all the vigor and intelligence of insulted nature. To be governed at all, they must be governed with a rod of iron."[174] Hastings's supporters also began to develop a rationale for empire that convinced a broader public. They portrayed the British empire in India as benevolent, paternalist, and authoritarian, and the Indians as degraded and in need of guidance.[175] In doing so, they strengthened the pseudoscientific notions of race that were becoming more predominant by the 1790s.[176] Although Hastings himself had long praised and studied Indian civilization, in 1792, Hastings's counsel Law declaimed "that until the English formed a settlement [in India] the inhabitants were a savage race of barbarians under a government of the most cruel tyranny."[177] In newspapers, pro-Hastings editorials began to argue not only that Hastings had benefited Britain by increasing revenues from India but also that the inhabitants of India were much better off under British rule than under their own princes.[178] Cornwallis began to defend "benevolent despotism" as the correct strategy in British India. He testified in the Hastings trial in 1794 that "the natives have been accustomed to despotic rule from time immemorial, and are well acquainted with the miseries of their own tyrannic Administrators."[179]

When they rose up against Europeans, as in the Saint Domingue slave revolt, colonized people could be seen as threateningly masculine enemies rather than passive feminine victims.[180] Indian princes who fought back against the British were now demonized as "dark foes" rather than heroic princes. In the age of the French Revolution, the British began to fear that strong Indian rulers would deliver the empire to France.[181] Critics scorned humanitarianism as a "relaxation and effeminacy of manners" more suited for the sentimental novel than the tough task of disciplining the colonies, preventing revolution at home, and aggressively competing for trade.[182]

Burke's own political philosophy began to change as well. Although Burke had long criticized the excessive power of the Crown, in 1790 he switched sides, beginning to defend the monarchy and denounce the French Revolution. His *Reflections on the Revolution in France* won him the favor of the king and the prime minister, William Pitt. Burke's attack on Hastings shifted from a republican emphasis on natural rights to a monarchist attack on rebellion.[183] Whereas in 1788 he portrayed India as a "republic of princes" and defended Cheit Singh's right to resist, in 1794 he merely emphasized that the people had a right to be ruled by their traditional princes. He equated tyrants and rebels: "The man who is a tyrant, would, under some other circumstances, be a rebel; and he that is a rebel, would become a tyrant." In France and India, both rebellion and despotism, proclaimed Burke, derived from the "wild unbridled lewdness of arbitrary power."[184] In Burke's rhetoric, the tyrant Hastings stormed the begums' zenana, just as the plebeian French rebels invaded Marie Antoinette's bedroom.[185] But even as Burke painted affecting pictures of victimized ladies, he also told lurid tales of uncontrolled females, such as Munny Begum who ruined Bengal, and the "savage women" who stormed Versailles during October 1789.[186] While Burke's vivid rhetoric persuaded many to oppose the French Revolution, it no longer worked in the impeachment.[187]

The trial dragged on until 1795. The scandal had become entangled once again in party politics, with Pitt, the prime minister, as the master manipulator. Pitt had seemed to distance himself from both sides in the 1780s, presenting himself as an objective yet humanitarian judge who believed Hastings should be prosecuted for attacking Cheit Singh but rejected other counts. However, by the 1790s he seemed to prolong the impeachment to embarrass the opposition Foxite Whigs. Fox and Sheridan had split from Burke over the French Revolution; Fox lost interest in the impeachment altogether. But as managers of the trial, they had to continue to work with Burke—and take the blame for perpetuating the unpopular impeachment.[188] Burke began to lose all credibility in the Hastings trial. In 1794, he tried to refute Hastings's defense of Munny Begum as a sentimental novel, and his whole administration as a "great Indian opera," but this argument was unconvincing given that satirists had already mocked Burke's speeches as a tragicomic burlesque.[189] When Burke rose, shaking with rage, to deliver his response to Hastings's defense, the Lords literally turned their backs on him.[190] By 1795, the House of Lords finally acquitted Hastings. Hastings was now lauded as the hero who had saved British India.

CONCLUSION

This analysis of the Hastings impeachment trial reveals that sexual rhetoric can help attract public attention in the short term by portraying complicated issues as a simple scandal. But in the long term Burke and Sheridan's attempt to transform the impeachment into a scandal failed to have a political impact. Their scandalous language burgeoned out of control into voyeurism and inadvertent titillation and could not compensate for their lack of evidence against Hastings. Publications subsidized by Hastings and the government also undercut Burke's message with vicious satires.

Above all, Burke failed to transmute his personal attack on Hastings into a wider campaign to reform the empire. He refused to organize public opinion for his cause. Burke and his ally Fox still fundamentally believed in the primacy of Parliament over the people. Although Burke crafted his rhetoric to appeal to public opinion, he declared that public opinion "could not give judgment," unlike the House, that actually had the power to "come to a Decision."[191] In 1789, Fox even charged the Reverend John Logan with libel for daring to suggest that "private, personal and malicious motives" were behind the Commons' motion to impeach Hastings, thus damaging the respect due to Parliament as a judicial body. However, Logan's counsel, Thomas Erskine, pointed out that Fox, the champion of liberty, was trying to muzzle the freedom of the press.[192] By 1794, Burke even complained against the press for reporting the speeches at the trial.[193]

Burke did not mobilize public opinion because he did not believe that associations had a legitimate place in the constitution. However, this deprived him of a potent weapon. In contrast, the antislavery movement organized public opinion to pressure Parliament successfully. As in the Hastings impeachment, emotional rhetoric overcame the initial indifference among British people who could not see their own interest in empire.[194] In the Hastings affair, however, all audiences could do was applaud, weep, or laugh, unless they had a vote in the House of Lords. But in the abolitionist movement, men could feel a part of the movement by joining the abolition societies and local committees and petitioning Parliament, and women could write antislavery poetry and boycott West Indian sugar and rum. By 1792, the antislavery movement successfully impelled the Commons to pass a bill gradually abolishing the slave trade. However, the outbreak of war against revolutionary France and the Saint Domingue slave revolt gave the Lords the excuse to scuttle the proposal. Yet these actions set an important precedent for the power of organized public opinion.[195]

The failure to mobilize the humanitarian constituency against the empire in India was especially notable in the debate over the 1793 renewal of the EIC charter. Many liberals sharply criticized the injustices of the empire's policies.[196] But few advocated British withdrawal from India, instead calling for free trade, for progressive systems of law and land reform, or for the introduction of missionaries.[197] No doubt preoccupied with the war and the French Revolution, none organized into associations for India, and few petitioned. Sheridan did call for reparations to be paid to India, but he never made clear who was to receive them, and he did not start a campaign to pressure Parliament. Burke remained silent as the EIC retained its monopoly over trade.[198] Fox refused to investigate egregious EIC abuses in 1806.[199]

Nonetheless, the scandal over impeachment forced each side to articulate its philosophy of empire for a wider British audience. Burke presented himself as a defender of oppressed Indians and a critic of empire, a characterization sometimes accepted by political philosophers today. However, by using metaphors of victimized females and emasculated princes, Burke strengthened the rationale for an empire that denied Indians self-determination. In contrast, Burke criticized British oppression in the American colonies and in Ireland, but he did not depict Americans and the Irish as passive and effeminate. Instead, he regarded the Americans as manly lovers of liberty with "kindred blood" to the "chosen race and sons of England." They should enjoy "similar privileges, and equal protection" from the British constitution, the "sacred temple" of freedom."[200] Nor does his rhetoric on Ireland feature the highly gendered, sexualized images characteristic of his speeches on India in the 1780s. Burke spoke out less on Ireland, facing political constraints and his own ambiguous position, descended from a converted Catholic Irish family. But he believed that respectable, propertied Catholic men, often "fathers of families," could be trusted with the vote and incorporated into the British constitution.[201] By portraying the Indians as feminine, Burke attempted to reconcile a fundamental contradiction in his philosophy. He believed that government was a "trusteeship" to be exercised benevolently to protect the people, who at the last resort could theoretically "control" an op-

pressive government. Burke was never ready to imagine the people exercis-
ing this control, however, and believed that non-European peoples, unlike
the Americans and Irish, were totally incapable of it.[202]

Burke claimed to defend the right of Indians to preserve their own valid
culture, religion, and civilization, but he felt that this right was perfectly
congruent with British rule over India. He accused Hastings of violating
these customs by invading the begums' zenana. But in fact, Hastings was
much more knowledgeable about Indian culture than Burke. He instructed
his subordinates to respect customs regarding women, and he implemented
Hindu and Muslim codes in the juridical system of India. Hastings regarded Indian leaders as formidable individuals rather than as orientalist
stereotypes. Of course, Hastings used his knowledge to extend and solidify
British power in India; he simply found it more effective to rule using Indian techniques. Similarly, Hastings's successor, Lord Cornwallis, believed
that the British should rule India efficiently without interfering in Hindu or
Muslim religious customs concerning the family. Many generals and governors feared that interference in religion would spark dangerous revolts and
undermine the empire.

The impeachment, however, made it necessary to justify Britain's empire
to public opinion at home. As a result, Hastings's supporters created a new,
racist rationale for empire by portraying Indians as barbarians who needed
the strong hand of British rule. Although Burke tried to refute the idea that
Indians were barbarians, his orientalist fantasies of victimized begums and
emasculated princes contributed to the notion that Indians were strange
and different creatures who could never rule themselves. Commentators
began to argue that Britain could "atone" for the guilt of empire by ruling
more humanely than the Mughals.[203] Hannah More hoped that conquest,
"after having deluged a land with blood, involved the perpetrator in guilt,
and the innocent victim in ruin, may yet be the instrument of opening to
future generations the way to commerce, to civilization, to Christianity."[204]

Burke's attack on the French Revolution deployed family imagery more
successfully to justify a conservative, antidemocratic political order. But
as the next chapters will show, he faced an old adversary—Catherine
Macaulay—and a new one—Mary Wollstonecraft—who vigorously refuted his antidemocratic arguments. Wollstonecraft criticized Burke's emotional rhetoric as stirring up "sensibility," the bodily response of "sympathetic emotion." "Humanity," she argued, "discriminates the active exertions
of virtue from the vague declamation of sensibility." Wollstonecraft argued
that women, like slaves, needed rights, not pity.[205]

❧   ❧   ❧

CHAPTER FIVE

Scandal in an Age of Revolution

On the eve of the French Revolution, Marie Antoinette epitomized corrupt petticoat influence. Scandalmongering pamphlets depicted the queen as indulging in affairs, ruining her husband's politics, and squandering the French treasury on her jewels, châteaus, and orgiastic parties. Across the Channel, the British continued to fear petticoat influence as well. The Whigs rumored that Queen Charlotte would intrigue behind the throne as King George III struggled with dementia. Tales of aristocratic adultery, gambling, and bankruptcies in high life enlivened newspaper columns.

When the French Revolution erupted, moralists feared that scandals about aristocratic decadence would sap Britain's resolve to withstand the contagion. In response, the ruling elite needed to develop new, more convincing rationales for royal rule and aristocratic dominance. In his famous *Reflections on the Revolution in France* (1790), Edmund Burke contributed to this project by redeeming Marie Antoinette. But he was met by a fierce counterattack, as radicals used scandals to fuel their larger campaign against the social privileges of the aristocracy. Female radicals such as Catherine Macaulay and Mary Wollstonecraft played an important role in this campaign, denouncing Burke's call for chivalry as sentimental.

The British elite withstood these scandals and emerged unscathed from the era of the French Revolution. Historians debate whether Britons turned against reform and revolution because conservatives won the argument against revolution, or because the government harshly crushed reform.[1] I will argue that conservatives effectively defused scandals against the monarchy and aristocracy by combining repression and counterpropaganda. The conservative Hannah More, for instance, defended the aristocratic social order but also called upon aristocrats to abandon their fashionable ways and convert to true Christianity—or risk losing all.

SCANDALS AGAINST THE RULING ORDER

Royal scandals acquired a new meaning on the eve of revolution. Throughout the 1780s, Britons had heard rumors of the diamond necklace affair,
which discredited Marie Antoinette in the eyes of the French people.[2] A
swindler had persuaded Cardinal Rohan to buy an elaborate diamond
necklace, supposedly for Marie Antoinette, in hopes of regaining her favor
at court. Marie Antoinette was entirely innocent in the plot, but the French
public found it all too easy to believe that diamonds could obtain the
queen's political—and perhaps her sexual—favors.[3] As the French government teetered on the brink of bankruptcy, radicals blamed Marie Antoinette when the king dismissed reformist ministers.

In 1788, Britain met its own royal crisis. George III suffered a severe attack of dementia (caused by the disease porphyria) in 1788. As he raged under the strict care of doctors, Parliament had to decide who would become
regent. Allied with the prince, the Whigs Charles James Fox and Edmund
Burke anticipated his regency and their accession to power. But the prime
minister, William Pitt, wished to install Queen Charlotte in the position. In
response, the Whigs revived their old theory of "backstairs influence" over
the king by insinuating that the queen might exert illicit petticoat influence.
Burke protested that if the queen became regent, she would gain "power of
an enormous description," such as patronage, which might prove a "temp-
tation [that] may pervert the purest mind, and draw it aside from the path
of rectitude."[4] But soon, the king recovered.

When the French Revolution erupted in the summer of 1789, politics
changed across Europe. The French National Assembly abolished aristocratic privileges, and six thousand Parisian women forced Louis XVI and
Marie Antoinette to go from their palace at Versailles to Paris. The French
king ceded most of his power to the National Assembly. Many Britons, including Charles James Fox, greeted the outbreak of the Revolution with
enthusiasm. They hoped that France might become a constitutional
monarchy, like Britain. Others feared that the revolution might spread to
Britain. Conservatives knew that the aristocratic elite and the Crown must
be reconciled in order to survive, and they had to provide more convincing rationales for their rule. The ruling elite needed propagandists to combat radical arguments; it found them among those who were not aristocratic themselves but who had gained entrée into high society through their
talents.

Edmund Burke was one of the first, and most influential, to respond to
this crisis. Although he lacked dynastic connections, being the scion of an

Burke

obscure Irish family, his political and rhetorical brilliance impressed patrons who helped his parliamentary career. But he repudiated his former allies, Fox and the reformist Whigs, over the French Revolution and joined the king's side. As he tearfully broke with Fox, Burke flung a dagger on the Commons floor to symbolize the thousand daggers revolution aimed at England's heart.[5]

In his *Reflections on the Revolution in France*, Burke implicitly defended Marie Antoinette against scandal and used her dazzling image to bolster monarchy against revolution.[6] In doing so, he seemed to repudiate two of his previous principles: his long campaign against the excessive influence of the Crown, and his ambivalence toward female (especially queenly) influence in politics.[7] By focusing his description of the French monarchy on the frail person of Marie Antoinette instead of the actual ruler, Louis XVI, Burke justified aristocratic power while seeming to defend the Crown. The monarchy, he implied, could not rule on its own; it needed the aristocracy to rescue it. He hardly mentioned Louis XVI—when the king appeared in the story, Burke immediately dismissed his significance, adding, "to say no more of him," and returned his attention to the queen. Burke redeemed Marie Antoinette from the stigma of petticoat influence and instead portrayed her as an inspiration to a chivalrous social order. He painted a vivid picture of the queen as he first saw her in happier days, "glittering like the morning star, full of life, and splendor, and joy." As with the Begums of Oudh, Burke used the image of a vulnerable woman to exemplify France in danger from the Revolution. Ravening hordes of French revolutionaries, including "savage" women "lost to shame," invaded the queen's bedroom in Versailles and forced her and the king back to Paris to live under the eyes of the mob. Burke mourned that "the age of chivalry is gone," asking why "ten thousand swords" did not leap to her defense.[8] As in the Hastings affair, he implicitly positioned himself as the chivalrous hero who could rescue the doomed princess—and the aristocracy as the last best hope of chivalry.

Burke therefore implicitly continued conservative Whig traditions by regarding the aristocracy as even more important than the monarchy as a ruling elite. To be sure, Burke criticized the French aristocracy for foolishly imitating "the worst part of the manners of England" and flirting with "licentious philosophy." But the aristocratic French law courts, the *parlements*, checked "the excesses and vices of the monarchy." Indeed, the English Crown was more stable than the French because the monarch "must submit to the soft collar of social esteem" by associating with the aristocracy and taking the advice of his ministers. The British aristocracy maintained its power through its "austere and masculine morality," its vast acres and long traditions, and its openness; Burke believed that the French had erred by closing the ranks of the high aristocracy to merchants and bankers. Burke did not simply defend the constitution; he used familial imagery to celebrate the hierarchical nature of British society as a whole and emotive language to stir up Britons' loyalty.[9]

Many Britons greeted Burke's *Reflections* with acclaim, convinced by his fears that revolution would spread to Britain, but others scorned him as an apostate. The pension a grateful king bestowed on Burke proved to his critics that he sided with the government for opportunistic reasons.[10] Philip Francis, his ally in the Hastings affair, ridiculed his high-flown language about Marie Antoinette as "foppery." For others, Burke's lurid rhetoric confirmed their fears about his sanity.[11] Hannah More commented to William Wilberforce that "to enhance the horrors of anarchy" Burke represented "despotism as rather a desirable thing."[12]

A pamphlet war soon erupted around Burke's ideas, as Britons debated whether the aristocracy was necessary, what impact parliamentary reform would have on Britain, whether Thomas Paine's notion of rights was feasible, and whether economic progress and equality could be reconciled.[13] Two women were among the first, and "boldest," to refute Burke in print, an indication that some women could gain recognition as public intellectuals.[14] Catherine Macaulay and Mary Wollstonecraft scorned Burke's pity for Marie Antoinette and demolished his reverence for the hereditary aristocracy. Macaulay's reply to Burke was to be her last political pamphlet. Her work inspired Mary Wollstonecraft, a much younger and less privileged writer. Although they wrote in different styles—Macaulay in the stately language of earlier days, Wollstonecraft in more personal, heightened prose—their arguments followed the same lines.[15] Both insisted that reason, not emotion or tradition, should shape political argument. Macaulay rejected Burke's sentimental effusions over the French queen, pointing out, "The high colouring given to these scenes of regal distress" will "captivate the imagination," but "the delusions of fancy are apt to subside in men of cool minds" concerned with the public good. Wollstonecraft later declared that "the state had been fleeced, to support the unremitting demands of the queen; who would have dismembered France, to aggrandize Austria, and pamper her favorites."[16]

Macaulay and Wollstonecraft also mocked Burke's celebration of the hereditary aristocracy in order to reject conventional politics altogether. Macaulay described aristocratic chivalry as "the train of pompous ostentation" that puts "naked virtue . . . out of her rank," neatly reversing Burke's celebration of Marie Antoinette's virtue.[17] In a private letter to Samuel Adams, Macaulay used even stronger language, hoping that the Revolution would "bring after it the final emancipation of every other society in Europe from those Monarchic and Aristocratic chains imposed by the violence of arms and riveted on mankind by ignorance credibility and Priestcraft."[18] Wollstonecraft reviled the aristocracy as "profligates of rank, emasculated by hereditary effeminacy."[19] Following Macaulay's long-standing critique of the parliamentary system, Wollstonecraft depicted Parliament as so corrupted by aristocratic influence that it became "a convenient handle for despotism."[20] She asked, how are "hard-working mechanic[s] . . . represented, whose very sweat supports the splendid stud of an heir apparent, or varnishes the chariot of some female favorite who looks down on shame?"[21] Yet Macaulay's and Wollstonecraft's writings were mild in comparison to the productions of another radical.

Charles Pigott deployed sexual scandal to undermine the aristocracy in his best-selling *Jockey Club* and *Female Jockey Club* (1792–94). Pigott knew the aristocracy all too well. The scion of a gentry family, he socialized among them at horse races and married—unhappily—an aristocratic woman. His ramblings in high society enabled him to pick up juicy stories to fuel his radical ire against aristocratic corruption. His *Jockey Club* volumes compiled rumors and personal slanders about individual royals, aristocrats, and politicians. This was an old genre—the *Town and Country Magazine* and the *Bon Ton Magazine* published similar profiles in every issue. But whereas these periodicals accepted aristocratic vices such as gambling and keeping mistresses as the way of the world, or as subjects for titillating rumors, the *Jockey Club* used scandal for a radical republican purpose, as Nicholas Rogers has shown.[22] Wilkes and Fox had insisted that private vices were irrelevant to public virtues, but Pigott claimed that private vice contributed directly to public corruption. Pigott justified attacking individual personalities as a way of undermining the privileges of the aristocracy, for only then would the lash of scandal sting them into reform.[23] Pigott repudiated his former friends, the Whigs, as just as corrupt as the rest. Despite their talents, Whigs such as Fox and Sheridan betrayed radical principles, and Sheridan was now "much bloated and disfigured by nocturnal orgies."[24]

By his third and fourth volumes, Pigott began to focus on corrupt petticoat influence, and his language became more violent and obscene. This change mirrored the increased intensity of French royal scandal. As the Revolution in Paris accelerated, the trickle of underground literature depicting the sexual escapades of the elite became a torrent of pornographic, violent tracts. These pamphlets depicted Marie Antoinette in rather athletic sexual contortions with various combinations of aristocratic ladies, male courtiers, bishops, and her own children. These naked, obscene images desacralized the French monarchy and paved the way for the executions of Louis XVI and his queen.[25] In Britain, *The Memoirs of Antonina* (1791) described Marie Antoinette's lascivious conversations with her female lovers and her political intrigues with her male lovers.[26] Echoing these sources, Pigott depicted Marie Antoinette as a fiendish libertine whose poor subjects' taxes purchased her "scandalous and unnatural pleasures." By 1793, he wrote, "she still pants to sacrifice the regenerated liberty of France, and to gratify her vengeance, in oceans of blood at the altar of German despotism."[27]

In contrast to the French court, the British monarchy had a virtuous and domestic image, but Pigott wished to rip away its mask. Like other radicals of the time, he rejected the image of George III as a good father to his people.[28] He dismissed the king's "soberness, temperance and chastity" because he did not contribute enough to charity, and because he only observed the outward forms of religion.[29] Pigott and others also decried the influence of Queen Charlotte, for a "love of power" was "in some degree inherent in the female mind." She seemed to be a pure domestic mother, but "R——y——l G——e never decided on any measure, without having first deliberated with the prudent and artful C——l——tte." Similarly, James Gillray caricatured Queen Charlotte as a naked hag who protected her alleged lover Pitt.[30]

Pigott emulated the Roman poet Juvenal to criticize many other British ladies for using paint, taking lovers, and gambling. Pigott praised the duchess of Devonshire as beautiful and benevolent (perhaps she had rescued him from debts), but he savaged the duchess of Gordon. The duchess of Gordon was the supposed mistress of Henry Dundas, who controlled Scotland and ruthlessly repressed radicalism. Pigott claimed that the duchess of Gordon used her considerable political clout to aid Pitt and Dundas, and, in return, gained lucrative positions for her many male relatives. Indeed, radical member of Parliament Nathaniel Wraxall remembered her acting "as a *whipper-in* of ministers. Confiding in her rank, her sex, and personal attractions, she ventured to send for members of Parliament to question, to remonstrate, and to use every means for confirming their adherence to government."[31] But the fact that Pigott could find just a few women to criticize for political clout indicates that he only attacked petticoat influence as a weapon in his larger campaign against aristocratic power.

Pigott and other radicals viewed the aristocracy as a parasitic, destructive force. He claimed that among the aristocracy "the most affluent fortunes are squandered or consumed in the idlest and often criminal pursuits—in profligate schemes of sensual pleasure, or personal ambition . . . to corrupt inferior orders of the people."[32] Pigott expressed the resentment, common among middle-class people of his time, that "aristocratic connections sweep all before them, leaving poor plebeian merit under a total eclipse."[33] Mary Hays, a friend of Wollstonecraft, accused the aristocracy of being "the contagious example, that with pestilential influence pervades all society." While others maintained them "by the sweat of their brow," aristocratic idleness meant they "must necessarily be corrupt."[34] Wollstonecraft showed how corruption forced women to curry favor with servile submission, middle-class men to debase themselves to gain the influence of a powerful patron, and the poor to "acquiesce to their landlords."[35] This attack on aristocratic luxury also represented a shift away from the classical republican denunciation of commerce as leading to luxury and corruption; while radicals disagreed among themselves about the value of commerce, they agreed that luxury caused aristocratic dependence, unlike the productive work of the middle class and the poor.[36]

Radicals also broadened the definition of aristocracy beyond the titled few to the larger elite who were complicit in their wealth. They were responding to Burke's definition of the legitimate public, whose opinions the government must respect, as the four hundred thousand aristocrats, clergymen, men of talent, merchants, and bankers, and in an early version of his definition, twenty thousand women.[37] For Pigott, the aristocracy included "the opulent bankers, the mitred, pampered pluralists [bishops and clergymen], the mercantile aristocracy of this country, the stockjobbers"; they all made their living through influence and corruption rather than honest work. Radical writer John Thelwall described Burke's "favored four hundred thousand" as "a mixed herd of nobles and gentles, placemen, pensioners and court-expectants, of bankers and merchants, manufacturers, lawyers, parsons and physicians, warehousemen and shopkeepers, pimps and king's messengers, fiddlers and auctioneers, and twenty-thousand petticoat allies—ladies of the court, and ladies of the town."[38] Like aristocratic ladies and prostitutes, Thelwall implied, bankers, auctioneers, and parsons were also complicit in the aristocratic system.

Pigott's scandalous volumes contributed to a general atmosphere of denunciation of aristocratic sexual vice and political corruption in the 1790s. A poem called *The Hymen* (1794) directly linked the sexual decadence of the aristocracy with their political corruption, contrasting the domestic virtue of the city merchant and the wicked seductions of the titled lord.[39] The *Morning Chronicle* criticized ministers for "regaling themselves in voluptuous indulgence, and strengthening their interests by Matrimonial treaties and Cabinet arrangements," while failing to help the suffering poor and "middling classes" in a time of crisis.[40] As part of its larger critique of the system of corruption, the radical *Argus* denounced the aristocratic women who organized gambling clubs and married for money.[41]

Adultery trials, which increased in number in the 1790s, also buttressed this message of aristocratic decadence, as Katherine Binhammer has shown.[42] Many newspapers profited by publishing accounts of these trials, appealing to "the men of middling rank [who] chuckled to read the amours and intrigues of Lords and Ladies."[43] Lawyers sometimes took these trials as an occasion for portraying the aristocracy as engaging in loveless marriages for financial advantage, in contrast with the domestic bliss of romance among the poor. In summing up one adultery case, Thomas Erskine argued that neither "vice and corruption . . . wars or treaties . . . nor all the tricks and artifices of the State" could ensure the happiness of the nation if the aristocracy lived "in cold and alienated embraces, amidst the enervating rounds of shallow dissipations." National unity could be ensured only if the aristocracy married for love and lived in benevolent rural felicity.[44] In another adultery trial, the defense lawyer argued that "the loss of comfort— the privation of happiness was by no means so great in fashionable life," in contrast to humble couples where the wife was "the constant partner of her husband's pleasures, or his discomfitures," the nurse of his children, and his companion in industry.[45]

Critiques of the aristocracy by these middle-class intellectuals also influenced more plebeian radicals.[46] Pigott's expensive *Jockey Club* tomes reached few plebeians, but his *Political Dictionary* was often reprinted in cheap editions available to the laboring poor. It defined "harlot" as "the wife of a prince" and an aristocratic woman as a "hag—a fury; a she-monster."[47] As William Hodgson proclaimed, the rich "pillage and ravage their fellow-citizens to support themselves in the most shameful debauchery," resembling "the caterpillars and locusts who destroy, without remorse, the produce of the industry and labor of others."[48] Some used religious language to denounce the rich: one satirist warned, "Thou hath lived in pomp, and in pride, and in luxury, and hath been wanton," but now the "pensioned tribe" must "redress the grievances of the starving Swine, lest the multitude devour them like hogs-wash."[49] (Burke had infamously referred to the poor as the "swinish multitude.") These sentiments contributed to violent, anti-monarchical feeling. *The Happy Reign of George the Last*, sold at a radical pub along with a sheet entitled "King-killing," told "little tradesmen and the laboring poor" to "refuse to consent to have needless and enormous contributions raised upon you, for the gratification of the vicious and depraved, however high in title."[50]

These scandalous attacks on aristocratic morality contributed to a larger assault on the system of corrupt political influence. Radicals and reformers argued that rampant electoral bribery proved the bankruptcy of the parliamentary system.[51] Their long-standing suspicions were confirmed as a scandal erupted over government intervention in Westminster elections. When a publican sued the government's publicist, George Rose, for unpaid bills from the 1788 contest, the court case proved that Rose had used government funds to bribe voters and hire thugs to help Pitt's candidates. But the radicals pointed out that the Foxite Whigs were equally guilty of bribery and corruption and repudiated them as just another aristocratic faction.[52]

Liberals and radicals wanted to revolutionize the political system and society. Liberals wanted genuine parliamentary reform and an end to corruption, while radicals demanded that all—or almost all—men be given the vote. They began to consider the grievances of the laboring poor, the high taxes, low wages, and high food prices that harmed their families. Between 1791 and 1795, associations formed all over Britain to demand reform, ranging from the elite Friends of the People, which charged a guinea for admission to its banquets, to the plebeian London Corresponding Society, where working men met in pubs to organize politically for the first time.

How was the government to defuse antiaristocratic scandal and defeat the wider threat of reform and radicalism? The French revolutionary Terror, of course, horrified and frightened many liberals back into the government fold. More important, the government defeated the revolutionary potential in British society with repression and counterpropaganda.

In 1792, the government intensified its prosecutions of the press. "At least four booksellers were prosecuted for selling Pigott's work," as Nicholas Rogers has found, and Pigott himself, like several other radicals, spent a month in jail for insulting the king.[53] The traditions of common law did put some limits on government repression, however. Fox's Libel Act of 1792 enabled juries to find writers "not guilty" of seditious libel, even if the fact of publication were proved. Many radicals evaded conviction for libel by writing fables and parodies that could not be pinned down as seditious to insinuate that royalty was scandalously corrupt and decadent.[54] Nonetheless, the prosecutions had a chilling effect, scaring off many writers from articulating their radical ideas and forcing debating societies to turn away from political topics. In 1794, the government suspended habeas corpus, meaning radicals could be arrested without trial, and in 1795, a series of acts broadened the definition of treason to include speaking against the king and almost completely suppressed public political meetings and organizations. By 1796, many middle-class reformers had faded from the scene.

Conservatives turned scandal against radicals: government allies and subsidized hacks wrote myriads of pamphlets attacking Paine, often denigrating his humble beginnings and alleging that he was a wife beater.[55] His supporters were portrayed as drunken "levelers" who indulged in "idleness and debauchery," "turbulence and licentiousness."[56] The conservative propagandists built upon the Protestant, anti-French elements of traditional British patriotism by whipping up patriotic fervor against the perfidious French, especially after war broke out in 1793.[57] Caricatures depicted French revolutionaries as savage beasts who would spear babies and eat the corpses of massacred aristocrats, and accused British radicals of wishing to emulate them.[58]

To answer scandalous attacks such as *The Jockey Club*, many antireform propagandists asserted the superiority of the British common law and constitution.[59] Some opponents of the French Revolution, often former reformers, argued that British government was superior because it had responded to middle-class concerns, because the king upheld the constitution, and because Pitt had bolstered the financial system.[60] Other conservative writers of the 1790s blatantly justified the system of influence. Arthur Young, who had sympathized with the French Revolution in its first year, now totally turned against reform, declaring that "influence is the oil in the machine of the constitution." He explained that "an unequal representation, rotten boroughs, long parliaments, extravagant courts, selfish ministers, and corrupt majorities" are "so intimately interwoven with our practical freedom" that we may "owe our liberties" to these seeming evils. Influence and prerogative enabled the Crown and great families to control the Commons against the wild passions of democracy, keeping them from destroying property and instituting anarchy. When the king promised government offices in return for votes in the Commons, or when great lords bribed voters, Young and other writers maintained, they did not corrupt the system but maintained the balance of the constitution. If great lords could choose talented men to serve in Parliament, the nation benefited. Conservatives termed the aristocracy the "landed orders" rather than high society, giving them a more respectable image as benevolent, stable country squires quite different from the frivolous, dissipated creatures of the scandal sheets.[61]

The image of the monarchy was also redeemed. The government successfully depicted the king as a splendid monarch, a devoted father, and a defender of the constitution.[62] Although many caricatures mocked the king as the excessively frugal and clumsy Farmer George, this image could also endear the people to the king, or at least allow them to see him as a domesticated and somewhat pitiful figure instead of a threatening despot.[63] Middle-class moralists ignored the insinuations that Queen Charlotte interfered in politics: contrasting her with French queens, they praised her morality as a domesticated wife.[64]

Scandals about the Prince of Wales also deflected hostility away from the king. Throughout the 1780s, moralists had criticized the prince and his Foxite allies for gambling and womanizing. Tory newspapers, for instance, slammed the morality of the Prince of Wales, Fox, and the duchess of Devonshire and accused Fox and his associates of being too sympathetic to the French Revolution.[65] Satires insinuated that Fox and the Whigs plotted to overthrow the monarchy and torture the king.[66] The king, therefore, could be seen as a positive alternative to a scandal-ridden aristocracy.

Hannah More became one of the most convincing conservative counterpropagandists because she acknowledged that the aristocracy needed reform—moral reform, that is. She could make this argument with credibility, since she had lived in the fashionable world and then rejected it. Aided by patrons, she attained success as a serious playwright in London and joined the glittering circle of Elizabeth Montagu, the wealthy and erudite *salonière*. She helped Edmund Burke's electoral campaign in Bristol in 1774 and lobbied members of the House of Lords for the antislavery cause in 1787.[67] Then More experienced an Evangelical conversion in the late 1780s; even staid and stuffy London life seemed distracting, and she refused to attend an oratorio concert because it was too public. More retreated to Somerset with her sisters, writing moral tales and establishing charity schools. But her seclusion gave her a moral platform.[68]

Even before the French Revolution broke out, Hannah More had warned the aristocracy that they must give up their dissolute ways and embrace the true religion of the heart. Charity could not compensate for "corrupt manners, ruinous extravagance, and a passion for play." When the Revolution broke out in 1789, her moral message acquired a new urgency, which she conveyed through *An Estimate of the Religion of the Fashionable World* (1790). Previously, she argued, the great had lived at their country seats, sheltering the poor like a great oak, but now, "All the shades of discrimination in society seem to be melting into each other," for Britons were "turning our liberty into licentiousness." As a result, she believed, "bankruptcies are grown more frequent, robberies more common, divorces more numerous, forgeries more extensive," and suicide all too prevalent. To solve this problem, the upper classes must truly reform their souls.[69] More warned that irreligion caused the French Revolution, and Britain faced the same danger: "The same contempt of order, peace, and subordination, which makes men bad citizens, makes them bad Christians."[70]

More criticized the system of patronage that rewarded connections more than merit. In her poem "The Bad Bargain, or the World Set Up for Sale," she depicted the devil offering "a peerage, or a star and garter," as mortals "sell their souls for reputation" and a virgin "grants her virtue as the price" of a title.[71] In her famous tale "Village Politics," she contrasted the ideal squire, benevolent and caring toward his villagers, with his "rantipolish" wife, who "begged him to pull down [his] fine old castle, and build it up in her frippery way." The old castle, of course, symbolized British traditions, and the wife's French aspirations might have alluded to the Whig aristocracy, with their fashionable French styles.[72]

More became one of a phalanx of conservative ladies helping the British government combat the French Revolution and the radical threat. She wrote a pamphlet against the Revolution for a committee of ladies organized to help French refugees, asking women to sacrifice their luxuries.[73] However, she refused to join the committee herself, reluctant to engage in public life.[74] Furthermore, she did not yet focus on the role of women, preferring to concentrate on attacking the Revolution. More preferred to exert her power behind the scenes.

More realized that to combat the French Revolution, the aristocracy not only must reform, but plebeians must be persuaded away from the radical cause. To accomplish this, she published scores of "Cheap Repository Tracts," which were inexpensive ballads, songs, and stories warning of the dangers of social leveling. Although she closely imitated the popular literature of the poor, the tone of these tracts was rather condescending. More believed that the laboring poor must be manipulated from above, not allowed to express their own opinions. In her charity schools, she taught most of her charges only to read, not to write, to prevent the correspondence of revolutionary ideas.[75] She even warned middle-class men to avoid discussing national politics. Her ideal tradesmen met in their club "not to reform parliament, but their own shops; not to correct the abuses of government, but of parish officers; not to cure the excesses of administration, but of their own porters and apprentices; to talk over the news of the day without aspiring to direct the events of it."[76] But the poor had their own, more amusing and often radical popular literature. These tracts became best-sellers, but middle- and upper-class philanthropists may have purchased many of them.[77] While many plebeians celebrated "church and king" and attacked radicals, they hated both the liberal Dissenters and the conservative Evangelicals for trying to suppress their popular amusements and drinking habits; More's pious tracts were unlikely to appeal to them.[78]

Nonetheless, Hannah More may have played a more important role than

Burke in turning public opinion away from revolution because she realized the importance of appealing to a wider audience. While Burke believed that only the privileged four hundred thousand counted as public opinion, and scorned the rest as the "swinish multitude," More at least aimed her propaganda at the middle class and the laboring poor. She also differed from Burke over the basis of morality. For him, tradition was the basis of morality; a few aristocratic peccadilloes did not matter in the face of centuries of inherited privilege. He eloquently redefined influence and corruption as chivalry and tradition. More, in contrast, regarded Evangelical religion, not tradition, as the source of morality.

Britain escaped the contagion of revolution in the 1790s, in part, because the British government skillfully encouraged the production of counterpropaganda much more effectively than had the French crown. Yet it did not rely solely on the persuasive power of propaganda; it responded to radical organization by mobilizing conservative public opinion. Loyalist associations distributed cheap pamphlets to counter radical tracts and organized middle-class men to ferret out Jacobins (supporters of the French Revolution) and regulate the political beliefs of their workers. Of course, these associations faced a paradox: traditional conservatives had long argued that the people should not associate outside of Parliament, but to combat the radical threat, the government had to allow, even encourage, the formation of conservative associations and increase the political involvement of the middle class.[79] To defeat scandal, the government had to widen the public. But only certain publics were allowed: repression and censorship also played a key role in suppressing scandal and crushing hopes for reform.

CHAPTER SIX

From Petticoat Influence
to Women's Rights?

Mary Wollstonecraft and Hannah More were widely regarded as each other's antithesis. Known as the pioneer of feminism, Mary Wollstonecraft claimed the right to love freely, to defend liberty in print, to stride through the streets of London and Paris and argue with philosophers in austere salons. Portraits depict her with her hair romantically tumbling about her face, framed by a Grecian scarf in the French revolutionary manner, or jauntily wearing a man's top hat. In contrast, Hannah More secluded herself in the green and murky Cheddar countryside, quietly opening Sunday schools and writing tales. Despite her influence, she appeared to be a sweet, feminine, elderly spinster, her face surrounded by the ruffles of a respectable cap (figure 10). But surprisingly, they had some characteristics in common: both were hailed as female geniuses, both denounced female vice and aristocratic corruption, and both became the subject of scandal.[1]

After Wollstonecraft died in childbirth in 1797, her grief-stricken husband, the philosopher William Godwin, published an honest account of her life and loves. Conservatives seized this opportunity to stir up scandal against all feminists, arguing that female sexual freedom disrupted society and destabilized politics. Hannah More turned her moral ammunition against Wollstonecraft's notion of women's rights. But More herself subsequently became the subject of scandal. Ultraconservative churchmen claimed that her informal influence undermined the established authority of the church. Why did More succeed in shrugging off this scandal while Wollstonecraft's supporters failed to reclaim her reputation from posthumous scorn? The answer can contribute to debates over whether women gained access to the public sphere or retreated from it in the era of the French Revolution.[2]

FIGURE 10   Portrait of Hannah More, from frontispiece to *The Works of Hannah More*, vol. 1 (Philadelphia, 1832). From author's collection.

BEYOND PETTICOAT INFLUENCE

By recasting the basis of morality, the feminists of the 1790s tried to defy the threat of scandal that hovered over any woman who acted unconventionally. Mary Wollstonecraft was joined by Catherine Macaulay, Mary Darby Robinson, and Mary Hays in this task. Although the word had not yet been invented, they can be termed feminists, since they denounced women's subordination and advocated female rights.

First, they needed to work through the suspicions of petticoat influence that pervaded their own radical tradition. In her *Letters on Education* (1790), Catherine Macaulay wrote, "By the intrigues of women, and their rage for personal power and importance, the whole world has been filled with violence and injury."[3] Similarly, Wollstonecraft portrayed aristocratic women as frivolous, spoiled, and shallow, like birds with "nothing to do but plume themselves, and stalk with mock majesty from perch to perch."[4] Yet Macaulay, and Wollstonecraft, moved significantly beyond the masculine classical republicanism of earlier radicalism to invent a new paradigm: the solution to petticoat influence was not to expel femininity from politics but to give women rights.[5] Macaulay argued that "when the sex have been taught wisdom by education, they will be glad to give up indirect influence for rational privileges."[6] Similarly, Wollstonecraft wrote, "If women are not permitted to enjoy legitimate rights, they will render both men and themselves vicious, to obtain illicit privileges."[7]

Robinson, a friend of Mary Wollstonecraft, knew all too well the perils of petticoat influence. Originally from a middle-class family, she became an actress and caught the eye of the Prince of Wales. When the affair ended, she handed over his incriminating love letters—in return for an annuity. Robinson exerted petticoat influence herself, campaigning with Charles James Fox in 1784 and canvassing for her lover Banastre Tarleton in Liverpool elections. But she was not content to serve men as an auxiliary; in her feminist tract, she demanded the right to speak in the "British senate." Petticoat influence was illusory, she knew; clearly referring to her former lovers Fox and Tarleton, she asked why a British patriot "would rather pass his hours . . . dall[ying] with an unlettered courtesan" than conversing with an intelligent woman. Faced with illness and forced to make her own living, Robinson proved her intelligence by publishing novels and poetry.[8]

Like Robinson, Macaulay, Wollstonecraft, and Hays were all outsiders even within radical circles. Catherine Macaulay became a feminist only at the end of her life. When she married a younger man, radicals ridiculed her, forgetting her contribution to constitutional thought. Although she never met Wollstonecraft, they corresponded, and she greatly inspired the younger woman.[9] Wollstonecraft lacked Macaulay's political connections and wealth. The daughter of a failed gentleman farmer, she supported herself and her sisters through teaching and writing. She learned to hate aristocratic women when serving as a governess to Lady Kingsborough and her spoiled daughters. A strong, passionate personality, Wollstonecraft vacillated between despair at the hardships of her life and an arrogant assurance in her own intellectual abilities.[10] Her friend Mary Hays, the daughter of a middle-class family of London Dissenters, educated herself in theology and philosophy.[11]

These women found intellectual sustenance in the circles of radical poets and Dissenting intellectuals in Norwich and London, among middleclass Unitarian preachers, schoolteachers, writers, and publishers. The Dissenting men who served as mentors to these women were themselves excluded from many of the institutions of English life, such as universities and high politics, since they did not belong to the Church of England. Many of them were deists or Unitarians who based their religious beliefs on reason, not just faith or ritual, and challenged the political system as violating reason.[12]

The feminists took these men's ideas much further by asserting that sexual morality must be based on reason, not prejudice. They argued that female rights must extend to private life, and to self-determination in the private sphere. Liberals and radicals had defined men's rights as public: the right to participate in politics. Wilkes had defined a man's right to privacy as the right to do what he wished in his own home, and implicitly, to do what he wished to women. As Hays noted, "It is astonishing . . . that principles of private and domestic justice, do not at least keep pace in the minds of men, with those of a public and political nature."[13] While male radicals had long described the British government as a despotism, these women pointed out the despotic character of traditional masculine tyranny, ruled by passions and augmented by unjust laws.[14]

Macaulay pointed out that the sexual double standard infringed upon women's private rights. Once a woman lost her sexual reputation, her honor was gone. The double standard did not derive from religion, she opined, but from primitive ideas of women as property. Morality should be the same for both sexes if it is to be founded in reason. Why should a woman be forgiven all faults but be utterly rejected for the single flaw of unchastity, she asked? Chastity was an important virtue, Macaulay argued, not because of convention, but because it indicated continence and self-control for both sexes. A wise, just woman would forgive female sexual frailty and repudiate male rakes, overturning contemporary conventions.[15] Like Macaulay, Hays called for a single standard of morality: "Till one moral and mental standard is established for every rational agent, every member of a community, and a free scope afforded for the exertion of their faculties and talents, without distinction of rank or sex, virtue will become an empty name, and happiness elude our most anxious research."[16]

Mary Wollstonecraft went even further to critique both public and private oppression of women.[17] She carried her arguments beyond those of Macaulay and Hays to suggest that women should be able to vote.[18] Transforming the classical republican tradition, which held that only independent citizens should participate in politics, she said that women should become economically independent so they could be good citizens.[19] Because she denigrated Parliament as a legitimate forum, however, personal politics outweighed conventional politics in her thought. The Dissenting moralists who were Wollstonecraft's friends praised the good husband and father and declared that domestic life was the foundation of political virtue. But Wollstonecraft redefined what this virtue meant: women needed economic independence not only to be citizens but also to be good wives and mothers. Women's dependence on men distorted marriage, making women "cunning, mean and selfish." Men treated their wives as competent servants but looked elsewhere for entertainment. Instead, marriage should be the union of two rational minds.[20]

Wollstonecraft and other feminists met with a mixed reception in the early and mid-1790s. Of course, conservatives found their ideas to be scandalous. Burke wrote to a friend that he hoped "virtuous Wives and Mothers . . . would save themselves and their families from the ruin [which] . . . all that clan of desperate, wicked and mischievously ingenious Women" will bring.[21] Writing privately to Horace Walpole about Wollstonecraft, Hannah More declared, "To be unstable and capricious, I really think, is but too characteristic of our sex; and there is perhaps no animal so indebted to subordination for its proper behavior as woman." However, she did not publicly denounce Wollstonecraft until 1799.[22] In her moral advice to women, Mary Dawes Blackett criticized the "Political and Scientifical Ladies" and the "new order of females" who "run all risques; fearless and insensible to the dangers and allurements of an unrestrained connection with the other sex, setting scandal at defiance."[23] In 1793, Laetitia Hawkins, a conservative polemicist, denounced all women who commented on politics, not just feminists, and warned women to stay away from scientific, historical, and political writing. Placing herself in the "middle rank" of society, she argued that all women needed to know about politics was to support their king and country unquestionably. While mainly attacking writer Helena Maria Williams for her support of the French Revolution, Hawkins also impugned "Miss Mary" (Wollstonecraft) and insinuated that the liberty she sought was the liberty to marry the footman or have affairs, referring to a rumor that one of Mary Wollstonecraft's pupils had run off with a servant.[24] But this was one of the few allusions to Wollstonecraft's personal life at the time. Many found her ideas alluring, if alarming. In her letters to a friend, Elizabeth Greenly seemed fascinated and horrified by Wollstonecraft. When she heard that most in society regarded her as "very indelicate," she replied, "I pity the want of genius in the present age."[25]

In contrast, liberal writers greeted Wollstonecraft's ideas with more enthusiasm. A few even expanded on her brief suggestion that women be allowed to vote.[26] But most reviewers objected to women's participation in politics, although they accepted Wollstonecraft's suggestion that women should be educated in order to be suitable companions for their husbands.[27] If women engaged in politics, the *Critical Review* feared, "the state would lose ten thousand useful domestic wives, in the pursuit of one very indifferent philosopher or statesmen."[28] Another article warned women not to "abandon their needles or their charms" for politics.[29] Norwich intellectual William Pattison joked to a friend that if his mother became absorbed in Wollstonecraft's book, she would not wash his shirts, and Norwich barrister Thomas Amyot privately wrote, "Woman is far more amiable in a domestic than a public Station."[30]

As the debate over the French Revolution became more polarized by 1795, so did the controversy over Wollstonecraft's ideas. The *Monthly Magazine*, founded to discuss "liberal" ideas of science, manufacturing, and philosophy, published a fierce exchange on feminism. "A.B." argued that ladies should study only literature, not science, philosophy, or history, but Mary Hays and other writers indignantly rebuked this author's prejudices against women's education. "Eliza" declared that it was not enough for a woman to be a wife, daughter, or mother, for "women, in common with men, are rational beings, and have an equal right with them to all the pleasures of intellect; and that it should be a woman's first object, as a human being, to cultivate her understanding." While liberals argued that public virtues were founded in private life, feminists argued that oppression in the family produced oppression in the state. But the responses to this debate also reveal the hardening of ideas about women by the later 1790s; commentators portrayed women as weak in body and mind, suited only to be wives and mothers.[31]

Most of the men and women in the liberal, Dissenting circles that nurtured the feminists espoused rather conventional ideas about domesticity and marriage. As a result, unmarried women like Mary Wollstonecraft and Mary Hays felt somewhat marginal. To be sure, some male writers also questioned the conventional basis of sexual morality. The novelist Thomas Holcroft portrayed intrepid heroines defying the double standard; the philosopher William Godwin queried the necessity of marriage.[32] But these were intellectual questions for male writers, who could engage in flirtations of the mind without consequence. For women such as Wollstonecraft and Hays, romance and marriage were matters of emotional and financial survival; they rejected conventional marriage but struggled with the alternatives. The feminists could not fully articulate their dilemmas in conventional political writing, so they turned to novels to explore their moral critiques. While they criticized the conventions of sensibility for portraying women as weak and sentimental, they used sensibility for more radical ends through the genres of gothic romance.[33]

Mary Hays fell into a deep depression after her fiancé died young. When she recovered, she fell in love with Dissenting thinker William Frend, pouring out her soul to him in passionate letters. After he declined her advances, she explored the subject of thwarted female desire and the drive for reason in her novel *Memoirs of Emma Courtney* (1796). Compulsively rewriting her frustrated affairs, she included incidents from her own life and even excerpts from Godwin's and Frend's letters in this novel. But her associates in liberal circles sometimes mocked her for this unrequited love, and reviewers attacked the novel for provoking women to give in to their passions.[34]

Mary Robinson also explored both ideas and her life in her novels. She had been separated from her husband since the early 1780s. Her long relationship with Banastre Tarleton ended bitterly when he flirted with her daughter and then married a young heiress. She faced middle age alone and sick, partially paralyzed after a miscarriage. Her impassioned gothic novels allowed her to take revenge on her unfaithful lover Tarleton by portraying him as a dastardly aristocratic villain, but they also presented daring ideas about women's role, the false pretensions of the aristocracy, and revolutionary intrigue. Like many of her friends, Robinson had become disillusioned by the excesses of the French Revolution and lamented Marie Antoinette's death, but she still clung to her hopes for a radical transformation of society.[35]

Mary Wollstonecraft saw the unhappiness that marriage brought both to her sister and to a close friend. She preferred independence but also sought love in an affair of the mind with the painter Henry Fuseli. She later formed an intense sexual relationship with the American merchant and adventurer Gilbert Imlay, the passion of her life and the father of her first child, but she hesitated to marry him, for financial dependence on him would be the equivalent of prostitution. However, she called herself "Mrs. Imlay" and depended on him emotionally; when he left her, she tried to commit suicide by jumping into the river Thames. Rescued, she slowly rebuilt her life and eventually met and fell in love with the philosopher William Godwin.

A radical philosopher, Godwin rejected organized religion and personal sentiment—until he met Wollstonecraft. In his *Political Justice*, he had infamously asserted that one must abandon a personal relation in order to rescue a philosopher from a burning building because the philosopher would contribute more to the happiness of all mankind. But Wollstonecraft had helped him see that one could recognize the value of affections while still upholding individual private judgment. At first, they lived together, refusing to conform to society by marrying. Wollstonecraft believed in marriage if she could attain equality within it, but Godwin critiqued marriage as a ridiculous, false ceremony that trumpeted before the world of "all things most sacredly private": the "climax" of the "overflowing" of two souls.[36] When Wollstonecraft became pregnant by Godwin, however, they married, in hopes of protecting their child from prejudice. By marrying Godwin, Wollstonecraft revealed that she had not been legally married to Imlay, thus shocking their friends and acquaintances. Now they realized Imlay had been her lover, and that her child, Fanny, was illegitimate. Most rallied round, but some dropped her, like the novelist Elizabeth Inchbald (whom Wollstonecraft satirically referred to as "Mrs. Perfection") and the actress Sarah Siddons. As the gossip spread through London society, such women depended too much on public opinion to risk associating with a woman of Wollstonecraft's reputation.[37] But in 1797, these rumors remained private, not yet erupting into public scandal.

Wollstonecraft defended herself to her friend Amelia Alderson (later Opie), declaring, "My conduct in life must be directed by my own judgment and moral principles."[38] Although she was deeply religious, she believed in the importance of private, individual conscience rather than empty forms and ceremonies.[39] Above all, she believed that the conventional laws of marriage oppressed women rather than upheld morality. She explored this theme by working on her novel, *Maria, or the Wrongs of Woman.* In this radical gothic romance, she illustrated the oppression faced by women of different social classes, ranging from the genteel heroine, confined in a madhouse by her mercenary husband, to Jemima, the former prostitute, raped by her master and forced onto the streets, to her landlady, whose drunken husband deserted her only to return and appropriate all her hard-earned savings. At its apogee, her heroine's husband turns to the law to regain his wife, but she appeals "to my own sense of justice" to refuse an empty, oppressive marriage. Rather, she insists on living with her lover, considering him to be her true husband since their union was based on love rather than convention. Wollstonecraft never finished the manuscript, for she died soon after giving birth to her daughter (who was to become Mary Shelley, author of *Frankenstein*).

Heartbroken, Godwin consoled himself by publishing an honest memoir of her life and the unfinished novel in 1798. These works contributed to an efflorescence of feminist publishing in 1798–99. In 1798, Mary Hays published a work she had written earlier, inspired by Wollstonecraft, the passionate *Appeal to the Men of Great Britain on Behalf of Women*, criticizing women's subordination in marriage and education, followed in 1799 by her novel *The Victim of Prejudice*, which showed how the double standard oppressed a victim of rape. Mary Robinson anonymously published her rigorous critique of women's oppression, *A Letter to the Women of England on the Injustice of Mental Subordination*, under the name Anne Frances Randall, and her novel *The Natural Daughter* in 1799, under her own name. Two less radical works, by Priscilla Wakefield and Mary Anne Radcliffe, advocated greater opportunities for women in the professions and trades to enable them to support themselves and their families instead of having to resort to prostitution.[40]

These works unstintingly confronted the double standard and argued that chastity should not be the measure of a woman's worth. They asserted that scandal should not attach to women victimized by unjust laws, abusive husbands, and rapists but, instead, the public should scorn men who lied, coerced, and even raped women and then manipulated the law to destroy them. Women who had sex outside marriage should not be condemned; rather, they should be enabled to become economically independent. These works were also closely associated with women who had become known for their sexual unconventionality. Mary Robinson, for instance, had long been notorious as "Perdita," mistress of the Prince of Wales in the early 1780s, and Hays was known for her roman à clef *The Memoirs of Emma Courtney*. Above all, in his memoir Godwin recounted Wollstonecraft's passion for Fuseli, her extramarital relationship with Imlay, her suicide attempt, and her two children conceived out of wedlock.

Why did Godwin reveal Wollstonecraft's love life with such honesty? He may have been oblivious to the perils of publication because the government had not prosecuted his very radical philosophical writings. This lack of censorship may be attributed to the expense and abstraction of his tomes, which would not appeal to a volatile plebeian audience. Godwin scorned the hypocritical conventions of traditional society. By publicizing Wollstonecraft's life, he may have wished to put forth an alternative morality in the strongest possible terms. Godwin believed that "sincerity" motivated Wollstonecraft's public and private actions; she followed her heart and passions rather than bowing to unjust conventions; furthermore, the intimacy of their relationship contributed to their ability to make moral and political judgments.[41]

By focusing on the private, sexual lives of these women, however, Godwin's memoirs and the associated novels made feminism vulnerable to scandal. In 1798 and 1799, a debate erupted around his revelations about Mary Wollstonecraft's life and the writings of other feminist authors. This controversy about feminism became a scandal because the private lives of Wollstonecraft, Hays, and Robinson were used to discredit their political and intellectual ideas. This was also a tense moment in the struggle against revolution both at home and abroad. To conservatives fearful of revolution in England, the feminist call for a transformation of private life seemed incredibly dangerous. Conservatives feared that liberalism might revive; in the previous year liberals had unsuccessfully tried to get Parliament to extend the franchise, and the plebeian London Corresponding Society defied the government to hold a mass meeting. By 1798, the huge fleet on the Nore estuary had erupted in mutiny, and insurrection had broken out in Ireland. The government responded with another wave of political prosecutions and censorship. For instance, Joseph Johnson, a friend and publisher of Mary Wollstonecraft, was imprisoned; radical ideas could not be printed.[42]

For the liberals who reviewed Godwin's memoirs of Wollstonecraft, her personal life damaged the credibility of her ideas. Since they celebrated domesticity as an antidote to corrupt politics, these liberals could not understand why anyone would critique the family. To be sure, a few of the more liberal periodicals recognized the principles that lay behind Wollstonecraft's unconventional actions but believed she behaved recklessly. While lauding Wollstonecraft as a genius, the *Monthly Review* criticized Godwin for publishing these memoirs, which could not advance "public welfare and improvement."[43] The *Edinburgh Magazine* understood the philosophical basis behind her critique of marriage but concluded that given the current corrupt state of men, "We are inclined to conclude her confidence too great, and her conduct imprudent and hazardous."[44] The liberal *Analytical Review*, for which Wollstonecraft had worked, criticized Godwin for not paying enough attention to her intellectual development: "We think it was due to Mrs. Godwin to have stated how those opinions were formed and the reasons by which she supported them."[45] Similarly, the *Monthly Mirror*, which had earlier printed a flattering portrait of her, lamented that Godwin wrote too much on her personal life, whereas if she had lived, we would have "discovered her ardent and vigorous mind busied every day in fresh pursuits for the amelioration of mankind."[46] The liberal *Monthly Magazine* was more equivocal: "It is not for us to vindicate Mary Godwin from the charge of multiplied immorality. . . . her character, in our estimation, is far from being entitled to unqualified praise; [but] she had many transcendent virtues."[47]

Mary Wollstonecraft's allies met with similar responses. Only two reviews acknowledged Mary Hays's feminist tract.[48] The *Edinburgh Magazine* published extracts from Anne Randall's *Letters on the Position of Women*, not knowing, however, that the notorious Mary Robinson was the real author.[49] Even so, a reviewer in the *Gentleman's Magazine* attacked her tract: "Mrs. R. avows herself of the school of Wollstonecroft [*sic*]; and that is enough for all who have any regard to decency, order, or prudence, to avoid her company."[50]

For her few enthusiastic supporters, Wollstonecraft could be seen as an "extraordinary genius" who was "not to be estimated by common rules." The idea of "female genius" helped make women acceptable as public intellectuals, but it also detracted from the plausibility of their feminist ideas. They could be lauded as celebrities, as exceptional women, the female muses, without being seen as patterns or inspirations for women as a whole.[51] Furthermore, as a romantic, individualist genius, Mary Wollstonecraft believed public opinion to be the "shallow herd" moved only by the "squally gusts of passion."[52] As a result, she did not try to mobilize a constituency that might have upheld her legacy. There were no radical women's groups in the 1790s equivalent to the London Corresponding Society or the Parisian women who formed a revolutionary republican society.[53]

Yet a public forum remained where feminist ideas had long been discussed—the London debating societies. To be sure, no female societies seemed to have survived after 1788. But the London societies turned to debating women's roles because they had been prohibited from discussing politics from the mid-1790s onward. The forums had twice debated women's intellectual capacities in 1797, and in April 1798 Wollstonecraft's ideas became the topic du jour, inspiring at least five more debates. For instance, a society considered whether "the fair sex" acted more properly "when fulfilling all the domestic duties of the Wife and Mother, or when writing Histories, Plays, Romances, etc and pursuing the attainment of those masculine functions," as Wollstonecraft had supposedly advocated.[54]

The woman who proposed this idea to the London and Westminster Forums had studied with Wollstonecraft, but she already had been excluded from another debating society.[55] Furthermore, the question itself retreated from earlier responses to feminism; whereas in 1793, reviewers of Wollstonecraft's work argued that more education would improve wives' character, by 1798 intellectual achievement and domesticity seemed to be irreconcilable goals.

Government repression, however, played a more decisive role than liberal ambivalence in closing down the possibilities for feminism. Pitt found the debating societies' discussions of feminism just as dangerous as their political critiques. As he proclaimed in Parliament, debating societies "agitated" questions "which operate to loosen the foundations of morality, religion, and social happiness." So Pitt prohibited all debating societies in late 1798, leaving no forum where liberal views could be publicly discussed.[56] Even if Wollstonecraft had left a legacy of organized feminism, any woman's group would then have been suppressed.

Conservatives also undermined liberal ideas with counterpropaganda. Now that French political principles seemed discredited, they focused their attack on the liberal critique of conventional morality. A newspaper, the *Anti-Jacobin*, was founded specifically to combat attacks on chastity, and other sins. Its successor, the *Anti-Jacobin Review*, was published by clergymen whose sinecures derived from the government, and took as one of its chief tasks rebuking female intellectuals. In 1797, they had satirized Godwin and Holcroft for their deist views and radical sympathies in the poem "The New Morality."[57] By 1798, they took Godwin's memoirs of Wollstonecraft as an excuse to fight feminism.

Godwin's sexual frankness about Wollstonecraft predictably horrified *Anti-Jacobin* and other reviewers. The *Anti-Jacobin Review* took a very scurrilous tone, claiming that Godwin did "not mention many of her amours" and cross-listing Wollstonecraft under "prostitution" in the index.[58] As the *Anti-Jacobin* reviewer proclaimed, "It is our province, and our duty, to meet the legion of Wollstonecrafts . . . [who] diffuse the poison of corruption through the mass of society . . . and to endeavor to cast them out!"[59] The journal also denounced "Randall's" (Robinson's) *Letter to the Women of England* as a "mass of corruption." It claimed that Wollstonecraft inspired Robinson to excuse female unchastity as the outgrowth of genuine passion in her novel, *The False Friend*. Women writers should stick to writing about the feelings, the reviewer opined, and avoid moral and political questions.[60] Similarly, a reviewer claimed that Mary Hays advocated a "corrupt and vicious system of education" that would fit women to be "revolutionary agents or heroines . . . setting aside all the decencies, the softness, the gentleness of the female character, and enjoying indiscriminately every envied privilege of man."[61]

Conservatives used Mary Wollstonecraft's irregular sex life to symbolize the disorder that French principles threatened to bring to England. Once the Revolution broke out, "female infidelity" and the "monstrous lust" of French women were seen as some of its causes.[62] "Leaving women to the exercise of . . . their natural and social rights," the reviewer warned, would encourage promiscuity, "annihilate virtuous principle," and advance "Jacobin morals [which] . . . dissolve . . . the tie of marriage [and] destroy one of the chief foundations of political society."[63]

While Wollstonecraft had derived her principles from rational, individual private judgment, conservatives based their morality on tradition and accepted public opinion. The religious journal the *British Critic* warned that Godwin and Wollstonecraft would "eradicate from the minds of their readers all respect for establishments deemed venerable for their antiquity, and . . . inspire them with enthusiastic admiration of daring and untried theories in morals, in politics, and in religion."[64] In a more general tirade about women's influence for good or ill, the Reverend Handley Norris warned against the "illuminized females" who spread "disorganizing principles" in society instead of following their proper chaste, submissive role.[65] The *European Magazine* portrayed Wollstonecraft's memoirs as a "warning to those who fancy themselves at liberty to dispense with the laws of propriety and decency, and who suppose the possession of perverted talents will atone for deviations from rules long established for the well government of society, and the happiness of mankind."[66] This review, written by the Reverend Richard Polwhele, focused on Wollstonecraft's failure to attend church and raked up scandal from the past, blaming her for the fact that one of her pupils, Lady Kingsborough's daughter, ran off with her lover.

Polwhele expanded his critique into a more general invective, *The Unsexed Females.* This long poem, heavily and favorably publicized in the *Anti-Jacobin Review*, denounced all the prominent liberal female intellectuals.[67] A poor cleric, Polwhele wrote satires to express his horror at the French Revolution—and to support his family. The genre of this poem also demonstrates how satirical slander undermined the gothic, romantic mode of Mary Wollstonecraft's radicalism. While earlier writers such as Charles Churchill and Charles Pigott imitated Juvenal to savage the decadent aristocracy, Polwhele, like other 1790s conservatives, adopted the Roman poet's misogyny to critique feminists, ostentatiously displaying his Latin learning in the notes.[68]

Polwhele

Polwhele insinuated that Wollstonecraft, "the arch-priestess of female Libertinism," lured gentle female poets such as Mrs. Barbauld and novelists such as Charlotte Smith away from proper feminine literary accomplishments to the unnatural arts of free love, science, and politics. Polwhele particularly feared that the study of botany, with its descriptions of the sexual parts of plants, posed a danger to women; hence, he used botanical imagery to sexualize the dangers feminists posed to society. He imagined that "unsex'd women"

> With bliss botanic as their bosoms heave,
> Still pluck forbidden fruit, with Mother Eve,
> For puberty in signing florets pant,
> Or point the prostitution of a plant;
> Dissect its organ of unhallow'd lust—[a flower's pistil].

Somehow, gazing at "the titillating dust" of a garden would lead a feminist to

> With liberty's sublimer views expand,
> And oe'er the wreck of kingdoms sternly stand;
> And, frantic, midst the democratic storm,
> Pursue, Philosophy! thy phantom-form.

Interestingly, as a young man Polwhele had known both Catherine Macaulay and Hannah More—two different models of female intellect. He chose the latter as an ideal. Polwhele counterposed Hannah More to Wollstonecraft as the exemplar of her sex, citing More's celebration of women's separate and different talents. Polwhele could accept female genius, as long as femininity constrained it.[69]

While several women had achieved renown as public intellectuals in the early 1790s, by 1798 they could no longer comment on politics with propriety. For instance, Anna Laetitia Barbauld had been a respected commentator on Dissenting politics in the early 1790s. By 1798 the *Ladies Magazine* praised her husband for "naturally and properly sequester[ing] [his wife] from the world" and lauded Mrs. Barbauld for breathing "the real spirit of patriotism, without debasing it by the little vulgar impurities of party politics." Perhaps the author did not know that Mrs. Barbauld withdrew from the public world because her husband was insane and that she wrote for the public in order to support her family.[70]

After the scandal against Wollstonecraft, female novelists turned away from daring expositions of passion and reason and instead made their names by ridiculing feminism. Elizabeth Hamilton of Scotland, for instance, believed women should be educated and philanthropic. But in her

Memoirs of Modern Philosophers (1800), she caricatured Mary Hays as "Bridgetina Botherim," a ridiculous bluestocking whose doctrines of free love impel the beautiful Julia to run away from her parents with an evil seducer.[71] Amelia Alderson Opie, a liberal Norwich Dissenter, turned against her former friend Mary Wollstonecraft to write *Adeline Mowbray* (1802) as another warning to any woman who followed feminism or free love. Although Opie regarded Wollstonecraft as principled and idealistic, she thought that given society's present mores she was imprudent and foolish to reject marriage.[72] In their novels, Hannah More and Maria Edgeworth also ridiculed feminists as the mannish "Miss Sparkes" or the obnoxious "Harriot Freke."[73] Similarly, Jane West, a conservative novelist and the wife of a yeoman farmer, rebuked Wollstonecraft for undermining religion and chastity.[74] In contrast to its earlier debates on female education, in 1800 the *Scots Magazine* published an article that ridiculed "Female Accomplishments," arguing that "a man might think his wife better employed in making custards than in making syllogisms; in pickling cucumbers than in extracting the square roots."[75] Feminist ideas disappeared from the liberal press for decades to come.

THE SCANDAL AGAINST HANNAH MORE

Hannah More joined her voice in the chorus against Mary Wollstonecraft. In her *Strictures on the Modern System of Female Education*, first published in 1799, she took Wollstonecraft to task for advocating adultery, encouraging infidelity, and condoning suicide.[76] She had already ridiculed William Godwin's morality in her *History of Mr. Fantom*.[77] Her conservative clerical friends, convinced that radical philosophy and aristocratic adultery would make Britain vulnerable to revolution, encouraged her to write a new tract addressing the problem of private life.[78] Although More had long criticized aristocratic morality, in 1799 she began to focus her attack on aristocratic women, denouncing them for tolerating gambling, libertinism, and unchastity and for using their influence for evil rather than good. She wanted to replace traditional aristocratic female petticoat influence not with women's rights but with female domestic influence. However, More herself eventually bore the brunt of scandal.

Throughout her life, More had struggled to manipulate traditional femininity into a source of power. Lacking aristocratic wealth or family ties, she could not exert petticoat influence, so she tried to find new sources of influence that would give her clout without defying convention. After all, her mentor, Dr. Stonhouse, preached that women could improve their minds only by staying at home.[79] In the 1770s, she wrote a tract advocating conventional restrictions in feminine education, but she also playfully explored masculinity and femininity in her plays' prologues, as Wahrman notes.[80] To negotiate her progress in the fashionable world, More deployed the resources of her personality: deferential yet witty, she shone as a "female genius" yet overcame any threat she posed by flattering male patrons with fulsome praise.[81] It is not surprising, then, that More carefully cultivated a reputation as, in Dr. Stonhouse's words, "extremely modest—& yet has the most amazing talents, of which she seems insensible."[82] A friend described her as "masculine in her person, but extremely feminine and pleasing in her manner . . . without any display of that knowledge and understanding, she so eminently possesses."[83]

Behind the scenes, More was fiercely ambitious: she carefully negotiated royalties with her publisher.[84] But she faced scandal when she took a more public role. She aspired to become a patroness: in the mid-1780s, she helped a milkwoman, Anna Yearsley, publish her poetry, but controlled her protégée's profits herself. Outraged at this condescending coercion, Yearsley stirred up a controversy in the newspapers.[85] In the 1790s, Charles Pigott accused More of defending the aristocracy in hopes of obtaining "an appointment, suitable to her talents, equal to her deserts," like the other hack writers who supported the administration.[86] Indeed, she later campaigned, unsuccessfully, to be tutor to the Princess of Wales.[87] These mini-scandals, and More's Evangelical conversion, impelled her decisive retreat from the public world.

More claimed she was trying to develop a dignified and responsible role for women far removed from the old-fashioned domestic drudge or the contemporary fashionable lady. She decried those who believed that women should not be educated and suggested that female intellectual potential might be much greater than contemporaries thought. At the same time, she admonished other women to keep their learning within certain limits, to avoid science and other unfeminine pursuits.[88] On a visit to Paris, she was horrified that ladies "neglected their families" to attend lectures on anatomy at a lyceum: "I hope we shall never have such institutions here," she sniffed to her sister.[89] She and Jane West explicitly warned women of the middle ranks that learning could distract them from their domestic duties; West haughtily declared that middle-class women would be better employed "picking out the seeds of currants" or embroidering than reading novels from circulating libraries (although she herself was a middle-class woman who wrote novels).[90]

More resolved the paradox of denigrating women's actions yet celebrating feminine influence by delineating the ideology of separate spheres. Nature ordained that women and men are different, she declared: "A firmer texture of mind was given to man, that he might preside in the deep and daring scenes of action and of council; in the complicated arts of government, in the contentions of arms, in the intricacies and depths of science, in the bustle of commerce, and those professions which demand a higher reach, and a wider range of powers."[91]

She and her ally West attacked both radical and aristocratic women who engaged in politics. When More hoped women would stir up patriotism against Napoleon, she quickly cautioned, "I am not sounding an alarm to female warriors, or exciting female politicians; I hardly know which of the two is the most disgusting and unnatural character." She may have been alluding to the ladies who publicly presented colors to militias and made patriotic speeches in 1798.[92] Her reference to female politicians could include not only Mary Wollstonecraft but also the duchess of Devonshire or the duchess of Gordon. Similarly, West wrote with horror that "female letter-writers [presumably such as Robinson and Hays] teach us the arcana of government, and . . . recommend manners and actions at which female delicacy should blush."[93] She also warned against canvassing female politicians, declaring that "a conscientious attachment to our King and country . . . will be a preservative from party violence, and from that agitating interest in local disputes which overpowers weak minds." Instead, West argued that women should "become *legislators* in the most important sense of the word . . . by resisting the corruption of the times."[94]

More asked women, "Is it not desirable to be the lawful possessors of a lesser domestic territory, rather than the turbulent usurpers of a wider foreign empire?"[95] More ruled this "lesser domestic territory" through religious philanthropy and education. Together with her sisters, she set up a Sunday school for the children of local farmworkers near Cheddar, Somerset. In some ways, More built upon the tradition that local great ladies would grant philanthropy and in return receive deference. However, she also reshaped this notion of "influence." Her influence did not derive from her family's landholdings or the ability to pick a member of Parliament, or even from benevolent charity. Instead, it derived from religious belief: she aimed to reshape the minds of the poor rather than to fill their purses. Hannah More enforced the social order by inculcating ideas of subordination into her charges in Somerset. As her sister wrote, they tended to parishes "as dark as Africa," but they regarded not only the poor but also the local farmers as heathen barbarians.[96] In introducing Sunday schools, More herself had to contend with Mr. C., a rich farmer, "rough, cold, ignorant, unfeeling," the "chief despot of the village, who thought religion would be the ruin of agriculture."[97]

This tension hinted at the paradox that eventually caused a larger scandal against her. She wanted women to stay at home and submit to men and hierarchical authority in general, but her religious influence over charitable institutions clashed with local male authorities.[98] Ultraconservatives realized, to their horror, that by allowing Evangelicals to stir up patriotism, they had inadvertently encouraged them to "strike down . . . localism, the elitism, the structures of traditional deference" and the rigid institutions of the Church of England, as Gerald Newman observes.[99] The philanthropy of a lady could interfere with middle-class and gentry men's control over villages and parishes. For instance, in one story, More celebrates Mrs. Jones, a widow, who gets the smith to inform on the baker for selling shortweight bread; gets the squire to prosecute the shopkeeper who keeps shop open on Sundays, gives credit, but has higher prices; gets the gentry to buy good cuts of meat so the poor can get cheap cuts.[100] Not surprisingly, such an interfering lady could annoy parish notables. More herself quarreled with the farmers and tradesmen of Nailsea over the appointment of a schoolmaster and incited the squire to prosecute a woman who held dances.[101]

Furthermore, More's Evangelical moralism could collide with the rougher, more traditional "church and king" boisterous conservatism, with its kneejerk hostility to Catholicism and Dissenters.[102] She rebuked men who thought that drinking to "church and king" was enough to prove their patriotism. Instead, only true religion could inspire a meaningful love of country.[103] She criticized a clergyman who gave a sermon "upon good Tory principles, upon the laws of the land and the Divine right of kings; but the Divine right of the King of kings seemed to be a law above his comprehension."[104] "True religion," she argued, "does not consist in an external conformity to practices, . . . forms, modes, and decencies. It is being transformed into the image of God . . . a change in the human heart."[105] The tensions among conservatives were becoming particularly acute around 1800–1802. The right wing had moved sharply away from their earlier constitutional language to emphasize uncompromising "church and king" principles.[106]

More was a member of the Evangelical movement in the Church of England, but she ran up against the traditional wing of the church's distrust of newfangled innovations—such as Sunday schools.[107] Conservatives believed that Evangelicalism's enthusiasm brought it uncomfortably close to Methodism, the movement that proved an increasingly powerful alternative to the Church of England among the lower and middle classes. Methodism's association with female preachers gave Anglican opponents a potent weapon. In the Church of England only Anglican divines could rightly proclaim on religion. As the *Anti-Jacobin Review* noted, "We wish our students in divinity ... to consult the best commentators ... and not to learn the way of salvation from experiences, inward calls, sovereign grace, female devotées."[108] When More entered into theological disputes in 1799, clergymen cited the epistle of Saint Paul against women preaching and criticized even the *Strictures on the Modern System of Female Education* as insufficiently orthodox.[109]

In the Blagdon controversy of 1801–3, these tensions erupted into a scandal about Hannah More's personal influence.[110] She had a long-running feud with the local rector of Blagdon, who, as she indignantly wrote William Wilberforce, "keeps a mistress, gets tipsy before dinner and last week treated forty of the poorest wretches he could find to a strolling play."[111] More and her sisters had established a Sunday school and various local clubs and charities in Blagdon. But this rector dismissed her protégé, the curate John Boak, suspecting him of Methodism and radical sympathies. His replacement, Thomas Bere, joined local farmers who complained that More allowed male and female Sunday school teachers to pray extemporaneously, instead of waiting for an ordained clergyman to read from the Book of Common Prayer. The Church of England distrusted all extemporaneous prayer as suspiciously "enthusiastic" and as undermining the authority of the priest and Scriptures. The worst, of course, was to have a woman lead prayers. Bere and his allies took More to court for hiring a schoolteacher without the license needed for Dissenting instructors.[112]

Bere turned this local quarrel into a national scandal by publishing pamphlets in London spreading vicious personal rumors about More. Over thirty pamphlets and innumerable newspaper articles for and against Bere and More were produced.[113] Bere alleged that "under the mask of Sunday Schools and a professed attachment to the Church, [More introduced] ... the extemporaneous effusions of silly women ... bringing the Liturgy ... into contempt and ridicule." The *Anti-Jacobin* criticized her as too "enthusiastic"; her tolerance of Dissenters could easily slide into sympathy for revolution. But it also personalized the controversy, portraying More as a "spleenish, peevish," and "cunning" woman who encouraged Methodism in her parish.[114] Edward Spencer called her an "Amazon" who failed to superintend the morality of her flock, and alleged that her servants and teachers indulged in "fornication" and produced illegitimate children. Picking up on her tale of conversion from fashionable life to strict Evangelicalism, he wondered what debaucheries converts had experienced before they saw the light.[115] As More herself lamented, gossip circulated that she was having affairs with an officer and two actors.[116] Indignantly, she wrote to the bishop of Bath, "I am accused of being the abettor, not only of fanaticism and sedition, but of thieving and prostitution."[117]

When this controversy erupted, More took refuge in the older techniques of female influence. However, she only worsened the scandal by manipulating clerical appointments behind the scenes. Using her connections with Sir Abraham Elton, the dean of Wells, and Minister of War William Windham, she spread rumors that Bere was a Jacobin and blocked his appointment to the rectory of Brockley; instead, her protégé, Boak, was appointed. The "lower clergy" resented this heavy-handed use of influence. As one opponent alleged, "Bishops, Deans and Dignitaries not only bestow Vicarages, Rectories, and valuable Curacies upon Mrs. Hannah More's friends, but even rob their own ministers, to do it."[118] More refused to defend herself in print; in a letter, she attributed the attack "to the defenseless state of our sex."[119]

Yet More eventually recovered her reputation. Far from defenseless, she instructed her friends on every nuance of the campaign. She quietly "circulated supportive material among London politicians and the episcopacy, gathered and transmitted information about Bere . . . and kindled various anti-Bere sermons and pamphlets," as Mitzi Myers has found.[120] The conservative journal the *British Critic* and her powerful allies in Parliament and the church openly defended her. By 1805, the *Anti-Jacobin* favored her once again, and More continued to win respect for her moral and religious writings. The Blagdon scandal vanished into obscurity.

CONCLUSION

Why did More succeed in overcoming scandal when scandal destroyed Wollstonecraft's legacy? More shaped her idea of female genius to gain patronage and acceptability. By relying on male allies to defuse scandal, she took a risk, but it paid off. She was too valuable as a conservative ideologue to be abandoned. Mary Wollstonecraft and the other feminists lacked these powerful allies. The feminists had also failed to organize a constituency around their ideas, but government repression played a significant role as well.

Which woman had a longer-term impact? Clearly, the feminists were ahead of their time, but some historians have argued that despite her separate spheres ideology, Hannah More actually advanced women's position in public by advocating a philanthropic feminine role.[121] However, many other women had long been advocating and carrying out such philanthropic activities. Plebeian women had long founded their own female-friendly societies without ladies' help, and plebeian communities organized their own Sunday schools.[122] Mary Wollstonecraft herself advised wealthy women to visit the poor and organize charities.[123] And, indeed, some aristocratic ladies had set up charities to provide work for poor women. Liberal women were probably most influential in carving out a philanthropic role for women because they established formal institutions that gave women practice in management. In 1797, a liberal magazine publicized Unitarian Catherine Cappe's organization of schools, female benefit clubs, and hospitals. Liberal Edinburgh activist Eliza Fletcher defied conservative magistrates to establish a society for poor women in 1798.[124] In contrast, Hannah More refused to join a patriotic ladies' committee in the 1790s; she may have had a loose network of charitable women in Somerset, but she did not create open, accountable, charitable associations. Eventually, More joined in campaigns to send missionaries to India and became a member of the first female antislavery society in 1826, but she was following, rather than leading, more liberal women.[125]

More was also praised for advancing women's learning, and, indeed, middle-class women seemed to be steadily increasing their intellectual activities by the first decades of the nineteenth century. In liberal Dissenting circles, women began to found female and mixed-sex book clubs after 1800.[126] Some lectures on intellectual topics were open to women, enabling them to cultivate their minds. However, as the playwright Joanna Baillie observed, men approved of women's intellectual activities only if they did not interfere with domestic responsibilities; to be free of such tasks, a woman needed a large independent income.[127] Margaret Wodrow lamented that she could not attend more scientific lectures, for, as she wrote to Mary Kenrick, "all my sublime genius evaporated in the contrivance of Dinners."[128]

The role of the female intellectual became constrained after 1798.[129] Reviewers praised women writers for concentrating on feelings but denigrated their reason. For instance, a critic in the *Edinburgh Review* noted that Amelia Alderson Opie "does not reason well; but she has, like most accomplished women, the talent of perceiving truth, without the process of reasoning, and of bringing it out with the facility of the effect of an obvious and natural sentiment."[130] When Mrs. Barbauld published her impassioned radical poem *1811*, the poet Robert Southey admonished her to return to her knitting needles.[131] Not surprisingly, middle-class women found it impossible to articulate feminist ideas. For instance, in her poem *An Epistle on Women* (1810), Lucy Aikin, niece of Mrs. Barbauld, expressed extreme ambivalence about feminism. She revealed her anger by asking, "be our sex content to knit and spin / To bow inglorious to a master's rule?" but she answered in the affirmative. She disclaimed "the absurd idea that the two sexes ever can be, or ever ought to be placed in all respects on a footing of equality" and concluded that she preferred "shy and retiring domestic English women" to heroines such as Charlotte Corday and Madame Roland (French revolutionary women).[132] Aikin seems to have sensed that a straightforward celebration of women's intellect would no longer be acceptable.

Hannah More also helped conservatives to narrow significantly the sphere of politics for men. She and Jane West joined government hack John Bowles to argue that only the elite should discuss politics; the rest of the populace must trust them to manage the government. More admonished middle-class men to stay by their firesides instead of demanding the vote. If More's admonitions did not persuade them, government repression drove many liberal middle-class men out of politics by the late 1790s. Afraid to speak out, they also retreated to domestic concerns and turned away from the possibility of feminism.[133] But by moralizing politics, More perversely set a precedent for middle-class reengagement in public life by the first decade of the 1800s.

More had helped to create a patriotism based on morality, family, and a love for Britain that could unite liberals and conservatives. By 1806, conservatives began to see the middle class as a repository of political virtues who would defeat the radical plebeians. They also praised George III as a good husband and father. But this focus on family life created a conditional loyalty. If the monarch did not display domestic virtues, did his subjects still owe him loyalty? If family life was necessary for public virtue, perhaps men must engage in politics to defend their family life.[134]

The problem of petticoat influence had not gone away. Looming on the scenes were incidents in which saucy women defied the power of the British Crown—one, Mary Anne Clarke, revealing that her lover, the Duke of York, took money from her to promote army officers and the other, Queen Caroline, exerting her own radical political influence. The new conservative morality may have saved Britain from the French Revolution, but it left royalty vulnerable to scandal.

CHAPTER SEVEN

The Mary Anne Clarke Affair
and the System of Corruption

In 1809, a saucy young woman with a retroussé nose and fashionable blue pelisse stood before the House of Commons. With pert self-confidence, Mary Anne Clarke testified that the duke of York, the king's second son and commander in chief of the army, had set her up in a grand mansion. To furnish it, she bought the duc de Berri's silver plate and sparkling chandeliers—and paid for these luxuries by selling promotions to officers. The duke had put the advancement of army officers in the hands of a kept mistress (figure 11).

The Mary Anne Clarke affair became one of the most effective scandals in British history. Her revelations exposed a seething morass of corruption beyond the army, for offices in the government, and even seats in Parliament, were bought and sold. For once, petticoat influence could be documented, as a related inquiry revealed that ladies trafficked in East India Company positions. The scandal undermined the credibility of the state in a time of war. Thousands of citizens met and petitioned the government, demanding that Parliament be reformed and government cleansed.[1] The scandal temporarily overcame censorship and forced the government to take action on corruption.

The Mary Ann Clarke scandal undermined the patriotic consensus that had seemed to unite Britons at a time of war. Britons had rallied around the Crown, for they loved George III for his domestic virtues and for his role as defender of the Constitution. By 1802, even liberals supported the war against Napoleon, the ambitious dictator who betrayed the Revolution's democratic principles and threatened to invade England. Both liberals and conservatives believed they were fighting for the British constitution and British liberty.[2] By deliberately energizing the whole country into patriotic parades, militias, and loyalist associations, the government acknowledged the place of the people in the nation. The government also seemed to be more efficient and accountable after Pitt's reforms from the 1780s onward.

FIGURE 11   Portrait of Mary Anne Clarke, from frontispiece to *Les Princes Rivaux, ou Mémoires de Mistress Mary-Anne Clarke, favorite du Duc d'York, écrits par elle-meme* (Paris, 1813). Reproduced by permission of the University of Minnesota.

Most civil servants, military officers, and East India Company servants, unlike those in other European countries, worked long and regular hours and earned promotions on the basis of their merit.[3] Service in the government, the army, and the East India Company promised opportunities for middle-class men and kept them loyal to the empire.[4] The Mary Ann Clarke affair, as Philip Harling observes, revealed that this patriotism was conditional.[5] Middle-class trust in the army's strength, the government's efficiency, and the king's domestic virtue could be easily eroded.

For liberals, true patriotism meant supporting a just war but criticizing the government if the war seemed oppressive and the army became corrupt and inefficient. Radicals such as William Cobbett asked why the heroic common soldier could not enjoy the privileges of citizenship, why aristocratic generals bungled battles.[6] Loyal officers who had served the army in dangerous imperial outposts became frustrated when their promotions were inexplicably blocked as well-connected young men swanned into lucrative offices.

Tensions between efficiency and patronage persisted in the government. The government paid generous sinecures to those favored by the Crown or politicians. For instance, the brother of Lord Grenville, the prime minister in 1807, received a sinecure worth £35,000 a year, without performing any duties in return.[7] Once attained, offices were also seen as a form of property to be transmitted to relatives. While many officials were paid salaries, others gained most of their incomes from monopolies or fees from the public.[8] The fundamental problem remained that merit alone could not earn a position; officers had to purchase their commissions in the army, which favored men from genteel families; candidates for the civil service and East India company still needed a patron to obtain an office.

Middle-class men had long expressed their frustration at this state of affairs. As Adam Smith put it, a man of "rank and distinction" only "hopes to . . . succeed in an intrigue of gallantry," so the government must rely on "men who were educated in the middle and inferior ranks of life, who have been carried forward by their own industry and abilities, though loaded with the jealousy, and opposed by the resentment, of all those who were born their superiors."[9] J. Burton celebrated the merchant's hard work as more useful to the state than the "political servitude" of those who gain titles by corruption.[10]

George III, however, earned middle-class support with his reputation for probity, hard work, and domestic virtue. It was the behavior of his sons, George, the Prince of Wales, and Frederick, Duke of York, that endangered royalty's reputation. They spent their youth pursuing women, guzzling wine, gorging on food, spending extravagantly, and gambling excessively. To settle them down, marriages to German princesses were arranged, but their philandering continued. As described in the next chapter, George flaunted his mistresses while secretly investigating his wife, Caroline, for adultery in 1806.

At least Frederick, the duke of York, could earn a reputation as a military man. In 1795, at the age of thirty-two, he was appointed commander in chief of the British army. He had trained in German armies and led troops against the French, but he clearly owed his position to his royal blood. Once in office, he seemed to dedicate himself to improving the education, food, and housing of the British soldier. He equipped palace guards with bearskin helmets and paraded them in strict order to impress the public. The duke also took credit for reforms in the system of promotions. Formerly commanders pocketed the money officers had to pay for commissions and promotions, but now this cash was to be deposited in a fund for superannuated officers. Officers were to serve for two years before promotion, to prevent privileged young cadets from leapfrogging over experienced army officers to obtain promotion while they were still at school. But agents continued to buy and sell commissions and promotions, and the duke retained much patronage himself. Questions remained about his competence—and his private life.

Mary Ann Clarke became one of a long series of the duke's women. Unlike the titled mistresses of the Prince of Wales, Clarke came from an artisan family and married a stonemason at sixteen. The romance soon faded: her husband may have infected her with venereal disease, and they lived a miserable life in the Kensington Gravel pits. To escape, Clarke took several lovers in search of a wealthy keeper, including a Mr. Ogilvie, an agent who sold army commissions, before getting lucky with the duke of York.[11] The duke expected her to maintain a grand establishment, furnished with pier mirrors and silver plate and tended by several servants, including a talented cook for intimate dinner parties. He even encouraged her to take lessons in harp playing and painting on velvet.[12]

Mary Anne Clarke wanted to make the most of the duke's assets. As she wrote in her memoirs, she preferred the quality of "ambition" to "prudery."[13] When the duke procrastinated in paying the bills for their lavish lifestyle, she took bribes to gain promotions for officers from him, keeping a list of candidates tacked over the bed (figure 12). Clearly, the recent reforms in army promotion had been ineffective, for the favorites of the duke and Clarke could disregard seniority. The duke even appointed Clarke's footman, Samuel Carter, as an ensign. Mary Anne traded the duke's favors

FIGURE 12 Thomas Rowlandson, *The Bishop and his Clarke, or a Peep into Paradise* (1809), BMC 11227. © The British Museum. The duke of York held the title (and income) of the bishop of Osnaburgh. A "List for Promotion" is tacked over the bed. The duke says, "Ask anything in reason and you shall have it my dearest dearest Love," quoting from one of his letters that emerged in the trial. Clarke says, "Only remember the promotions I mentioned I have penn'd up the list at the head of the bed."

for cash to a network of agents and anxious officers. As Rowland Maltby, one of her agents, wrote her, "You would be quite a treasure *in every way* to any Secretary of State."[14]

The relationship made the duke of York vulnerable to the scandalmongers of the London press, who threatened to publicize embarrassing incidents in hopes of receiving hush money. The *Morning Post* tried to publish paragraphs about their relationship, but the duke bribed a Mr. Wright to suppress them.[15] The duke's man of business, Mr. Adams, became even more worried when tradesmen threatened to sue Clarke for refusing to pay her bills (on the grounds that as a married woman she was not responsible for her own debts). These lawsuits, he feared, would expose the duke to harmful publicity, so he advised him to abandon her. In 1806, the duke left Clarke and then reneged on his earlier promise to pay her a £400 annuity. Mary Anne Clarke was left with the debts for their large, grandiose household—but with the assets of the duke's letters.

This scandal did not explode for three years. Why did it take so long? First, Mary Anne Clarke preferred the secretive means of blackmail to the publicity of scandal. Like many in London's seamy world of kept mistresses, shady journalists, and hangers-on, she thought she could profit from promising her silence and so for several years tried to negotiate with the Duke and other interested parties.[16] After all, "Perdita" Robinson had earned a comfortable annuity from the Prince of Wales after surrendering his love letters. In addition, though, in the atmosphere of 1806, radicals had failed to sustain other scandals about governmental malfeasance, so it was unlikely that the tale of Mary Anne Clarke and the duke could break through repression and public indifference.

The government accused any critics of endangering Britain in a time of war, and Pitt ruled with an iron hand. Many Whigs and most Tories justified the system as legitimate influence rather than corruption. Royalty, the aristocracy, and the gentry could reward merit by bestowing offices on deserving but impecunious men (like Edmund Burke), thus infusing talent into the system. To be sure, there were limits to acceptable patronage. For instance, in 1805, it was revealed that Lord Melville (Henry Dundas), architect of the repression of the 1790s, controller of almost all the Scottish members of Parliament, president of the Board of Control of India, with power over its patronage, had embezzled thousands of pounds from the government. Whigs, Evangelicals, and radicals banded together in the House of Commons to impeach him, but the House of Lords acquitted Melville in 1806. Public meetings called for wider investigations into corruption, even parliamentary reform, but the Whigs did not take up this cause. Melville only lost his office and escaped further punishment. Pitt managed to recover by instituting ineffectual inquiries into reform.[17]

The Whigs, in a coalition ministry from 1806 to 1807, refused to respond to a potential scandal about India. Neither the home government nor the company could control the army in India. As a result, Lord Wellesley, the governor-general of India from 1798 to 1805, had invented excuses for wars to conquer further territory, and when no wars seemed to be necessary, he forced princely rulers, such as the nawab of Oudh, to cede most of their sovereignty to the British. In sharp contrast to their earlier prosecution of Hastings, Fox and Sheridan refused to support a move to impeach Wellesley.[18] After all, Wellesley cultivated extensive connections in Parliament.[19]

In response, a radical candidate, James Paull, ran against the Whig Richard Brinsley Sheridan in the Westminster election of 1806, linking royal corruption and imperial oppression. Paull claimed that English taxpayers paid for Wellesley's oppressions in India and "vice in splendor," while they suffered hardships at home.[20] His radical supporters contrasted the "Honest Men of the *middling* Classes Struggling with Adversity!" and "The *lower* Order without a *Bed left* to satisfy the rapacity of the TAX GATHERER! " with the aristocratic Whigs, tainted by their association with the decadent Prince of Wales.[21] The allusion to "vice in splendor" may have been an oblique reference to the duke of York and Mary Anne Clarke, for Paull's pamphlet ironically promised to prove the duke "a good general."[22] But the Whigs defeated Paull, their electoral influence stronger than radical outrage.[23]

The next year, however, the duke of York scandal began to simmer beneath the surface, when radicals Sir Francis Burdett and Lord Cochrane ran against the Whigs in Westminster. Lord Cochrane was a popular military hero who became frustrated after parliamentarians receiving sinecures blocked his inquiries into the corruption and inefficiencies of the Admiralty.[24] His uncle, Andrew Cochrane Johnstone, served as governor of Dominica. But when he applied for promotion, he faced a court-martial on unspecified charges; although he was acquitted, he never gained promotion. Although Cochrane Johnstone had been a tyrannical, cruel, and corrupt governor, he persuaded Cobbett and Burdett that he himself was the victim of the duke of York's corruption.[25] The radicals, supported by Cobbett, linked peculation and sinecures at home with corruption in the war; they called upon voters to defy the system of ministerial influence and vote independently as honest Englishmen.[26] In response, the Westminster voters threw out the Whigs.

The conduct of the war against Napoleon also became problematic. Through the Convention of Cintra in 1808, the British allowed Napoleon's forces to crush Spanish nationalist guerrillas. The British government supported a corrupt monarchy against constitutionalist forces. This led to a large public outcry.[27] The case was worsened when the duke of York pressured the government to allow him to command forces in Spain, despite doubts about his competence.[28] In 1807–8, public agitation had become more open. Public meetings protested a myriad of issues and debating societies of radicals revived in London.[29]

The time was ripe for the Mary Anne Clarke scandal, but for the affair to emerge, it needed instigators who had information and the power to do something with it. Some of the scandal's instigators were seedy journalists connected to the "radical underworld," making their living by blackmail; they needed to connect to more credible instigators.[30] They also feared censorship and libel, so they tended to allude to the affair indirectly.

First, in 1807, a caricature entitled *Military Leapfrog* (figure 13) portrayed prosperous young officers giving cash to a figure who suspiciously resembled the duke of York and then leapfrogging over the backs of elderly officers crippled from their services in the war. As they bounded to the end of the line, the officers threw a purse into the bag of a beautiful woman, who says, "I am the Principal *Clark*." Caricatures could insinuate what newspapers could not say openly, because to prosecute caricaturists for libel would require spelling out the scandal only hinted at visually.

Then, in 1808, Eaton S. Barrett, a barrister and satirist, published a pamphlet entitled *The Miss-Led General; a Serio-Comic, Satiric, Mock-heroic, Romance.* Emulating the savage satires of Juvenal, Barrett portrayed the army as a decadent world where generals' aides-de-camp "pimp[ed] for them and escort[ed] their mistresses to all public places." The army could not be efficient "where a commander-in-chief has succeeded to his high station through any other channel than his intrinsic merit." All this corruption formed a blood-sucking monster that ate away at the middle class through excessive taxes. He concluded, "We must neither be *miss-led* nor *old-woman-led*, if we would not be *slave-led*."[31] But radicals had been exposing the corruption of aristocratic mistresses and the system of influence for decades without effect. Barrett's satirical style could be dismissed like other scurrilous effusions of the radical underworld where pamphleteers attempted to blackmail vulnerable aristocrats.[32] Without hard evidence, the duke's activities could be defended as part of the legitimate system of influence.

The duke's brother, the duke of Kent, then turned against him. A puritanical commander, he resented the duke of York's louche lifestyle. Kent had incited a mutiny in Gibraltar by forbidding his men to drink on Christmas, so his brother removed him from command. Kent probably paid Thomas

FIGURE 13   George Cruikshank, *Military Leapfrog, or Hints to Young Gentlemen* (1807), BMC 10740. © The British Museum. The duke requests, "Throw in your purse of 300 pounds and you will finish much quicker." The young men leapfrog over military veterans. They throw bags of money into Clarke's purse. She says, "Throw in your 700 here and I'll give you a Majority, I am the Principal Clark" ("clerk" is pronounced "clark" in England).

Hague to publish two pamphlets in 1808 that indirectly linked Mary Anne Clarke to the problem of army promotions. Hague lambasted the duke of York as an incompetent general, denouncing his "ignorance, thoughtless profligacy, negligence, drunkenness, barefaced debauchery, open adultery, dark malice and cold craft." But Hague's praise of the duke's rival brothers, the duke of Kent and the duke of Sussex, undermined his credibility.[33]

    Major Denis Hogan, another officer victimized by the system of corruption, became a more believable instigator of scandal. Unlike the scurrilous pamphleteers, Hogan was a loyal army officer with no political connections, and he wrote in a straightforward, indignant style that could not be dismissed as sexual satire. He raised 145 recruits and served with distinction but saw 40 captains promoted over him. He was told that he could pay several hundred pounds to obtain a higher rank but disdained to engage in bribery. Hogan actually confronted the duke with the rumors that several women served as intermediaries for promotions, but the duke failed to respond. Hogan truly believed in the goals of the empire and a system based on bravery and merit, and he felt deeply outraged "that parliamentary, personal or family influence, is allowed to supersede the highest pretensions of professional excellence; or, that the allurements of Venus are suffered, in any respect, to interfere with the interests of Mars."[34] Fearing prosecution for libel, Hogan then fled to America.

Radicals still hesitated to link Mary Anne Clark and the duke of York directly because they faced government repression. Indeed, the government prosecuted Hogan's publisher, Peter Finnerty, for libel.[35] Similarly, the editor of the *Independent Whig*, who combined intense radical commitment with connections to the radical, blackmailing underworld, was imprisoned for libel after he fearlessly denounced corruption and called for a convention to push through parliamentary reform.[36] Even radical William Cobbett only obliquely declared, "We know but too well what patronage is worth" when he denounced the duke of York's power at a meeting. The crowd seemed to know what he meant, roaring in response "upon the subject of this curious statement."[37]

Leigh Hunt, a literary-minded liberal who appealed to a smaller, more elite audience in his *Examiner*, took the matter further.[38] Like Cobbett, Hunt had been denouncing the duke of York's command. Unlike Cobbett, Hunt reprinted large sections of Hogan's pamphlet. He felt it was his duty to expose this "petticoat influence" to redeem the efforts of men such as Hogan. Now we have, claimed Hunt, gray-haired "officers almost starving . . . to enable a courtesan to keep her country house and give royal parties on a birthday!" Normally, Hunt reassured his readers, he would not "intrude upon the firesides of men who will keep their follies to themselves." But when "*private vice becomes a public curse*, and when a man's fireside, for want of common care, bursts out into a conflagration, and threatens everything with destruction," then it was his duty to expose scandal, "to break in to the domestic walks . . . and to endeavor to quench the fire, even though it arises from a Lady's chamber." He concluded, "Let the People look to it," calling for public meetings to demand parliamentary reform.[39] In response, the government also prosecuted Hunt and others for libel.[40]

It took a politician to bring the affair to the more powerful stage of the House of Commons. To be sure, efforts had already been made to expose corruption; for instance, in 1807, the reformer Samuel Whitbread raised Cochrane-Johnstone's case in the Commons. But Cochrane-Johnstone's case was weak, and at the time, evidence linking Mary Anne Clark and the duke of York was not available.[41] An ambitious politician needed a journalist with connections in the seedy underworld to find the evidence that would light the fuse of scandal.

Pierre MacCallum and Colonel Gwillim Wardle became the successful instigators of the Clarke scandal. Wardle, a Welshman, served the empire in the dragoons, which viciously repressed the Irish rebels at Vinegar Hill in 1798. Something of a playboy, Wardle also concerned himself with the inadequate defenses of England and the general incompetence of the military. Perhaps, as an ambitious politician, he hoped the other members of Parliament would take him more seriously if he presented explosive evidence of corruption. To find it, he drew upon the aid of an opportunistic journalist, Pierre MacCallum, who knew about Mary Anne Clarke. MacCallum claimed that he had fought in the black army of Haiti for Toussaint Louverture. MacCallum also served in the West Indies but had run afoul of the harsh governor there, Thomas Picton, who imprisoned him. In retaliation, MacCallum exposed Picton's sadistic tortures of a young West Indian woman.[42] For MacCallum, the Mary Anne Clarke affair promised financial advantage and another opportunity to embarrass the hated military system. Meanwhile, Mary Anne Clark had been facing money difficulties and threatened the duke of York with publication of his letters. His agent fobbed her off, so she was looking for other sources to capitalize upon her incriminatory documents. MacCallum brought Wardle and Clarke together. Armed with Clarke's letters, Colonel Wardle and Sir Francis Burdett moved for a parliamentary investigation into the corruption of the duke of York.[43]

Colonel Wardle succeeded in sparking the scandal because unlike his predecessors he had hard evidence of the duke of York's corruption (the letters) and because as a member of Parliament he enjoyed freedom of speech. If a civilian raised such allegations, he or she would be subject to a libel action, but Colonel Wardle and Sir Francis Burdett were immune from such prosecution. When Wardle and Burdett introduced their motion to investigate the duke of York, the government dropped the libel cases against the newspapers because this publicity made them moot.

Some conservative writers denounced the affair as a foul "Jacobinical conspiracy . . . formed not only for the destruction of his Highness, but all the Royal Family, and the monarchical principles of the Constitution."[44] Others admitted the duke was indiscreet but portrayed *him* as a victim of a criminal conspiracy.[45] Ironically, one commentator revived the old Whig argument that a man's private vices had nothing to do with his public service. Reflecting the tensions between traditional and Evangelical conservatives, he argued that "there is a boisterous over-acted morality which is as pernicious to a state as corruption itself."[46] But most conservative commentators violently attacked the duke, even the ultraright *Anti-Jacobin.*[47]

Conservatives had long argued that the people should not debate contentious issues or organize themselves because Parliament would respond to their grievances. However, this argument would hold water only if Parliament responded to the issue of the duke of York instead of sweeping the affair under the rug. But they debated whether Parliament should hold an open or closed inquiry. William Wilberforce, an Evangelical, hoped that a private inquiry could solve the problem without discrediting the monarchy and openly discussing sexual issues. Wilberforce believed that high-placed men such as himself, not popular agitation, should pressure the monarchy to reform. But Spencer Perceval, the formidable government spokesman in the Commons, insisted on a public inquiry. Also an Evangelical, he believed that publicity would prove that the allegations against York were false.[48]

The Commons could not initiate impeachment proceedings against the duke, since he was a member of the royal family. Therefore, the Commons faced a choice between slowly appointing a special commission, where evidence could be taken on oath (as the duke of York wished), or speedily meeting as a committee of the whole and taking public evidence from witnesses not under oath. The government decided on the latter course of action. However, the conduct of the inquiry undermined the Commons' credibility as an independent judicial body. In interrogating the witnesses, Perceval and other government ministers clearly acted on the side of the accused, the duke of York, by trying to discredit the witnesses. Indeed, Perceval insinuated that one witness, Mrs. Clarke's friend Elizabeth Taylor, was a prostitute and revealed that she was the illegitimate daughter of a stockbroker and a woman imprisoned for debt. The publicity destroyed her boarding school, her only means of earning a living.[49]

The royal status of the duke of York also undermined the Commons' judicial credibility. As a prince, the duke did not have to testify, but he wrote a letter to the Commons asking them to take his word as a "man of honor" that he was innocent. His letter undercut the constitutional promise that the law treated all equally and decided innocence or guilt according to the evidence, not the social status of the accused.[50] His intervention also threatened the constitutional separation of Parliament and the Crown, foreshadowing his brother's use of the House of Lords to persecute his wife.

In contrast to her former lover, Mary Anne Clarke had to face several hundred male members of Parliament, who assumed she would be intimidated and deferential. Indeed, she burst into tears when the people crowded around her carriage outside of Parliament.[51] However, she soon recovered, coming through the galleries of Parliament "with a light step and a smirking countenance," dressed "as if she had been going out to an evening party, in a light blue silk gown and coat, edged with white fur, and a white muff."[52] Clarke took control by making the politicians laugh at her double entendres; she refused to answer some questions and talked back to others, challenging the Commons on points of procedure. When the attorney general examined Mrs. Clarke with his hat on, she whispered, "Is it usual for Members to put questions to witnesses with their hats on; or does the Learned Gentlemen think that he serves his cause by insulting me?" She objected to a witness being called and asked, "May I not take the sense of the Honourable House on that?" When asked how long she spent with one of her lovers, she evaded the question by asking "is this a proper question, whether it is not unbecoming to the dignity of the house?"[53] As Sir Francis Burdett told the house, "She stood at the bar like a potent witch, and no sooner did the sable band [of Crown lawyers] encounter her, than their faculties seemed to be withered, as it were, by the wand of an enchantress." Perceval indignantly criticized her "sarcastic insolence . . . her art and wit" in "continually evading the questions which she wished to avoid" and "misleading" the examiner.[54] A satirist described Clarke as a "shark, whose wits . . . cut keen . . . [in] the *quorum* . . . with *snip, snap, snorum*."[55]

The investigation riveted the public and overcame press censorship. Free from the threat of libel prosecutions, newspapers published detailed daily accounts of the proceedings. The government subsidized newspapers in order to control them, but high circulation proved more profitable than payoffs.[56] Even the conservative *Sun* gave in to its readers' curiosity to report on the investigation, and the usually loyal *Courier* became "unmanageable."[57] Provincial newspapers reprinted these accounts and criticized royal immorality.[58]

Some conservatives denounced the press as licentious and demanded that the government control it. But other conservatives supported the inquiry, arguing that it was necessary to redeem the army from the danger of corruption. The *Courier* ridiculed those who saw the whole affair as a "Jacobin plot." It was not the "licentiousness of the press," it observed, but the immorality of the duke's behavior, which threatened Britain.[59] Of course, as several newspapers commented, the duke of York's love life distracted attention from the "disastrous excursion to Spain."[60]

This inquiry stimulated scandal where others had faltered, such as the Dundas impeachment, in part because it built upon familiar romantic genres. As the *Morning Chronicle* observed, the inquiry could easily become a popular drama, with its "*plot, interest, . . . overflowing audiences, new performers*, and an excellent MORAL."[61] But radicals and conservatives interpreted the story through different versions. For conservatives, Clarke might have represented the villainess Milwood, the wicked courtesan who led an innocent man astray.[62] Olivia Wilmot Serres claimed that Clarke was vain, ungrateful, and avaricious: "She loved *variety . . . extravagance*, . . . she liked *power*, and was a stranger to the prudent managing of it."[63] The duke was compared to Samson, robbed of his strength by Delilah.[64]

But the duke of York's defenders in the House of Commons drew upon a more louche genre of erotic fiction that gaily recounted the adventures of aristocrats and prostitutes.[65] They admitted that the duke kept Mary Anne Clarke as his mistress but denied that he allowed her to sell promotions. Indeed, they claimed, he was such a generous keeper that she had no need to resort to such tactics; to prove this argument, they compared her expenditures with the amounts he allegedly gave her. However, by so blatantly admitting that the duke kept a mistress, his supporters offended powerful Evangelicals and became contaminated by the very sexual language they used to defend him. The *Courier* lamented seeing "the Duke of York's moral character abandoned that his military character as Commander-in-Chief may be preserved. He may triumph in coffeehouses and on parades; but what will be thought of him at family firesides, and in churches."[66]

To defend herself, Mary Anne Clarke had to create her own story. Clarke portrayed herself according to a somewhat more sophisticated narrative of prostitution sometimes found in novels, that of the genteel woman down on her luck, forced to become a kept mistress. She claimed to be educated beyond her station by her father, supposedly a professor at Oxford. Clarke implicitly placed herself in the geneology of radical scandal by claiming that her father "had been the intimate friend and companion of Wilkes and Churchill."[67] Evoking radical gothic novels, her supporters soon began to portray her as a plucky heroine who defied the aristocratic libertine.[68] One sympathetic editor claimed that she was forced to leave her "dissolute and depraved husband" and live with her mother until "she consented, after numberless solicitations, to place herself under the protection of the Duke of York."[69] A pamphlet portrayed her as a biblical heroine like Judith, who seduced the enemy in order to destroy him: "Say no more of the weakness of woman, or that this person was but a concubine; remember such in the days of yore have entertained great and wise men. . . . She spake of liberty to the guardian of the isles."[70] Veteran reformer Capel Lofft wrote, "That Woman has manifested no ordinary force of Mind; and may it enlighten and conduct her to a more honorable and happier Life!"[71]

It may seem "strange that the whole nation should be absorbed in listening to the examination of a prostitute," the moderately radical *Tyne Mercury* editorialized, but "nothing can be more natural or reasonable," since the affair tested "the soundness of our boasted constitution."[72] The inquiry began with an investigation into the sale of promotions in the army but quickly threatened to reveal the persistence of the sale of positions and promotions in the government, the church, the East India Company, and, finally, Parliament.

First, the investigation documented in Parliament what radicals had been rumoring for years: that many officers who had proudly served the empire could not obtain promotions unless they could pay off agents or the duke's mistresses. Clarke and her agents claimed that their influence was more powerful than that of the older generals and members of Parliament whom ambitious men usually turned to for promotion. For instance, Colonel Shaw asked General Harry Burrard, who had fought with his father, to recommend him for promotion to the duke, but the duke ignored Burrard's letters. Shaw then promised Mrs. Clarke £1,000 pounds in exchange for a position as barrack master at the Cape of Good Hope. This does not sound like a very enticing position, but perhaps he hoped that as a barrack master he could profit by skimming off supplies. But Mrs. Clarke was not satisfied with the £500, which was all she received from him. She complained to the duke, who "said, he had told me all along, that I had a very bad sort of man to deal with, and that I ought to have been more careful, and that he would immediately put him on half pay."[73]

Major Hogan's failed promotion also contrasted with Colonel Huxley Sandon and Colonel French's sham levy. Major Hogan had raised 145 recruits without reward. But the duke of York gave Colonel Huxley Sandon and Colonel French permission to raise a levy of troops, allowing them considerable profits from the expenses allowed for each recruit. However, the whole enterprise was so corrupt they recruited only a few dozen fit men. In turn, Colonel Huxley Sandon used his connection with Clarke to demand £500 from a Major Tonyn for a promotion.[74] The duke also promoted Colonel Clavering to a brigadier generalship upon Clarke's urging. Promising a further £1,000 pounds, he then prevailed upon her to get the duke to allow him to raise a regiment. The duke, however, refused. In a letter addressed to "My Darling Love" and "My Angel," he protested that "never was a woman adored as you are!" but went on to insist that no new regiments were to be raised for Clavering. This letter both documented the fact that the duke discussed army affairs with Clarke and revealed him as ridiculously love-stricken.[75]

The duke's supporters alleged that he had actually reformed the army. However, it turned out that his aide, Colonel Gordon, impelled him to issue the 1804 order forbidding the trafficking in promotions. Gordon testified that he had cautioned army officers against selling commissions and promotions for profit, but an "eminent Counsel" told him that these practices were "not even a misdemeanor, and I could have no address." However, he was able to persuade the secretary of war to insert a clause in the Mutiny Act to impose a fine on such trafficking.[76] But clearly, Gordon's efforts came to naught.

It was clear, however, that the problem was not just Mary Anne Clarke but a widespread system of corruption in the army that blocked the promotion of competent men and rewarded those who exploited their dubious connections. Army agents traded openly in commissions, obtained through a string of go-betweens.[77] The duke of York also responded to pressure from other women, such as Lucy Sutherland—possibly a former mistress—who asked him to obstruct the transfer of an officer who had offended a friend of hers. The Baroness Nollekens also wrote to him for favors for her connections. Charles Greenwood, an army agent, testified that he reluctantly acquiesced to the duke's orders in such cases.[78] In fact, Mrs. Carey, who had supplanted Mrs. Clarke in the duke's affections, employed two agents in a public office in Threadneedle Street in the city to trade offices at the very time the inquiry began. Newspapers advertised government positions for sale.[79] To be sure, the government then prosecuted Mrs. Carey and three others for trafficking in offices, but the public wondered how many positions were bought and sold behind the scenes.[80]

Spencer Perceval, the Chancellor of the Exchequer, lamely tried to defend the system on constitutional grounds, claiming it was "the royal prerogative to appoint officers."[81] But for reformers, the inquiry exposed the problem at the heart of the army system. How could officers appointed on such grounds run an army efficiently? As the usually conservative *Courier* asked, "Is the honor of the army supported by making the Footman of the Duke of York's mistress . . . an officer?"[82] The editor of the *Circumstantial Report* declared that until merit, not money, obtained promotion, "we may expect to see generals who have neither courage nor skill, entrusted with important commands, the bravest men in the world sacrificed to ignorance and cowardice."[83] Cobbett asked, "If men give money, or render secret services, for their offices, to a kept mistress, how can it be expected, that any service should be performed by them to the public?"[84]

The problems the inquiry revealed were not confined to the army but extended to the Church of England. Members of the royal family, for instance, could appoint bishops. In fact, the king had given the duke of York the position of bishop of Osnaburgh, which did not require any duties but brought him £30,000 a year. Not surprisingly, Mary Ann Clarke's agents thought that clerical appointments could be gained by bribery. Hoping to obtain a bishopric, a Dr. O'Meara of Ireland offered Clarke an unspecified sum of money to arrange for him to preach before the king. The duke obligingly arranged the sermon, in which Rev. O'Meara preached to the king and royal family on the danger of French deists who "transfer all the lovely train of social affections from our relatives and friends to distant and unknown myriads." As Cobbett hinted, this was a somewhat ironical message, given that the aristocracy rewarded their "relatives and friends" with lucrative positions.[85] Unfortunately for Dr. O'Meara, the duke of York's influence could not overcome his father's prejudice against the seemingly Catholic "O" in his name.

Undeterred, Mary Ann Clarke and her agent Jeremiah Donovan hurried to arrange another clerical preferment before the queen aggrandized all the patronage in the church. Donovan asked Clarke to influence the duke of Portland to obtain a deanery for the Reverend Mr. Bazeley. Apparently Lady Cardigan and several other ladies deposited 3,000 guineas with Donovan in hopes of surprising Bazeley, their favorite, with this plum position. Lady Cardigan liked him because he was recommended by "many persons of fashion, the Bishops of Norwich and Salisbury," and because he wrote an anti-Catholic pamphlet "for the benefit of administration." Unfortunately for him, at this point Clarke, having been rejected by York, had no influence with Portland. When Bazeley himself wrote a rather obsequious letter to Portland openly promising £3,000 for a position, the duke of Portland warned the bishop of London against this "wretched creature."[86]

Mary Anne Clarke, her agents, and the duke also trafficked in civil service positions. For instance, in one letter Jeremiah Donovan asked if she could procure "a surveyorship of customs in Jamaica," "a Landing Waiter's place" in the custom house, and a paymaster second battalion.[87] Donovan also informed Clarke that "the place of Inspector of the Customs is now vacant by the death of Mr. Booty, and I learn that the Queen and the Duke of Dorset are about to apply for it."[88] William Dowler first purchased a job as lottery commissioner through Mrs. Clarke, but his claim was overridden by a connection of Pitt's, so she accommodated him by obtaining a position in the account department at the Commissariat at Lisbon.[89] Far more damagingly, it came out that the duke had instructed his agent, Mr. Adams, to ask

Pitt to appoint Robert Kennett, a former upholsterer, as collector of customs in Surinam. At the same time, Mr. Kennett was trying to arrange a loan of £30,000 for the duke. Pitt had already promised the appointment to someone else, and the loan fell through, but the duke's corrupt intentions were clear.[90]

Members of the government tried to explain away many of these cases by arguing that positions in the army, the civil service, and the church could be obtained only through the recommendation of someone who could vouch for an individual's merit, such as a member of Parliament, an officer in the government, or a wellborn relative. But these explanations simply ratified the suspicion that merit alone did not obtain promotion in the government or army, that only connections sufficed.[91] All the great public boards seemed controlled by "parliamentary influence"—or worse—which hampered the coordination of the government in a time of war.[92] As the *Morning Chronicle* wrote, the "representative of a rotten borough is constituted the judge of military merit."[93] This reliance on connections was what frustrated hardworking middle-class people.[94] As a satirical poet wrote,

In general vile interest guides
Each man in office who presides:
The meritorious, oft we find
Most shamefully are left behind,
From further services deterr'd
While the unworthy are preferr'd.[95]

Far more seriously, Mary Ann Clarke also alleged that she had influence over votes in Parliament, obtained through her trafficking in positions in the civil service. She testified that she had demanded that William Dowler "procure some votes for the Defense Bill" to obtain promotion over a rival. Mr. Russell Manners, a member of Parliament, apparently hoped to gain a place through Clarke's mediation; presumably, he would thus become amenable to political pressure in exchange. Charles Long and General Clavering both denied Clarke's claim that they would vote as the duke wished.[96] But then the House read a letter she had written to Colonel Huxley Sandon, one of her agents, asking him to "drop me a line Monday morning, saying if you have been able to influence any person who is with Pitt, to attend the House on Monday to give his *Vote*."[97]

Mary Anne Clarke and her agents Jeremiah Donovan and Rowland Maltby also traded in East India Company positions. For instance, she wrote to an agent, "Will you ask again about an India Lieutenancy? as the Duke assures me there are two for sale."[98] These revelations led to a second parliamentary inquiry, immediately following the Clarke investigation, into allegations that East India Company commissions were bought and sold, and even exchanged for a seat in Parliament. Cadetships and writerships— positions in the East India Company—were highly sought after because they enabled young men to earn their fortunes in India. The directors enjoyed the power to bestow these offices, but their patronage could conflict with the East India Company's ethos of advancement by merit.[99] As the *Morning Chronicle* wrote, it was "notorious" that writerships could be exchanged for seats in Parliament and clerical livings, but that was not defined as corruption unless cash was involved.[100] In 1798, "higher powers" blocked an investigation into the persistent rumors that directors sold cadetships and writerships to agents, rather than dispensing them to deserving, well-connected young men. The directors did have to swear on oath that they gave no cadetships or writerships for personal gain, but their social and political acquaintances begged them to give them such appointments, ostensibly for reputable friends. These connections then sold the appointments on to intermediaries, and the intermediaries sold them to agents, who advertised in the *Morning Post* that they had positions or spread the news by word of mouth. The cost for an appointment ranged from £300—a comfortable middle-class yearly salary—to many thousands of pounds.[101] As the *Examiner* indignantly noted, agents took positions "to market, and sold them by known brokers, like any common commodity, he knew not, he cared not to whom, so the highest price of the day was paid."[102] The investigation thus undercut the fiction that patronage and influence rewarded merit; instead, it exposed the fact that offices were traded in a capitalist market.

The cash value of these positions meant that deserving candidates could not enter the service of the East India Company. For instance, a friend of Daniel Beale became very depressed after he sent one of his six sons to learn Persian at Oxford at great expense but failed to obtain an EIC position for him. Hoping to help his friend, Beale paid £3,675 to obtain an appointment for the young man through an agent found in the newspaper. Samuel Lewis could not take the requisite EIC exam to enter its service, since he was a "mulatto," blocked by the company's increasingly racist restrictions. So Lady Lumm arranged for another man to impersonate Lewis in an interview before the board. Conversely, families could rescue ne'er-do-well young men by buying them EIC positions. One young man trained as a doctor but did not like it; his friends got him into the stock exchange, but he lost money and married a young lady of no property; so they rescued him once again by trying to get him sent out as a surgeon to India.[103]

petticoat
influence

Women played a prominent role in these transactions because directors gave writerships and cadetships to those connected to them by social, political, or familial ties. The East India Company, therefore, seemed riddled by petticoat influence that came dangerously close to implicating the court. The investigation exposed a seamy underworld of mercenary tradesmen and women, down-at-the-heels aristocrats, women pretending to be titled ladies, and titled ladies trading in commissions. For instance, John Fuller gave Mr. Shee £150 to obtain a letter of introduction to Mrs. Cottin in hopes she could obtain an EIC position for his friend. He went to visit Mrs. Cottin in Hampton Court Palace, where she enjoyed a "grace-and-favor" apartment (usually granted courtesy of the royal family). Upon reading the letter, Mrs. Cottin "put on her hat, took me across Hampton Court Green, and introduced" him to Captain Poplett, deputy lieutenant for the County of Middlesex. Fuller was to give £500 to Mrs. Cottin and deposit £2,500 "for the lady in whose possession the Patronage was." This lady supposedly enjoyed "very considerable influence with the Duke of Cambridge," who would give her a position thinking it was for a friend of hers. The transaction, however, fell through. Some of these characters were imposters, such as Mrs. Byng, who bragged of her connections at court but tried to obtain a position for a young lady who was an "improper character."[104]

Several other directors bestowed cadetships on plebeian intermediaries. George Thelluson, a director, gave a situation to Mrs. George, his wife's milliner. Mr. John Manship, who had been a director until 1808, gave a cadetship to Mrs. Welch, his landlady in Lambs Conduit Street. When asked why he did so, he explained it was out of charity. He admitted he had asked Mr. Welch to take a glass of wine with him, "but I never asked him to sit down." Despite this social distance, Manship gave Mrs. Welch three cadetships, one of which she sold. Why would a wealthy East India Company director give his landlady or his wife's milliner such valuable positions? Clearly, they would not know anyone of the proper social position. It is probable, but only distantly hinted at in the evidence, that directors gave such positions in lieu of paying their debts to tradesmen. After all, gentlemen were notorious for punctiliously paying their gambling debts but neglecting to respond to tailors' bills. Another reason emerged when Sir Theophilus Metcalfe gave William Scott, a tailor, a cadetship. Scott and his wife met Metcalfe "when he was canvassing for Maldon" but denied that Metcalfe gave him tailoring work—and a cadetship—in return for electoral favors. Metcalfe testified that he passed on the office as thanks for receiving game from Mrs. Scott from the country. But clearly Scott had turned these supposedly gracious favors into cash.[105]

Female parliamentary influence could also help obtain commissions. The director Robert Thornton testified that the Reverend Corsellis urged him to give Elizabeth Spinluffe a cadetship, thinking it was for her fiancé. Thornton seems to have owed both Corsellis and Spinluffe favors for their support during past elections at Colchester. He testified, "I have seen Miss Spinluffe at my very first election twenty-five years ago, wearing my colors, and giving me every assistance in her power." He also knew she had connections with Mr. Wilson, a member of Parliament. Miss Spinluffe, however, sold the cadetship to Mrs. Morrison, an agent, who was impressed when Spinluffe rode in a coach emblazoned with a coronet.[106]

More significantly, these disreputable men and women negotiated to exchange East India Company positions for a seat in the House of Commons. The inquiry made brutally clear what had been common knowledge: that seats in Parliament were for sale.[107] One witness testified that "most men know that [seats of Parliament] were sometimes sold," although another knew that "it was understood these things are not to be publicly said in downright English language." Emporer John Alexander Woodford, a cousin of EIC director G. W. Thelluson, hoped to parlay the writerships Thelluson had given him into a seat in Parliament through the intervention of solicitor Gabriel Tahourdin.[108] This did not come off, but another case came closer to the seats of power.

Lord Castlereagh, a powerful politician with Irish connections who served as president of the EIC Board of Control, admitted that he gave two writerships to Lord Clancarty, one of which Clancarty was to trade for a seat in Parliament. However, he insisted that he would only recommend someone who could properly receive a political favor from a member of government. But to find this seat, Clancarty went through Jeremiah James Reding, whom he knew because Reding's stepmother, Mrs. Grove, was a friend of Lord Clancarty's aunt. Reding knew the Marquis of Sligo—as "intimately" as a middle-class man "could know a peer"—and Sligo wanted to exchange his seat in Parliament for a writership for a young relative of his. However, the negotiations foundered when the Marquis of Sligo blocked Reding from revealing his name or title. It soon became apparent that Reding was a swindler, however, who wanted the other writership for his own profit. He offered to lay £3,000 on Lady Clancarty's toilette in exchange for the writership; Lady Clancarty also received a letter from Charlotte Johnson offering Reding £3,000 to "use her influence" to obtain a writership, offers which she indignantly refused. Mrs. Grove, Reding's stepmother, also intended to take a cut on the exchange.[109] Despite the failure of these transactions, it was clear that Castlereagh was willing to trade EIC positions for a seat in Parliament. While the inquiry was going on, Castlereagh moved from the presidency of the Board of Control to become secretary of state, at the heart of power. Despite the evidence of his corruption, the House of Commons voted against censuring him.[110]

The outcome of the duke of York affair undermined the Commons' credibility as representatives of the people. Wilberforce introduced a motion that cleared the duke from charges of corruption, but he urged the duke to resign because as commander in chief, he should have discovered and prevented such abuses, which were "hurtful to the public morals and religion."[111] But the motion went down, 294 to 199. Wardle's more forthright motion that the duke should resign due to corruption was defeated even more decisively, 354 to 123. It was clear that the government and the royal family's allies were able to threaten and bribe members of Parliament to save the duke of York from humiliation. The liberal *Tyne Mercury* claimed that "when we remember the brothers, the brothers-in law, the cousins and dependents of men in rank and office all looking for preferment," it was no surprise that even 125 members of Parliament voted against the duke.[112] Even the conservative *Courier* pointed out that "the sense of the Country is not to be found in the majority of the House of Commons, whereof so many hold places at the will of [the duke of York's] Father, but in the minority, voting free from such influence."[113] For instance, the duke of York allegedly obtained a seat in the Commons for Mr. Adams, his agent.[114] Conversely, when Mr. Dick, member of Parliament for Cashel, voted against York "according to his conscience," Castlereagh informed him that he must resign his seat. Dick had to follow Castlereagh's instructions because he had purchased his seat through Henry Wellesley, who acted on behalf of the Treasury.[115] However, the Crown *was* forced to respond to the public outcry against the duke. As figure 14 reveals, "John Bull," standing for the British people, held the scales of justice, and public opinion judged the duke as guilty. Perceval and members of the royal family presumably pressured the duke behind the scenes, and he resigned as commander in chief a few days later.

Whigs and moderate conservatives asserted that the outcome showed the strength of the British constitution, proving even a king's son could be investigated by the "representatives of the people." Both liberal and conservative patriots argued that the investigation demonstrated the superiority of the British constitution over France, for "there is no other country in Europe where the people dare breathe a syllable against their rulers."[116] For the Whigs, the outcome proved that the House of Commons deserved its constitutional place as the legitimate representative of the people because it

FIGURE 14   George Cruikshank, *John Bull as Justice* BMC 11304. © The British
Museum. John Bull, the symbol for the British people, carries a scale with Mary
Anne Clarke on one side, carrying the duke's love letter and other evidence, and the
duke on the other. Three men pull down on him in vain; the bishop says, "Pull away,
pull away, the Church is in danger," the politician says, "We'll lose all our places,"
and the soldier says, "We shall lose our Noble Commander."

"feelingly sympathizes" with their "enlightened understanding."[117] The *Bury and Norwich Post* declared that "if corruption does prevail," the remedy lay in "those legitimate powers with which the valor of our ancestors invested the Commons of Great Britain."[118] However, the Whigs were discredited by the fact that most of them (with the exception of Samuel Whitbread and T. W. Coke) voted for the duke out of loyalty to the Prince of Wales.[119]

For many others, Parliament's failure to condemn the duke proved the necessity for parliamentary reform. Even the conservative newspapers acknowledged "the necessity of gradual, gentle reformation" to "shield the just prerogative and dignity of the Crown, and . . . the rights, the liberties, and the happiness of the People, against ruin from internal enemies, or subjugation by a foreign foe."[120] Others demanded radical surgery. Eaton Barrett, one of the original instigators of the scandal, claimed the Whigs' and Tories' "sole aim is . . . to prevent the *corrupting maggots,* that is to say themselves, *from being discovered to the naked eye* of the public."[121] Tracing the movement back to Wilkes, the *Independent Whig* argued that Parliament could not be trusted to reform itself. Instead, the people must form themselves into a convention *outside* of Parliament to restructure the constitution.[122]

Fifty large meetings took place around the country to denounce York and demand parliamentary reform. Most of the accounts of these meetings do not give numbers, but 10,000 met in Westminster, 2,000 in Manchester, 1,500 in Wiltshire, 15,000 in Sheffield, and 4,000 in Glasgow.[123] One government informant heard from a constable that 60,000 planned to meet secretly in various Lancashire public houses, an "alarming" state of affairs.[124] But on the whole, the press regarded these meetings as composed of "respectable" middle-class citizens, whom Cobbett admonished to take charge of reform lest irresponsible plebeians destroy the movement. Some of these meetings voted to demand very moderate parliamentary reform to prevent the Crown from controlling members of Parliament through bribery, patronage, corruption, or sale of seats. A Norfolk meeting, however, demanded "an entire change of system," for by acquitting the commander in chief, the Commons majority "was in direct opposition to the sense of the people." Westminster, of course, was most radical, holding a meeting on 29 March demanding parliamentary reform.[125]

These meetings also revived the debate over the constitutional place of the people in the public. The repression of the late 1790s had diminished the number of public protest meetings, but they had revived by 1808.[126] Traditionally, local officials, the sheriffs, common councils, and borough corporations called these meetings, which were attended by inhabitants and freeholders. But the meetings also revealed conflict over who would control these local "publics." In many cities, such as Carlile, Lynn, Pontefract, North-ampton, Norwich, and Manchester, mayors refused to call the meetings their inhabitants demanded. In response, townspeople asserted the people's right to meet and discuss public measures, to consider the conduct of their representatives, and to address the king and the House of Commons.[127]

Conservatives argued that the people should trust Parliament to respond to their needs; it would be dangerous, they asserted, for Parliament to respond to public meetings. John Tinney wrote, "The great body of the people, actuated by human passions, and subject to error and deception, are to be governed by the legislative power, and cannot be superior to that power."[128] Perceval proclaimed that "the House had better cease to exist, and become itself a wild democracy, than be an instrument in the hands of popular frenzy."[129] The police magistrates should act, fulminated one writer, to repress seditious meetings and censor the press.[130] Playwright Olivia Wilmott warned that these proceedings "render[ed] the industrious and lower orders of people perverse and discontented with the rulers they may have placed over them"; such people, she believed, had no right to discuss, let alone even know about, these scandals. Conservatives claimed that patriots supported the government and stayed by their firesides.[131]

In response, liberals and radicals crafted justifications for their activism out of traditional materials. They defined patriotism as serving the public by exposing corruption, thus protecting the rights of the freeborn Briton.[132] As the *Independent Whig* noted, "All opposition to a bad or weak administration either in or out of Parliament, is the strongest visible mark, which any man can give his Country of *Patriotism and Public Virtue*."[133] Many meetings praised Wardle for his patriotism in exposing the affair. For Cobbett, it was a man's obligation as a father and an Englishman to join the parliamentary reform movement.[134] The *Tyne Mercury* proclaimed, "This is not a time for a man to sit quietly by his fireside, or think only of his own concerns."[135]

The parliamentary reform movement faced a blow, however, when Mary Anne Clarke and Colonel Wardle became embroiled in a lawsuit. In June 1809, Francis Wright, an upholsterer, sued Clarke because she had not paid for furniture he provided. In response, she alleged that Wardle was her lover and had promised to pay for her luxurious furnishings. Both Clarke and Wardle were revealed as unreliable narrators of scandal. It also became public that Clarke received £10,000 from the government to suppress her memoirs, which included further extremely embarrassing stories about the royal family.[136] As Clarke later confessed, self-interest, not patriotism, motivated her. If the duke had paid her a sufficient annuity and given her a lavishly furnished house, "not all the Jacobinical parties in Europe should have introduced my letters and person to the notice of Parliament." Clarke tried to depict Wardle as an unreliable narrator of scandal, an opportunist who "*Proteus* like, changes his nature with every gale."[137] For conservatives, this mini-scandal proved that Mary Anne Clarke had lied; they denounced Wardle for exposing the duke's adultery at the same moment as he committed adultery with Clarke.[138] For some reformers, Wardle's public services outweighed his private vices; for others, the movement for reform was more important than the quarrels of a politician and his mistress. *The Independent Whig* rebuked the government for trying to discredit Wardle's sexual morality, just as it had tried to injure the reputation of Wilkes as a pornographer and Fox as a gambler.[139] The parliamentary reform movement transcended its unreliable narrator, continuing to meet and organize.

As the popular movement surged forward, the government responded with concession, distraction, and coercion, forcing radicals to invent new strategies. In hopes of defusing calls for fundamental parliamentary reform, several members asked for inquiries into the sale of places in the Commons and moved that the House pass a motion requiring members to swear on oath that they had not purchased their seats. During the debate, some members of Parliament openly defended the system of buying and selling places in the Commons as a private matter of confidences between gentlemen, which "inquisitorial proceedings" should not invade.[140] Perceval argued that only an impossible transformation of human nature and human passions could do away with corruption.[141] William Windham claimed that patronage brought brilliant young men into Parliament: as he cavalierly admitted, "It is the way the world works on every level of society."[142] But as Capel Lofft, the distinguished constitutionalist, pointed out, these talented men represented only their patrons, not their constituents.[143] After great difficulty, Curwen's act finally passed, prohibiting the buying and selling of parliamentary seats. Perceval also pushed through an act "prohibiting the purchase, solicitation and sale of public offices," and Viscount Folkestone forced an amendment extending "the ban to offices in the gift of the Governor General of India."[144] However, Parliament decisively turned down Sir Francis Burdett's motion to enfranchise all taxed male householders, and the movement continued to agitate.[145]

Popular royalism could distract attention from the duke's embarrassment, but it could also inspire calls for reform. A few months later, after the duke of York resigned, the country celebrated George III's jubilee with magnificent spectacles and plebeian processions. Yet Britons did not uncritically acquiesce to royal power and aristocratic hierarchy, for the country was deeply divided after the Clarke affair. Norwich, for instance, failed to organize royal festivities, perhaps because the mayor and corporation had alienated the townspeople in the Clarke affair.[146] By praising George III's domestic virtues, radicals and liberals highlighted the decadence, incompetence, and corruption of his sons. The *Examiner* quoted George III's proclamation "that all Persons of Honor, or in Place of Authority, will give good example by their own virtue and piety."[147] They made it clear that their love for the king was conditional on his virtue and could be withdrawn. As one writer pointed out, "It is not . . . because he is our *King* that we love him, but because he is a good King." Kings existed for the convenience of the public.[148] Eaton Barrett wrote, "A king is neither more nor less than a chief magistrate, selected by and from the people, for the *public good*; and he who does not make that his chief business, is no king."[149] Radicals appropriated the notion of the king as a good father to demand that he prevent his ministers from violating the liberties of the subject. One letter called upon the people to "invoke the King, as our common father, that we may be treated as children, not as aliens—that we may be shorn, not flayed—that we may be ruled with whips, rather than with scorpions, and that we may be led by conscientious guides, not driven by desperate hirelings!"[150] Radical royalism also enabled activists to evade prosecution for seditious libel, or even treason, which they would have faced if they criticized the monarchy more directly.

The popular outrage over the duke of York affair, its exposure in Parliament, and its seamy details had forced the government to drop twenty libel publications during the inquiry. But the government soon reimposed press censorship. The *Independent Whig* was accused of libel for characterizing the duke of York as a "*Gamester*" and "Duelist" who indulged in bacchanals, sold "commissions through an abandoned woman," and "bribe[d] or influence[d] votes in Parliament."[151] Leigh Hunt also faced imprisonment for criticizing the Prince of Wales as a "corpulent gentleman . . . a libertine . . . [and] a despiser of domestic ties."[152] Parliament also asserted its privilege to serve as the only legitimate public. In the beginning of 1810, John Gale Jones was jailed for sponsoring a public debate on whether Parliament was right to enforce "the Standing Order for excluding strangers [such as parliamentary reporters] from the Commons," and Burdett was also jailed for "denying the Commons' right to imprison the people of England."[153]

The parliamentary reform movement, however, had set a precedent for the power of organized public opinion. The 1809 inquiry and subsequent probes forced the East India Company to professionalize its bureaucracy and crack down once again on the civil servants who traded privately on the side.[154] Two constituencies, those of merchants and Evangelicals, mobilized to demand amendments when the company's charter was renewed in 1813, mounting public meetings and sending thousands of petitions to Parliament. The EIC lost its monopoly, opened up its trade to all merchants, and finally allowed missionaries in its territories.[155]

CONCLUSION

In some ways, the Mary Anne Clarke affair was the perfect scandal. By exposing the tawdry affair of the duke of York and his mistress, reformers created a story that excited public opinion in a way that previous issues, such as the Dundas impeachment or Wellesley's conquests, had not. The simple affair of the duke and Mary Anne Clarke revealed a much wider system of corruption in the army, the church, the civil service, the East India Company, and even Parliament, laying bare the contradiction between the ethos of meritorious service to the public and the system of influence and patronage. Previously, the elite justified patronage as motivated by honor and influence, but when the machinations of a mistress obtained promotion, the whole system seemed illegitimate. Offices could be traded just like any other commodity, as titled gentlemen and ladies swapped favors with tailors and milliners. The civil service and empire had promised the middle class opportunities to advance through merit and hard work, but instead the scandal undermined the rationale for aristocratic dominance and strengthened the ethos of the middle class frustrated at their failure to advance in government.

The scandal worked because it appealed to several constituencies: Evangelicals, middle-class citizens, and radicals. It revived a parliamentary reform movement that transcended the scandal's narrators, Wardle and Clarke, and sustained itself after they were discredited. However, the Clarke affair seems to have outraged a mostly middle-class constituency, perhaps because they were angered by the patronage system that prevented their advancement.[156] Plebeian radicals do not seem to have been as active in this phase of the movement, which organized itself as "respectable" instead of inclusive. Such class divisions and government repression hampered the parliamentary reform movement from 1809 to 1815, but the movement eventually revived.

The scandal forced the government to make significant concessions. As Philip Harling argues, ministers did not begin to reform the British state out of an abstract, idealistic belief in justice and efficiency. Instead, they feared popular pressure for even more radical reform. Buying and selling of places, at least in the government if not in Parliament, declined if not ended; sinecures were phased out and replaced with proper pensions for those who had devoted their lives to the civil service.[157] But the fundamental contradiction still remained that positions were not open to all on the basis of merit, and that high birth, connections, and "influence" still determined a man's ability to obtain a job regardless of his abilities and education. The duke of York regained his position in the army and continued to promote officers on the basis of family influence, even if bribery no longer motivated him.[158] This flaw in the system continued until the late nineteenth century.

The widespread evidence that some royal mistresses, titled ladies, and plebeian tradeswomen trafficked in offices cemented the association of petticoat influence with corruption. As an individual woman, Mary Anne Clarke temporarily overcame the association of femininity with corruption by defying Parliament. Although conservatives denounced her as an abandoned prostitute, liberals and radicals lauded her as a radical heroine, disregarding her sexual reputation. But it soon became clear that she was an opportunistic schemer when she exposed Wardle and sold her memoirs to the government. But what choice did she have? Wardle could parlay the scandal into a parliamentary career, but as a woman, Clarke could only exchange her sexual secrets for money; she could never enjoy the privileges of office, or even prove her merit by serving in government. The parliamentary reform movement continued to associate citizenship with patriotic, militaristic, and paternal manliness.

The royal family did its part by continuing to provide raw material for public outrage. The Prince of Wales had long been even more notorious for his mistresses than his brother, and he became regent in 1811. The duke of York's troubles had damaged his brother's already shady reputation. When George attempted to divorce his wife in 1820, the scandal surpassed Mary Anne Clarke's revelations in shaking the foundations of monarchy.

❧ ❧ ❧

CHAPTER EIGHT

Queen Caroline and the Sexual Politics of the British Constitution

There have been disembarkations on the British coast, bringing
war and producing revolutions in the state, ere now. . . . Henry VII
and William III brought with them . . . a train of armed followers.
But this woman comes arrayed only in native courage, and . . .
conscious innocence; and presents her bosom, aye, offers her neck,
to those who threatened to sever her head from it, if ever she
dared to come within their reach.[1]

This woman was Caroline of Brunswick, a buxom, gregarious woman of fifty-two who had spent seven years in exile traveling around Europe with her handsome Italian valet. When her estranged husband, George IV, finally ascended the throne in 1820, he determined to put her on trial for adultery and divorce her, despite his own notorious womanizing. But Caroline was not "arrayed only in native courage": she forged alliances with Whigs and radicals, and huge crowds cheered her all the way to London. Soldiers threatened to mutiny, working-class people demonstrated, and middle-class petitioners sent addresses of support.

Caroline had long caused scandal, but now she turned scandal to her own ends. Her followers also used the scandal to revive the radical movement, for her cause symbolized a myriad of political and social issues. For working-class people, Caroline's persecution by the king served as a powerful metaphor for the oppression they faced from the government, as I and others have argued in earlier work. The affair also reflected anxieties about the changing sexual moralities of Regency Britain.[2]

The scandal also had serious implications for the constitution. The king posed a threat to the constitutional balance of king, Lords, and Commons by forcing his ministers and the Lords to solve his marital problems. In response to massive popular mobilization, conservatives, Whigs and radicals each had to develop new images of royalty that depended on public opinion. Some wondered whether the constitutional monarchy would survive; a few hoped it would not.

AN UNHAPPY MARRIAGE

The Prince of Wales had sparked scandal for years, endangering George III's image as a paternal monarch. The prince prided himself on his patronage of the arts, but he also squandered thousands at the racetrack and indulged in low brothels. In the 1780s, he spent £80,000 per year in excess of his income of £62,000 (at least one thousand times the income of an artisan) and owed more than £269,000. He allied himself with the Whig opposition to his father yet depended on the government to support his lavish lifestyle. But Parliament would pay his enormous debts only if he married a suitable bride.[3]

The prince could not just marry anyone he fancied, not even among the nobility of Britain, for an unsuitable marriage could upset the constitution. The Royal Marriage Act of 1772, which limited his choices, had responded to three concerns: the prince had to serve as a moral example to his subjects by obtaining the permission of the monarch for his marriage; second, he had to marry a Protestant to ensure the Protestant succession; and third, he could not marry a British subject, only a foreign princess. If the prince married into one of the great aristocratic families, he could grant its members government offices and patronage, which would disturb the balance of power between Parliament and monarch.[4] In 1786, however, the Prince of Wales surreptitiously married, without the king's permission, a Catholic British subject: the widowed Mrs. Maria Fitzherbert. The marriage became an open secret, but since he had violated the Royal Marriage Act, the wedding was considered invalid.

By the early 1790s, the Prince of Wales's debts had skyrocketed to £550,000. Marriage became even more urgent. The prince's minions searched throughout Europe for a suitable bride and eventually resorted to George's cousin Princess Caroline, from the small German state of Brunswick.[5] Thomas LeMesurier, sent out to scrutinize the princess, described her as "a very handsome Woman, at least as far as we could judge through a very thick layer of rouge which was on her cheeks. Her eyes have much fire, but there is a sharpness in them which was not pleasant." Although the prince's defenders later alleged that Caroline lost her virginity before marriage, LeMesurier observed chaperones carefully supervising her.[6]

The prince and Caroline disliked each other immediately upon their first encounter. The prince offended Caroline by sending his mistress, Lady Jersey, to serve as her lady of the bedchamber. Freed from her chaperones, Caroline was gregarious, friendly, outspoken, and sometimes forgot to wash, horrifying the prince, who prided himself on his exquisite dress and toilette. That is, when he was not intoxicated—as he was during their wedding, when his aides had to push him to the altar. Caroline later confided in a friend that he fell down dead drunk in the grate on their wedding night.[7] Somehow, they managed to consummate the marriage, and the princess gave birth to the heiress to the throne, Charlotte, in nine months.

The prince hated his new wife and separated from her after a year. Exaggerated rumors spread throughout London that he struck her and infected her with venereal disease.[8] The estrangement soon became a public scandal, which endangered royalty's popularity in the dangerous years of the French Revolution.[9] After all, only the year before, a London mob stoned the king's carriage. In 1796, crowds cheered Caroline when she appeared on a balcony with baby Charlotte or in her box at the opera. They jeered the prince and even the queen, who was rumored to side with Lady Jersey against Caroline; the queen's carriage was stoned. Newspapers took sides. Those allied with or subsidized by the prince's friends the Whigs tried to blame Caroline for refusing to submit to her husband, but conservative newspapers feared that the fracas could undermine royalty's tenuous popularity.[10] The conservative *St. James Chronicle* admonished the prince that he might lose his "splendid patrimony" if he continued in this course of action. "It is not enough," warned the paper, "for the friends of Order, throughout the country, to be peaceable and rational—they must use active virtue."[11]

Eventually, the prince exiled Caroline to Blackheath, a two-hour ride outside of London. There, Caroline established a miniature court in exile, freed from the stiff formality of George III's rather austere palace. A sociable and kindhearted woman, she opened her house as a salon for raffish intellectuals and politicians of her era, including the romantically disreputable poet Lord Byron and politicians such as George Canning. One partygoer saw her "in a gorgeous dress, which was looped up to show her petticoat, covered with stars, with silver wings on her shoulders, sitting under a tree, with a pot of porter on her knee."[12] She certainly flirted with several men and may have taken lovers; after all, her adulterous husband abandoned her for years, and many high-society ladies took lovers after giving their husbands an heir. She also adopted a little boy from a poor family, seeking a substitute for her daughter, who was being brought up apart from her in the palace.

The "Delicate Investigation"
1806-7

In 1806–7, the prince tried to stir up a scandal behind the scenes by accusing Caroline of adultery. He needed a distraction from his own problems, for creditors publicly attacked him for failing to pay his debts "at a time when the middle and lower classes of society could not obtain the common necessaries of life."[13] The prince instructed the king's ministers to initiate a Delicate Investigation of Caroline's morality on the grounds that her behavior endangered the succession to the throne. Two of her former friends, Sir John and Lady Douglas, alleged that Caroline had given birth to the little boy, the result of an affair with either Sir Sidney Smith or Captain Thomas Manby.[14] Embittered against Caroline because she evicted them from a rented house, the Douglases were unreliable witnesses. The commission concluded that Caroline had not given birth to an illegitimate child, but it rebuked her for "improper levity"—such as being alone with a gentleman in the morning or sitting on a sofa with him.

Caroline's treatment under the Delicate Investigation underlined the vulnerability of women, especially royal women, to sexual gossip and innuendo. But Caroline enterprisingly sought allies to help her fight back against scandal. As her friend Lady Charlotte Bury observed, Caroline had "a bold and independent mind, which is a principal ingredient in the formation of a great queen or an illustrious woman." Well acquainted with politicians, she "took great pleasure in explaining the state of politics and parties" but also manipulated politicians against each other.[15] She gained the assistance of Tory politician Spencer Perceval, who helped her write a letter to the king protesting her treatment. She protested that the commission was not a properly constituted legal body such as the Privy Council but an ad hoc arrangement established by the king's warrant, and witnesses did not testify under oath. As a result, Sir John and Lady Douglas could not be charged with perjury in their testimony, leaving Caroline unable to redeem completely her reputation. Furthermore, she could not defend herself against the allegation of "levity," which was a vague insinuation, not a crime. Nor could she sue for defamation, as could ordinary London women. Unlike the duke of York, she had no official position, patronage, or prestige.

Perceval proved unreliable as an ally. At first, he supported her in hopes of embarrassing his political rivals, the prince's friends the Whigs, briefly in power as the Ministry of All the Talents. But the Prince of Wales was furious at the ministry for failing to protect him in the affair. When its members resigned, Perceval became a minister in the new government.[16] Perceval apparently rebuked the prince for refusing to let Caroline attend the queen's birthday, because he feared that this would stir up the crowd's wrath against the king and queen.[17] But he stopped helping Caroline.

Caroline also sought to turn publicity to her cause in 1807 by trying to publish her letter of protest and the report exonerating her, but the Crown quickly foiled these efforts. Nonetheless, word of the investigation leaked out.[18] However, radicals divided over her cause. Some saw her as a victim of the decadent prince. As one commentator warned the prince, "What perils await the monarch who rules not in his people's hearts, what horrors his country has to dread from internal discord and conflicting parties."[19] Others saw Caroline as just another immoral upper-class woman. William Cobbett asked why the vice society ignored her immorality but prosecuted poor applewomen for selling on the Sabbath.[20] Another pamphlet, *The Royal Eclipse*, implied that "a Dignified Prostitute [by implication, Caroline] . . . TRIUMPHS in her turpitude, and insults virtue with impunity," while the poor streetwalker was "driven by NECESSITY . . . to the bitter and humiliating resources of prostitution . . . afraid of the beadle and his lash."[21]

In 1811, George III lapsed permanently into insanity, and the Prince of Wales became the regent. On one hand, he seemed to turn away from his private interests toward the responsibilities of government by abandoning his former Whig friends and retaining his father's Tory ministers, such as Perceval. To be sure, some thought that Perceval blackmailed him over the Delicate Investigation to hold on to office.[22] On the other, the prince remained self-absorbed, so drunk and indolent that he had to be cajoled into signing state papers instead of carousing.[23] The Whigs now sided with Caroline, irked at the prince's betrayal, and the rising young Whig barrister Henry Brougham took up her cause.

In 1813–14, Caroline once again became a heroine of the people. The Prince of Wales had turned against his daughter, Princess Charlotte, because she was fond of her mother; he severely restricted Charlotte's freedom of movement and forbade her to see Caroline. Charlotte was so upset that she fled Carlton House to her mother in the middle of the night. When newspapers reported on these events, this family quarrel became public. Vast crowds gathered outside the regent's palace to protest his treatment of his daughter—and his government's policies. Brougham warned Charlotte that she must leave her mother's home, for if she defied the regent, the crowds could burn down Carlton House (the regent's palace) and endanger the government. Chastened, she returned to the control of her father, who exiled her to the suburbs under a strict governess.

To prove that Caroline was an unfit mother, the regent leaked the 1806 depositions from the Douglases to the *Morning Herald* and the *Morning Post*.[24] He hoped that public opinion would see Caroline as a debauched woman and turn against her, but instead, Caroline and the Whigs turned publicity against him. Whig publishers brought out the report of the Delicate Investigation that had exonerated Caroline of adultery. Aided by Brougham, Caroline published a letter claiming that this private family quarrel was a public, and constitutional, concern. She wrote that she had a duty "to my Husband and the People committed to his Care" both to defend her own reputation and to ensure that Charlotte was educated to be a future ruler of empire.[25]

Parliament began to debate the regent's actions on the grounds that the behavior of the princesses had implications for the constitutional succession of the monarch. The prince and the Tories argued that the monarch must ensure the legitimacy of the succession, which depended on the purity of the Hanover dynasty. The prince's supporters claimed that Parliament had no business deciding how the king should raise his daughter or conduct his marriage.[26] For Whigs, the Glorious Revolution established that Parliament must consent to the succession, and therefore had the right to interfere. Cochrane Johnstone, who had triggered the investigation into the duke of York, pointed out that disputes over the succession to the throne had sparked revolutions. Hence, only a legal investigation could officially absolve Caroline and ensure the succession of Princess Charlotte. The Commons rejected his motion, many Whigs arguing that since the Commons believed Caroline to be innocent, no investigation was necessary.[27] Barrister Charles Dunne proclaimed that the prince grossly insulted "the leading constitutional authorities of the state, which had absolved her from every accusation." He asked, "Will the principles of the constitution be unhinged to please the prejudices of a Prince?"[28] This constitutional protest indicated that loyalty to the throne was conditional and could be withdrawn.

Radicals seized upon the controversy to protest against the Crown. After the duke of York affair, they saw the utility in royal scandal. While the radicals were not united on this issue, Cobbett now supported Caroline and Charlotte against the regent, and addresses poured in supporting them from London, Westminster, and indeed all over the country. Unlike the Whigs, the radicals did not fear that the prince was upsetting the balance between the Commons and the Crown; instead, they regarded both Parliament and the prince as equally oppressive. For instance, the freeholders of Middlesex linked the treatment of Caroline and Charlotte to the "defective state of representation." They declared to Charlotte that "the Borough-Mongering Faction, the detestable oligarchy of Great Britain, [was] united in one impenetrable Phalanx, against the Cause of her Royal Mother, [and] . . . the abused People of England."[29] In their eyes, the corrupt system unjustly attacked Caroline and fattened the rich at a time when the poor suffered under the hardship of war.[30]

Indeed, the situation could be dangerous, for the prince regent was extremely unpopular. When members of the royal families of Europe visited London in 1814, crowds flocked to see the czar and other luminaries, including Caroline, but hissed the regent. As Hannah Colfax of Dorset noted of her visit to London, she did not get to see the regent's carriage because he maneuvered away from the main streets "to escape the fury of the mob."[31] Dunne noted that not only "the mechanic or lower orders" hissed at the regent but the "higher ranks" as well; disaffection deeply "infect[ed] the very guards that surrounded his person."[32] This popular support could not help Caroline, who went into exile in 1814. But the prince's unpopularity intensified when the Napoleonic Wars ended, bringing high taxes, high food prices, and unemployment.

Radicals revived the old theme of oriental despotism, comparing the prince to a sultan, a Grand Mogul, or the Grand Turk, and indeed, the prince fit this image much better than his father had. In 1815, the regent handed his critics a golden opportunity for satire by rebuilding the Brighton Pavilion as an orientalist extravaganza. The pavilion resembles a miniature Taj Mahal, with its gleaming white onion domes and turrets, its interior a grandiose concoction of palm tree columns, writhing dragons, and crimson chinoiserie. By comparing George to an oriental despot, critics implied he lusted for absolute power; his series of mistresses proved he could not control his appetites, and his government policies that he would not rule according to the law.

Caricatures and pamphlets had depicted the pavilion as "the British seraglio." Many believed that this prince was too vulnerable to the petticoat influence of his mother, his morganatic wife, Maria Fitzherbert, and his mistress Lady Hertford. One work blamed Lady Hertford for many measures that were "obnoxious to the people." Her husband supposedly "connived" to his wife's seduction in consequence of the "mighty political influence which such an intrigue must naturally throw into the hands of himself and his family."[33] Indeed, the regent demanded that his mistresses' relatives receive lucrative sinecures.[34] In the theory of oriental despotism, as we have seen in Burke's rhetoric on Hastings, excessive masculine lust could lead to effeminacy. As an effeminate dandy, the prince was controlled by women. For instance, Cruikshank depicted the "Pleasures of Petticoat Government": George IV dressed as a woman, surrounded by his fat and buxom mistresses who managed the privy purse.[35] The theme of oriental despotism could also implicitly mock Britain's growing empire. In 1816, Cruikshank caricatured the regent as grotesquely fat and dressed in a Chinese hat, about to send missives to the court of China—although the Chinese had little interest in British influence. The caricature also paralleled the rotund profile of the regent with that of Saartje Baartman, the "Hottentot Venus" put on public exhibition in 1812. While the caricature was thus complicit in the racist objectification of Baartman, it also mocked British imperial pretensions of superiority to the Chinese and Africans by equating the regent with a Chinese emperor and with the Hottentot Venus.[36]

Government repression of radicals strengthened the allegation that the prince was a despot who ruled without law (although the ministers were much more responsible for the actual policy, given the prince's indolence). The movement for parliamentary reform revived once again, but it was now dominated by radical, working-class activists who organized strikes and mass demonstrations. In response, the government suspended habeas corpus, censored newspapers, prohibited "seditious" meetings and organizations, and imprisoned radicals. Worst of all, in the Peterloo massacre of 1819, the cavalry charged a peaceful mass meeting in Manchester, killing several and wounding dozens, including women. Radicals claimed that the suspension of habeas corpus and freedom of the press threatened the constitutional liberties of England and proved it was in danger of despotism. The government argued once again that Parliament was the only legitimate public; the people had no right to meet in public or publish their opinions.[37]

Meanwhile, Caroline enjoyed her exile in Europe. Freed at last from the constraints of English society, she poked into archaeological digs, called upon the bey of Tunis, who allowed her to visit his seraglio, and entered Jerusalem on a donkey and inquired into the historical evidences of ancient Christianity, finally settling by the shores of Lake Como in Italy. The handsome, mustachioed, six-foot-tall valet Pergami, an Italian, accompanied Caroline so closely that he slept under her shipboard tent.[38] He also consoled her when she heard that her daughter, Charlotte, died giving birth in 1816. Princess Charlotte was mourned as "England's Only Hope"—a pointed rebuke to her father.

Confident of his power despite his unpopularity, the regent prepared to divorce Caroline, sending emissaries to Italy to spy on her every movement and gather dirt against her.[39] Her case was not helped by the presence of Pergami and her love of low-cut dresses and rouge. But even some of those who came to spy were won over by her good-hearted nature. John Galiffe, for instance, had heard that she had ruined young men in Europe and discredited royalty by associating with people of the lower classes, such as Pergami. Upon meeting her, he became convinced of her innocence.[40] The

Milan Commission sent to investigate her gathered a green bag of evidence against Caroline that was to be famously caricatured, but it could not find conclusive proof of adultery. When the old king died in early 1820, the situation became more urgent.

George's ministers wished for a quiet agreement of separation, but both Caroline and George refused to resolve their marital problems privately—Caroline because she knew public opinion was her only power, the prince because he felt he could use the government for his own ends. Caroline was furious at the Milan Commission and feared that the vicious rumors it had spread would discredit her in the courts of Europe. Brougham negotiated with the king's agents on her behalf, but their offer of £50,000 a year to renounce the title of queen and stay away from Britain affronted her.[41] By turning down the cash, she disproved claims that she was just another self-interested parasitical princess (although, of course, she was already receiving £35,000 a year). Furthermore, on his accession to the throne George immediately removed her name from the prayers for the royal family in the Church of England liturgy. Outraged by this slight, Caroline prepared to return to England.

George wrote Lord Liverpool that a private arrangement would be "an unnecessary sacrifice of important public interests, as well as of [his] personal feelings."[42] He probably wished to remarry and father a new successor, so he ordered his ministers to find constitutional strategies to get rid of the queen. She could be tried for high treason, they pointed out, but the high court judges rejected this possibility.[43] Divorce by act of Parliament was an option, but it first required divorce in the ecclesiastical courts. There, Caroline could plead ill-usage, George's own adultery, and—what remained unspoken—his illegal marriage to Maria Fitzherbert. Secret proceedings would cause an uproar in the press. Above all, his ministers warned, it was important to avoid actions likely "to disturb the peace of the country."[44]

Furious, the king threatened to dismiss his ministers. Technically, he had the power to do so, but he was supposed to use this prerogative for public issues, not private affairs.[45] But only Canning resigned, because he had been a close friend—rumor had it, a lover—of the queen and could not, with honor, sit in judgment on her.[46] The ministers leaked news of the dispute to the newspapers, but this evidence of division in the government strengthened Caroline's hand.[47] A caricature depicted the king as an oriental despot, dressed in eastern robes and surrounded by his minions, facing his ministers and the judges dressed in judicial robes, who represented the constitution (figure 15). But the ministers gave in to the king with a compromise. The king's adviser Lord Eldon found a precedent for Parliament to consider

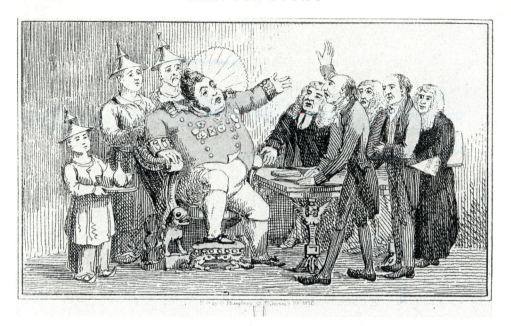

FIGURE 15   *Horrida Bella. Pains and Penalties versus Truth and Justice* (London, 1820), p. 3, in TS 11/120. Reproduced by permission of the Public Record Office. The king, dressed as an oriental ruler with his minions, faces his ministers, dressed in legal regalia.

a "Bill of Pains and Penalties," which, if the queen was found guilty of adultery, would strip her of her titles and send her into exile. As Flora Fraser notes, this allowed the king to "achieve what no adulterous subject of his could achieve—divorce without 'clean hands.'"[48] It was also of dubious constitutionality, having been used rarely, and only in those cases "where the proofs of wrongdoing were unlikely to secure conviction under the law."[49] By giving in to the king's insistence on a public trial, the ministers lost credibility. Even very conservative Scotsmen thought the proceedings showed that "they were ruled by a ministry so servile to the King that, in order to please him, they would not scruple to endanger royalty."[50] The king's ministers began preparing a dossier for Parliament in an atmosphere of high tension, for the Cato Street conspirators had just been discovered plotting to blow up the cabinet.

Caroline returned to England to claim her crown as queen on 4 June 1820, four months after the old king died. Vast crowds greeted her at Dover and accompanied her all the way to London. Her supporters plastered her image on building walls and broke the windows of those who would not illuminate them in her honor.[51] Caroline responded eagerly to this effusion of public sentiment, which allowed her to go beyond the Whigs in her search for allies. Brougham had long supported her in hopes of advancing his own political career, but she felt he was too prone to compromise. As Lady Cowper wrote, Caroline "jockeyed" Brougham, whose "vanity made him believe his influence with her to be very great," but they both used each other for their own interests.[52] When J. C. Hobhouse told her that "the nobility or higher gentry . . . and the Whig aristocracy would come to her if she triumphed—She said—I will not let them then—snapping her fingers."[53]

Caroline knew she had to reach beyond Parliament, which she mistrusted, to gain the support of public opinion, especially plebeian folk. The Alderman Mathew Wood of London, a radical, had urged her to reject Brougham's negotiations and return to England. Lady Charlotte Lindsay acidly observed that he hoped "to make himself a consequence with the Radicals, which on account of his silliness and inefficiency, he would not otherwise have obtained.[54] Woods welcomed Caroline on her arrival and made his house the center of Carolinite organizing. Brougham resented Wood's influence; as he wrote to a colleague, the prince's supporters ought to put out "all manner of hints and squibs against him" to "keep her from listening to so great a blockhead."[55] Caroline was undeterred and also sought help from William Cobbett, an influential radical who had been so important in publicizing the duke of York affair. He sent her letters advising her to stand firm and trust to "public opinion," not Parliament. He and his daughter, Anne, eventually wrote many of the queen's addresses to the people and pamphlets supporting her cause.[56] The radicals knew that here was a heaven-sent opportunity to embarrass the government and safely redeem themselves after Peterloo.

As the summer drew on and Parliament prepared for the trial, Caroline's radical supporters and the Whigs protested against the proceedings, but they followed different strategies. The radicals denounced the trial as unconstitutional, just like the government's suspension of habeas corpus. Caroline herself published an open letter to the king (probably ghostwritten by Cobbett) linking her cause to the radical critique of the constitution. "Royalty rests on the basis of the public good," and on this ground, the trial would be unconstitutional, illegal, and unfair. She demanded to be tried by a jury of the people, since the peers sitting in judgment on her "hold, by themselves and their families, offices, pensions and other emoluments solely at the will and pleasure of Your Majesty."[57] Radicals explicitly equated "the vile system of espionage and perjury by which they are seeking to overwhelm your Majesty" with the imprisonment of "our best and bravest . . .

for having constitutionally sought for a restitution of their inborn and imprescriptable privileges."[58]

The Whigs tried parliamentary maneuvering to avoid a trial. The Commons had advised the king's ministers to continue to negotiate with Caroline and felt outraged when they faltered.[59] Lord Grey moved in the House of Lords that Caroline should be impeached. If the queen were found guilty of adultery under this procedure, she could have been beheaded, an alternative so drastic and dangerous to public order that no peer would dare vote for it. By this strategy, it was surmised, Grey hoped to save the queen. But the Lords voted down this motion; after all, impeachment had failed spectacularly in the cases of Warren Hastings and Lord Melville.[60] Because public personages could be charged with offenses not known under the law, impeachment was a vague remedy that easily sprawled out of control, as in the case of Hastings, or discredited the Lords, as with Melville's embezzlement.

The trial began in late August and continued until early November, with a brief intermission. The very duration of this event sustained the scandal. Lord Holland wrote to Wilberforce, "It seems to me that for the honor of the Crown the King's advisors are determined to make him yield every point piecemeal, exhibit his spite and lose his power & for the sake of morality to occupy the country for half a year with the licentious conduct of a Princess."[61] Descriptions of Caroline sitting as a lone woman, surrounded by hundreds of black-robed men, stirred up sympathy for the queen. As the Lords weighed the testimony and tried to decide whether to vote for or against the Bill of Pains and Penalties, they knew that the eyes of the country were upon them.

Through the summer and into the fall of 1820, Caroline appeared at the balcony of her new residence, Brandenburgh House, before vast processions of London artisans, who proudly marched through the streets with their trade emblems and tools. All over the country, townspeople met to send the queen addresses of support with thousands of signatures, and she responded warmly, waving from the balcony and delivering speeches with radical sentiments. For radicals, the queen became a symbol of working-class oppression.[62] As the townspeople of Nottingham told her, "The addressers felt for the wrongs of the Queen as they felt for the various oppressions under which they themselves labored."[63] Cotton and silk weavers specifically tied the queen's woes to their own industrial suffering.[64]

Most of this organization was peaceful, but the government feared that this disaffection would infect the soldiers—with good reason. Spies reported that soldiers drank to Caroline's health in London pubs.[65] An anonymous writer warned Lord Liverpool that as the guards "marched through

Brompton, they cheered God save the Queen and the address of the commanding Officer at the Barracks was answered by a general groan." Liverpool received death threats from a soldier, and another soldier told him that "any soldier would draw his sword in defense of the Queen."[66]

The affair overwhelmingly stimulated an expansion of the press and completely swamped the government's efforts at censorship and control. Caricatures proved to be a particularly good way of overcoming censorship. While the king and Treasury paid off some of the more egregious caricaturists to keep their worst—or best—efforts out of circulation, the tide of ridicule against the king could not be stopped.[67] The king's supporters tried to produce their own caricatures and pamphlets against the queen, but as Hannah More lamented, "they have all the wit as well as all the zeal" on Caroline's side.[68]

Most newspapers published the complete proceedings of the trial. Although the government may have attempted to bribe papers to support George against Caroline, to do so caused precipitous declines in circulation and the danger of mob attacks. Even most conservative newspapers supported Caroline.[69] One exception was the scurrilous *John Bull*, founded solely to combat Caroline's popularity. Its principles were traditionally conservative, supporting the king, the church, and the army and opposing Evangelicals, as had Hannah More's opponents. But it was not a respectable paper, using insult and scandal to its own ends. For instance, it called Wilberforce "that little man," impugned addressers to the queen as "a very inferior shoemaker" and "Mr Slight an humble staymaker," and revealed that a banker's wife who visited the queen was originally a servant maid.[70] Anne Hamond, wife of a Norfolk gentleman, described *John Bull* as pervaded with a "dirty, mean spirit."[71]

Radicals were much more successful in transforming the affair into familiar narratives, drawing upon the popular genres of melodrama and satire to depict the controversy.[72] William Hone, imprisoned a few years earlier for seditious libel, simplified elaborate and expensive caricatures into easily publishable and cheap woodblock images against the king, most notably his *Queen's Matrimonial Ladder*.[73] A spy for the Home Office reported that Carolinite propaganda now supplied "the Place of Tales and Ballads in every village. . . . All the People are of one mind that Revolution has pervaded the Continent and will succeed here."[74] But whether the tale was told as a cuckolded husband and insubordinate wife, or wicked libertine and innocent maiden, these narratives enabled Britons to debate the constitution once more.

The divided conservatives, Whigs, moderate reformers, and radicals all used the occasion to express their views on the constitutional place of the monarchy. Conservative supporters of the king proclaimed that the public should support him because the queen's adultery could contaminate the succession to the crown. A conservative Whig argued that the "the People, for whom the King holds the sovereignty in trust," had an interest in ensuring that "the stream of Royal blood flows pure and uncontaminated."[75] To defend the king against the accusation that he unconstitutionally interfered in politics, his supporters declared that the nation as a whole needed morality to be protected from Caroline's "contagion." For instance, Henry Crabb Robinson argued that a "vagabond princess" roaming around Europe affronted the British Empire's dignity.[76]

The king's supporters linked unquestioning support for the king with the empire.[77] *The Palace of John Bull* praised George for ensuring the prosperity of the empire, its "ships laden with India's treasures."[78] "Patraie Fides" celebrated empire and warned the middle class to trust the "paternal" government. Caroline's addresses, feared one commentator, exhibited "disaffection to His Majesty's sacred person . . . disrespect and contempt for our established religion—for our admirable system of public justice . . . leading to the overthrow of constitution, pillage of property, rebellion."[79]

Yet the more conservatives stressed the king as symbol of church, state, and empire, the less important the individual king became and the more important the Crown as symbol of government. The same commentator pointed out that the king was "the constitutional hereditary guardian" not of one particular administration but of the "*form and constitution* of government."[80] For instance, Hannah More honored the "kingly *office*" more than the king himself because she regarded the king as "imprudent" and much less than saintly.[81] As R. N. Bacon, editor of the *Norwich Mercury*, noted, "We regard the Monarchy as part of the Constitution, and only as a part of the Constitution."[82]

Two competing pamphlets put the conflict between the conservative and moderate views of the constitution in a visual form. The pamphlet *The Real or Constitutional House that Jack Built* depicted the constitution as a temple supported by the columns of Lords, Commons, and monarchy; the monarchy column was ornamented with an elaborate canopy and a throne (figure 16). Yet the throne in this depiction was empty. The constitutional place of the monarch was more significant than the monarch himself. This work had been published to counteract Hone's famous pamphlet, *The Political House that Jack Built*, which presented a different notion of the place of the Crown in the constitution: in Hone's depiction, the constitution is presented as a temple with three equal, unadorned pillars, standing for the Commons, Lords, and Crown (figure 17). This illustration shows that the

FIGURE 16 *This is the House that Jack Built*, in *The Real or Constitutional House that Jack Built* (London, 1819), p. 2. From author's collection.

FIGURE 17   *This is the House that Jack Built*, in William Hone, *The Political House that Jack Built*, 51st ed. (London, 1821), p. 2. From author's collection.

Crown was not supposed to predominate over the representatives of the people.

For many Whigs, the power of Parliament had to balance the power of the Crown. According to Whig doctrine, the Glorious Revolution and the Hanoverian succession established the principle that only Parliament had the right to alter the succession of the Crown; therefore, the king had no right to put his wife on trial for adultery. Whigs soon pointed out that the Bill of Pains and Penalties endangered the constitutional balance between king and Parliament. Although Charles Tennyson, a member of Parliament, also felt Caroline was immoral, he reasserted the classic Whig doctrine that the king's private life should never become a public issue. He criticized the king for using the ministers of the government to prefer the charges, "injudiciously afford[ing] ground also for imputing that His Majesty acted rather in his private than his public capacity." Even worse, the king as an injured husband also served as "the Prosecutor" who would "deliver final judgment in this cause."[83] Lord Archibald, who believed the queen guilty, was reported to have said "he should still vote for her acquittal, because he thinks the K[ing] has no right to a divorce or to embroil us in a Civil War for a thing which signifies so little."[84]

The Whigs' loyalty to the Crown was conditional. As Mr. Bigge argued at a meeting in Morpeth, "loyalty did not consist in an almost superstitious attachment to the person of the sovereign" or "a uniform acquiescence in the measures of his Majesty's ministers—but in a rational and steady attachment to the sovereign . . . and a warm attachment to the liberties of the country."[85] Similarly, another author disavowed "the absurd and dangerous principle, that a blind unlimited obedience to the ministers of state constitutes the criterion of loyalty, and the measure of patriotism."[86] Some pro-Caroline writers asserted that the sovereignty of the Crown depended on the assent of the people. Charles Phillips, an Irish barrister, wrote that "other crowns may be bestowed by despots and entrenched by cannon, but the Throne we honor is the people's choice. Its safest bulwark is the popular heart, and its brightest ornament, *domestic virtue.*"[87]

George IV's role as head of the Church of England was undermined by the hypocrisy he exhibited by flaunting his mistresses and then removing the queen's name from the liturgy of the Church of England. Many religious people felt that the king had to earn public support by serving as an example of virtuous family life.[88] Charles Tennyson pointed out that the proceedings introduced the principle that "royalty may be cashiered for a relaxation of morals."[89] Even the ultraconservative Protestant Irish Orange Order supported the queen.[90] Wilberforce wanted the king to reintroduce her name into the liturgy to help defend the church against incursions by the Methodists.[91] The inhabitants of Taunton told the queen, "The exclusion of Your Majesty's name from the Liturgy of the established church, we regard an indecent anticipation of an anomalous and unjust mode of trial that has been instituted against you, and as being irreconcilably at variance with the genuine spirit of Christianity."[92] The matter was more serious for the Scottish Kirk, which was not under the leadership of the king. A Presbyterian minister pointed out that the king may have been titular head of the Church of England, but not of Scotland, and he had no right to instruct Kirk ministers for whom to pray. Furthermore, the king inflamed the sentiments of those who criticized the church for being dominated by the state.[93] A Scottish minister defied the liturgy by preaching for the queen "as an ornament and a blessing to the nation" and celebrated the independence of the Church of Scotland "who can without restraint send up their prayers unto Thee on behalf of any injured or oppressed individual."[94]

Radicals and plebeian activists were united in their hostility to George IV, but they also expressed some differences in their views of monarchy. Some radicals had long argued that the king should defend the constitution against an oppressive Parliament. This idealized view of a monarch who could take care of the people was now appropriated for Queen Caroline. One spy wrote, "How should I glory . . . if that his Majesty should appear . . . and exclaim If she will be your Queen I will protect her If she will be a mother to my People I will be a Father and Protector to her through Life."[95] In a carnivalesque inversion of monarchy, Caroline could also be a queen of misrule, an icon for the plebeian populace. As Scottish weaver John Mackinnon remembered, "She reigned as Queen in the hearts of the people."[96]

Some radical activists revived the theme of the king as an oriental despot. Intellectual reformers had long suspected the king had pretensions to absolute monarchy, especially because Britain supported the restoration of absolute monarchies after the defeat of Napoleon.[97] By the time of the Caroline affair, the mob shouted that the king was the Grand Turk in his seraglio.[98] George Cruikshank ridiculed the Brighton Pavilion to portray George IV as "the Joss in his Folly" (figure 18). W. J. Fox, a unitarian minister, warned that "only in despotisms is the personal character of the monarch important." He implied that George IV's involvement of Parliament in this divorce, and his own "luxuriating and wantoning in the gratification of every passion," violated the constitutional principle of limited monarchy as well as religious morality.[99] However, while earlier versions of oriental despotism reviled petticoat influence as its essential element, during the Caroline agitation the queen became the heroine of the working

FIGURE 18   George Cruikshank, *The Joss and his Folly*, in William Hone, *The Queen's Matrimonial Ladder*, 44th ed. (London, 1820), p. 18. From author's collection.

classes defying Sultan Sham or Khouli Khan.[100] This trope enabled radicals to contrast Caroline with Queen Charlotte, long suspected of being grasping, avaricious, and power hungry.[101]

The king's body lost its sacred, metaphysical character, instead becoming reduced to a grotesque physicality. One pamphlet compared the king's blubberlike body to cat food.[102] As had Wilkes, caricaturists mocked the regent's phallic potency. For instance, Hone transformed a cannon-shaped "bomb" presented to George by Ferdinand of Spain into a caricatured "bum," and another print claimed to be "A Representation of the Regent's

Tremendous Thing Erected in the Park."[103] Pamphlets described George as an ignorant ne'er-do-well (figure 19):

> All he thinks of is eating, and getting dead drunk,
> Or putting his friends in a deuce of a funk.[104]

Ultraradicals believed that as a despot, the king could legitimately be overthrown. As a radical pamphlet warned,

> That power that made a duke or king,
> Can to the dust the proudest bring![105]

A broadsheet of 1820 called "The Pig of Pall Mall" threatened that the king's throat would be cut; a woman from Commercial Road in the poor East End of London heard some men say "they would have no King, if there was no necessity of a Queen . . . they would draw the inference they could do without a King."[106] Rumors of planned insurrections in the North and Scotland also worried the government. In Newcastle, seven thousand men marched through the streets in "military array" to a meeting in support of the queen.[107]

The huge number of organized, peaceful assemblies again raised the constitutional question of public opinion. The Tories vainly reasserted the notion that Parliament was the only legitimate public. The Reverend Richard Blacow "supported the sacred shield of protection, the banner of the sovereign," against the "democratic mob, under the many-headed mob, the majesty of the people," and furthermore, quoted Burke's address to the electors of Bristol to refute the importance of public opinion.[108] As John Harvey, former mayor, stated at a Norwich public meeting, "I acknowledge to its fullest extent the right of free and fair Political discussion; but I shall as unequivocally maintain that the House of Commons is the legal, constitutional, representative voice of the People."[109]

The constant meetings, addresses, and processions for the queen completely overwhelmed the government's efforts to control what it saw as sedition.[110] In Scotland, Henry Cockburn claimed that the Queen Caroline affair broke the hold of the Tory ministry and local oligarchy over public expression. Defying the provost's prohibition, a largely "middle-class" meeting "was the first modern occasion on which a great body of respectable persons had met, publicly and peaceably, in Edinburgh, to assail this fortress" of conservative hegemony.[111]

The debate over public opinion often centered around the question of class. For Tory J. Webster Wedderburn, the Whigs had usurped the proper predominance of the nobility. Middle-class men stepped beyond their al-

whigs | middle class

FIGURE 19   George Cruikshank, *Qualification*, in William Hone, *The Queen's Matrimonial Ladder*, 44th ed. (London, 1820), p. 18. From author's collection.

lotted sphere of competence, "ill calculated for the great and arduous work inseparable from the counsels of that multifarious thing called a state . . . wholly unacquainted with the constitution with which they are ever attacking and new modeling."[112] When the *Times* dared to question the plausibility of loyalist addresses to the king on the grounds that they were attended only by officeholders, churchmen, aristocrats, and their dependents, *John Bull* responded that these were the only proper people to make such addresses. *John Bull* repudiated any thought that public opinion should matter in the constitution or even that petitions were a legitimate way to address Parliament or the king. The paper did not even accept the constitutionality of the loyal opposition.[113] *John Bull*'s opinions were echoed by the *Loyalist Magazine*, which warned the "different ranks of artisans, trades, companies, orders and classes in this busy nation . . . to be quiet and to mind their own business,—to fear God and the King, and meddle not with those that are given to change."[114]

Conservatives had long warned middle-class and laboring men to stay by their firesides and out of politics. Yet in this time of crisis, some conservatives believed it was necessary to mobilize middle-class political opinion to defend the Crown. To do so, they appealed to their sense of domestic virtue. For instance, one antiqueen commentator declared that in the middling ranks "the virtue and the strength of the Empire mainly rest," but "if the Crown be cast to the ground . . . the pride and comfort of domestic life must perish with it."[115] Opponents of the queen admonished "those men in the middle and humbler ranks of life, to whom domestic peace is dear; . . . who love their King and Country, adore their God" to speak out against Caroline.[116] Conservatives seemed somewhat more likely to mention domesticity than those who demanded political representation for the middle classes, for the liberal Whigs had long insisted on a strict separation of public politics from private virtues or vices.[117]

For many, the Caroline affair demonstrated that the "middling and lower classes" were now the foundation of the constitution instead of the upper classes. Even some conservatives now believed that the middle class could defend the monarchy. At a conservative Norfolk meeting, Mr. Skipper proclaimed, "While the middling Classes (upon whose strength [the constitution] mainly rests), shall continue to take an interest in preserving [the constitution] we shall be safe."[118] Far more often, middle-class language was used to support the queen. As an address from Chipping Sudbury proclaimed, "The highest rank . . . is become the most unsound part of the Constitution. Hence the middle and subordinate ranks must check corruption" and prevent "the total destruction of liberty . . . by a firm and energetic union among themselves."[119] Charles Tennyson asserted that the threat of persecution for sedition deterred "enlightened and disinterested men in the middle and upper walks of life" from "freely declaring their political sentiments," which they had the right to do under the constitution.[120] A poem linked the king's indolence to the wider critique of aristocratic parasitism, which contrasted with industry:

> He has not a penny, save what he obtains
> By making those drudge of less desperate brains
> Nor would he exist, were his victuals confin'd
> To the earnings of either his *hands* or his *mind!*[121]

The conservative Tories, however, tried to impugn the Whigs by linking them with radicals who endangered the constitution.[122] In response, the Whigs explained that the people meant the middle class, not the laboring people. As Lord John Russell argued, "The middle class of people are the determined enemies of both ultra conservatives and seditious radicals."[123] In Newcastle, "Merchants, Bankers, and other inhabitants" called for parliamentary reform in order to save the country from anarchy on the one hand and despotism on the other.[124]

For radicals, as in the duke of York scandal, the affair discredited Whigs, Tories, and Parliament altogether.[125] In fact, the role of the House of Lords in enacting the trial made Parliament complicit in the affair. They were all the corrupt, libertine, borough-mongering faction in the radicals' eyes.[126] One pamphlet questioned the right of the House of Lords to sit in judgment on Caroline, since that institution was full of "rank adulterers, gross libertines, or men of prejudiced minds."[127] A constituent wrote to his member of Parliament that "a corrupt house of commons" unconstitutionally influenced by "an hereditary house of peers" caused low wages, high prices, and the persecution of Caroline.[128]

The Caroline affair also raised the question of women's place in public opinion. It stimulated widespread, organized political mobilization by women of both the working and middle classes. Working-class women were especially prone to identify Caroline with their own woes not only of poverty and taxes but also of their problems in marriage, as I have previously written. But many middle-class women also spoke out on this issue. When the "Ladies of Edinburgh" presented her with a laudatory address, Caroline responded, "The reasons which are employed to annul my marriage have a tendency to render every nuptial obligation fluctuating and insecure. The permanence of the institution would thus be made to depend more on inclination than on principle."[129]

Women's activism was also differentiated by class. While working-class women had taken a public role in elections, radical organizations, and strikes for two decades, they were often reviled as prostitutes for doing so.[130] Middle-class women had just begun organizing associations for missionary and charity work, but the Caroline affair was much more risky for them. As a result, female supporters of Caroline tended to stress their class status and respectability. For instance, a petition to the queen was signed by 17,652 women, all "respectable . . . married women and mistresses of families." Anne Cobbett recounted that one hundred ladies in "full dress" processed to meet the queen in twenty-eight private carriages. They defined them-selves as safe from poverty, from the "middle classes of society," and "unac-customed to public acts, and uninfluenced by party feelings," but they felt that the treatment Caroline faced forced them to leave their "domestic cir-cles" and express their indignation. Of course, they represented the more liberal and radical sector of middle-class opinion, since Mrs. Thelwall, pre-sumably the wife of the radical John Thelwall, read the address. Yet they were not exceptional: as well as the women of London and Edinburgh, women of Aylesbury, Greenwich, and many other locales addressed the queen. The *Times* of London, the pillar of the establishment, supported the middle-class women who processed for the queen.[131] In September alone, a procession of 135 carriages containing the "Married Females, Inhabitants, and Householders of St. Marylebone" visited the queen, and 10,000 "fe-males of Sheffield," 8,000 Halifax women, and 8,321 Edinburgh women signed addresses to her. The affair was also notable for an address to the queen from the Freemason's tavern that was signed by both men and women.[132] Similarly, 150 male and female inhabitants of Taunton signed an address that lauded Caroline's "heroism in personally daring a judicial in-quiry into every part of your conduct."[133] All in all, Nicholas Rogers has cal-culated, "twenty-seven female addresses were presented to Caroline," with over seventy thousand signatures.[134]

Conservatives were horrified at the activism of women of all classes in favor of Caroline.[135] The *Morning Post* described the women who presented addresses to her as "shameless females, who tearing off the veil of modesty with unprecedented audacity, insulted the King."[136] One pamphlet told the story of an army officer who rejected his fiancée because she supported the queen; the writer blamed middle-class women for indulging in expensive habits and encouraging their husbands' ambitions instead of accepting the paternal government.[137] Another writer forthrightly declared, "Let the fe-male look to her family! and leave to the male the management of poli-tics."[138] J. W. Cunningham, the vicar of Harrow, wrote, "This is not a question of mere politics, but of morals . . . all the decencies, virtues, and comforts, of public and domestic life."[139]

Conservatives believed that for a lady to even mention or know of the existence of the trial of Queen Caroline would tarnish her own chastity.[140] However, it was impossible for women to follow this admonition, and instead, they seem to have been intently interested in the trial, if surviving diaries are any evidence.[141] The wife of J. W. Cunningham followed the trial through her husband's participation in the controversy. Similarly, even though Lady Charlotte Grimston disapproved of the queen and feared the mob, she knew details of the trial, since her brother was one of the Lords sitting in judgment.[142] The pious Anna Maria Larpent, wife of the censor of plays, confessed to her diary that she neglected her usual serious historical and religious studies for months, reading little but accounts of the trial. But she, too, disapproved of the king; having toured Carlton House, she found it "gaudy," dirty, and in "bad taste," especially when she noticed a portrait of Madame de Pompadour.[143] The erudite lesbian Anne Lister lamented to herself that gossiping about the queen's affairs distracted her from investigating Latin and Greek poetry.[144] Hannah More found herself obsessed with Caroline, writing to Wilberforce that she feared "her sins occupy my thoughts more than my own."[145]

Paradoxically, the Queen Caroline affair gave a few conservative women an excuse to write on politics, if only to attack the queen.[146] Jane Alice Sargant was the woman most active in writing against Caroline. She justified her intervention in the affair by denying it had anything to do with politics and advised the queen to submit to her husband. After all, when her own husband abandoned her, she at first tried to win back his heart, then retreated to a "dignified retirement." Ironically, her husband's desertion forced her to work as a professional writer.[147]

A few aristocratic women and Whig women stood up for the queen, most notably Lady Jersey (a different Lady Jersey from the king's mistress in the 1790s), Marianne Brougham, and Lady Francis, out of both personal and political sympathies. They visited her at Brandenburgh House, conveying social approbation of her cause. But *John Bull* waged a vicious campaign against any woman who dared visit Caroline. It exposed the fact that Mrs. Brougham had been pregnant before her marriage and revived the rumors of Anne Damer's lesbianism.[148] One lady was even reviled as a servant maid before her marriage to a banker and therefore unfit for elite drawing rooms.[149] Another lady was discredited because her sister once had an affair with a servant, although this accusation opened up *John Bull* to a libel charge.[150] Through its attacks, *John Bull* explicitly warned even aristocratic women to stay out of politics, contributing to the long-term trend.[151] Eventually, it successfully deterred most Whig women from siding with Caroline.[152] As it was, most aristocratic women seem to have disapproved of Caroline, both on moralistic grounds and because it was expedient to do so. Although the king did not control high society, alienating him could cut off a lady from favor at court and the patronage available to her family. Ironically, the king's mistresses still waged a great deal of political influence and patronage, but because they used their sexuality to please a man, not themselves as Caroline had, they could still be received in society.

The Caroline scandal also sustained itself for so long because the country was deeply divided over sexual morality. As in *John Bull*, the government and its sympathizers tried to stir up the power of sexual scandal against Caroline, but loyalist satires tended to be crude and unconvincing.[153] One caricature depicted Caroline in her bath with her breasts exposed, attended by a leering Pergami.[154] However, by explicitly recounting her alleged sexual affairs, counterpropaganda risked being contaminated by the very sexuality it wished to denounce. For instance, a pamphlet entitled *Gynecocracy* blatantly justified the king's adultery in comparison with the queen's on the grounds that female adultery brought with it the dangers of false heirs and female insubordination.[155] *John Bull* and an anti-Caroline pamphlet were both sued for libel for insulting the queen.[156] Fairly or unfairly, the nobility and princes had long been identified with libertinism, so by attacking Caroline's sexual adventures, conservatives risked exciting antagonism against the elite. Indeed, Benbow published a guide to the Lords sitting in trial against Caroline that delineated their individual adulteries and corruptions.[157]

Evangelicals were scandalized by the behavior of both the king and the queen; indeed, they found that the whole affair was much too lubricious. However, they were horrified in large part because the king's and queen's behavior seemed, rightly or wrongly, to typify the upper aristocracy and the royal family. They believed George IV should have settled the affair quietly. The Reverend John Clayton, a Dissenter, rebuked both sides for allowing the affair to "introduce discord into their families" and believed that the "royal and noble should henceforth set a fine pattern of domestic purity and peace to the humble orders."[158]

But Caroline's behavior was not very different from that of other aristocratic women. It was quietly rumored in royal circles that one of George's sisters had given birth to a child after George III and Queen Charlotte refused their consent to her marriage.[159] The duchess of Devonshire and several other women of her circle had children by men not their husbands. The wife of Caroline's own adviser, Brougham, was probably pregnant at the time of their very quiet wedding.[160]

Many radicals and plebeians did not care that Caroline may have had an affair, especially since George IV had abandoned her for so long and flaunted his own mistresses. Philosophic radicals such as Leigh Hunt of the *Examiner* also believed in sexual freedom as a cause. As I have written elsewhere, many plebeians also engaged in common-law marriage and bigamy themselves, so they did not see Caroline's behavior as unusual or unjustifiable.[161] Caroline's supporters simply did not accept the idea that chastity was the most important female virtue. Instead, they admired Caroline for her kindhearted, generous nature. In response to queries from female readers, one woman wrote to the *Norfolk Chronicle* in December 1820 defending Caroline on the grounds of her many charities.[162] Women could also identify with Caroline as a grieving mother.[163] After her death, Dissenting minister John Evans preached that even though she was not "entirely faultless," British females should "imitate" her qualities of "affection and benevolence of soul," "firmness of principle, and fidelity of conduct" when facing persecution, her patience even when ill, her gratitude for the people's support, and her forgiving spirit.[164]

As evidence damaging to the queen emerged in the trial, divisions over sexual morality became more apparent. The government had imported Caroline's former servants from Italy to testify against her. Theodore Majocci told the Lords that he saw Pergami go into the queen's bath and alleged that they slept together under a tent on board ship. Chambermaid Barbara Kress saw the queen's cloak on Pergami's bed and the imprint of two bodies on her sheets.[165] But the witnesses' reputations were undermined when it became clear the government paid their expenses: Majocci famously responded, "Non mi ricordo" (I don't remember) when asked how much he received. Brougham had ably defended the queen, discrediting the witnesses as foreign hirelings, and pointed out that there was no concrete evidence that she had committed adultery. In response, the inhabitants of Taunton regarded the trial as "a tissue of testimony from discarded servants invited by an inquisitorial commission."[166] Caroline's supporters indignantly argued that Pergami had to stay close to her to protect her from the king's hired assassins.[167] For others, the witnesses' testimony was horrifying evidence of the queen's immorality, but the government, by bringing forward such prurient sexual evidence to be printed in the newspaper, damaged the cause of morality as well.[168] Toward the end of the trial, middle-class opinion seemed to turn against the queen.

In weighing their judgment, however, the Lords considered not only the evidence but also the consequences of a verdict. Above all, the constant meetings, processions, and addresses outside of Saint Stephens Hall seemed to threaten dire consequences if they defied the wishes of the people and voted to condemn the queen. Lady Harrowby indignantly asked Greville, "If the House of Lords was to suffer itself to be influenced by the opinions and wishes of the people, it would be the most mean and pusillanimous conduct, and that after all what did it signify what the people thought or what they expressed if the army was to be depended upon?" Greville answered, "I never had expected that the day would come in which I should be told that we were to disregard the feelings and wishes of the people of this country, and to look to our army for support."[169] The Lords realized that it was not politically feasible to keep on prosecuting the queen. The bill against the queen, it was finally realized, would win with a majority of only nine, not strong enough to send it to the Commons. The government dropped the bill, and the persecution of the queen ended.

Radicals celebrated the queen's acquittal as the triumph of liberty and the free press over the heavy-handed government, army, and oppressive legal system (see figure 20). Caroline's supporters organized a massive thanksgiving ceremony at Saint Paul's Cathedral, which demonstrated the rare and temporary unity of moderates and radicals, middle-class and working-class support. Charles Churchill, a London wood broker, described the procession as "very good humoured & peaceable—Lord Mayor and Sheriffs in State . . . Lady Ann Hamilton etc. Queen very fat but good looking—numerous cavalcades of horsemen, journeymen, masters, clerks, tinkers, and tailors—and one bumpkin, absolutely dressed in a smock frock, round hat covered with laurel."[170] All across the country, even in sleepy towns and tiny villages such as Berkampstead, bells rang and windows were illuminated in her support.[171] The outpouring of support for Caroline also demonstrated the determination of working-class and liberal citizens to assert their independence of traditional Tory urban oligarchies that attempted to block celebrations of the queen's acquittal, as Nicholas Rogers observes.[172] For instance, the "small tradesmen and working classes" of Lynn defied the mayor, aldermen, "and most respectable inhabitants" to illuminate their windows in honor of the queen.[173]

Many feared—or hoped—that the vote would be enough to fell the government and deeply embarrass the king. Some Whig members of Parliament introduced a motion two months later rebuking the government for its persecution of the queen and "calling for parliamentary reform." But the motion failed; although the Lords may have voted for the queen to "appease the

FIGURE 20 George Cruikshank, *Transparency,* in William Hone, *The Political Showman—at Home* (London, 1821), p. 3. From author's collection. This transparency, printed on very thin paper, was intended to be pasted up in windows and illuminated from behind to celebrate the queen's acquittal.

lower orders," they seem to have instructed their clients in the Commons to vote against the motion, perhaps to ensure the government's survival.[174]

By 1821, the tenuous alliance of Whigs and working-class radicals had broken down. Whigs and moderates tended to recast their politics to differentiate themselves from working-class radicals, but they continued to call for reform. The *Declaration of the People of England to their Sovereign Lord the King* criticized the queen and emphasized the loyalty of the "plain people, in the *Middle ranks* of life," to the established order but hinted that a "reasonable reform" would benefit the country.[175] At a meeting in Morpeth, Northumberland, in January 1821, called in defiance of the sheriff, Whigs asserted their loyalty to the Crown but called for parliamentary reform.[176] For Charles Maclean, the only way to save the crown was to institute parliamentary reform.[177]

Eventually, much of the middle-class support of the queen faded away, but working-class people wildly defended her. However, her heart was broken, and she was humiliated when she tried to attend her husband's coronation and was turned away at the door. She also lost allies by accepting a large annuity from the government. Caroline died a few months later, in 1821, of a bowel obstruction. Many in the nation grieved. In the tiny village of Bishops Hull, Somerset, the churchwardens voted to borrow black cloth to cover "the Clergyman's desk and pulpit in our parish on the occasion of the death of our late Queen Caroline Consort of the Realm."[178] Ministers preached sermons on her death combining religious sentiment with radical opinion.[179] The Unitarian W. J. Fox articulated the conditional loyalty of many middle-class people. For him, monarchy may be necessary, but the king should, like his late father, prove his domestic virtue instead of allowing his private passions to interfere with the state.[180] Independent preacher John Evans preached in Malmsbury, Wiltshire, that religion justifies radical political action: he prayed that "the Tree of Liberty may strike its roots throughout the world . . . that Religion may extend its sacred influence."[181] In London, sorrow became more dramatic, as Caroline's funeral procession sparked a riot and the military shot two supporters dead. But lacking a focus, the scandal was over.

The king's popularity rebounded, but more than ever it was recognized that it depended on public opinion. Henry Bathurst, the archdeacon of Norwich, was thankful "that the influence of public opinion" saved the queen from ruin, but also "preserved the original compact of a free government from at least an apparent violation."[182] As Dror Wahrman shows, all now agreed that public opinion had a legitimate place in the constitution.[183]

CONCLUSION

The prime instigators of this scandal, the king and queen, had tried to deploy the power of politics to solve their personal problems. The king, taking actions many saw as unconstitutional, manipulated ministers and Parliament in an unsuccessful effort to obtain a divorce. Caroline forged alliances with Whigs and radicals, turning to the power of the street to embarrass her husband. In turn, politicians took advantage of the scandal for their own political ends. The Whigs, such as Brougham, wished to advance their own party's interest. Radicals wanted to overcome severe censorship and repression to revive the parliamentary reform movement. They succeeded because this scandal enabled them to use sexual narratives to represent larger issues of the constitution and class, and because, at least at first, the scandal appealed to both middle-class and working-class audiences.

What was the long-term impact of the Caroline scandal? Over the course of the 1820s, its impact on women's place in politics was mixed. The vicious right-wing attacks on Caroline's female supporters made it difficult for women, especially those in the middle class, to address their own woes in public.[184] However, middle-class women did start to form their own associations, such as antislavery associations, by 1826; could their public activity in 1820 have provided a precedent? For working-class women, processing in public was nothing new, and later in the 1820s ultraradicals began to explore the sexual politics of marriage.

The working-class movement, however, did not sustain its momentum immediately after the scandal ebbed, unable to transcend the cause of Caroline and build a more massive movement. The push for parliamentary reform took a backseat to industrial action in the hard times of the 1820s. The always-tenuous alliance with the Whigs dissolved once again.

The Whigs capitalized most successfully on the affair. While they "failed to topple the government" and lost their 1821 motion for moderate parliamentary reform, they succeeded in justifying public meetings for reform and portraying themselves as the movement's leaders.[185] In 1822, they persisted with reform motions, changing the paradigms of the debate to emphasize middle-class respectability.[186] In Scotland, the Caroline affair contributed to the eventual passage of borough reform, destroying the hold of the Tory oligarchy.[187]

In the end, the Caroline affair may have affirmed popular royalism, but it also changed it. According to conservative doctrine, the people owed unquestioning obedience to the monarch and should trust in Parliament to represent their political opinions. Ever since the 1790s, popular royalism depended on the individual behavior of the monarch as well as his position; people loved George III for his domestic virtues as much as he awed them by his splendor. But the Mary Ann Clarke and Queen Caroline affairs damaged the prestige of both Crown and Parliament, exposing a system of corruption and injustice. To defend the established order, conservatives tried to combat scandal with counterpropaganda, but given the royal brother's libertinism, they risked being contaminated by the very vices they abhorred. More successfully, they tried to stir up popular loyalism and patriotism, organizing meetings to defend the Crown. In doing so, conservatives continued to establish a precedent for middle-class participation in politics, as they had done with loyalist and patriotic associations during the Napoleonic Wars. And conservatives could not credibly inculcate loyalty to George IV by lauding his personal virtues. Instead, they celebrated the Crown as a symbol of the established order, of church, king, and empire—the throne rather than its occupant.

" the m.c.'s blood is its ok"

⊷ ⊷ ⊷

CHAPTER NINE

Sexual Scandals and Politics,
Past and Present

L ate eighteenth-century and early nineteenth-century scandals followed distinctive patterns. These patterns contributed to changes in British politics, society, and gender roles that became evident at the beginning of the nineteenth century. Furthermore, by anatomizing scandal in the past, the significance of scandal in the present can be better understood.

PATTERNS OF SCANDAL

Scandals began when gossip became public; the instigators of scandal chose specific moments to reveal rumors that had long circulated behind the scenes. For instance, Mary Wollstonecraft's love life only stirred up gossip during her life, but after her death, Godwin's memoirs enabled conservatives to discredit both radicalism and feminism at a moment of crisis during the Napoleonic Wars. Pamphleteers hinted for two years that mistresses of the duke of York bought and sold army commissions, but Mary Anne Clarke's role did not become public until two preconditions were met: first, her efforts to blackmail the duke had failed, so she was willing to exploit the public concern of politicians; second, activism had revived, and reformers felt able to defy government censorship. Caroline did not become a radical heroine in 1806, when the prince regent first investigated her behavior; in that year, William Cobbett criticized her as just another immoral parasite. By 1820, the year after the Peterloo massacre had almost crushed their movement, Cobbett and other radicals seized her cause as a chance to embarrass the new king.

Scandals about private behavior also acquired a public significance when they were used to symbolize wider political debates. To serve as a symbol, sexual rumors could be invented, as when Wilkes claimed the princess dowager had sex with the prime minister, or when Burke portrayed Hastings as a vicious violator of Indian princesses. Despite their implausibility, these images of sexual malfeasance served to represent constitutional issues through symbols and stories. Burke, for instance, was trying to arouse public anger against British abuses in India.

If governments attempted to censor sexual stories and images about royalty or ministers, they ran the risk of further publicizing embarrassing rumors. For instance, when the government prosecuted Wilkes for privately publishing his pornographic *Essay on Woman*, it inspired incredible curiosity about the suppressed essay's contents. As a result, others wrote their own faux essays, which contained even more virulent denunciations of alleged petticoat influence and sodomy at court: Instigators of scandal had to use explicit language to expose sexual misbehavior, but they risked being contaminated by sexual language themselves. Burke tried to draw public attention to Hastings's actions in India by blaming him for sexual tortures of Indian women, but the explicit, voyeuristic tone of his speech eventually tainted his testimony. George IV undercut his own popularity by forcing Parliament to air his wife's dirty laundry in public—in the most literal sense, as her maid testified as to the state of her sheets.

Scandals personified political issues, but reputations could change quickly. The target of a scandal could try to reverse the plot, depicting the instigator as a villain and himself as a victim. When the government tried to turn scandal against Wilkes by prosecuting him as a blasphemous pornographer, Wilkes accused the government of repressing the people's freedom. Supporters celebrated his libertinism as a love for liberty. Even if people knew he was a rogue playing a part, they enjoyed his flair. Burke tried to portray himself as the hero who would rescue India; but over the course of the impeachment, Hastings's supporters cleverly manipulated the press to depict Burke as a fiendish prosecutor with a vendetta against Hastings, the hero who saved India. George IV tried to destroy his wife's reputation with the Delicate Investigation, but eventually, his people saw him as hypocritical for persecuting the wife he had abandoned.

Instigators of scandals often became unreliable narrators when their plausibility was damaged and their self-interest revealed. Wilkes's status as popular hero eroded when he used funds raised for the people's rights on his mistresses and fine wines. Burke lost credibility when his audience realized that he had exaggerated or misread much of the evidence against Hastings; his emotive rhetoric now seemed like castles in the air. Radicals lauded Mary Anne Clarke as a heroine for revealing royal corruption, but when she sold her memoirs to the Crown, it became apparent that she would sell her story to the highest bidder.

Politicians effectively exploited scandal by arousing the fears of the broadest possible audience. In the 1784 elections, Pitt's supporters denigrated Charles James Fox and the duchess of Devonshire as libertine gamblers. In doing so, they appealed both to moralistic provincial liberals who trusted Pitt to push moderate reform and to conservatives who feared Fox's populist message. Hastings initially restricted his pragmatic defense to a narrow group of East India Company stockholders and politicians, while Burke aimed beyond Parliament to the humanitarian public. Hastings's defenders gained ground only when they reached out to this wider audience, arguing that "barbaric" India needed Britain to rescue it.

Allies could also help women defy scandal. The duchess of Devonshire drew upon the Whig organization to defend her from insult, and some debating societies celebrated female canvassing. Queen Caroline appealed to radical organizations—and skillfully manipulated politicians—to further her case. However, the feminists of the 1790s did not form associations that could have pressured society to change unfair laws that oppressed women or defended Mary Wollstonecraft posthumously against scandal.

Ultimately, scandals could have a long-lasting political impact only when they transcended their instigators and protagonists to focus on wider issues, and when they generated political associations with the power to pressure Parliament. Wilkes equated his persecution at the hands of the government with the dangers British people faced from censorship and excisemen. He organized Middlesex voters and helped begin the Bill of Rights Society, which provided an important precedent for the later Association movement. As the Mary Anne Clarke affair accelerated, citizens called public meetings to protest against Parliament and revive the movement for reform. Burke failed in his campaign against Hastings, in part, because he did not mobilize humanitarian public opinion, unlike the antislavery movement. When activists did organize public opinion in 1813, they forced significant changes to the East India Company's charter.

SCANDAL AND POLITICAL CHANGE IN BRITAIN

Scandals contributed to changes in British politics in the late eighteenth and early nineteenth centuries. Some historians have argued that a conservative consensus united British society, as the people deferred to royal and aristocratic leadership. While Britain, unlike France, did not experience a revolution, in part this was because the government responded more effectively to scandals. Even so, scandals seriously undermined the consensus by exposing conflict over three main constitutional issues around the monarch, Parliament, and public opinion.

Wilkes used scandal to undermine the king's prerogative to choose personally a minister who did not have support in Parliament. Wilkes satirically alleged that George III chose Lord Bute as prime minister because Bute had a sexual affair with the king's mother. Similarly, after the king and Pitt engineered Fox's fall from power, Fox accused Pitt of exerting "backstairs influence" over the Crown and even insinuated that Pitt sexually desired men. By linking a prime minister's power with illicit sex, Fox and Wilkes wished to sabotage the legitimacy of his influence. Of course, neither Fox nor Wilkes succeeded in abolishing the king's prerogative to appoint his minister. By defeating Fox in the 1784 election, Pitt firmly buttressed the king's right to choose his chief minister, recasting the king as the defender of the people against an aristocratic faction. However, because Pitt triumphed in an election largely on the strength of public opinion, the king's popularity increasingly rested on the people's assent.

The government constructed an image of the king as a splendid monarch, a defender of the constitution, and a benevolent father of his people. But many radicals and Whigs insisted that the king's private virtues as a father could not compensate for the public oppressions of his government. Even for those who loved the king as father, this image still depended on the individual monarch's virtues. The duke of York and George IV squandered their father's popularity with their outrageous decadence and corruption. Radicals revived the motif of oriental despotism to depict George IV as ruling without law, indulging his mistresses, building Chinese palaces, and suppressing the legal rights of the people to freedom of speech and assembly. Although the monarchy survived the Queen Caroline affair, its personal clout had been discredited, and the monarchy now depended almost totally on public opinion.

Parliament's function as a court also lost credibility in many of these scandals. Royalty exploited Crown influence over Parliament for their personal purposes. In the Clarke affair, the government hoped that a public inquiry at the bar of the House of Commons would defuse public outrage, but the ministers did not follow the legal rules of evidence. The duke of York also declared that Parliament should just take his word as a "man of honor" that he was innocent. This process, however, undermined the belief that the English legal system treated a prince and a commoner the same. Most egregiously, George IV went against his ministers' advice to put his wife on trial for adultery in the House of Lords, revealing that Parliament still had to follow the personal whims of the sovereign. However, the defeat of the Bill of Pains and Penalties also revealed Parliament's vulnerability to public opinion.

The Whigs tried to use scandal to portray Parliament as the defender of the people against an overweening Crown. But they also abused Parliament's function as a court in the Hastings impeachment. Burke and Fox turned the process into an inquisition by suppressing the conventional rules of evidence. When a critic impugned Parliament's motive in persecuting Hastings, Fox charged him with seditious libel for undermining the dignity of the House of Commons.[1]

Scandals helped radicals shift constitutional debates away from the problem of king versus Parliament, to the problem of Parliament versus the people. Wilkes had first defended himself against a charge of sedition by arguing that as a member of Parliament, he was guaranteed free speech by the Bill of Rights. But he quickly realized that the privileges of Parliament excluded the rest of the people from rights—the Bill of Rights had failed to extend freedom of speech to them. The Commons revealed its scorn for the people when it overturned Wilkes's victory in the Middlesex election. In the 1784 Westminster election, Fox tried to present the Whigs as the defenders of the liberties of the people in the struggle against the Crown. But radicals believed that illicit aristocratic influence in Parliament posed the real problem. In the 1784 election, for instance, they accused the duchess of Devonshire of exerting petticoat influence to give the peers unconstitutional power in the Commons. By the 1790s, feminists such as Catherine Macaulay and Mary Wollstonecraft denounced the whole parliamentary system as irredeemably corrupt. The Commons lost credibility in the duke of York affair by refusing to vote for him to resign, revealing that many members responded more to royal and aristocratic influence than to public opinion. However, the Whigs most successfully took advantage of the Queen Caroline affair to revive their version of parliamentary reform.

In the long term, these scandals contributed to the recognition that the people belonged in the constitution as the public. Until the Caroline affair, most conservatives insisted that Parliament was the only legitimate forum for political debate and organization. But the outrage inspired by scandal sometimes helped radicals and reformers to organize the people as the public. During the Wilkes agitation, the movement for constitutional reform mobilized, sowing the seeds for the later Association movement. By the time of the French Revolution, the government realized that it needed to encourage conservative associations such as "church and king" and loyalist clubs to form—implicitly allowing people to organize independently of Parliament.[2] The duke of York affair broke down the fragile patriotic consensus that all public opinion had to support the government and resurrected the parliamentary reform movement. By the time of the queen's trial, conservatives had to acknowledge the power of public opinion.

Scandals had their greatest impact in opening up the press to public debate. Of course, in times when scandals did not rock the nation, radicals often challenged government control of the press and prosecutions for seditious libel.[3] But during times of crisis, scandal could overcome repression. For instance, Wilkes demonstrated that the general warrant the government used to seize his papers was unconstitutional. Wilkes also pushed for the 1771 Printers' Case, which allowed newspapers to publish parliamentary debates, opening the Commons to public scrutiny. Governments had tried to control the press through subsidies, paying newspapers to spin rumors off or suppress scandals. But by 1809, large circulations outweighed government subsidies. Readers bought newspapers at times of war, political crisis—or scandal. If newspapers failed to print every detail of the Mary Anne Clarke investigation or the queen's trial, no one would read their columns. Scandals produced more satirical material than the government could control, especially caricatures and parodies. This was most striking in the Queen Caroline affair, which erupted a few months after the severe repression following Peterloo.

Scandals also reveal some of the nascent class tensions of eighteenth-century and early nineteenth-century England. Aristocratic and royal influence and patronage dominated eighteenth-century politics. For the aristocratic elite and those who depended on them, this system was legitimate. However, instigators of scandals undercut the excuse that benevolence or the public good motivated influence and patronage because they alleged that personal, even sexual, interest lay behind influence. Even before middle-class people explicitly articulated their own separate interests, they often expressed resentment at royals and aristocrats who gained high positions and lucrative sinecures through influence and connections instead of merit; they wished Britain would live up to its ideals as an efficient, competent government. By the first two decades of the nineteenth century, scandals contributed to a growing middle-class consciousness and helped set the stage for the 1832 Reform Act.[4] Laboring people felt angry that the taxes that deprived their families of bread paid for the gambling, mistresses, and palaces of the elite. Scandals about aristocratic and royal sexual corruption thus appealed to both middle-class and plebeian audiences, potentially overcoming class divisions. As a result of the Clarke affair, Parliament was forced to pass significant legislation prohibiting the sale of seats in the Commons and positions in the government. Influence and patronage remained, but they began to diminish. To be sure, these scandals only eroded aristocratic dominance; they did not destroy it. Even with the 1832 Reform Act, the aristocracy still largely controlled Parliament.

When politicians acknowledged the place of the people during the Caroline affair, they considered the middle class to be the people, not the working class.[5] When politicians tried to manipulate these scandals to incite crowds, they could not always control working people, who had their own agendas, as Nicholas Rogers points out.[6] Radicals responded to scandals with much more fundamental goals: to transform the parliamentary system with universal suffrage and to change the economic system that oppressed the working class.

SCANDAL, SEXUALITY, AND GENDER

Some scandals became so drawn out during this period because British people did not experience a consensus around sexual morality. Many British people, from the laboring poor, to middle-class tradesmen, to aristocrats, espoused a strict sexual code based on self-control and chastity, often derived from Evangelical, Dissenting, or Church of England beliefs. But others followed looser sexual codes: aristocratic men who kept mistresses, great ladies who took lovers, tradesmen who frequented prostitutes, laboring people who engaged in common-law marriages. When conservatives attacked Wilkes or Fox and the duchess of Devonshire as libertines, their supporters responded by celebrating libertinism and liberty. Many Britons felt that Caroline was justified in taking a lover, since the prince abandoned her and committed adultery himself. Evangelicals, however, warned the aristocracy that they must reform their morals or lose their dominance.

In contrast to traditional conservatives, who tended to equate order in the family and the state, many liberals and radicals insisted that the public and the private must be judged on different terms. Wilkes, for instance, declared that his debauchery was irrelevant to his service to the public; all that mattered was his political contribution. He asserted his right to try out radical religious, political, and even sexual ideas in the privacy of his own study, and he attacked the government for prosecuting him for pornography. But sexual scandals also exposed the double standard behind liberal understandings of the public and private. Wilkes failed to respect the privacy of others, obsessively attacking what he termed "sodomites" and denigrating his former ally Catherine Macaulay when she married a younger man. For Wilkes, privacy was the right to do what he wanted in his own home, but only the male head of household could enjoy those rights. In contrast, by the 1790s, Catherine Macaulay and Mary Wollstonecraft asserted that women needed private as well as public rights. Women needed the right to leave unhappy marriages and to support themselves, as Wollstonecraft argued. Women's character should not be judged solely on their chastity, they argued, but according to their wisdom, benevolence, and courage.

Scandals can also illuminate the debate about women in public in the late eighteenth and early nineteenth centuries. Some historians assert that women advanced into the public sphere during this period; others see attitudes toward women in politics becoming increasingly negative.[7] Most of the scandals described in this book aimed to push women out of politics, but to assess their success, we must differentiate women by class and nation and delineate the different roles women took in public.

Some aristocratic women had long been able to exert power in politics through their dynastic influence, social connections, or control over their tenants' votes. But radicals vastly exaggerated the importance of petticoat influence in order to attack aristocratic dominance as a whole. Wilkesite caricatures alleged that the road to preferment lay beneath the princess dowager's skirts; radicals criticized the duchess of Devonshire for pressuring tradesmen to vote for the Whigs. Only when Mary Anne Clarke arrived on the scene could petticoat influence be proved as a reality, as she and other ladies were exposed as trading in places in the army, church, and state. Interestingly, although both she and Queen Caroline profited from the system of patronage, Clarke by selling promotions and Caroline by receiving £30,000 a year from the Crown, they enjoyed the approbation of radicals who usually scorned petticoat influence, because they defied Parliament and the king. But they could not gain any independent power themselves.

Conservatives also used the motif of petticoat influence to punish their political enemies. The scandal against the duchess of Devonshire drove her away from canvassing for years. In 1806, conservative Norfolk Whigs insulted two Tory ladies who had canvassed for their opponent, flamboyantly waving pink and purple party colors. To imitate them, the Whigs hired two prostitutes, dressed them in pink and purple, and drew them in a carriage about town; the message was clear.[8] Of course, some aristocratic women continued to campaign without exciting comment: scandal would be incited only if they acted too autonomously as political entrepreneurs, or if radicals attacked them as exerting unfair aristocratic influence. By the mid–nineteenth century, most aristocratic women withdrew from party politics, which had become much more formal; their public participation might remind voters of unseemly aristocratic influence.[9]

Like aristocratic ladies, the Begums of Oudh and Munny Begum derived their considerable clout from their dynastic connections. While they were not typical of Indian women, their power confused British officials. These officials often assumed that Indian women would be passive and confined in purdah, but following the discourse of oriental despotism, they also feared that Indian women would intrigue behind the veil and disrupt the polity. As with the scandal involving the duchess of Devonshire, politicians used women's activities to symbolize larger political concerns about who should govern India.

The female public intellectual exerted a different kind of influence, respected more for her opinions than her connections. A few middle-class and elite women had long enjoyed access to literary culture, but Catherine Macaulay was one of the first late eighteenth-century women to attain acclaim as a public intellectual speaking out on politics and history. Scandal discredited her when she married a much younger man. By the 1780s, the debating society women established a more collective female presence in the realm of public discussion and began to stir up debate over women's political position. In the 1790s, even more women became respected for their writings on politics and religion. Mary Wollstonecraft, after all, made her name by refuting Burke's *Reflections on the Revolution in France* before she began to revolutionize ideas of women's place. By 1798, scandal significantly muted women's ability to function as public intellectuals, let alone feminists. The conservative Richard Polwhele used the revelations of Godwin's memoirs of the late Wollstonecraft to stigmatize as a prostitute any woman who wrote on politics, science, or religion.

Hannah More publicized an alternative, and much more successful, role for middle-class women—that of female domestic influence. She advised women to shrink from the rough-and-tumble political world but to exercise a beneficent moral influence through their families, churches, schools, and neighborhoods. Middle-class women could aid the conservative cause by inculcating submission into the poor. Yet scandal turned against More as well. When she asserted too much authority over religion, Church of England traditionalists accused her of Methodism—and taking lovers. This ridiculous allegation reveals that when women were accused of sexual misconduct, the real trigger for scandal was often their autonomy, not their sexuality.

Working-class women also faced scandal when they stepped into politics. For instance, in 1802, twenty-four young working-class women processed for a radical candidate in Nottingham, dressed in white and supporting their community's cause of manhood suffrage. As part of an effort to overturn the radical victory, a conservative pamphleteer claimed that these women were prostitutes accompanying a half-naked Goddess of Liberty. He equated their alleged unchastity with the radical threat of universal manhood suffrage. However, for the working-class voters, these young women, ornamented with wreaths of flowers and laurel leaves, represented the solidarity of their community.[10] Similarly, in an 1807 Yorkshire election, working women who joined crowds for a radical candidate were stigmatized as "cyprians," or women of the street.[11] Eventually, working-class women defied the fear of scandal to form their own radical political associations between 1815 and 1819, ignoring conservative caricaturists who mocked them as animalistic, half-naked harridans. Unlike the feminists of the 1790s, however, they concentrated on the collective rights of their communities, speaking out for their families' survival rather than individual female rights. Yet by 1820, working-class and more radical middle-class women organized to defend Queen Caroline—and their own marital rights.

Scandal pushed most middle-class and aristocratic women out of politics; to avoid its sting, female activists had to defy conservative proscriptions and create alternatives to conventional politics, or evade scandal by portraying their actions as feminine and apolitical. In 1802–7, middle-class women helped in elections in Norwich and Yorkshire, for instance, but they stayed behind the scenes. Their husbands and fathers toasted them as "female patriots" but did not invite them to join the victory banquets.[12] Perhaps for this reason, middle-class women organized formal associations much later than middle-class men or working-class women; the first female antislavery organization came in 1826. Until the 1840s, middle-class women tended to define their activities as philanthropic or humanitarian rather than political.

Masculinity also changed during this period as instigators took advantage of scandal to develop notions of manhood that could potentially transcend class. Wilkes's political rhetoric drew on the learned traditions of classical republicanism, celebrating the Roman citizen, but he also exploited the male bonding of plebeian club culture to organize London voters. In contrast to the polished, obsequious manner of the gentleman seeking favor from the court, Wilkes asserted the freedom of the independent man, whether he were an entrepreneur or an artisan. His hard-drinking manly image allowed the adventurer Andrew Stoney Bowes to gain support from Newcastle radicals despite his aristocratic connections. But this libertine masculinity could excuse abusive behavior toward women; Newcastle voted for Bowes as a member of Parliament despite the rumors that he savagely beat his wife, the countess of Strathmore. Fox and Wilkes also tried to appeal to popular hostility against men who desired other men, solidifying the stereotype of the "sodomite" as cowardly, effeminate, corrupt, and exclusively interested in men.

Libertine masculinity, however, faced competition from a different model of manhood: the sober, restrained fatherhood of religious, often Dissenting, middle-class men. Rejecting classical republicanism's focus on public rather than family life, these men believed that private life was the source of political virtue. For liberals and humanitarians, this new model of manhood could impel political engagement. Conservatives, in contrast, advised middle-class men to stay by their own firesides and trust the government with affairs of state, especially during the Napoleonic Wars. Yet middle-class men entered politics when concern over taxes—or a fresh scandal—outraged them once again.[13]

The increasing influence of the Evangelical movement also forced aristocratic men to curb their excesses, especially after George IV so egregiously took advantage of the double standard to prosecute his wife while flaunting his own mistresses. Of course, many aristocratic men never lived up to this stereotype, being as family-oriented and quiet as middle-class men. But public image was all; politicians had to adjust to new political realities. Mid-eighteenth-century politicians, such as the duke of Grafton, could strut at court like peacocks with their mistresses and condescend to inferiors expecting patronage. William Pitt the younger was a transitional figure, still enmeshed in patronage and drinking heavily, but ruthlessly efficient. But, as Paul Langford argues, the acceptable mid-nineteenth-century statesman, with notable exceptions, was "discreet in manner, unpretentious in appearance, keeping his warmth for his home and hearth, disdainful of men and their wants, devoted to public duties."[14]

SCANDALS CHANGE FROM THE EIGHTEENTH TO THE NINETEENTH CENTURY

Between 1763 and 1821, the style of scandalous stories began to shift. Satire dominated the Wilkes affair and other attacks on political personalities. It bridged the old personal politics of scandal, aimed at individuals, and the newer radical politics, aimed at the whole political order. Sexual satire, in particular, undermined the dynastic clout of the monarchy by casting doubt on the legitimacy of the heir—or on the whole concept of dynastic privilege. Radical satire could neatly skewer conservative claims that order in the family was necessary for order in the state, pointing out the hypocrisy of ministers calling for Christian virtue by day and calling for their mistresses by night.

By the time of the Hastings affair, a new genre, gothic romance—the ancestor of melodrama—appeared on the stage of scandal. Burke and Sheridan used the conventions of orientalist novels to depict Hastings as a villain who oppressed Indian princesses. While satire focused on the villain, destroying him through ridicule, gothic romance concentrated on the victim, eliciting sympathy for her sufferings. Furthermore, the victim could stand for a category of the oppressed—in the Hastings affair, the people of India. Mary Wollstonecraft also used the genre of gothic romance to convey her anger at women's mistreatment in marriage.

Burke's use of gothic romance failed, trumped by satire. Hastings and the government often paid caricaturists to ridicule Burke's bombastic rhetoric, but many unsubsidized satirists found him to be an irresistible target. By the 1790s, conservatives turned satire to their own ends. These shifts in the use of satire can be seen in changing imitations of Juvenal, the Roman poet. For instance, Charles Churchill, Wilkes's friend, emulated Juvenal to attack the court as riddled by "sodomites" and aristocratic petticoat influence. But by the 1790s, conservatives also took up Juvenal, alluding to his Sixth Satire to portray feminists such as Mary Wollstonecraft as promiscuous harridans who undermined the social order.[15]

By 1820, radicals deployed both satire and melodrama in the Caroline affair. Satire turned the king's royal body into a ridiculous mound of flesh, as in the poem depicting George IV as "pig's meat." Melodrama enabled working people to identify with the queen's woes, as both felt they were victims of royal oppression. By the 1830s, satire and caricature seriously declined in the press, while melodrama flourished both on the stage and in radical rhetoric.[16] Melodrama may be a more powerful weapon than satire. Satire incites laughter, but laughter can just serve as a safety valve or a form of entertainment; the spectator stands at a safe remove from the action. Melodrama stirs up sorrow and anger, pity and empathy, shame and guilt; the spectator identifies with the victim or feels impelled to rescue her. In the 1830s, radicals took up the motif of melodrama, especially the image of the aristocratic libertine seducing the poor girl, to symbolize exploitation of the working class, as I have written earlier. Melodramatic rhetoric helped motivate the rage of antifactory and anti–poor law movements.[17]

In the eighteenth century, sexual scandal had focused on the aristocracy and their influence as individuals, which seemed to corrupt the state. In the nineteenth century, the sexuality of collective groups—working class, prostitutes, homosexuals—seemed to threaten the state and impel it into action. The government regulated their sexual behavior through the New Poor Law, the Contagious Diseases Acts, and the criminal justice system. By the second half of the nineteenth century, Victorian society also seemed to form a greater consensus around sexual morality than had been apparent in the eighteenth century. Scandals could flare up about the adultery of prominent politicians, but Victorians generally agreed that adultery was wrong: a contrast with the duke of York, who flaunted his affair with Mary Anne, or Queen Caroline, whose supporters argued that she was justified in taking a lover. Beneath the surface, cracks in this consensus appeared, as radicals and feminists objected to the exploitation of women that Victorian probity concealed.

The White Slave Scandal became one of the largest controversies in late nineteenth-century England. Female activists had already been agitating against the Contagious Diseases Acts, which forced many women in garrison and port towns to register as prostitutes and submit to medical examinations for venereal disease. This led to a wider attack on the exploitation of prostitution. As Judith Walkowitz has written, crusading journalist W. T. Stead fueled the flames of the controversy when he purchased a thirteen-year-old girl from her mother in order to expose the problem of child prostitution in the pages of his *Pall Mall Gazette*. Nevertheless, Stead was revealed as an unreliable narrator when he was put on trial for the abduction of the girl. He was contaminated by the very sexuality he wished to expose. However, the scandal transcended its unreliable narrator and created a political impact because female activists and working-class men organized monster demonstrations in protest at the sexual exploitation of poor girls that Stead had revealed. In response, Parliament changed the age of consent for girls to sixteen and passed the Criminal Law Amendment Act of 1885, which punished indecent assault, regulated prostitution—and further criminalized sexual behavior between men.[18]

SEX SCANDALS AND CONTEMPORARY POLITICS

What are the implications of these scandals for today? The monarchy lost its political power in the nineteenth century, replaced by a raison d'être as a fantasy of ideal family life. But the unhappy marriages of the British royal family now reflect the changes in contemporary marriage. Royal scandals continue to fascinate, but instead of serving as political metaphors, they tell us about society's lost illusions. Conservative Tory politicians such as Margaret Thatcher and John Major attempted to revive "Victorian values" and traditional family mores, in an effort to stigmatize feminism, the lesbian and gay rights movement, and the left as immoral and irresponsible. However, John Major's government faced a series of sex scandals in 1997, when his ministers and leading members of Parliament were revealed to be carousing with seventeen-year-old girls—or boys. Far more serious scandals brought down his government, of course, as the media revealed that members of Parliament received huge bribes in brown paper bags. But since sex scandal fuels circulation, some of the traditionally Tory tabloids published the sexual shenanigans of ministers even though they damaged the Conservative cause.[19]

More seriously, Britain's unwritten constitution is in the process of revision. The issue of freedom of speech has long been vexed; after all, Margaret Thatcher tried to censor news about the IRA, and her government imprisoned a young civil servant who sent news of nuclear cruise missiles stationed in Britain to the *Guardian* newspaper. At the same time, tabloids managed to expose the most intimate details of even ordinary people's lives. The overweening power of Parliament, so eloquently revealed by Catherine Macaulay and other eighteenth-century radicals, remains a continuing problem, albeit in a different guise. The monarch, of course, has no power over Parliament; the House of Lords has been purged of most of its peers. Instead, the prime minister, with a majority in the Commons, can push through almost any measure without facing serious opposition. The parliamentary party can override local constituencies. However, the press has not been able to articulate constitutional issues in a way that seizes the public imagination.

In American society, commentators deride sex scandals as trivial distractions, but in fact, they reflect deep political conflicts. The patterns that emerged from eighteenth-century scandals persisted in the Hill-Thomas and Clinton-Lewinsky scandals of the 1990s. Today as in the past, scandals reflect serious divides over sexual morality. Rumors of sexual misbehavior become public only in charged political circumstances. Anita Hill did not report that Clarence Thomas, her boss, sexually harassed her until he was nominated as a Supreme Court justice, and even then, she took the stand reluctantly. Conservatives exploited President Clinton's dalliance with Monica Lewinsky only because they had failed to find convincing proof of malfeasance in the Whitewater financial scandal; they were searching for a weapon to bring down his presidency.

Both scandals hinged on the ability of key players to find convincing narratives for their sexual experiences. Anita Hill testified that Thomas used crude sexual terms to her, joking about "Long Dong Silver" and pubic hair on Coke cans, but as a result, the public's disgust at this language rubbed off on her.[20] Clarence Thomas could draw upon the narrative of lynching, claiming that as a black man he was subject to a "high-tech lynching," but American society did not recognize the story of an African-American woman's sexual harassment.[21] Clinton, of course, lost credibility when he lied about his relationship with Monica Lewinsky, but he also drew upon popular understandings about what counted as sex. Kenneth Starr, the independent prosecutor, tried to incite horror at a president sexually serviced by a much younger woman, but his report read like a badly written soft-porn novel, contaminated by the very sexuality it wished to denounce. Clinton came to be seen as a victim of a Republican vendetta, much the same way as Hastings triumphed over Burke. In the year after the Thomas hearings, David Brock's book *The Real Anita Hill* discredited Hill as a liar and seemed to bolster Thomas's status as a victim of scandal, but more recently Brock himself revealed that he had fabricated lies against Anita Hill.[22]

The ability of constituencies to mobilize in response to scandal made a difference in the Anita Hill affair. Feminist groups, such as the National Organization for Women, generated letters and calls in support of Hill. Although the Senate confirmed Thomas as a Supreme Court justice, the fact that almost a dozen women were successful in the next election was widely seen as a result of feminist organization around Anita Hill. In contrast, despite its intense organization, the right-wing assault on Clinton did not persuade more than 30 percent of the population; in fact, Democrats gained in the 1998 midterm elections after the conservatives began pushing for impeachment.

While many thought that these scandals served as distractions from real political issues, such as Clarence Thomas's right-wing agenda and lack of judicial qualifications, or Clinton's welfare reforms and reduction of the deficit, the Thomas and Lewinsky affairs did have more serious implications. The effort to impeach Clinton continued the conservative assault on the federal government's expanded role and New Deal heritage, as Eli Zaretsky argues, but the impeachment failed because Republicans could not link a sexual affair to any abuse of constitutional powers.[23] Anita Hill broke down the barrier between the public and the private by asserting that sexual harassment was a matter of power, not just a conflict between individuals. As Catherine Macaulay and Mary Wollstonecraft asserted so long ago, women need private as well as public rights. Conservatives tried to portray

Clinton's affair with Monica Lewinsky as sexual harassment, but they saw sex itself as contaminating instead of admitting that it is the abuse of power that defines harassment. Bill Clinton, however, confused the right to privacy with the right to secrecy, as Ellen Willis has pointed out. The right to secrecy implies that a man can do what he likes in private, even if such actions might be considered shameful, adulterous, or even abusive. The right to privacy includes the right to sexual freedom without intrusion—and with responsibility.[24]

To conclude, scandals can be used to push women out of politics, to discredit feminism, or to distract attention from more serious political issues. But scandals can bring a wider public into politics and undercut corruption. If instigators can use sexual stories to create metaphors for deeper political and constitutional conflicts, transcend the individual protagonists to focus on these deeper problems, and use the outrage aroused by scandal to organize constituencies around these issues, scandals can democratize politics.

NOTES

CHAPTER ONE: INTRODUCTION

1. For a narrative of these events, see Flora Fraser, *The Unruly Queen: The Life of Queen Caroline* (New York: Knopf, 1996), pp. 225–35.

2. See the articles in Anne Phillips, ed., *Feminism and Politics* (New York: Oxford University Press, 1998), especially Susan Moller Okin, "Gender, the Public and the Private," pp. 116–42, and Irene Diamond and Nancy Hartsock, "Beyond Interests in Politics," pp. 201–20.

3. For a recent exploration of these themes, see Anthony Fletcher, *Gender, Sex and Subordination in England 1500–1800* (New Haven, Conn.: Yale University Press, 1996), pp. 78–98; Tim Hitchcock, *English Sexualities, 1700–1800* (New York: St. Martin's Press, 1997), pp. 30–40.

4. Thomas Laqueur, *Making Sex: Body and Gender from the Greeks to Freud* (Cambridge: Harvard University Press, 1990), pp. 190–245.

5. For the term "political entrepreneur" applied to the late eighteenth and early nineteenth centuries, see Charles Tilly, *Political Contention in Great Britain, 1758–1834* (Cambridge: Harvard University Press, 1995), p. 50.

6. For the notion of the bourgeois public sphere as rational, see Jürgen Habermas, *The Structural Transformation of the Public Sphere* (Cambridge: MIT Press, 1989). Peter Stallybrass and Allon White argue that the bourgeois public sphere defined itself in opposition to the "grotesque" popular sphere, but the grotesque remained its "political unconscious"; Stallybrass and White, *The Politics and Poetics of Transgression* (Ithaca, N.Y.: Cornell University Press, 1986), p. 199. However, the bourgeois public sphere itself was never as independent, unitary, or rational as Habermas imagined.

7. Such stories can also be conceived of as allegories, a common narrative device of the eighteenth century. See J. Hillis Miller, "The Two Allegories," in Morton W. Bloomfield, ed., *Allegory, Myth, Symbol*, Harvard English Studies 9 (Cambridge: Harvard University Press 1981), p. 356; Claude Rawson, *Satire and Sentiment 1660–1830* (Cambridge: Cambridge University Press, 1994), p. 5.

8. M. M. Bakhtin, *The Dialogic Imagination*, ed. Michael Holquist, trans. Caryl Emerson and Michael Holquist (Austin: University of Texas Press, 1981), p. 23.

9. Peter Pindar, *The Eldest Chick of the R——l Brood; the Trial of the Dove before Judge Bear; and her Appeal to the Assembly of Birds. Including the Accusations of the Toad and the Viper* (London, 1813?), p. 37.

10. J. Ann Hone, *For the Cause of Truth: Radicalism in London 1796–1821* (Oxford: Clarendon Press, 1982), p. 221; *Address of the Freeholders of Middlesex* (London, 1813), p. 3.

11. Joan Landes, *Women and the Public Sphere in the Age of the French Revolution* (Ithaca, N.Y.: Cornell University Press, 1988).

12. Sarah Maza, *Private Lives and Public Affairs: The Causes Célèbres of Prevolutionary France* (Berkeley: University of California Press, 1993); Jeffrey Merrick, "Sexual Politics and Public Order in Late Eighteenth-Century France," *Journal of the History of Sexuality* 1 (1990): 68–84.

13. Lynn Hunt, *The Family Romance of the French Revolution* (Berkeley: University of California Press, 1992).

14. Linda Colley, *Britons: Forging the Nation 1707–1837* (New Haven, Conn.: Yale University Press, 1992), p. 206; Linda Colley, "The Apotheosis of George III: Loyalty, Royalty and the British Nation, 1760–1820," *Past and Present* 102 (1984): 94–129; J.C.D. Clark, *English Society 1688–1832*, rev. ed. (Cambridge: Cambridge University Press, 2000), pp. 178–82.

15. John Brewer, *The Sinews of Power: War, Money and the British State 1688–1783* (New York: Knopf, 1989).

16. Clark, *English Society*, p. 170; for a subtle account of the difficulties of maintaining deference and alternative forms of authority in a changing society, see Paul Langford, *Public Life and the Propertied Englishman 1689–1798* (Oxford: Oxford University Press, 1994).

17. For the tensions in constitutional interpretations between influence and representation, especially royal and aristocratic influence in Parliament, see J.A.W. Gunn, "Influence, Parties, and the Constitution: Changing Attitudes, 1783–1832," *Historical Journal* 17 (1974): 309–13.

18. Susan Amussen, *An Ordered Society: Gender and Class in Early Modern England* (New York: Columbia University Press, 1988), pp. 54–64; David Underdown, *A Freeborn People: Politics and the Nation in Seventeenth-Century England* (Oxford: Clarendon Press, 1996), p. 12; Johann P. Sommerville, *Royalists and Patriots: Politics and Ideology in England, 1603–1640*, rev. ed. (London and New York: Longman, 1999) p. 33.

19. Alastair Bellany, *The Politics of Court Scandal in Early Modern England: News Culture in the Overbury Affair, 1603–1660* (Cambridge: Cambridge University Press, 2002), pp. 1–23; Paul Hammond, "The King's Two Bodies: Representations of Charles II," in Jeremy Black and Jeremy Gregory, eds., *Culture, Politics and Society in Great Britain, 1660–1800* (Manchester: Manchester University Press, 1991), p. 14; Cynthia B. Herrup, *A House in Gross Disorder: Sex, Law, and the Second Earl of Castlehaven* (New York : Oxford University Press, 1999).

20. Rachel J. Weil, "The Politics of Legitimacy: Women and the Warming Pan Scandal," in Lois G. Schwoerer, ed., *The Revolution of 1688–1689: Changing Perspectives* (Cambridge: Cambridge University Press, 1992), p. 74; Rachel Weil, "Sometimes a Sceptre Is Just a Sceptre: Pornography and Politics in Restoration England,"

in Lynn Hunt, ed., *The Invention of Pornography* (New York: Zone Books, 1993), pp. 146, 148; Robert L. Woods Jr., "Charles II and the Politics of Sex and Scandal," in Charles Carlton, ed., *State, Sovereigns and Society in Early Modern England* (New York: St. Martin's Press, 1998), pp. 119–37.

21. For antipatriarchal ideas in the Glorious Revolution, see Julia Rudolph, "Rape and Resistance: Women and Consent in Seventeenth-Century English Legal and Political Thought," *Journal of British Studies* 29 (2000): 157–85.

22. Marilyn Morris, *The British Monarchy and the French Revolution* (New Haven, Conn.: Yale University Press, 1998) p. 149.

23. For more detail on the origins of this theory, see chapter 4. Charles-Louis de Secondat Montesquieu, *The Spirit of the Laws*, ed. David Wallace Carrithers (Berkeley: University of California Press, 1977 [1757]), bk. 4, chap. 14, pp. 144–45.

24. Diana Schaub, *Erotic Liberalism: Woman and Revolution in Montesquieu's Persian Letters* (Lanham, Md.: Rowman and Littlefield, 1995), p. 138.

25. *Secret Memoirs of a Prince, or a Peek behind the Scenes* (London, 1816), p. 59.

26. The office of prime minister was not formally defined in the eighteenth century, but the First Lord of the Treasury usually functioned as the prime minister.

27. J. V. Beckett, *The Aristocracy in England 1660–1914* (Oxford: Basil Blackwell, 1986), p. 22; Lawrence Stone and Jeanne C. Fawtier Stone, *An Open Elite? England 1540–1880* (Oxford: Clarendon Press, 1984) more generally.

28. Naomi Tadmor, *Family and Friends in Eighteenth-Century England: Household, Kinship, and Patronage* (Cambridge: Cambridge University Press, 2001), pp. 73–82.

29. Elaine Chalus, " 'To Serve My friends': Women and Political Patronage in Eighteenth-Century England," in Amanda Vickery, ed., *Women, Privilege, and Power: British Politics, 1750 to the Present* (Stanford, Calif.: Stanford University Press, 2001), p. 86; Elaine Chalus, " 'That Epidemical Madness': Women and Electoral Politics in the Late Eighteenth Century," in Hannah Barker and Elaine Chalus, eds., *Gender in Eighteenth-Century England: Roles, Representations and Responsibilities* (London and New York: Longman, 1997), pp. 151–78; and Elaine Chalus, " 'My Minerva at My Elbow': The Political Roles of Women in Eighteenth-Century England," in Stephen Taylor et al., eds., *Hanoverian Britain and Empire* (Rochester: Boydell Press, 1998), pp. 210–20.

30. Frank O'Gorman, *Voters, Patrons and Parties: The Unreformed Electoral System of Hanoverian England, 1734–1832* (Oxford: Clarendon Press, 1989), p. 179; and John A. Phillips, *Electoral Behavior in Unreformed England: Plumpers, Splitters and Straights* (Princeton, N.J.: Princeton University Press, 1982).

31. Clive S. Emden, *The People and the Constitution* (Oxford: Oxford University Press, 1956), p. 12; J.A.W. Gunn, *Beyond Liberty and Property: The Process of Self-Recognition in Eighteenth-Century Political Thought* (Kingston and Montreal: McGill–Queen's University Press, 1983), p. 278.

32. Diana Donald, *The Age of Caricature: Satirical Prints in the Reign of George III* (New Haven, Conn.: Yale University Press, 1996), pp. 1–23.

33. For bribery and government control, see Lucyle Werkmeister, *The London Daily Press 1772–1792* (Lincoln: University of Nebraska Press, 1963); Werkmeister, *A Newspaper History of England, 1792–93* (Lincoln: University of Nebraska Press, 1967). For the press as representative of the public, see Hannah Barker, *Newspapers, Politics, and Public Opinion in Late Eighteenth-Century England* (Oxford: Clarendon Press, 1998), p. 19.

34. Edmund Burke, *Works*, ed. R. B. Macdowell (Oxford: Clarendon Press, 1991), vol. 9, p. 224.

35. Dror Wahrman, *Imagining the Middle Class: The Political Representation of Class in Britain, c. 1780–1840* (Cambridge: Cambridge University Press, 1992).

36. Margaret R. Hunt, *The Middling Sort: Commerce, Gender and the Family in England 1680–1780* (Berkeley: University of California Press, 1996), pp. 103–19.

37. Langford, *Public Life*, p. 502.

38. John Smail, *The Origins of Middle-Class Culture* (Ithaca, N.Y.: Cornell University Press, 1994), p. 121; see also Nicholas Rogers, "The Middling Sort in Eighteenth-Century Politics," in Jonathan Barry and Christopher Brooks, eds., *The Middling Sort of People. Culture, Society and Politics in England 1550–1800* (London: Macmillan, 1994), p. 167; Kathleen Wilson, *The Sense of the People: Politics, Culture and Imperialism in England, 1715–1785* (Cambridge: Cambridge University Press, 1995).

39. Nicholas Rogers, *Crowds, Culture and Politics in Georgian Britain* (Oxford: Clarendon Press, 1998), pp. 58, 85.

40. For the sexual politics of plebeian and working-class culture, see Anna Clark, *The Struggle for the Breeches: Gender and the Making of the British Working Class* (Berkeley: University of California Press, 1995).

41. Amanda Vickery, "Golden Age to Separate Spheres: A Review of the Categories and Chronology of English Women's History," *Historical Journal* 36 (1993): 383–414; Amanda Vickery, *The Gentleman's Daughter: Women's Lives in Georgian England* (New Haven, Conn.: Yale University Press, 1998); Colley, *Britons*; Amanda Foreman, *Georgiana, Duchess of Devonshire* (London: HarperCollins, 1998); Hannah Barker and Elaine Chalus, eds., *Gender in Eighteenth-Century England: Roles, Representations and Responsibilities* (London and New York: Longman, 1997).

42. For changes in masculinity, see Tim Hitchcock and Michele Cohen, eds., *English Masculinities 1660–1800* (London and New York: Addison Wesley Longman, 1999).

43. Classical republicanism was also known as civic humanism; David Wootton, ed., *Republicanism, Liberty, and Commercial Society, 1649–1776* (Stanford, Calif.: Stanford University Press, 1994).

44. J.G.A. Pocock, *The Machiavellian Moment: Florentine Political Thought and the Atlantic Republican Tradition* (Princeton, N.J.: Princeton University Press, 1975), p. 37.

45. *Oxford English Dictionary* (Oxford: Oxford University Press, 1971); *1811 Dictionary of the Vulgar Tongue*, unabridged from original 1811 edition with foreword by Robert Cromie (Northfield, Ill.: Digest Books, 1971 [1785]). The *Oxford*

English Dictionary also quotes a 1611 citation from the King James Bible that equated "effeminates" with "sodomites."

46. Gerald Newman, *The Rise of English Nationalism: A Cultural History 1740–1830* (New York: St. Martin's Press, 1997), p. 132.

47. Seyla Benhabib, "Models of Public Space: Hannah Arendt, the Liberal Tradition, and Jurgen Habermas," in Craig Calhoun, ed., *Habermas and the Public Sphere* (Cambridge: MIT Press, 1994), p. 78.

48. For private interests contaminating the public, see Daniela Gobetti, *Private and Public. Individuals, Households, and Body Politic in Locke and Hutcheson* (London and New York: Routledge, 1992), p. 64.

49. This is not to say that the family was not valuable; a citizen's property in his family and household was his hostage to fortune, his incentive to defend the state. See J.G.A. Pocock, "Introduction," in J.G.A. Pocock, ed., *The Political Works of James Harrington* (Cambridge: Cambridge University Press, 1977), p. 44.

50. G. J. Barker-Benfield, *The Culture of Sensibility: Sex and Society in Eighteenth-Century Britain* (Chicago: University of Chicago Press, 1992), p. 259, and in general, for an excellent introduction.

51. Lawrence E. Klein, "Gender, Conversation and the Public Sphere in Early Eighteenth-Century England," in Judith Still and Michael Worton, eds., *Textuality and Sexuality* (Manchester: Manchester University Press, 1993), p. 108; Barbara M. Benedict, "Service to the Public: William Creech and Sentiment for Sale," in John Dwyer and Richard B. Sher, eds., *Sociability and Society in Eighteenth-Century Scotland* (Edinburgh: Mercat Press, 1993), p. 133; Catherine Gallagher, *Nobody's Story: The Vanishing Acts of Women Writers in the Marketplace, 1670–1820* (Oxford: Clarendon Press, 1994), pp. 109, 151.

52. Boyd Hilton, *The Age of Atonement* (Oxford: Oxford University Press, 1988), pp. 19–26.

53. Frances Harris, *A Passion for Government: The Life of Sarah, Duchess of Marlborough* (New York: Oxford University Press, 1991). For an approving view of Queen Anne, see Robert Bucholz, "Queen Anne: Victim of Her Virtues?" in Clarissa Campbell-Orr, ed., *Queenship in Britain 1660–1837: Royal Patronage, Court Culture and Dynastic Politics* (Manchester: Manchester University Press, 2002), pp. 94–130.

54. Rachel Weil, *Political Passions: Gender, the Family and Political Argument in England, 1680–1714* (Manchester: Manchester University Press, 1999). This is an excellent examination of gendered political discourse and scandal in the earlier period.

55. Margaret Rose, *Political Satire and Reforming Vision in Eliza Haywood's Works* (Milan: Europrint Productions, 1996), p. 38.

56. Derek Jarrett, *Britain, 1688–1815* (New York: St. Martin's Press, 1965), pp. 174–75.

57. J.C.D. Pocock, *Virtue, Commerce, and History* (Cambridge: Cambridge University Press, 1985) p. 114.

58. Jeremy Black, *Robert Walpole and the Nature of Politics in Early Eighteenth Century Britain* (London: Macmillan, 1990), p. 40.

59. Betsy Bolton, *Women, Nationalism and the Romantic Stage: Theatre and Politics in Britain, 1780–1800* (Cambridge: Cambridge University Press, 2001), p. 146.

60. Robert Halsband, *Lord Hervey, Eighteenth-Century Courtier* (Oxford: Clarendon Press, 1963), p. 177; Thomas Sheridan, *Juvenal's Satires Translated, with Explanatory and Classical Notes, relating to the Laws and Customs of the Ancient Greeks and Romans* (London, 1739), pp. vi, 31, 37, 51, 229, 269.

61. Lois G. Schwoerer, "Women's Public Political Voice in England: 1640–1740," in Hilda Smith, ed., *Women Writers and the Early Modern British Political Tradition* (Cambridge: Cambridge University Press, 1998), p. 72.

62. Catherine Ingrassia, *Authorship, Commerce, and Gender in Early Eighteenth-Century England: A Culture of Paper Credit* (Cambridge: Cambridge University Press, 1998), pp. 40–76; Gallagher, *Nobody's Story*, p. 135; Rose, *Political Satire*, p. 108.

63. Vincent Carretta, *The Snarling Muse: Verbal and Visual Political Satire from Pope to Churchill* (Philadelphia: University of Pennsylvania Press, 1983), p. 227.

64. Black, *Robert Walpole and the Nature of Politics.*

65. Jarrett, *Britain*, p. 212.

66. Howard D. Weinbrot, "Politics, Taste, and National Identity: Some Uses of Tacitus in Eighteenth-Century Britain," in A. J. Woodman and T. J. Luce, eds., *Tacitus and the Tacitean Tradition* (Princeton, N.J.: Princeton University Press, 1993), pp. 168–84.

67. H. T. Dickinson, "Popular Politics in the Age of Walpole," in Jeremy Black, ed., *Britain in the Age of Walpole* (London: Macmillan, 1984), p. 40.

68. O'Gorman, *Voters, Patrons and Parties*, p. 179.

69. Nicholas Rogers, *Whigs and Cities: Popular Politics in the Age of Walpole and Pitt* (Oxford: Clarendon Press, 1989), pp. 194, 250.

70. For these scandals and patriotism, see ibid., p. 374; Wilson, *Sense of the People*, pp. 185–205.

71. Wilson, *Sense of the People*, p. 137.

72. Newman, *Rise of English Nationalism*, p. 172.

73. Colley, *Britons*, p. 101.

74. Ibid., p. 110; Linda Colley, *In Defiance of Oligarchy* (Cambridge: Cambridge University Press, 1982); Clark, *English Society*, p. 123.

75. David Armitage, *The Ideological Origins of the British Empire* (Cambridge: Cambridge University Press, 2000), p. 172, points out that patriotism was an ideology, not an identity, and could therefore be questioned. As Linda Colley's earlier work stressed, the dominant meaning of patriotism in the eighteenth century was opposition to the government. Linda Colley, "Radical Patriotism," in Raphael Samuel, ed., *Patriotism: The Making and Unmaking of British National Identity* (London: Routledge, 1989), pp. 169–87.

76. Donald, *Age of Caricature*, p. 1.

77. Barker, *Newspapers, Politics, and Public Opinion*, p. 19.

78. Rogers, *Whigs and Cities*, p. 250, points out that earlier movements and pamphlets against corruption in the 1740s did not advocate the enfranchisement of the laboring poor, although they would allow them to debate politics.

CHAPTER TWO: WILKES, SEXUALITY, AND LIBERTY: HOW SCANDAL TRANSFORMS POLITICS

1. John L. Bullion, "The Origins and Significance of Gossip about Princess Augusta and Lord Bute, 1755–1756," in Patricia B. Craddock and Carla H. Hay, eds., *Studies in Eighteenth-Century Culture*, vol. 21 (East Lansing, Mich.: Colleagues Press/American Society for Eighteenth-Century Studies, 1991), p. 256.

2. Horace Walpole, *Memoirs of the Reign of George III* (London, 1844), vol. 1, p. 16.

3. Audrey Williamson, *Wilkes: A Friend to Liberty* (New York: Dutton, 1974), pp. 16–17, 20, 22, 30; for a negative depiction of Medmenham Abbey, see Charles Johnstone, *Chrysal, or the Adventures of a Guinea* (London, 1765), vol. 3, p. 150.

4. Peter D. G. Thomas, *John Wilkes: A Friend to Liberty* (Oxford: Clarendon Press, 1996), pp. 1–7.

5. Anthony Fletcher, *Gender, Sex and Subordination in England, 1500–1800*, (New Haven, Conn.: Yale University Press, 1996), pp. 334, 344.

6. Temple to Wilkes, 3 Apr. 1762, and Wilkes to Temple, 9 July 1763, Guildhall Library, London, Ms. 14, ff. 240, 175/5.

7. John Brewer, *Party Ideology and Popular Politics at the Accession of George III* (Cambridge: Cambridge University Press, 1976), p. 48. This is the best work on Wilkes and his era.

8. *A Select Collection of the most Interesting Letters on the Government, Liberty and Constitution of England, which have appeared in different newspapers from the elevation of Lord Bute to the death of the Earl of Egremont* (London, 1763) vol. 2, p. 61, Letter XV; *The History of Prime Ministers and Favorites, in England, from the Conquest down to the Present Time* (London, 1763), p. 103.

9. For these debates, see Herbert Butterfield, *George III and the Historians*, rev. ed. (New York: Macmillan, 1959); Frank O'Gorman, "The Myth of Lord Bute's Secret Influence," in Karl W. Schweizer, ed., *Lord Bute: Essays in Re-interpretation* (Leicester: Leicester University Press, 1988), pp. 66–72.

10. *North Briton*, no. 5 (1762): 38.

11. *North Briton*, no. 36 (1763): 168; George Nobbe, *The North Briton: A Study in Political Propaganda* (New York: AMS Press, 1966), pp. 46, 26, 64.

12. *North Briton*, no. 13 (1762): 122.

13. Catherine Macaulay, *The History of England, from the Accession of James I to That of the Brunswick Line* (London, 1763–68), vol. 6, pp. 26, 27.

14. Bridget Hill, *Republican Virago: The Life and Times of Catherine Macaulay, Historian* (Oxford: Clarendon Press, 1992), pp. 135, 7–20; Barbara B. Schorenberg,

"The Brood-Hen of Faction: Mrs. Macaulay and Radical Politics, 1765–1775," *Albion* 11 (1979): 33–45.

15. Kathleen Wilson, *The Sense of the People: Politics, Culture and Imperialism in England, 1715–1785* (Cambridge: Cambridge University Press, 1995), p. 218.

16. "The Loaded Zebra or the Scotch Paperie Pedlar," in *The British Antidote to Caledonian poison: Consisting of the most humorous Satirical Prints, for the year 1762* (London, 1763), no. 14; see also Frederick George Stephens, *Catalogue of Political and Personal Satires* (London: British Museum, 1978), vol. 4, 1761–1770, BMC 3899.

17. "The Scotch Broomstick and the Female Besom," in Stephens, *Catalogue*, vol. 4, BMC 3852.

18. J.C.D. Clark, *English Society 1660–1832*, rev. ed. (Cambridge: Cambridge University Press, 2000), pp. 121, 234.

19. *North Briton*, no. 19 (1762): 174; no. 32 (1763): 87; John Wilkes, manuscript review of Locke's Two Treatises on Government (1764), Wilkes letters (on microfilm), Clements Library, University of Michigan, vol. 3, f. 9; Macaulay, *History of England*, 4: 427.

20. Walpole, *Memoirs*, 1: 16.

21. *North Briton*, no. 19 (1762): 177.

22. *North Briton*, no. 2 (1762): 28.

23. Michael Seidel, *Satirical Inheritance: Rabelais to Sterne* (Princeton, N.J.: Princeton University Press, 1979), pp. 31, 127, 263.

24. Charles-Louis de Secondat Montesquieu, *The Spirit of the Laws*, ed. David Wallace Carrithers (Berkeley: University of California Press, 1977 [1757]), bk. 4, chap. 14, pp. 144–45. For other mentions of oriental despotism, see *A Select Collection of the most Interesting Letters on the Government, Liberty, and Constitution of England; which have appeared in the different newspapers from the elevation of Lord Bute to the death of the Earl of Egremont* (London, 1763), vol. 1, p. 43; vol. 2, p. 163.

25. Catherine Macaulay, *Loose Remarks on Certain Positions to Be Found in Mr. Hobbes' Philosophical Rudiments of Government and Society with a Short Sketch of a Democratical Form of Government in a Letter to Signior Paoli* (London, 1767), p. 20.

26. Joan Landes, *Women and the Public Sphere in the Age of the French Revolution* (Ithaca, N.Y.: Cornell University Press, 1988), p. 36.

27. Rachel Weil, "Sometimes a Sceptre Is Just a Sceptre: Pornography and Politics in Restoration England," in Lynn Hunt, ed., *The Invention of Pornography* (Cambridge: Zone Books, 1993), pp. 146, 148.

28. [John Wilkes], *An Essay on Woman* (London, 1763), reprinted in Adrian Hamilton, *The Infamous Essay on Woman, or John Wilkes Seated between Vice and Virtue* (London: Andre Deutsch, 1972), p. 18.

29. "Provision for the Scotch Convent," in *The British Anecdote to Caledonian Poison* (London, 1763), vol. 2, p. 49.

30. *North Briton*, no. 3 (1763): 42.

31. Jeffrey Merrick, "Sexual Politics and Public Order in Late Eighteenth-Century France: The *Mèmoires secrets* and the *Correspondance secrete*," *Journal of the History of Sexuality* 1 (1990): 79.

32. Francoise Meltzer, "Unconscious," in Frank Lentricchia and Thomas McLaughlin, eds., *Critical Terms for Literary Study* (Chicago: University of Chicago Press, 1987), p. 160; Homi K. Bhabha, *The Location of Culture* (New York: Routledge, 1994), p. 75. For another instance of metonymy in which a woman represents unstable male rule, see Sandra R. Joshel, "Female Desire and the Discourse of Empire: Tacitus's Messalina," *Signs* 21 (1995): 72.

33. *The Group; composed of the most shocking figures, though the greatest in the Nation* (London, 1763), p. 23.

34. *The Three Conjurors, a Political Interlude Stolen from Shakespeare, as it was performed in sundry places in* Westminster, *on 30 April and 1 May* (London, [1763]).

35. "The Life of John Wilkes" (manuscript autobiography), BL, Add. Ms. 30,865.B, vol. 2, f. 16.

36. *The Demi-Rep by the Author of the Meretriciad* (London, 1766), p. 10.

37. *An Essay on Woman, in Three Epistles* (London, 1763], British Library 11631.g.31 (18).

38. Anna Clark, *The Struggle for the Breeches: Gender and the Making of the British Working Class* (Berkeley: University of California Press, 1995).

39. *Freeholders' Magazine*, November 1769, p. 161.

40. Walpole, *Memoirs*, 1: 141.

41. Thomas, *Wilkes*, p. 48.

42. Papers of Phillip Carteret Webb, Solicitor General, on the Prosecution of the *North Briton* and the *Essay on Woman*, and Phillip Carteret Webb, "A Genuine Account of the Proceedings against Mr. Wilkes for being the Author, printer and publisher of the *Essay on Woman*," Guildhall Library, Ms. 214, vol. 1; Ms. 214, vol. 2.

43. Wilkes's manuscript defense in the prosecution of the *Essay on Woman*, BL, Add. Ms. 30,885, ff. 155–57.

44. For analysis of the anticlerical aspects of Wilkes's libertinism, see John Sainsbury, "Wilkes and Libertinism," *Studies in Eighteenth-Century Culture* 26 (1998): 151–74.

45. Boulanger asserted that both oriental despotism and European despotisms regarded the king as a god, almost becoming a theocracy, and regarding any criticism of him as blasphemous. *The Origins and Progress of Despotism* (Amsterdam, 1764), pp. 14, 150. A note in the Huntington Library copy suggests Wilkes translated this book, and a note in the copy at the University of Minnesota suggests Wilkes published it; the book is mentioned in a letter from Percival Stockdale to Wilkes, 16 Oct. 1773, BL, Add. Ms. 30,871, f. 200.

46. [Wilkes], *Essay on Woman*, p. 6. For the first appearance of these insinuations, see *A Letter from a P——M——E in I——l——d to a Certain Great Man, who was Out of Town on the First of August Last* (Dublin and London, 1759), p. 28. See also Stephens, *Catalogue*, vol. 4, BMC 3680, "Who Shewd his Rear at Minden

1759"; BMC 3682, "General Pompadour or the Minden Hero. A great Satire or the Effeminacy and Cowardice of a Noble, or rather Ignoble, General"; and BMC 3681, "Pompadour General," all from 1759.

47. Thomas Farmer, *The Plain Truth: being a Genuine Narrative of the Methods made use of to procure a Copy of the Essay on Woman, with Several Extracts from the Work itself, given as a Specimen of its astonishing Impurity* (London, 1763); papers concerning prosecution of Wilkes's Essay, Guildhall Library, Ms. 214, vol. 4, f. 34.

48. Walpole, *Memoirs*, 1: 247.

49. Rev. J. Kidgell, *A Genuine and Succinct Narrative of a scandalous, obscene, and exceedingly profane Libel, entitled an Essay on Woman* (London, 1763), p. 16.

50. Webb, Proceedings against Mr. Wilkes, Guildhall Library, Ms. 214, vol. 2, f. 134.

51. Kidgell, *Genuine and Succinct Narrative*, p. 12.

52. N.A.M. Rodger, *The Insatiable Earl: A Life of John Montagu, Fourth Earl of Sandwich, 1718–1792* (New York: Norton, 1993), pp. 100–103. Rodger discounts the rumors that Sandwich knew Wilkes and the *Essay on Woman* well, as well as his motive for inventing the sandwich, but he admits that Sandwich was a gambler, libertine, and member of Medmenham Abbey.

53. [John Horne, later Tooke], *The Petition of an Englishman* (London, 1765), p. 23. For general comments on sodomy and antiaristocratic feeling, see Michael McKeon, "Historicizing Patriarchy: The Emergence of Gender Difference in England, 1660–1760," *Eighteenth-Century Studies* 28 (1995): 313.

54. J.W. Senator, with notes, by the Bishop of G., *An Essay on Women* (London, 1763), British Library 11631.g.31 (15); in catalog, listed under Julius Wanlovius, Senator of Lucca, pseudo. notes by Bishop of Grenoble, i.e., Bishop of Gloucester, William Warburton, *An Essay on Woman, in Three Epistles* [London, 1763], British Library 11631.g.31 (18).

55. Randolph Trumbach, "Sodomy Transformed: Aristocratic Libertinage, Public Reputation, and the Gender Revolution of the Eighteenth Century," *Journal of Homosexuality* 19 (1990): 105–24.

56. Margaret R. Hunt, *The Middling Sort: Commerce, Gender and the Family in England 1680–1780* (Berkeley: University of California Press, 1996), pp. 103–19.

57. Rictor Norton, ed., "Molly Exalted, 1763," Homosexuality in Eighteenth-Century England: A Sourcebook. Updated 1 Dec. 1999, http://www.infopt.demon.co.uk/exalted.htm. See also "This is not the Thing, or, Molly Exalted" (1762), in Stephens, *Catalogue*, vol. 4, BMC 3993.

58. L. Dyer to Wilkes, 13 Jan. 1761, Guildhall Library, Ms. 214, vol. 3, f. 272; Wilkes may have also been familiar with discussions of this theme in France. Helvetius, with whom he was familiar, defined sodomy as an "act of indecency" but nonetheless pointed out that many cultures accepted it as virtuous—such as the ancient Greeks. Discussed in Bryant T. Ragan Jr., "The Enlightenment Confronts Homosexuality," in Jeffrey Merrick and Bryant T. Ragan Jr., *Homosexuality in Modern France* (New York: Oxford University Press, 1996), p. 21.

59. Paul Hammond, "The King's Two Bodies: Representations of Charles II," in Jeremy Black and Jeremy Gregory, eds., *Culture, Politics and Society in Great Britain, 1660–1800* (Manchester: Manchester University Press, 1991), p. 29; Cynthia B. Herrup, *A House in Gross Disorder: Sex, Law, and the Second Earl of Castlehaven* (New York: Oxford University Press, 1999); W. A. Speck, "William—and Mary?" in Lois G. Schwoerer, ed., *The Revolution of 1688–1689: Changing Perspectives* (Cambridge: Cambridge University Press, 1992), p. 141.

60. [Charles Churchill], *The Times. A Poem* (London, 1764), pp. 18, 21.

61. Macaulay, *History of England*, 1: 265.

62. For a contemporary translation that presented Juvenal in this light, see that by Thomas Sheridan: *Juvenal's Satires Translated, with Explanatory and Classical Notes, relating to the Laws and Customs of the Greeks and Romans* (London, 1739), p. vi: "Rage and resentment against the unnatural and shocking Vices of the Age, . . . the monstrous enormities of a debauched and corrupted Court, of a starving, sharking, and dependent Nobility, of a slavish, beggarly and mercenary Set of Commons, may be exposed, and lashed, and reformed." Tobias Smollett also took up this theme. See Cameron Macfarlane, *The Sodomite in Fiction and Satire 1660–1770* (New York: Columbia University Press, 1997), p. 135.

63. Catherine Edwards, *The Politics of Immorality in Ancient Rome* (Cambridge: Cambridge University Press, 1993), pp. 53, 63–65, 71.

64. *Middlesex Journal*, 12–14 Mar. 1771, referring to an earlier incident.

65. *The Group* (London, 1763), pp. 31, 32, 36.

66. Nobbe, *The North Briton*, p. 60.

67. *The Controversial Letters of John Wilkes, Esq., the Rev. John Horne, and their Principal Adherents* (London, 1771), p. 39.

68. William Purdie Treloar, *Wilkes and the City* (London: John Murray, 1917), p. 9; Thomas, *Wilkes*, pp. 21, 48.

69. Although I agree with David Kuchta's overall argument, this interpretation of Wilkes complicates his chronology. David Kuchta, "The Making of the Self-Made Man: Class, Clothing, and English Masculinity, 1688–1832," in Victoria de Grazia, with Ellen Furlough, eds., *The Sex of Things: Gender and Consumption in Historical Perspective* (Berkeley: University of California Press, 1996), pp. 54–78.

70. For a discussion of dueling, see Donna Andrew, "The Code of Honor and Its Critics: The Opposition to Dueling in England 1700–1850," *Social History* 5 (1980): 416–20.

71. Laurence Senelick, "Mollies or Men of Mode? Sodomy and the Eighteenth-Century London Stage," *Journal of the History of Sexuality* 1 (1990): 59–60.

72. Thomas, *Wilkes*, pp. 30–31.

73. *North Briton*, no. 5 (1762): 36; no. 19 (1762): 174; no. 36 (1763): 130.

74. Thomas, *Wilkes*, p. 31.

75. *Daniel Cast into the Den of Lions, or True Blue will never stain* (1763), engraving, Huntington Library; *The Butiad, or Political Register* (London, 1763), p. 6.

76. Thomas, *Wilkes*, p. 68.

77. Ian R. Christie, *Wilkes, Wyvill and Reform: The Parliamentary Reform Movement in British Politics, 1760–1785* (London: Macmillan, 1962), p. 26.

78. Edmund Burke, *Thoughts on the Causes of the Present Discontents,* in Ian Harris, ed., *Burke: Pre-revolutionary Writings* (Cambridge: Cambridge University Press, 1993), p. 126.

79. *A Select Collection of the most Interesting Letters on the Government, Liberty, and Constitution of England,* vol. 1, p. 39.

80. Catherine Macaulay, *Observations on a Pamphlet, entitled, Thoughts on the Causes of the Present Discontents* (London, 1770), p. 10.

81. [John Wilkes], *A Letter to Samuel Johnson, LLD* (London, 1770), p. 23; *A Select Collection of the most Interesting Letters on the Government, Liberty, and Constitution of England,* vol. 1, pp. 92, 102.

82. *Political Electricity, or an Historical and Prophetical Print in the Year 1770* (London, 1770), in Huntington Library.

83. George Rudé, *Wilkes and Liberty: A Social Study* (London: Lawrence and Wishart, 1983), pp. 100–104.

84. Ibid., p. 173, quoting *Gentleman's Magazine* (1768): 241.

85. *The Drivers: A Dialogue* (Cambridge, 1770), pp. 4, 20.

86. "A Friend of Liberty" to Wilkes, 3 Jan. 1770, BL, Add. Ms. 30,870, f. 1, Jane Blenkinsopp sent Wilkes a turkey; Blenkinsopp to Wilkes, 22 Jan. 1769, BL, Add. Ms. 30,870, f. 103.

87. [Richard Godfrey], *English Caricature, 1620 to the Present* (London: Victoria and Albert Museum, 1984), plate 23, p. 59.

88. *Battle of the Quills* (London, 1768), p. 52.

89. [Samuel Johnson], *The False Alarm* (London, 1770), p. 16.

90. John Brewer, "Commercialization and Politics," in Neil McKendrick, John Brewer, and J. H. Plumb, eds., *The Birth of a Consumer Society: The Commercialization of Eighteenth-Century England* (London: Hutchinson, 1982), p. 383; John Brewer, "The Number 45: A Wilkite Political Symbol," in Stephen B. Baxter, ed., *England's Rise to Greatness, 1660–1763* (Berkeley: University of California Press, 1983), p. 361.

91. J. Free, *The Political Songster; addressed to the Sons of Freedom, and Lovers of Humour* (Birmingham, 1771), p. 99.

92. "An Election Entertainment at Brentford," reproduced in Diana Donald, *The Age of Caricature: Satirical Prints in the Age of George III* (New Haven, Conn.: Yale University Press, 1996), p. 122.

93. L[auchlin] Macleane to Wilkes, 24 Dec. 1765, BL, Add. Ms. 30,868, vol. 2, f. 221.

94. For a good discussion of scandal and the press at this time, see Donna T. Andrew and Randall McGowen, *The Perreaus and Mrs. Rudd* (Berkeley: University of California Press, 2001), p. 57.

95. Brewer, "Commercialization and Politics," p. 257.

96. Richard Sennett, *The Fall of Public Man* (New York: Knopf, 1977), pp. 99, 103.

97. Wilkes to Suard, 1 Dec. 1769, Wilkes letters (microfilm), Clements Library, vol. 3, f. 26.

98. *Remarks on the Importance of Studying Political Pamphlets* (London, 1765), p. 3.

99. Thomas, *Wilkes,* p. 96; *Essay on Patriotism and on the Character and Conduct of some Late Pretenders to that Virtue, particularly of the present Popular Gentleman* (London, 1768), p. 21; for a criticism of this tactic, see *Public Advertiser,* 29 Mar. 1769.

100. [Andrew Henderson], *A Letter to the Right Honorable Earl of T——e: or, the Case of J——W——s, Esquire: with respect to the King, Parliament, Courts of Justice, Secretaries of State, and the Multitude* (London, 1768), p. 12.

101. *The Battle of the Quills: or, Wilkes Attacked and Defended* (London, 1768), pp. 25, 29, 31; see also *Gazetteer,* 18 Mar. 1768; [Francis Squires], *A Faithful Report of a Genuine Debate concerning the Liberty of the Press* (London, 1764 [1740]), p. 21.

102. *Gazetteer,* 10 Mar. 1769.

103. [Richard Bentley], *Patriotism: A Mock-Heroic,* 2d ed. (London, 1765), p. 78.

104. *A Vindication of the Whigs against the Clamours of a Tory Mob; with an Address to the City* (London, 1765), pp. 20–21.

105. *A Letter to a Noble Member of the Club in Albemarle-Street* (London, 1764), p. 15.

106. Marilyn Morris, *The British Monarchy and the French Revolution* (New Haven, Conn.: Yale University Press, 1998), p. 39.

107. Philip Francis to Major Baggs, 30 March 1771, in Joseph Parkes and Herman Merivale, *Memoirs of Sir Philip Francis, KCB with Correspondence and Journals* (London, 1867), p. 260.

108. John Cannon, *The Letters of Junius* (Oxford: Clarendon Press, 1978), pp. 23, 24, 136. The letters were probably written by Philip Francis.

109. *Public Advertiser,* 14 Jan. 1771.

110. *Middlesex Journal,* 26–29 Jan. 1771; similar in *Gazetteer,* 1 Apr. 1771.

111. *Middlesex Journal,* 18–20 Apr. 1771.

112. *Middlesex Journal,* 1–4 June 1771.

113. *Whisperer,* no. 3 (3 Mar. 1770): 15.

114. Cannon, *Letters of Junius,* pp. 24, 71, 85, 163, 21, 202, 293, 317.

115. Ibid., p. 202.

116. Ibid., p. 85.

117. From Domitian, 17 Jan. 1771, in Cannon, *Letters of Junius,* p. 483. For further obsessions on this theme, see *Public Advertiser,* 8 Jan. 1771; *Middlesex Journal,* 15–17 Jan. 1771; *Gazetteer,* 30 Mar., 1, 8, 9 Apr. 1771.

118. Free, *Political Songster,* p. 72.

119. Burke, *Thoughts on the Present Discontents,* p. 126.

120. *Middlesex Journal,* 18–20 June 1771; *Gazetteer,* 6, 30 May 1771.

121. *The Evidence, (As taken down in Court) in the Trial wherein the Rt. Hon. John, Earl of Sandwich, was Plaintiff, and J. Miller, Defendant, before William, Lord*

Mansfield, and a Special Jury, in the Court of King's Bench, July 8, 1773 (London, 1773); Paul Langford, *A Polite and Commercial People: England 1727–1783* (Oxford: Clarendon Press, 1989), p. 579; Andrew and McGowen, *The Perreaus and Mrs. Rudd*, p. 79.

122. *Town and Country Magazine* 1 (1769): 113–14, 272; 5 (1773): 123. The *Town and Country Magazine*, however, tended to regard the influence of mistresses as the way of the world, not a sign of corruption. See also *The Adulteress* (London, 1773), p. 11.

123. *Middlesex Journal*, 30 May–1 June 1771.

124. Cannon, *Letters of Junius*, p. 457.

125. "Woman—Enemy to Liberty," Walpole Library, photo 518, Apr. 1769.

126. Cannon, *Letters of Junius*, p. 393.

127. *Gazetteer*, 22 Mar. 1768; *Public Advertiser*, 3 Feb., 29 Mar. 1769.

128. [Joseph Towers], *Observations on Public Liberty, Patriotism, Ministerial Despotism, and National Grievances, with some Remarks on Riots, Petitions, Loyal Addresses, and Military Execution, in a Letter to the Freeholders of the County of Middlesex, and the Livery of London. By an Independent Citizen of London* (London, 1769), p. 9.

129. *Gazetteer*, 17 Mar. 1768.

130. Diary of Sylas Neville, 30 Apr. 1769, Norfolk and Norwich Record Office, MS MC 7/1; Macauley to Wilkes, [1769], BL, Add. Ms. 30, 870, f. 242.

131. *Gazetteer*, 14 Mar. 1768; *The Battle of the Quills: or, Wilkes Attacked and Defended* (London, 1768), p. 30

132. *A Letter, concerning Libels, Warrants, the Seizure of Papers, and Sureties for the Peace of Behavior; with a view to some late proceedings, and the Defense of them by the Majority*, 3d ed. (London, 1765), p.54.

133. *Public Advertiser*, 3 Feb. 1769; [William Bollan], *The Free Briton's Memorial. To all the Freeholders, Citizens, and Burgesses, who elect the Members of the British Parliament, presented order to the Effectual Defence of their Injured Right of Election* (London, 1769), p. 13.

134. [John Wilkes], *A Letter to the Worthy Electors of the Borough of Aylesbury in the County of Bucks* (London, 1764), pp. 20–21.

135. [Sir William Meredith], *A Reply to the Defense of the Majority, on the Question of General Warrants* (London, 1764), pp. 18–19; *A Letter, concerning Libels*, p. 54; Sir William Baker, a member of Parliament, sarcastically excused his dilatory response to a correspondence by noting that a publication may be "fatal though only a communication to the most intimate friend"; Sir W. Baker to William Baker, London, 9 Feb. 1764, Hertfordshire Record Office, D/EBk C3.

136. *Whisperer*, no. 33 (29 Sept. 1770): 202.

137. *The Memoirs of Miss Arabella Bolton, containing a Genuine Account of her Seduction, and the barbarous Treatment she afterwards received from the Honourable Colonel L——l, the present supposed M——r for the County of Middlesex* (London, 1770), pp. 29–33; *Freeholders' Magazine*, (December 1769), p. 217.

138. *Wilkes' Jest Book* (London, 1769), p. 151.

139. An Alderman of London, *A Letter to the Right Hon. Thomas Harley, Esq., Lord Mayor of the City of London* (London, 1768), p. 18.

140. *Form of the Grand Procession, as it was intended to have been made to W——m——r H——, on 20 April 1768* (London, 1768); broadsheet, Guildhall Library.

141. W. Shugg, "The Baron and the Milliner," *Maryland Historical Magazine* 83 (1988): 310–330. [Sophia Watson], *Memoirs of the Seraglio of the Bashaw of Merryland* [alias Lord Baltimore] (London, 1768); *A Letter on the Behaviour of the Populace, on a Late Occasion, in the Procedure against a Noble Lord*, 2d ed. (London, 1768).

142. For newspaper accounts and comments on the trial, see *Gazetteer*, 29–31 Mar. 1768.

143. Rudé, *Wilkes and Liberty*, pp. 86–88.

144. Sarah Wilkes to John Wilkes, 23 Oct. 1771, and anonymous undated letter, Wilkes letters (microfilm), Clements Library, vol. 2, ff. 95, 115.

145. Audrey Williamson, *Wilkes: A Friend to Liberty* (New York: Dutton, 1974), p. 149.

146. Wilkes to Suard, 3 May 1768, Wilkes letters (microfilm), Clements Library, vol. 2, f. 18.

147. *Middlesex Journal*, 1–4 June 1771.

148. *Middlesex Journal*, 11–13 June 1771.

149. *Public Advertiser*, 5 May 1771.

150. *Middlesex Journal*, 7–9 May 1771; *Public Advertiser*, 19 Jan., 5 May 1771.

151. *Public Advertiser*, 4, 5 May 1771.

152. [Thomas Hallie de la Mayne], *The Senators: or, a Candid Examination into the Merits of the Principal Performers of St. Stephens' Chapel*, 4th ed. (London, 1772), p. 24.

153. *Public Advertiser*, 5 May 1771.

154. *Pride: a Poem, inscribed to John Wilkes, Esq., by an Englishman* (London, 1766), pp. 10, 15; similarly, *Extraordinary North Briton*, no. 5 (11 June 1768): 25; no. 11 (23 July 1768): 66.

155. *The Controversial Letters of John Wilkes, the Rev. John Horne and their Principal Adherents* (London, 1771), pp. 98, 107, 121.

156. Gary Kates, *Monsieur d'Eon Is a Woman* (New York: Basic Books, 1997), pp. 87–95; for d'Eon and Wilkes, see Anna Clark, "Wilkes and d'Eon: The Politics of Masculinity, 1763–1778," *Eighteenth-Century Studies* 32 (1998): 19–48.

157. M. Dorothy George, *Catalogue of Political and Personal Satires* (London: British Library, 1978), vol. 5, 1771–1783, BMC 4865. For Mary Toft, see Lisa Cody, "The Doctor's in Labor; or a New Whim Wham from Guildford," *Gender and History* 4, no. 2 (1992): 175–96; Alan Shepard, "The Literature of a Medical Hoax: The Case of Mary Toft, the Pretended Rabbit-Breeder," *Eighteenth-Century Life*, n.s., 19 (1995): 59–77.

158. George, *Catalogue*, BMC 4870–73.

159. *Public Advertiser*, 6 June 1771.

160. Corporation Elections [collection of broadsheets], AN 20.3.7 f. 7, 9, 12, and Ms. 3332(2) ff. 157–61, 164, Guildhall Library; Thomas, *Wilkes*, p. 259. For general information, see Rictor Norton, *Mother Clap's Molly House: The Gay Subculture in England, 1700–1830* (London: GMP, 1992), p. 176.

161. For the trial, see *Gazetteer*, 22 July 1772; for crowds, *Morning Chronicle*, 14 Aug. 1772; *St. James Chronicle*, 6–8 Aug. 1772.

162. For this debate, see Randolph Trumbach, "Sodomy Transformed: Aristocratic Libertinage, Public Reputation, and the Gender Revolution of the Eighteenth Century," *Journal of Homosexuality* 19, no. 2 (1990): 105–24; Trumbach puts the moment of identification in the early eighteenth century, but Philip Carter disagrees. Philip Carter, "Men about Town: Representations of Foppery and Masculinity in Early Eighteenth-Century Urban Society," in Hannah Barker and Elaine Chalus, eds., *Gender in Eighteenth-Century England: Roles, Representations and Responsibilities* (London and New York: Longman, 1997), p. 32.

163. *Morning Chronicle*, 5 Aug. 1772.

164. Reprinted in *Middlesex Journal*, 29 Sept.–1 Oct. 1772.

165. *Middlesex Journal*, 1–3, 3–5, 8–10, 17–19, 26–29 Sept., 29 Sept.–1 Oct. 1772.

166. *St. James Chronicle*, 1–3 Sept. 1772. For another defense of Jones on this ground, see *Morning Chronicle*, 11, 20 Aug. 1772.

167. *St. James Chronicle*, 1–3 Oct. 1772.

168. *Morning Chronicle*, 6 Aug. 1772. See also *The Adulteress* (London, 1773), p. 26.

169. *Morning Chronicle*, 7 Aug. 1772. Mrs. Macaulay had alluded to James I's favorites.

170. *St. James' Chronicle*, 1–3 Oct. 1772.

171. *Morning Chronicle*, 21 Aug. 1772.

172. *St. James' Chronicle*, 5–7 Sept. 1772.

173. *St. James' Chronicle*, 12–14 Sept. 1772.

174. [James Murray], *New Sermons to Asses* (London, 1773), p. 20.

175. For this campaign, see John Brewer, "The Wilkites and the Law, 1763–74: A Study of Radical Notions of Governance," in John Brewer and John Styles, eds., *An Ungovernable People: The English and Their Law in the Seventeenth and Eighteenth Centuries* (London: Hutchinson, 1980), pp. 128–71.

176. *Middlesex Journal*, 26–29 Sept. 1772.

177. *Morning Chronicle*, 5, 6, 18 Aug. 1772.

178. *Morning Chronicle*, 11 Aug. 1772.

179. CB to Wilkes, June 1769, BL, Add. Ms. 30,870, f. 157.

180. "A Friend of Liberty" to Wilkes, 3 Jan. 1770, BL, Add. Ms. 30,870 f. 1.

181. Charlotte Forman to Wilkes, 12 June, 21 Aug. 1768, 2 Mar., 16 Aug. 1769, BL, Add. Ms. 30,870, ff. 52, 68, 117, 179; Forman to Wilkes, 9 Apr. 1770, BL, Add. Ms. 30,871, f. 26. See also Joel J. Gold, "'Buried Alive': Charlotte Forman in Grub Street," *Eighteenth-Century Life* 8 (1982): 28–45.

182. Isobel Grundy, "Mary Seymour Montague, Anonymity and 'Old Satyrical Codes,'" in Isobel Armstrong and Virginia Blain, eds., *Women's Poetry in the Enlightenment: The Making of a Canon* (Basingstoke: Macmillan, 1999), pp. 67–80.

183. Mary Seymour Montague, *An Original Essay on Woman* (London, 1771), pp. xi, 54.

184. Basil Cozens-Hardy, ed., *The Diary of Sylas Neville, 1767–1788* (London: Cumberlege/Oxford University Press, 1950), p. 29; manuscript diary of Sylas Neville, Norfolk and Norwich Record Office, MS MC 7/1 ff. 20–24.

185. Quoted in Norma Clarke, *Dr. Johnson's Women* (London: Hambledon and London, 2000), p. 88.

186. Catherine Macaulay to Wilkes, 1769, BL, Add. Ms. 30,870, f. 242.

187. Catherine Macaulay, *Loose Remarks on Certain Positions to be Found in Mr. Hobbes' Philosophical Rudiments of Government and Society with a Short Sketch of a Democratical Form of Government in a Letter to Signior Paoli* (London, 1767), p. 37.

188. Philip Hicks, "Catherine Macaulay's Civil War: Gender, History, and Republicanism in Georgian Britain," *Journal of British Studies* 41 (2002): 170–99.

189. Macaulay, *History of England*, vol. 5, p. 8.

190. Ibid., vol. 8, p. 62.

191. Ibid., p. 314.

192. *Public Advertiser*, 19 Dec. 1768.

193. Macaulay, *History of England*, vol. 1, p. x.

194. Macaulay, *Observations on Pamphlet, entitled, Thoughts on the Causes of the Present Discontents*, p. 1.

195. "On Mrs. Macaulay's History of England," 30 Nov. 1763, manuscript in Catherine Macaulay Graham Papers, Gilder Lehmann Collection, Pierpont Morgan Library, New York.

196. Montague, *An Original Essay on Woman*, p. 37; similarly, Mary Scott, *The Female Advocate: A Poem* (London, 1774), p. 27.

197. See letters to and from "Sophronia," Mrs. Knowles, Madame Deffand, and Mercy Otis Warren in Catherine Macaulay Graham Papers, Gilder Lehmann Collection, Pierpont Morgan Library.

198. *Public Advertiser*, 4 Jan. 1769.

199. *Public Advertiser*, 6 Jan. 1769.

200. *Political Register* 6 (1770): 152–54.

201. *Six Odes, presented to that justly celebrated Historian, Mrs. Macaulay, on her Birthday* (Bath, 1777), p. 26.

202. Hill, *Republican Virago*, pp. 101–2.

203. Ibid., pp. 113–17.

204. For a good account of this controversy, see Cecile Mazzucco-Than, "'As Easy as a Chimney Pot to Blacken': Catherine Macaulay 'the Celebrated Female Historian,'" in Paula Backscheider and Timothy Dystal, eds., *The Intersection of the Public and Private Spheres in Early Modern England* (London and Portland, Ore.: Frank Cass, 1996), pp. 78–104.

205. Hill, *Republican Virago*, p. 117.

206. [Richard Paul Jodrell], *The Female Patriot An epistle from C——t——e M——c——y to the Rev. Dr. W——l——n on her late Marriage* (London, 1779).

207. *A Bridal Ode on the Marriage of Catherine and Petruchio* (London, 1779), p. 8.

208. *The Patriot Divine to the Female Historian. An Elegiac Epistle, to which is added the Lady's Reply, or a Modest Plea for the Rights of Widows* (London, 1779).

209. John Wilkes, *Letters from the Year 1774 to the Year 1796, of John Wilkes, Esq., addressed to his Daughter* (London, 1804), vol. 2, pp. 145, 166.

210. Hill, *Republican Virago*, p. 117.

211. Catherine Macaulay, *The History of England from the Revolution to the Present Time, in a Series of Letters to a Friend* (Bath, 1778).

212. Montague, *An Original Essay on Woman*, pp. 1–52; Sarah Scott, *Millenium Hall* (London, 1762).

213. Walpole, *Memoirs*, vol. 1, pp. 353–54; *Town and Country Magazine* 3 (1772): 66, 308.

214. *Gazetteer*, 16 Mar. 1771.

215. Nicholas Rogers, *Crowds, Culture and Politics in Georgian Britain* (Oxford: Clarendon Press, 1998), pp. 121–60; see also Wilson, *Sense of the People*, pp. 252–59.

216. J.A.W. Gunn, *Beyond Liberty and Property: The Process of Self-Recognition in Eighteenth-Century Political Thought* (Kingston and Montreal: McGill–Queen's University Press, 1983), p. 170.

CHAPTER THREE: INFLUENCE OR INDEPENDENCE:
WOMEN AND ELECTIONS, 1777–1788

1. Linda Colley, *Britons: Forging the Nation 1707–1837* (New Haven, Conn.: Yale University Press, 1992), p. 250; Amanda Foreman, *Georgiana, Duchess of Devonshire* (London: HarperCollins, 1998), chap. 9.

2. Most notably, Elaine Chalus, "'That Epidemical Madness': Women and Electoral Politics in the Late Eighteenth Century," in Hannah Barker and Elaine Chalus, eds., *Gender in Eighteenth-Century England: Roles, Representations and Responsibilities* (London and New York: Longman, 1997), pp. 151–78; Elaine Chalus, "'To Serve My friends': Women and Political Patronage in Eighteenth-Century England," in Amanda Vickery, ed., *Women, Privilege, and Power: British Politics, 1750 to the Present* (Stanford, Calif.: Stanford University Press, 2001).

3. After the early eighteenth century, Elaine Chalus finds only two instances in which women's political patronage became controversial, but she mainly relies on the letters of elite families and politicians who accepted and benefited from the system. Chalus, "'To Serve My Friends,'" p. 77.

4. Lewis Namier, *The Structure of Politics at the Accession of George III* (London, 1967), depicted the system as so controlled by the Crown and aristocratic families that elections were basically meaningless.

5. Frank O'Gorman, *Voters, Patrons and Parties: The Unreformed Electoral System of Hanoverian England, 1734–1832* (Oxford: Clarendon Press, 1989), p. 19.

6. [George Tierney], *The State of the Representation of England and Wales. delivered to the Society, the Friends of the People, associated for the Purpose of obtaining a Parliamentary Reform, on Saturday the 9th of February 1793* (London, 1793), p. 34.

7. O'Gorman, *Voters, Patrons and Parties*, p. 140.

8. Chalus, "'To Serve My Friends,'" p. 86; Chalus, "'That Epidemical Madness,'" pp. 151–78.

9. Edward Porritt, *The Unreformed House of Commons* (New York: Kelley, 1963 [1903]), vol. 1, pp. 154–64.

10. Anne Damer to Mr. Grenville, 14 Aug. 1817, BL, Add. Ms. 41,858, f. 265.

11. O'Gorman, *Voters, Patrons and Parties*, p. 343. O'Gorman downplays the efficacy of this pressure, but landlords would not pressure their tenants how to vote unless they expected them to comply.

12. Ibid., pp. 179, 280.

13. John A: Phillips, "Popular Politics in Unreformed England," *Journal of Modern History* 52 (1980): 599–625.

14. Kathleen Wilson, *The Sense of the People: Politics, Culture and Imperialism in England, 1715–1785* (Cambridge: Cambridge University Press, 1995), p. 225.

15. For women in electoral crowds, see Nicholas Rogers, *Crowds, Culture and Politics in Georgian Britain* (Oxford: Clarendon Press, 1998), p. 219.

16. O'Gorman, *Voters, Patrons and Parties*, pp. 2, 10, 19, 218; Foreman, *Georgiana*, p. 141.

17. John A. Phillips, *Electoral Behavior in Unreformed England: Plumpers, Splitters and Straights* (Princeton, N.J.: Princeton University Press, 1982), p. 77.

18. Wilson, *The Sense of the People*, and Rogers, *Crowds, Culture and Politics in Georgian Britain*, are important works that stress the frustrations of voters' independence in an aristocratic system.

19. O'Gorman, *Voters, Patronage and Parties*, p. 179. O'Gorman stresses that the size of the electorate grew, but his figures show that the electorate declined as a percentage of the growing population.

20. George Stead Veitch, *The Genesis of Parliamentary Reform* (London: Constable, 1964 [1913]); John Cannon, *Parliamentary Reform 1640–1832* (Cambridge: Cambridge University Press, 1973).

21. For examples, see *Newcastle Journal*, 2 Apr. 1777; *New Election Budget* (Norwich, 1786), p. 3; *Norfolk Chronicle*, 26 Aug. 1786; *Nottingham Journal*, 8 Apr. 1803.

22. For instance, Lady Spencer had to canvass in Northampton because her male relatives, the peers, were debarred from interfering in elections. Foreman, *Georgiana*, pp. 28–29.

23. Matthew Cragoe, "'Jenny Rules the Roost': Women and Electoral Politics, 1832–68," in Kathryn Gleadle and Sarah Richardson, eds., *Women in British Politics, 1760–1860: The Power of the Petticoat* (New York: St. Martin's Press, 2000), p. 162. A story circulating in 1802 involved agents giving voters' wives lottery

tickets instead of cash; *Norwich Chronicle*, 3 July 1802; *Nottingham Journal*, 25 June 1802.

24. *The Country Election. A Farce* (London, 1768), p. 15.

25. *The General Election: a series of letters between two female friends* (London, 1775), vol. 1, pp. 17, 26. For an astute analysis of this novel, see Clare Brant, "Armchair Politicians: Elections and Representations, 1774," *Tulsa Studies in Women's Literature* 17 (1998): 269–82.

26. Mrs. Sarah Osborn to her son Jack Osborn, 9 Feb. 1768 and 3 May 1768, in Emily F. D. Osborn, ed., *Political and Social Letters of a Lady of the Eighteenth Century 1721–1771* (London, 1890), pp. 181–82.

27. For conservatism, see James J. Sack, *From Jacobite to Conservative: Reaction and Orthodoxy in Britain, c. 1760–1832* (Cambridge: Cambridge University Press, 1993), pp. 30–45.

28. For this point, see Ian Harris, ed., *Burke: Pre-revolutionary Writings* (Cambridge: Cambridge University Press, 1993), p. 112.

29. Edmund Burke, "Thoughts on the Causes of the Present Discontents" (1770), in Harris, *Burke: Pre-revolutionary Writings*, p. 125.

30. Quoted in L. G. Mitchell, *Charles James Fox* (Oxford: Oxford University Press, 1992), p. 20.

31. Frederick A. Dreyer, *Burke's Politics: A Study in Whig Orthodoxy* (Waterloo: Wilfred Laurier University Press, 1979), p. 69.

32. Edmund Burke, *Letter to Sherriffs of Bristol* (1777), quoted in Harris, *Burke: Pre-revolutionary Writings*, p. 114. For this notion of family based on the aristocratic lineage, see Naomi Tadmor, *Family and Friends in Eighteenth-Century England: Household, Kinship and Patronage* (Cambridge: Cambridge University Press, 2001), p. 82.

33. Burke, "Thoughts on the Causes of the Present Discontents," pp. 167, 180.

34. James T. Boulton, *The Language of Politics in the Age of Wilkes and Burke* (London: Routledge and Kegan Paul, 1963), pp. 53, 62.

35. Catherine Macaulay, *Observations on a Pamphlet, entitled, Thoughts on the Causes of the Present Discontents* (London, 1770), pp. 20, 5.

36. Catherine Macaulay, *The History of England from the Revolution to the Present Time, in a Series of Letters to a Friend* (Bath, 1778), p. 34.

37. *The Westminster Forum* (London, 1784), p. 121.

38. For examples of such language, see *Substance of the Speech of the Rev. Mr. Walker at General Meeting of the County of Nottingham* ([London]: Society for Constitutional Information, 1780), p. 7; [John Short], *The Rights and Principles of an Englishman considered and asserted, on a Review of the late Motion at the Hotel, for a County Meeting in Devonshire* (Exeter, 1780), p. 15; *The Speeches of Thomas Day, Esq., at the General Meetings of the Counties of Cambridge and Essex* ([London]: Society for Constitutional Information, 1780), pp. 5, 16; *The Out-of-Door Parliament, by a Gentleman of the Middle Temple* (London, 1780), p. 68; *Four Letters from the Country Gentleman, on the Subject of Petitions* (London, 1780), p. 13.

39. Ian R. Christie, *Wilkes, Wyvill and Reform: The Parliamentary Reform Movement in British Politics, 1760–1785* (London: Macmillan, 1962), pp. 189, 109.

40. Rev. Thomas Northcote, *Observations on the Natural and Civil Rights of Mankind, the prerogatives of princes and the powers of government, in which the equal and universal right of the people to election and representation is proved by direct and conclusive arguments* (London, 1781), p. 10.

41. *The People the Best Governors; or a Plan of Government founded on the Principles of Natural Freedom* (London, 1776), p. 9.

42. Trevor Fawcett, "Eighteenth-Century Debating Societies," *British Journal for Eighteenth-Century Studies* 3 (autumn 1980): 21; for women in Scottish debating societies, see Davis D. McElroy, *Scotland's Age of Improvement: A Survey of Eighteenth-Century Literary Clubs and Societies* (Pullman: Washington State University Press, 1969), pp. 90–91; Donna T. Andrew, *London Debating Societies* (London: London Record Society, 1994), p. 131. See also Donna T. Andrew, "Popular Culture and Public Debate: London, 1780," *Historical Journal* 39, no. 2 (1996): 405–23.

43. *A Short History of the Westminster Forum* (London, 1780), p. 127.

44. Andrew, *London Debating Societies*, p. 89, 11 Apr. 1780.

45. Mary Thale, "Women in London Debating Societies, 1780," *Gender and History* 7 (1995): 22–25.

46. Andrew, *London Debating Societies*, p. 131, 13 Feb. 1781.

47. Ibid., p. 111, 14 Oct. 1780; p. 135, 23 Mar. 1781; p. 146, 28 Feb. 1782; p. 181, 27 Mar. 1786; p. 223, 17 Mar. 1788. These debates took place at both the female La Belle Assemblée and the mixed Coachmaker's Hall.

48. For instance, on 2 March 1780, some debaters argued that women were "too liable to be seduced from their attention to the public weal, by the smooth and silken parasites who constantly infest a court, to rule a state." Andrew, *London Debating Societies*, p. 99.

49. Andrew, *London Debating Societies*, pp. 98, 101; *La Belle Assemblée, or the Female Praters*, reviewed in *Monthly Review* 50 (1780): 7.

50. William Pulteney, *The Effects to be expected from the East India Bill, upon the Constitution of Great Britain, if passed into a law* (London, 1783).

51. Paul Kelly, "British Politics, 1783–4: The Emergence and Triumph of the Younger Pitt's Administration," *Bulletin of the Institute for Historical Research* 54, no. 129 (1981): 77.

52. Sack, *From Jacobite to Conservative*, p. 85.

53. Kathleen Wilson has presented an excellent account of Bowes's election in her *Sense of the People*, p. 360, stressing his role as an independent candidate of the radicals.

54. Volumes of extracts of her readings, Countess of Strathmore Papers, Glamis Castle, consulted in University of Dundee Archives, box 244; Mary Eleanor Bowes, Countess of Strathmore, *The Seige of Jerusalem* (London, 1774).

55. For a biography, see Ralph Arnold, *The Unhappy Countess and Her Grandson John Bowes* (London: Constable, 1957).

56. *The History of Stoney Bowes* (Newcastle, 1810), p. 1.

57. "Lady Strathmore's Marriage, from the Time of her Marriage until she left Mr. Stoney," Strathmore Papers, Glamis Castle, box 245, vol. 332.

58. Sir Lewis Namier and John Brooke, *The House of Commons 1754–1790*, vol. 2 (London: HMSO, 1964), p. 108.

59. *The Stoniad: Addressed to Andrew Robinson, Esq* (Newcastle, 1777) pp. 1–5; *History of Stoney Bowes*, p. 2.

60. For accounts of these elections, see Wilson, *Sense of the People*, pp. 340–373; T. R. Knox, "Popular Politics and Provincial Radicalism: Newcastle upon Tyne, 1769–1785," *Albion* 11 (1979): 224–241; H. T. Dickinson, *Radical Politics in the North-East of England in the Later Eighteenth Century* (Durham: Durham County Local History Society, 1979), pp. 1–10.

61. British Library, *A Collection of Papers, Speeches, etc etc, delivered at the Newcastle Election in 1777.* collected by William Garret (Newcastle, 1823), f. 9.

62. George Rudé, *Wilkes and Liberty: A Social Study* (London: Lawrence and Wishart, 1983), p. 173, quoting *Gentleman's Magazine* (1768): 241.

63. [James Murray], *Sermons to Asses* (London and Newcastle, 1768); [James Murray], *The Travels of the Imagination; a True Journey from Newcastle to London, in a Stage-Coach, with Observations on the Metropolis* (London, 1773); *Freeman's Magazine*, 12 May 1770, p. 145.

64. See also letter from "Marcus Aurelius," in *Freeman's Magazine*, 10 May 1774, p. 80.

65. Wilson, *Sense of the People*, p. 350.

66. *Newcastle Courant*, 8 Mar. 1777.

67. Wilson, *Sense of the People*, p. 356.

68. Election papers, 1777, Strathmore Papers, Glamis Castle, box 245, no. 7.

69. Arnold, *Unhappy Countess*, p. 51.

70. *Newcastle Journal*, 2 Apr. 1777; Correspondence of Andrew Bowes, undated broadsheet, Strathmore Papers, Glamis Castle, Box 245, vol. 41, f. 23.

71. [James Murray], *New Sermons to Asses* (London, 1773), pp. 124–25.

72. Broadsheet, "To the Worthy freemen of Newcastle" (1774); for other examples, broadsheet from "Young Cato" (1777); song "By a Lady" [1776]; Correspondence of Andrew Bowes, Strathmore Papers, Glamis Castle, box 245, vol. 41, ff. 37, 35, 41.

73. *A Full and Accurate Report of the Trial between the Rev. John Stephens, Trustee to E Bowes, commonly called the Countess of Strathmore, and Andrew Robinson Stoney Bowes, Esq., her second husband, in the court of Common Pleas* (London, 1788), pp. 17, 21.

74. Election papers, Strathmore Papers, Glamis Castle, box 245, no. 7, unpaginated.

75. Bell Collection, Society of Antiquaries, Newcastle on Tyne elections, 1777–80, Northumberland Record Office; *Newcastle Courant*, 1 Mar. 1777.

76. *A Full and Accurate Report of the Trial*, p. 17.

77. "Lady Strathmore's Marriage," Strathmore Papers, Glamis Castle, f. 15.

78. Arnold, *Unhappy Countess*, p. 78. This accusation was made by Mr. Montagu, a relation of the countess's former friend Mrs. Montagu, who was accused of instructing her agent to get her own voters drunk and acquiescent. *Electioneering Journal*, 4 Mar. 1777, in Bell Collection, Northumberland Record Office.

79. Samuel Haggerston to the Countess of Strathmore, 26 Feb. 1791, Durham County Record Office, D/ST/C1/9/17. He was referring to a promise made during an earlier campaign.

80. *Newcastle Journal*, 2 Apr. 1777.

81. *Newcastle Journal*, 8 May 1777. Although House of Commons reports on bribery in elections were usually secret, Bowes caused the newspaper to reprint it. Henry Gibson to Bowes, 6 May 1777, Bowes correspondence, Strathmore Papers, Glamis Castle, box 245, vol. 41, f. 10.

82. Cragoe, "Women and Electoral Politics, 1832–68," p. 162.

83. Election bills of Andrew Robinson Bowes, 1777, Durham County Record Office, D/ST/C1/13/6; *Newcastle Courant*, 19 Apr. 1777.

84. Copy of *General Advertiser and Morning Intelligencer*, 9 Feb. 1780, Durham County Record Office, D/ST/C1/13/9; see also *Newcastle Courant*, 5 Feb 1780.

85. Wilson, *Sense of the People*, p. 370.

86. Handbill, 12 Aug. 1780, "Mr. Murray will deliver a lecture on the nature of Election . . . to be concluded with a Eulogium on Bribery." See also "To None but the Independent Freemen of Newcastle, from So Be it," Election Papers, Northumberland Record Office, ZAN M17/38.

87. Cutting, 15 Sept. 1780, Election Papers, Strathmore Papers, Glamis Castle, box 245, no. 7; *Newcastle Courant*, 9 Sept. 1780.

88. "To None but the Independent Freemen of Newcastle, from So Be it," 1784, Election Papers, Northumberland Record Office, ZAN M17/38.

89. Jesse Foot, surgeon, *The Lives of Andrew Robinson Bowes, Esq and the Countess of Strathmore, written from 33 years professional attendance, letters* (London, 1810), p. 69.

90. "Bowes and Freedom," 1780, Bell Collection, Northumberland Record Office.

91. *Newcastle Chronicle*, 19 Aug. 1780.

92. *Newcastle Chronicle*, 2 Sept. 1780.

93. *Newcastle Journal*, 22, 26 Aug. 1780.

94. *Newcastle Courant*, 5 Aug. 1780, Bell Collection, Northumberland Record Office.

95. "A Famous Oration, at the Common Hall," 1780, Election Papers, Northumberland Record Office, ZAN M17/38.

96. Shortly after the 1777 election, he was depicted as an Irish adventurer who made a pact with the devil to exchange political office for an Irish peerage, *The Stoniad*.

97. *Newcastle Journal*, 9 Sept. 1780.

98. "An Excellent New Election Song," 1780, Election Papers, Northumberland Record Office, ZAN M17/38.

99. *Newcastle Chronicle*, 19 Aug. 1780.

100. Dickinson, "Newcastle," p. 11.

101. "To the Free Burgesses of Newcastle, from Serjeant Glynn," 1784, Election Papers, Strathmore Papers, Glamis Castle, box 245, no. 7.

102. "The Third Book of the Chronicles," 1784, Election Papers, Northumberland Record Office, ZAN M17/38.

103. "To the Free Burgesses of Newcastle," Election Papers, Collection for 1784, Northumberland Record Office, ZAN M17/38, f. 71.

104. *Newcastle Chronicle*, 3 Apr. 1784.

105. *Newcastle Chronicle*, 10, 17 Apr. 1784; "Queries to Charles Brandling Esq.," item found in both Bell Collection, Northumberland Record Office, and Strathmore Papers, Glamis Castle, box 245, no. 7; "Charly Crucifix," 1784, Election Papers, Collection for 1784, Northumberland Record Office, ZAN M17/38, f. 68.

106. Martin Brown, *Paddy's Progress: or, the Rise and Fall of Captain Stoney, being a Brief, yet circumstantial Narrative, of his various Schemes, Tricks, Plots and Contrivances, since his arrival to England, down to the present time* (Gateshead, 1808), in Durham County Record Office D/St/C1/13/17; Foot, *The Lives of Andrew Robinson Bowes*, p. 81.

107. "Lady Strathmore's Marriage," Strathmore Papers, Glamis Castle, f. 35.

108. Ibid., " f. 192.

109. *The Trial of Andrew Robinson Bowes, Esq. et al. . . . for a Conspiracy against the Rt Hon. Mary Eleonor Bowes, Commonly called Countess of Strathmore* (London, 1787), p. 44.

110. Arnold, *Unhappy Countess*, p. 124.

111. Susan Staves, *Married Women's Separate Property in England, 1660–1833* (Cambridge: Harvard University Press, 1990), pp. 53–54.

112. Arnold, *Unhappy Countess*, p. 125.

113. James Gillray, "Lady Termagent Flaybum going to give her Step Son a taste of her Desert after Dinner," BMC 7011, 1786, and "The Injured Count——s," BMC 7013, in Richard Godfrey, *James Gillray: The Art of Caricature* (London: Tate Publishing, 2001), p. 68, plates 24 and 25.

114. *Tyranny Displayed, a Poem* (London, [1790?]), by a Friend to Humanity.

115. *Fatal Follies: or, the History of the Countess of Stanmore* (London, 1788).

116. For a criticism of her on this point, see [William Combe], *A Letter to her Grace the Duchess of Devonshire* (London, 1777).

117. Judith Lewis, "1784 and All That: Aristocratic Women and Electoral Politics," in Vickery, *Women, Privilege and Power*, p. 95.

118. For a popular biography, see Foreman, *Georgiana*.

119. Anne Stott, " 'Female Patriotism': Georgiana, Duchess of Devonshire, and the Westminster Election of 1784," *Eighteenth-Century Life* 17 (1993): 60–84.

120. *History of the Westminster Election, containing Every Material Occurrence . . . by Lovers of Truth and Justice* (London, 1784), p. 342.

121. For another contrast between Fox and Pitt, see Lewis, "1784 and All That," pp. 116–17.

122. *The Genuine Review of the Political State of an Unhappy Country, as originally written, before it was mutilated by a Right Reverend Prelate* (London, 1787), p. 20.

123. The best biography is John Ehrman, *The Younger Pitt*, vol. 1 (London: Constable, 1969).

124. *A Political Sermon, preached before a R——t H——ble H——e, the First Day of the present Meeting of P——t, by the Reviving Shade of Patriotism and Public Virtue* (London, 1784), p. 11.

125. Ehrman, *The Younger Pitt*, vol. 1, pp. 68–69.

126. [Francis Annesley], *Five Minutes Advice to the People preparatory to the ensuing General Election* (London, 1784); [William Strickland], *Second Letter to a Country Gentleman* (London, 1784); *A Vindication of the Peer's Right to Advise the Crown* (London, 1784).

127. For a biography, see Mitchell, *Charles James Fox.*

128. *Popular Topics; or, the Grand Question Discussed, in which the following subjects are considered, viz. the king's prerogative, the privileges of Parliament, Secret Influence, and a System of Reform for the East-India Company* (London, 1784); *Secret Influence public Ruin! An Address to the Young Premier on the Principles of his Politics . . . with a Speech by Charles James Fox* (London, 1784), p. 26.

129. *The Wit of the Day, or the Humours of Westminster* (London, 1784), pp. 121, 129, 40–41. Of course, in return Pitt's supporters reminded voters of the supposed secret influence of Henry Fox over Lord Bute.

130. *History of the Westminster Election*, p. 310.

131. James Morwood, *The Life and Works of Richard Brinsley Sheridan* (Edinburgh: Scottish Academic Press, 1985), p. 110.

132. *Political Letters written in March and April 1784* (London, 1784).

133. Peter Pindar [John Wolcot], *Criticisms on the Rolliad*, 3d ed. (London, 1785), p. 95.

134. *History of the Westminster Election*, pp. 323, 338. Fox supporters claimed that a pro-government newspaper was "devoted to the panegyric of the principal crime, which disgraces the name of *man*, and which is rivetted to the purpose of rendering the female sex obnoxious."

135. *Intrepid Magazine*, 1784, p. 88. This journal was edited by Rev. William Hamilton, M.A. [and possibly Philip Francis].

136. *Wit of the Day*, p. 121.

137. Stott, "'Female Patriotism,'" pp. 60–84; *Wit of the Day*, p. 124.

138. *Wit of the Day*, p. 78.

139. For this theme, see the excellent article by Phyllis Deutsch, "Moral Trespass in Georgian London: Gaming, Gender and Electoral Politics in the Age of George III," *Historical Journal* 39 (1996): 637–56.

140. Paul Kelly, "Radicalism and Public Opinion in the General Election of 1784," *Bulletin of the Institute for Historical Research* 45, no. 3 (1972): 73–88; Deutsch, "Moral Trespass," pp. 637–56.

141. *History of the Westminster Election*, p. 252.

142. M. Dorothy George, *Catalogue of Political and Personal Satires* (London: British Library, 1978), vol. 5, 1771–1783, BMC 6487, "The Election Tate a Tate"; BMC 6493, "Female Influence; or, the Devonshire Canvas"; BMC 6533, "A Certain Dutchess kissing Old Swelter-in-Grease the Butcher for his Vote"; BMC 6548, "Wits Last Stake or the Cobling Voters and Abject Canvassers"; BMC 6549, "Dark Lanthern Business or Mrs. Hob and Nob on a Night Canvass with a Bosom friend"; BMC 6560, "The Tipling Duchess," all 1784.

143. For similar prints, see George, *Catalogue*, vol. 5, BMC 6490, "The Duchess of D——(Devonshire) in the Character of a Mother"; BMC 6546, "Political Affection," in which the duchess nurses a fox instead of her own infant; and *History of the Westminster Election*, p. 234.

144. Betsy Bolton, *Women, Nationalism and the Romantic Stage; Theater and Politics in Britain, 1780–1800* (Cambridge: Cambridge University Press, 2001), p. 30.

145. Susan Benforado, "Anne Seymour Damer (1748–1828) Sculptor" (Ph.D. diss., University of New Mexico, 1986).

146. Chalus, "'That Epidemical Madness,'" pp. 151–78.

147. Lewis, "1784 and All That," p. 121.

148. George, *Catalogue*, BMC 6597, "The Apotheosis of the Duchess"; see also BMC 6521, "Devonia, the Beautiful Daughter of Love and Liberty," both 1784.

149. Stott, "'Female Patriotism,'" p. 79; *History of the Westminster Election*, p. 313.

150. *History of the Westminster Election*, p. 346.

151. *Wit of the Day*, p. 139.

152. For the debating societies, see note 45. Although Linda Colley suggests (*Britons*, p. 244) that Fox later advocated suffrage for women in the 1790s, in a speech in 1797 advocating an expansion of the suffrage, Fox reassured Parliament that they were not espousing universal suffrage by using the idea of women voting to ridicule the notion of enfranchising the "lowest classes" such as soldiers and servants. *Parliamentary History of England*, vol. 33 (London, 1818), pp. 650, 661, 726.

153. Two historians have also suggested this interpretation. Amanda Foreman, "A Politician's Politician: Georgiana, Duchess of Devonshire and the Whig Party," in Barker and Chalus, *Gender in Eighteenth-Century England*, p. 180; Colley, *Britons*, p. 244.

154. *Sam. House and Sir Geoffry Dunstan, a Westminster Eclogue* (London, 1784); [Francis Annesley], *Five Minutes Advice to the People preparatory to the ensuing General Election* (London, 1784); *Wit of the Day*, p. 16; *History of the Westminster Election*, p. 105; the Garrat mock elections also linked the duchess with plebeian voters: John Brewer, "Theater and Counter-theater in Georgian Politics: The Mock Elections at Garrat," *Radical History Review* 22 (1979–80): 32–33.

155. *History of the Westminster Election*, p. 293.

156. Ibid., p. 343.

157. Mitchell, *Charles James Fox*, p. 51.

158. *Wit of the Day*, p. 125.

159. *History of the Westminster Election*, pp. 190–94.

160. *A Full and Authentic Account of the Whole of the Proceedings at Westminster Hall*, on Saturday, 14 Feb. 1784 (London, 1784).

161. *Political Letters written in March and April 1784* (London, 1784); George, *Catalogue*, vol. 5, BMC 6207, "An Analysis of Modern Patriotism," accuses Fox of rejecting Macaulay's principles.

162. John Disney, *Memoirs and Works of John Jebb* (London, 1787), p. 199.

163. *A State of Facts: or a Sketch of the Character and Political Conduct of the Right Hon. Charles Fox* (London, 1783), p. 7.

164. *The Modern Atalantis; or, the Devil in an Air Balloon. containing the Characters and Secret Memoirs of the Most Conspicuous Persons of High Quality, of Both Sexes, in the Island of Libertusia, in the Western Ocean* (London, 1784), contains many examples of the mistresses of prominent men exerting their patronage and influence.

165. See also George, *Catalogue*, vol. 5, BMC 6493, "Female Influence; or, the Devonshire Canvas."

166. *History of the Westminster Election*, p. 264.

167. Ibid., pp. 231, 233, 243, 264.

168. *A Political Sermon, preached before a R——t H——ble H——e*, p. 13.

169. Foreman, *Georgiana*, chap. 9; *Fox's and Pitt's Speeches in the House of Commons, upon the Business of the Westminster Scrutiny* (London, 1784); House of Commons, *Journals* 40 (20 May 1784); 9; [Sir Cecil Wray], *A Letter to the Independent Electors of Westminster, in the Interest of Lord Hood and Sir Cecil Wray*, 3d ed. (London, 1784).

170. William Thomas Laprade, "Parliamentary Papers of John Robinson 1774–1784," *Camden Miscellany*, 3d ser., 3 (1922): xvi. Radical John Horne Tooke argued that both sides had deployed a "regular system of the most barefaced and scandalous *bribery*" and that the government charged its officeholders a percentage of their salaries to finance electoral corruption. See *Proceedings in an Action for Debt between the R. Hon. Charles James Fox, Plaintiff and John Horne Tooke, Esq., Defendant* (London, 1792).

171. M. Dorothy George, "Fox's Martyrs: The General Election of 1784," *Transactions of the Royal Historical Society*, 4th ser., 21 (1939): 133–68.

172. *The Lounger* 1 (1785): 81–85; Grace A. Ellis, *A Memoir of Mrs. Anna Laetitia Barbauld, with many of her letters* (Boston, 1874), vol. 1, p. 119; [Anna Maria Bennett], *Juvenile Discretions* (London, 1786), vol. 3, p. 101.

173. *Norfolk Chronicle*, 3 Apr. 1784; Gerald Newman, *The Rise of English Nationalism*, rev. ed. (New York: St. Martin's Press, 1997), p. 218.

174. For an excellent electoral account of Norwich, see Wilson, *Sense of the People*, p. 422.

175. Sir Lewis Namier and John Brooke, *The History of Parliament: The House of Commons 1754–1790*, vol. 1 (London: HMSO, 1964), p. 339.

176. "An honest Freeholder's Reasons for voting against Mr Coke," 1784, Norfolk Record Office, BUL 14/17/11.

177. *The Election Magazine; or, Repository of Wit and Politics* (Norwich, 1784), p. 32.

178. Ibid., p. 15.

179. Ibid., p. 42.

180. Sophia Wodehouse to Sir Martin Folkes, high sheriff of Norfolk, 6 Apr. 1784, Norfolk Record Office, MC 50/36 503, f. 7.

181. E. Rolfe to Sir Martin Folkes, high sheriff of Norfolk, 25 Apr. 1784, Norfolk Record Office, MC 50/35.

182. Collection on 1788 Westminster Election, British Library, 8133.bb.54.

183. K. D. Reynolds, *Aristocratic Women and Political Society in Victorian Britain* (Oxford: Clarendon Press, 1998); for the exceptions, see Sarah Richardson, "The Role of Women in Electoral Politics in Yorkshire during the Eighteen-Thirties," *Northern History* 32 (1996): 141; Jill Liddington, *Female Fortune: Land, Gender and Authority. The Anne Lister Diaries and Other Writings, 1833–6* (London and New York: Rivers Oram Press, 1998).

184. Interestingly enough, a Gillray caricature portrayed the new La Belle Assemblée as controlled by Mrs. Hobart, who had canvassed for Wray in 1784; Godfrey, *James Gillray*, BMC 7218, plate 192, p. 210. Handwritten notations on the print give the names of Mrs. Hobart and other ladies.

185. Andrew, *London Debating Societies*, p. 223, 17 Mar. 1788.

186. Ibid., p. 181, 27 Mar., 3 April 1786.

187. Ibid., p. 237, 29 Oct. 1788.

188. W. Taswell, Aylsham, to William Wiggin Bulwer, 1784, Norfolk Record Office, BUL 14/4/122.

189. J. Williams, *A Novel: the Forty Days madness of a General Election in England* (London, 1784), pp. 6, 12, 39; see also [Eliza Ryves], *Hermit of Snowden, or Memoirs of Albert and Lavinia* (London, 1789); "A Lady," *The Twin Sisters; or the Effects of Education* (London, 1788).

190. William Cowper, "The Task," *Poems* (London, 1786), vol. 2, p. 141.

191. *Morning Herald*, 19 Nov. 1780.

192. William Roberts, *Memoirs of the Life and Correspondence of Mrs. Hannah More* (New York, 1836), vol. 1, p. 117. The epilogue to Frances Brooke's play *The Seige of Sinope* (1781) contrasts the gambling patriot with the genuine emotion of the female Poet.

193. Gary Kelly, *Women, Writing, and Revolution, 1790–1827* (Oxford: Clarendon Press, 1993), p. 4.

194. G. J. Barker-Benfield, *The Culture of Sensibility: Sex and Society in Eighteenth-Century Britain* (Chicago: University of Chicago Press, 1992).

195. Sara Suleri, *The Rhetoric of English India* (Chicago: University of Chicago Press, 1992), p. 60.

CHAPTER FOUR: EDMUND BURKE AND THE BEGUMS OF OUDH: GENDER, EMPIRE, AND PUBLIC OPINION

1. The managers of the impeachment sometimes referred to begums as princesses, but this was really a more general term for wives or concubines of rulers or governors. There are several versions of the Hastings trial, which cover different years: *Hastings' Trial* (London, 1787–88), 3 vols., abbreviated as *Trial* (1787–88); *The Trial of Warren Hastings: Printed from The World* (London, 1793), abbreviated as *Trial* (1793); *The History of the Trial of Warren Hastings, Esq.* (London, 1796), abbreviated as *Trial* (1796). Much of the evidence was printed in *Papers printed by the Order of the House of Commons in the years 1786 and 1787 relating to the Charges of Delinquency exhibited in that House against Warren Hastings* (London, 1787), abbreviated as *Papers printed by Order of the House of Commons.*

2. *The Speeches of Richard Brinsley Sheridan* (London, 1842), vol. 1, p. 374.

3. *Trial* (1793), p. 154.

4. The standard work is P. J. Marshall, *The Impeachment of Warren Hastings* (London: Oxford University Press, 1965); see also Geoffrey Carnall and Colin Nicholson, eds., *The Impeachment of Warren Hastings* (Edinburgh: Edinburgh University Press, 1989). For other important issues such as law, trade, and land reform, see Ranajit Guha, *A Rule of Property for Bengal* (Durham, N.C.: Duke University Press, 1996); Susan Staves, "Chattel Property Rules and the Construction of Englishness, 1660–1800," *Law and History Review* 12, no. 1 (1994): 123–53.

5. Peter Charles Hull and N.E.H. Hull, *Impeachment in America, 1635–1805* (New Haven, Conn.: Yale University Press, 1984), pp. 3–7, on British precedents.

6. Regina Janes, "Edmund Burke's Flying Leap from India to France," *History of European Ideas* 7 (1986): 509–27; David Musselwhite, "The Trial of Warren Hastings," in Francis Barker, ed., *Literature, Politics and Theory* (London: Methuen, 1986), pp. 77–103; Frans De Bruyn, "Edmund Burke's Gothic Romance: The Portrayal of Warren Hastings in Burke's Writings and Speeches on India," *Criticism* 29 (1987): 428–29; Sara Suleri, *The Rhetoric of English India* (Chicago: University of Chicago Press, 1992), p. 48; Kate Teltscher, *India Inscribed: European and British Writing on India 1600–1800* (Delhi: Oxford University Press, 1995), pp. 157–91; Jyotsna G. Singh, *Colonial Narratives, Cultural Dialogues: Discoveries of India in the Language of Colonialism* (New York: Routledge, 1996), pp. 52–79.

7. *Public Advertiser*, 4 June 1788.

8. Frederick Whelan, *Edmund Burke and India: Political Morality and Empire* (Pittsburgh: University of Pittsburgh Press, 1996), p. 292.

9. Elizabeth D. Samet, "A Prosecutor and a Gentleman: Edmund Burke's Idiom of Impeachment," *English Literary History* 68 (2001): 407.

10. François Catrou, *Histoire Génerale de l'Empire du Mogol dépuis sa fondation, sur la Mémoires Portugais de M. Manouchi* (La Hague, 1708); François Bernier, *Travels in the Mogul Empire, A.D. 1656–1668*, trans. Irving Brock and Archibald Constable (Delhi: S. Chand, 1968 [1670]).

11. Charles-Louis de Secondat Montesquieu, *The Spirit of the Laws*, ed. David Wallace Carrithers (Berkeley: University of California Press, 1977 [1757]), bk. 4, chap. 14, pp. 144–45; James Tracy points out that the phrase "oriental despotism" originated in Nicholas Boulanger's *Origins and Progress of Despotism* (Amsterdam, 1764), which, as we have seen, was influential for Wilkes. James Tracy, "Asian Despotism: The Views of European Sojourners in the Muslim Empires (1500–1700)" (unpublished manuscript, University of University of Minnesota, 1 Oct. 1989). Thanks to Professor Tracy for allowing me to consult this manuscript.

12. Catrou, *Histoire Génerale*, p. 87; Bernier, *Travels in the Mogul Empire*, p. 291; Robert Orme, *Historical Fragments of the Mogul Empire, of the Morattoes, and of the English Concerns in Indostan*, ed. J. P. Guha (New Delhi: Associated Publishing House, 1974 [1753]), p. 299; for later images of the "effeminate Bengali," see Ashis Nandy, *The Intimate Enemy: Loss and Recovery of the Self under Colonialism* (Delhi: Oxford University Press, 1983), p. 10; Mrinalini Sinha, *Colonial Masculinity: The "Manly Englishman" and the "Effeminate Bengali" in the Late Nineteenth Century* (Manchester: Manchester University Press, 1995), p. 15.

13. Bernier, *Travels in the Mogul Empire*, pp. 133–45; Catrou, *Histoire Génerale*, p. 160; Montesquieu, *Spirit of the Laws*, bk. 24, chap. 3, pp. 322–23; Rana Kabbani, *Imperial Fictions: Europe's Myths of the Orient* (London: Pandora, 1994), p. 25.

14. Roxann Wheeler, *The Complexion of Race: Categories of Difference in Eighteenth-Century British Culture* (Philadephia: University of Pennsylvania Press, 2000), p. 242; for an example, *A Letter to the Right Hon. Lord North, etc. etc. on the Present Proceedings concerning the East India Company* (London, 1773), p. 27.

15. Philip Lawson, *The East India Company: A History* (London: Longman, 1993), pp. 89–90.

16. Charles Caraccioli, *The Life of Robert Lord Clive Baron Plassey*, 4 vols. (London, 1776); Bruce Lenman and Philip Lawson, "Robert Clive, the 'Black Jagir,' and British Politics," *Historical Journal* 26 (1983): 801–29.

17. Philip Lawson and Jim Phillips, "'Our Execrable Banditti': Perceptions of Nabobs in Mid-Eighteenth-Century Britain," *Albion* 16 (1984): 225, 239; Samuel Foote, *The Nabob* (London, 1778); *The Nabob: or, Asiatic Plunderers. A Satyrical Poem, in a Dialogue between the Friend and the Author* (London, 1773); *Thoughts on our acquisitions in the East Indies; particularly respecting Bengal* (London, 1771), p. 23.

18. Peter N. Miller, *Defining the Common Good: Empire, Religion and Philosophy in Eighteenth-Century Britain* (Cambridge: Cambridge University Press, 1994), p. 190.

19. *A Letter to the Rt. Hon Lord North, etc etc. on the Present Proceedings concerning the East India Company* (London, 1773).

20. Lawson, *East India Company*, p. 122.

21. Hastings to Lord North, 4 Dec. 1774, Letters from Bengal, James Ford Bell Library, University of Minnesota, 1777 Ha.

22. C. A. Bayly, "The British Military Fiscal-State and Indigenous Resistance: India 1750–1820," in Lawrence Stone, ed., *An Imperial State at War: Britain from 1789–1815* (London and New York: Routledge, 1994), p. 324.

23. For debates on whether Hastings functioned as an oriental despot or an efficient British administrator, see Bayly, "The British Military Fiscal-State"; Marshall, *Impeachment*, p. 153; Neil Sen, "Warren Hastings and British Sovereign Authority in Bengal, 1774–80," *Journal of Imperial and Commonwealth History* 25 (1997): 59–81.

24. Lauren Benton, *Law and Colonial Cultures* (Cambridge: Cambridge University Press, 2002), p. 139.

25. For this theme in general, see Bernard S. Cohn, *Colonialism and Its Forms of Knowledge: The British in India* (Princeton, N.J.: Princeton University Press, 1996).

26. C. A. Bayly, *Rulers, Townsmen and Bazaars: North Indian Society in the Age of British Expansion 1770–1870* (Delhi: Oxford University Press, 1992), p. 199; Lawson, *East India Company*, p. 113.

27. Letter from Hastings To my dear Friends, 28 Mar. 1776, from Fort William, Letters from Bengal, Bell Library, University of Minnesota, 1777 Ha.

28. Guha, *A Rule of Property*, pp. 67–77; Sophia Weitzman, *Warren Hastings and Philip Francis* (Manchester: Manchester University Press, 1929), p. 23; Joseph Parkes and Herman Merivale, *Memoirs of Sir Philip Francis, KCB with Correspondence and Journals* (London, 1867), vol. 1, p. 324.

29. Eunuchs were men, castrated in their youth, who could serve as administrators in Mughal courts. Muhammed Faiz-Bakhsh, *Memoirs of Delhi and Faizabad*, trans. William Hoey (Allahabad, 1888), vol. 2, p. 86.

30. Alexander Dow, *The History of Hindostan, Second Revised, Corrected and Enlarged Edition* (New Delhi: Today and Tomorrow's Printers and Publishers, 1973 [1770]), vol. 3, p. xiv.

31. Montesquieu, *Spirit of the Laws*, bk. 16, chap. 10, p. 272. Interestingly, Islamic sources in the Ottoman empire originated the criticisms of women's power over the sultan in the seventeenth century. Leslie P. Peirce, *The Imperial Harem: Women and Sovereignty in the Islamic Empire* (Oxford: Oxford University Press, 1993), p. 174; for British knowledge of Montesquieu, for instance, Ketaki Kushari Dyson, *A Various Universe: A Study of the Journals and Memoirs of British Men and Women in the Indian Subcontinent, 1765–1856* (Delhi: Oxford University Press, 1978), p. 124; *Thoughts on Our Acquisitions in the East Indies; particularly respecting Bengal* (London, 1771).

32. For examples among earlier nawabs of Oudh, see Jagadish Sarkar, *A Study of Eighteenth-Century India*, vol. 1, *Political History 1707–1761* (Calcutta: Saraswat Li-

brary, 1976), pp. 408–15; elsewhere, see Mehendra Narain Sharma, *The Life and Times of Begam Samru of Sardhana* (Sahibabad: Vibhu Prakashan, 1985), p. 59; Fazl Rubbee, "Mir Jafar and Siraj-ud-Daulah," *Bengal Past and Present* 12 (1916): 249.

33. Rev. G. R. Gleig, *Memoirs of the Life of the Rt. Hon. Warren Hastings, First Governor General of Bengal* (London, 1841), vol. 1, pp. 261–69, reprinting Hastings's letters justifying his decision.

34. Peirce, *Imperial Harem*, pp. 144, 248, 274.

35. Marshall, *Impeachment*, pp. 134–38.

36. "Oudh" was also spelled "Oude" in the eighteenth century; in India today, it is now spelled "Awadh." I am using the form "begums" instead of "begams" and "Oudh" instead of "Awadh" because these were the most common eighteenth-century spellings.

37. The Rohillas invaded a northern province of India in the eighteenth century, coming down from Afghanistan. Charles Hamilton, *An Historical Relation of the Origin, Progress, and Final Dissolution of the Government of the Rohilla Afgans in the Northern Provinces of Hindostan. Compiled from a Persian Manuscript and other Original Papers* (London, 1787), for an account critical of the Rohillas and favorable to Hastings. Hamilton could not find any evidence of the plundering of the Rohilla women (p. 253). For a version that emphasizes Shujah's lust, see *The Fall of the Rohillas. An Historic Poem in Three Cantos* (London, 1788).

38. Michael H. Fisher, *A Clash of Cultures: Awadh, the British and the Mughals* (Riverdale, Md.: Riverdale Company, 1987), pp. 18, 38; K. S. Santha, *Begums of Awadh* (Varanasi: Bharati Prakashan, 1980), p. 7. Placing surplus treasure in the zenana was typical in such dynasties; see Gavin R. G. Hambly, "Armed Women Retainers in the Zenanas of Indo-Muslim Rulers," in Gavin R. G. Hambly, ed., *Women in Medieval Islamic Culture* (New York: St. Martin's Press, 1998), p. 433.

39. Isfahani Abu Talib ibn Muhamad, *History of Asafu'd Daulah Nawab Wazir of Oudh*, trans. William Hoey (Lucknow: Pustak Kendra, 1971 [1885]), pp. 9, 29.

40. Santha, *Begums of Awadh*, p. 175; Richard B. Barnett, *North India between Empires: Awadh, the Mughals and the British 1720–1801* (Berkeley: University of California Press, 1980), pp. 121–22; Michael Fisher, "Women and the Feminine in the Court and High Culture of Awadh, 1722–1856," and Richard B. Barnett, "Embattled Begams: Women as Power Brokers in Early Modern India," both in Hambly, *Women in Medieval Islamic Culture*, pp. 497, 532.

41. Fisher, *Clash of Cultures*, p. 73; Barnett, *North India between Empires*, p. 105; Amir Hasan, *Palace Culture of Lucknow* (Delhi: BR Publishing, 1983), p. 110; Muhammed Faiz-Bakhsh, *Memoirs of Delhi and Faizabad*, vol. 2, pp. 12, 246, 36, 184; and Isfahani Abu Talib ibn Muhamad, *History of Asofu'd Daulah*, pp. 9, 29.

42. Kabir-Ur-Rahm Khan, "The Impeachment: Certain Issues of International law," in Carnall and Nicholson, *Impeachment of Warren Hastings*, pp. 158–59; Gregory Kozlowski, "Muslim Women and Control of Property in North India," in J. Krishnamurty, ed., *Women in Colonial India: Essays on Survival, Work and the State* (Delhi: Oxford University Press, 1989), p. 122.

43. Cohn, *Colonialism and Its Forms of Knowledge*, p. 18.

44. Letter from Bow [Bahu] Begum to Board, received 20th Dec. 1775, *Papers printed by the Order of the House of Commons*, vol. 4, p. 7, from E to F.

45. *Trial* (1787–88), vol. 2, p. 449; Extract from Bengal Secret Consultations, 3 Jan. 1776, in *Papers printed by the Order of the House of Commons*, vol. 2, p. 212.

46. *Papers printed by the Order of the House of Commons*, vol. 3, p. 214.

47. Rudranghshu Mukherjee, "Trade and Empire in Awadh, 1765–1804," *Past and Present* 94 (1982): 87; P. J. Marshall, "Debate: Early British Imperialism in India," *Past and Present* 106 (1985): 164–69; Rudranghshu Mukherjee, "Rejoinder," *Past and Present* 106 (1985): 170–72; more generally, Sudipta Sen, *Empire of Free Trade: The East India Company and the Making of the Colonial Marketplace* (Philadelphia: University of Pennsylvania Press, 1998), p. 97.

48. Hastings may have been searching for an excuse to overthrow Cheit Singh; his ally General Eyre Coote observed that Cheit Singh's lands could serve as a useful buffer against the marauding Marathas; see Journal of a Tour from Ghyretty, 27 Sept. 1779 to Jan. 1780, Ames Library, University of Minnesota, MssB115, f. 44. This journal is attributed to Hastings in the University of Minnesota catalog, but it is not by Hastings; it was probably written by Richard Johnson, an East India Company servant, who accompanied General Eyre Coote on this tour (attribution from internal evidence, handwriting comparison to Johnson manuscripts in British Library, India Office Library, OIC 1/6/1 ff. 87–92; OIC Ms. Eur. F. 201/13).

49. Warren Hastings, *A Narrative of the Insurrection which happened in the Zemeedary of Banaris, in the Month of August 1781* (Calcutta, 1782); *Trial* (1787–88), vol. 1, p. 382.

50. Barnett, *North India between Empires*, p. 202, quoting Hannay to Middleton, 13, 20 Sept. 1781.

51. Copy of Bengal Persian *Correspondence*, 27 Dec. 1781, *Papers printed by the Order of the House of Commons*, vol. 1, p. 386; Muhammed Faiz-Bakhsh, *Memoirs of Delhi and Faizabad*, vol. 2, pp. 12, 246, 36, 184.

52. Barnett, *North India between Empires*, p. 123; Isfahani Abu Talib ibn Muhamad, *History of Asaf*, p. 46.

53. Bristow to Hastings, 31 Mar. 1783, and letter from Major Gilpin to Bristow, Fyzabad, 15 Nov. 1782, from Bengal Secret Consultations, *Papers printed by the Order of the House of Commons* vol. 1, pp. 531, 735, 736.

54. Weitzman, *Warren Hastings and Philip Francis*, p. 32.

55. Lawson, *East India Company*, p. 123.

56. Charles James Fox, *Substance of the Speech of the Rt. Hon. Charles James Fox, on a motion for the commitment of the Bill for vesting the affairs of the East India Company in the Hands of certain commissioners, for the benefit of the proprietors, and the public* (London, 1783), p. 4.

57. Edmund Burke, "A Philosophical Enquiry into the Origin of our Ideas of the Sublime and the Beautiful" (1757), in Ian Harris, *Burke: Pre-revolutionary Writings* (Cambridge: Cambridge University Press, 1993), pp. 63–77.

58. P. J. Marshall, ed., *The Writings and Speeches of Edmund Burke*, vol. 5, *India, Madras and Bengal 1774–1785* (Oxford: Oxford University Press, 1981), p. 403.

59. Burke, "Speech on Almas Ali Khan," 30 July 1784, in Harris, *Burke: Pre-revolutionary Writings*, p. 283.

60. Marshall, *The Writings and Speeches of Edmund Burke*, vol. 5, p. 411.

61. *An Authentic Account of the debates in the House of Lords, on 15 and 16 December, 1783, on the East India Bill* (London, 1783); *A Warning Voice; or, An answer upon the speech of the Rt. Hon. Mr. Secretary Fox, upon East-India Affairs* (London, 1783).

62. M. Dorothy George, *Catalogue of Political and Personal Satires*, vol. 5, 1771–1783 (London: British Library, 1978), BMC 6276, 6277.

63. Recos Jepphi [Joseph Price], *A Ministerial Almanack: addressed to the Right Hon. Lord Thurlow, in which is set forth and clearly explained, the Nature and Value of every Sort of Patronage now about to be transferred from the East India Company to the Crown* (London, 1783), p. 43; see also *Some Considerations in Regard to the Dangerous Consequences which might ensue to the Constitution from the passing of the East India Bill* (London, 1784), p. 12.

64. Lawson, *East India Company*, pp. 124–29.

65. C. A. Bayly, *Indian Society and the Making of the British Empire* (Cambridge: Cambridge University Press), p. 78.

66. Burke to Adam Smith, 7 Dec. 1786, in John E. Woods, ed., *The Correspondence of Edmund Burke* (Chicago: University of Chicago Press, 1963), vol. 5, p. 296.

67. Lori Fisler Damrosch, "Impeachment as a Technique of Control over Foreign Policy in a Parliamentary System," *University of Colorado Law Review* 70 (1999): 1533.

68. Jonathan Turley, "Senate Trials and Factional Disputes: Impeachment as a Madisonian Device," *Duke Law Journal* 49 (1999): 9–18.

69. John Nicholls, *Recollections and Reflections, Personal and Political, as Connected with Public Affairs during the Reign of George III* (London, 1822), vol. 1, p. 277.

70. Major John Scott, *Charge against the Right Honourable Edmund Burke* (London, 1789).

71. Lars E. Troide, editor and annotator, *Horace Walpole's Miscellany 1786–1795* (New Haven, Conn.: Yale University Press, 1978), p. 51.

72. N. W. Wraxall, *Posthumous Memoirs of his Own Times* (London, 1836), vol. 1, p. 171; Michael Edwardes, *Warren Hastings: King of the Nabobs* (London: Hart-Davis, MacGibbon, 1976), p. 174.

73. *A Full and True Account of the wonderful Diamond, presented to the King's Majesty, by Warren Hastings, Esq.,* (London, 1786).

74. [Eliza Ryves], *The Hastiniad: An Heroic Poem in Three Cantos* (London, 1785).

75. *A Letter to the Right Honorable Charles James Fox on the Late Debates upon the Declaratory Bill in Parliament, and in Leadenhall Street, by an India Proprietor*

(London, 1788); *An Appeal from the Hasty to the Deliberate Judgment of the People of England, containing a Statement of the Manifold Services Rendered by our Countrymen in India* (London, 1787).

76. *The Friends of Mr. Hastings, wishing to convey to the Proprietory at large as full an Account as possible of the Proceedings which took place at the East India-house on Thursday last* (London, 1782), p. 40; [Nathaniel Brassey Halhed], *A Hint upon the Present Debates on Indian Affairs* (London, 1782), pp. 8–13; *Letters, containing a Correct and Important Elucidation of the Subject of Mr. Hastings' Impeachment, which originally appeared in the Oracle* (London, 1790), p. 82.

77. *Morning Chronicle,* 9 Feb. 1787; hostility to female property owning was increasing in late eighteenth-century England; Susan Staves, *Married Women's Separate Property in England, 1660–1833* (Cambridge: Harvard University Press, 1990), p. 168.

78. *An Appeal to the People of England and Scotland, on behalf of Warren Hastings* (London, 1787), p. 23.

79. *The Defense of Warren Hastings, Esq. (Late Governor General of Bengal) at the Bar of the House of Commons* (London, 1786), pp. 85, 106; copy in the British Library with manuscript notations by Hastings.

80. Manuscript Transcript of Proceedings in the Impeachment of Warren Hastings, 15 Apr. 1788, Impeachment Trial papers, Bell Library, University of Minnesota, f. 193.

81. [Nathaniel Halhed], *Examination of Public Measures, proposed in 1782, both in the House of Commons, and at the India House, as far as they concern The Hon. Warren Hastings, Esq., Governor General of Bengal* (London, 1782), p. 12. See also [Nathaniel Halhed], *The Letters of Detector, on the Reports of the Select Committee of the House of Commons* (London, 1782), p. 4.

82. Fox tended to see the Hastings impeachment as a party matter, which could give advantage to the Whigs, but Burke and Sheridan took a more idealistic view; Burke to Philip Francis, 10 Dec. 1785, in Woods, *Correspondence of Edmund Burke,* vol. 5, p. 243.

83. As in Burke's *Thoughts on the Present Discontents,* in Harris, *Burke: Prerevolutionary Writings,* p. 185.

84. This description of Sheridan draws upon Fintan O'Toole, *A Traitor's Kiss: The Life of Richard Brinsley Sheridan* (New York: Farrar Straus and Giroux, 1998), pp. 166–99.

85. Sheridan, *Speeches* (1842), vol. 1, p. 241.

86. *Gazeteer,* 15 Feb. 1787. In another example, a gentleman inspired by Sheridan's speech on India sent in a letter against cock throwing; *Gazeteer,* 20 Feb. 1787. See also poem by J. Day, *Morning Chronicle,* 27 Mar. 1788; a similar poem in the *Gazeteer,* 15 Feb. 1787.

87. Marshall, *Impeachment,* p. 62.

88. Seymour Drescher, *Capitalism and Anti-slavery: British Mobilization in Comparative Perspective* (Basingstoke: Macmillan, 1986), pp. 61–66; Robin Black-

burn, *The Overthrow of Colonial Slavery 1776–1848* (London: Verso, 1988), pp. 133–42.

89. Donna T. Andrew, *London Debating Societies* (London: London Record Society, 1994), p. 222; Maria Falconar and Harriet Falconar, *Poems on Slavery* (London, 1788), p. 3; Hugh Mulligan, *Poems, Chiefly on Slavery and Oppression* (London, 1788), p. 9.

90. *London Chronicle*, 16–19 Feb., 22–24 Apr. 1788.

91. *Ladies Magazine* 18 (Feb. 1787): 59–64; 19 (Apr. 1788): 197–200; 19 (May 1788): 219–22; 19 (June 1788): 275–280; 19 (July 1788): 254–58; 19 (Aug. 1788): 393–99.

92. In a letter to William Eden, 17 May 1784, Burke criticizes the limited "sensibility" of the public; Woods, *Correspondence of Edmund Burke*, vol. 5, p. 151.

93. Markman Ellis, *The Politics of Sensibility: Race, Gender, and Commerce in the Sentimental Novel* (Cambridge: Cambridge University Press, 1996), pp. 88–104.

94. Burke praised Sir Gilbert Eliot for evoking tears in his speech; Burke to Lady Elliot, 13 Dec. 1787, Woods, *Correspondence of Edmund Burke*, vol. 5, p. 369.

95. Sheridan, *Speeches* (1842), vol. 1, p. 241.

96. Marshall, *Impeachment*, p. 70.

97. Burke also highlighted female victimization in his summation of the issues; see P. J. Marshall, ed., *The Writings and Speeches of Edmund Burke*, vol. 6, *India: the Launching of the Hastings Impeachment 1786–1788* (Oxford: Oxford University Press, 1991), p. 77.

98. *Trial* (1787–88), pp. 1–12.

99. Marshall, *Writings and Speeches of Edmund Burke*, vol. 6, pp. 125–258.

100. Ibid., p. 292; Marshall, *Writings and Speeches of Edmund Burke*, vol. 5, p. 51; Philip Francis, *Speech in the House of Commons on Tuesday the 7th of March 1786* (London, 1786), p. 45; *The Origin and Authentic Narrative of the Present Marratta War; and also, the late Rohilla War, in 1773 and 1774* (London, 1781), p. 12; for a lurid version of this imagery, see *The Fall of the Rohillas: An Historic Poem in Three Cantos* (London, 1788). For refutations of Burke's charges, see Examination of Major Balfour, 11 May 1786, *Papers printed by the Order of the House of Commons*, vol. 3, p. 51; Charles Hamilton, *An Historical Relation of the Origin, Progress, and Final Dissolution of the Government of the Rohilla Afgans in the Northern Provinces of Hindostan* (London, 1787).

101. Marshall, *Writings and Speeches of Edmund Burke*, vol. 6, p. 255.

102. Regina Janes, "Edmund Burke's Indian Idyll," *Studies in Eighteenth-Century Culture* 9 (1979): 3–13.

103. Sheridan, *Speeches* (1842), vol. 1, p. 369.

104. Conor Cruise O'Brien, *The Great Melody: A Thematic Biography of Edmund Burke* (Chicago: University of Chicago Press, 1992), pp. 271–72; Uday Mehta, *Liberalism and Empire: A Study in Nineteenth-Century British Liberal Thought* (Chicago: University of Chicago Press, 1999), p. 155.

105. For debates on race in the 1780s, see Wheeler, *Complexion of Race*, p. 253.

106. Sheridan's speech, 6 June 1788, Manuscript transcript of proceedings, Impeachment Trial Papers, Bell Library, University of Minnesota, 1786fHa, f. 42. See also version in *Public Advertiser*, 10 June 1788.

107. Burke to Miss Mary Palmer, 19 Jan. 1786, Huntington Library, HM 22523.

108. *Public Advertiser*, 10 June 1788.

109. *Morning Chronicle*, 14 June 1787. This version emphasizes "British justice." See also Sheridan, *Speeches*, (1842), vol. 1, p. 424, which just prints "justice".

110. Burke also claimed Hastings deprived other powerless widows of their inheritance. Marshall, *Writings and Speeches of Edmund Burke*, vol. 5, p. 41; vol. 6, p. 451. For other speeches at the first day of the impeachment that refer to the victimization of women, see speeches of Mr. Adams, Mr. Pelham, and Mr. Goring, *Trial* (1796), pp. 28, 73; speech of Pelham, 16 Apr. 1788, Manuscript transcript of proceedings, Impeachment Trial Papers, Bell Library, University of Minnesota, 1786fHa, f. 179.

111. Sheridan's notes for the begum speech contain reprints of the begums' letters; manuscript notes on Sheridan's begum speech, Duke University Library, Special Collections. His wife helped him considerably in preparing the speech; Linda Kelly, *Richard Brinsley Sheridan: A Life* (London: Sinclair-Stevenson, 1997), p. 147.

112. This speech represents a move away from Burke's earlier speech on the begums, in which he lauds their "courage" in acting against the British (Burke, "Speech on Almas Ali Khan," in Harris, *Burke: Pre-revolutionary Writings*, p. 273); in his notes for the speech, Sheridan says they drew upon the deference due to tradition, in lieu of "manly courage."

113. De Bruyn, "Edmund Burke's Gothic Romance," pp. 428–29, establishes the importance of gothic romance as a genre in Burke's speeches. However, he mainly compares Burke's speeches to Ann Radcliffe's *Mysteries of Udolpho*, which was published in 1794, while Burke used these literary tropes in the 1780s. A more likely model for both Sheridan and Burke would be Horace Walpole, *The Castle of Otranto*, in E. F. Bleiler, ed., *Three Gothic Novels* (New York: Dover, 1966). For similarities between gothic and oriental genres, see Anna Laetitia Aikin, "On the Pleasure Derived from Objects of Terror" (1773), in E. J. Clergy and Robert Miles, eds., *Gothic Documents: A Sourcebook 1770–1820* (Manchester: Manchester University Press, 2000), p. 128. For examples of oriental dramas, see Mr. Howard, *Almeyda, or the Rival Kings: A Tragedy* (London, 1769); Richard Paul Jodrell, *The Persian Heroine, a Tragedy* (London, 1786); and Isaac Bickerstaffe, *The Sultan, or a Peep into the Seraglio, a Farce, in Two Acts* (London, 1787), which was first performed in 1775. William Beckford combined the genres in his *Vathek* (1786), reprinted in Bleiler, *Three Gothic Novels*.

114. Burke to Philip Francis, 7 Jan. 1787, in Woods, *Correspondence of Edmund Burke*, vol. 5, p. 304. To be sure, Sheridan criticized gothic romance in *The Critic* (1779), but later he wrote his own gothic drama, *Pizarro*, which used the Spanish conquest of Peru to echo the injustices of the English in India. See Paul Ranger,

"Terror and Pity Reign in Every Breast": Gothic Drama in the London Patent Theatres, 1750–1820 (London: Society for Theatre Research, 1991), pp. 13, 132.

115. Stephen Bernstein, "Form and Ideology in the Gothic Novel," *Essays in Literature* 18 (1991): 151–65.

116. Frances Sheridan (the playwright's mother), *The History of Nourjahad* (London, 1767); Walpole, *Castle of Otranto*, p. 101; Ranger, *"Terror and Pity,"* p. 12.

117. Sheridan, *Speeches* (1842), vol. 1, pp. 230, 240, 241, 376.

118. Paula Backscheider, *Spectacular Politics: Theatrical Power and Mass Culture in Early Modern England* (Baltimore: Johns Hopkins University Press, 1993), p. 232.

119. As Sara Suleri suggests in her *Rhetoric of English India*, pp. 15–16.

120. Terry Eagleton, "Aesthetics and Politics in Edmund Burke," *History Workshop Journal* 28 (1989): 58.

121. Marshall, *Writings and Speeches of Edmund Burke*, vol. 6, p. 307.

122. In fact, Shujah tried to kill Asof because of Asof's exclusive sexual interest in men. See "Observations on the Family of his Excellency the Nabob Vizier Sujah-ul-Dowlah, and upon the Characters of the Principal People about his Court, and some of his Civil and Military Sirdars," by an unknown hand, written 1775, in BL, Add. Ms. 29,202, ff. 110–11. For Sheridan and Pitt, see James Morwood, *The Life and Works of Richard Brinsley Sheridan* (Edinburgh: Scottish Academic Press, 1985), p. 110; Burke was more sympathetic to men accused of sodomy. Woods, *Correspondence of Edmund Burke*, vol. 4, p. 350, referring to an incident in 1780; Isaac Kramnick, *The Rage of Edmund Burke* (New York: Basic Books, 1977), p. 84. For the general suppression of information about non-Western male-male eroticism, see Rudi C. Bleys, *The Geography of Perversion: Male to Male Sexual Behavior Outside the West and the Ethnographic Imagination, 1750–1918* (New York: New York University Press, 1995), pp. 72, 113.

123. Marshall, *Writings and Speeches of Edmund Burke*, vol. 5, p. 392.

124. Ibid., vol. 6, p. 160.

125. *Morning Chronicle*, 3 Mar. 1787.

126. Marshall, *Writings and Speeches of Edmund Burke*, vol. 6, p. 205. In the third article of impeachment, Burke charged that Hastings exposed another "unfortunate Prince [Muzuffer Jung] aforesaid to the ruinous Effects of his own Weakness, and the Knavery and Corruption of his Servants"; ibid., p. 160.

127. P. J. Marshall, *The Writings and Speeches of Edmund Burke*, vol. 7, *India: The Hastings Trial 1789–1784* (Oxford: Oxford University Press, 2000), p. 54.

128. Kramnick, *Rage of Edmund Burke*, p. 201.

129. George, *Catalogue*, vol. 5, BMC 7138, "Cicero against Verres," 7 Feb. 1787. Nathaniel Wraxall was not convinced by this comparison, pointing out that the Sicilians brought the case against Verres, unlike the Indians. Nathanial William Wraxall, *Historical Memoirs of My Own Time* (London: Kegan Paul, 1904 [1816]), vol. 2, p. 110.

130. Marshall, *Writings and Speeches of Edmund Burke*, vol. 6, p. 28; M. Tullius Cicero, *The Orations of Marcus Tullius Cicero*, trans. C. D. Yonge (London: George Bell and Sons, 1903).

131. Amy Richlin, *The Garden of Priapus: Sexuality and Aggression in Roman Humor* (New York: Oxford University Press, 1983), p. 102, notes that in Verres "the figure of Priapus comes alive."

132. Marshall, *Writings and Speeches of Edmund Burke*, vol. 5, p. 184.

133. Burke to Francis, 3 Jan. 1788, in Woods, *Correspondence of Edmund Burke*, vol. 5, p. 372.

134. *Trial* (1796), p. 3.

135. Narahari Kaviraj, *A Peasant Uprising in Bengal 1783: The First Formidable Peasant Uprising against the Rule of the East India Company* (New Delhi: People's Publishing House, 1972); Ranajit Guha, *Elementary Aspects of Peasant Insurgency in Colonial India* (Delhi: Oxford University Press, 1983), p. 158; Rajat Kanta Ray, "Colonial Penetration and the Initial Resistance: The Mughal Ruling Class, the English East India Company and the Struggle for Bengal 1756–1800," *Indian Historical Review* 12, nos. 1–2 (1985–86): 68–69.

136. Burke and Francis emphasized that the zemindars in this case were mostly women in order to prove their point that they were hereditary landholders, like the English gentry, who could not be deprived of their land rather than, as Hastings described them, officials of the Mughal empire whose lands provided their salaries, and who therefore could be deprived of their lands when stripped of their offices. See Francis's speech, *Gazeteer*, 19 Apr. 1787. See also Guha, *A Rule of Property*, pp. 54–55.

137. Marshall, *Writings and Speeches of Edmund Burke*, vol. 5, pp. 420–22.

138. *Letters, containing a Correct and Important Elucidation of the Subject of Mr. Hastings' Impeachment, which originally appeared in the Oracle* (London, 1790), p. 2.

139. Hugh Mulligan, *Poems, Chiefly on Slavery and Oppression* (London, 1788), p. 72.

140. Edmund Burke, *A Philosophical Enquiry into the Origin of our Ideas of the Sublime and the Beautiful*, in Harris, *Pre-revolutionary writings*, pp. 64, 69; Paul Hindson and Tim Gray, *Burke's Dramatic Theory of Politics* (Aldershot: Avebury/Gower, 1988), p. 75.

141. In this paragraph, I am applying arguments about humanitarianism developed by Halttunen and Ellis to Burke's speech. See Karen Halttunen, "Humanitarianism and the Pornography of Pain in Anglo-American Culture," *American Historical Review* 100 (1995): 309–11; Ellis, *Politics of Sensibility*, p. 128.

142. *Morning Chronicle*, 28 Apr. 1788; also printed in *Public Advertiser*, 28 Apr. 1788.

143. In Nicholas K. Robinson, *Edmund Burke: A Life in Caricatures* (New Haven, Conn.: Yale University Press, 1996), p. 109.

144. Marshall, *Writings and Speeches of Edmund Burke*, vol. 6, p. 479; *Trial* (1793), p. 171.

145. George, *Catalogue*, vol. 5, BMC 7307, "A Reverie of Prince Demetrius Cantemir, Ospidar of Moldavia. 26 Apr. 1788." See Demetrius Cantemir, *The His-*

tory of the Growth and Decay of the Othman Empire (London, 1714). But what Cantemir may have been referring to was the Queen Mother making marital alliances for her son, not choosing nightly concubines. For this influence, see Peirce, *Imperial Harem*, p. 109.

146. [Ralph Broome], *Letters from Simpkin the Second to his Dear Brother in Wales; containing a humble description of the trial of Warren Hastings, Esq., with Simon's Answer* (London, 1788), p. 6.

147. George, *Catalogue*, vol. 6, BMC 7273.

148. *London Chronicle*, 16–19 Feb., 1–3 Apr. 1788.

149. [Broome], *Letters from Simpkin*, p. 7; *The Tribunal, addressed to the Peers of Great Britain, about to sit in Judgment on Warren Hastings* (London, 1788), pp. 29–30.

150. *The Whole Proceedings on the Trial of an Information . . . against John Stockdale; for a libel on the House of Commons* (London, 1790), p. 20.

151. Adam Smith, *Lectures on Rhetoric and Belles Lettres. Delivered in the University of Glasgow by Adam Smith. Reported by a Student in 1762–63*, ed. John M. Lothian (London and Edinburgh: Thomas Nelson, 1963), p. 190.

152. *World*, 30 May 1789.

153. *Morning Chronicle*, 2 June 1794; *Oracle*, 7 June 1794. In 1788, Mr. Adams was also criticized for excessively crude rhetoric in his speech about the women of Shujah's harem; *Trial* (1796), p. 33.

154. James Wodrow to William Kenrick, 10 Jan. 1791, London, Dr. Williams Library, 24.157, f. 156; Eugene Richard Gaddis, "William Windham and the Conservative Reaction in England, 1790–1796: The Making of a Conservative Whig and the Norwich Electoral Response" (Ph.D. diss., University of Pennsylvania, 1979), p. 82; Francis Fowke to Margaret Fowke, 12 May 1789, British Library, India Office Library, Eur Ms. D/546/11, 546/26; William Miles, *A letter to Henry Duncombe, Esq., Member for the county of York, on the Subject of the very Extraordinary pamphlet lately addressed by Mr. Burke, to a Noble Lord*, 4th ed. (London, 1796), p. 26.

155. For instance, *World*, 22, 27 May 1789.

156. *Universal Register (Times)*, 23, 26, 30 May 1789.

157. *Trial* (1793), p. 376.

158. Susan Staves, "The Construction of the Public Interest in the Debates over Fox's India Bills," in Paula Backscheider and Timothy Dystal, eds., *The Intersections of the Public and Private Spheres in Early Modern England* (London and Portland, Ore.: Frank Cass, 1996), pp. 175–98.

159. *Maharaja Deby Sinha* (Nashipur: privately printed, 1914); this book reprints the evidence on this charge from Hastings's trial.

160. Anonymous manuscript journal of day-by-day proceedings during the impeachment proceedings against Warren Hastings, 28 May 1789, Huntington Library, STG box 199 (17).

161. *World*, 23 Apr. 1789.

162. Billie Melman, *Women's Orients: English Women and the Middle East, 1718–1918* (Ann Arbor: University of Michigan Press, 1992), p. 86; Felicity A. Nussbaum, *Torrid Zones: Maternity, Sexuality and Empire in Eighteenth-Century English Narratives* (Baltimore: Johns Hopkins University Press, 1995), p. 137; Isobel Grundy, "'The Barbarous Character We Give Them': White Women Travelers Report on Other Races," *Studies in Eighteenth-Century Culture* 22 (1992): 73–86. For an example, see *World*, 11 May 1789.

163. Edmund Burke, *Thoughts on the Prospect of a Regicide Peace* (London, 1796), p. 17. This was an unauthorized version of a draft of *Letters on a Regicide Peace*; the authorized version leaves out women; see R. B. Macdowell, ed., *Writings and Speeches of Edmund Burke* (Oxford: Clarendon Press, 1991), vol. 9, p. 187.

164. Susan Staves, "Investments, Votes, and 'Bribes': Women Stockholders in the Chartered National Companies," in Hilda Smith, ed., *Women Writers and the Early Modern British Political Tradition* (Cambridge: Cambridge University Press, 1998), pp. 259–78.

165. Eliza Ryves, *An Epistle to the Rt. Hon. Lord John Cavendish, Late Chancellor of the Exchequer* (London, 1784).

166. Fanny Burney's diary, 16 Feb. 1788, quoted in Carnall and Nicholson, *The Impeachment of Warren Hastings*, p. 11.

167. Sarah Scott to Elizabeth Montagu, 30 June 1786; Elizabeth Montagu to Sarah Scott (her sister), 22 June 1786; Matthew Montagu, 4th Baron Rokeby, to Elizabeth Montagu, June 1786, all in Huntington Library, MO 5438, MO 6130, MO 3831.

168. Marshall, *Impeachment*, p. xvi.

169. Elizabeth Hamilton, *Translations of the Letters of a Hindoo Rajah*, 5th ed. (London, 1811 [1796]), pp. xxx, xliv.

170. Lucyle Werkmeister, *The London Daily Press 1772–1792* (Lincoln: University of Nebraska Press, 1963), pp. 326, 368.

171. Suleri, *Rhetoric of English India*, p. 48; for instance, Nicholls supported Hastings but denounced the empire; Nicholls, *Recollections*, vol. 1, pp. 251–90; vol. 2, p. 208; similar opinions from George Dempster, see Woods, *Correspondence of Edmund Burke*, vol. 5, p. 164, n. 1.

172. The House of Lords refused to consider evidence on this point in 1794. Marshall, *Writings and Speeches of Edmund Burke*, vol. 7, pp. 223, 636.

173. John Waring Scott, *A Second Letter from Major Scott to Mr. Fox, containing the Final Decision of the Governor General and Council of Bengal on the Charges brought against Rajah Deby Sing* (London, 1789); Kaviraj, *Peasant Uprising in Bengal 1783*, pp. 40–50; *Maharaja Deby Sinha* (Nashipur: privately printed, 1914), which reprints letter from the Committee of Revenue, 31 Mar. 1784, in Minutes of Council Meeting, Fort William.

174. *The Whole Proceedings . . . against John Stockdale*, p. 86; also printed in *The Speeches of the Hon. Thomas Erskine (now Lord Erskine) when at the Bar, on Subjects connected with the Liberty of the Press, and against Constructive Treasons* (London, 1810), vol. 2, p. 118.

175. Eliga H. Gould, *The Persistence of Empire* (Chapel Hill: University of North Carolina Press, 2000), p. 210; P. J. Marshall, "Empire and Authority in the Later Eighteenth Century," *Journal of Imperial and Commonwealth History* 15 (1987): 118; C. A. Bayly, *Imperial Meridian: The British Empire and the World 1780–1830* (London: Longman, 1989), p. 148.

176. Susan Bayly, "Caste and 'Race' in Colonial Ethnography," in Peter Robb, ed., *The Concept of Race in South Asia* (Delhi: Oxford University Press, 1997), pp. 168, 172.

177. *Trial* (1796), pp. 3, 21.

178. *Oracle*, 17 Apr. 1794; *Morning Chronicle*, 24 Apr. 1794.

179. George D. Bearce, *British Attitudes towards India 1784–1858* (Westport, Conn.: Greenwood Press, 1982 [1961]), p. 86; *Morning Post*, 17 June 1794; Eric Stokes, *The English Utilitarians and India* (Delhi: Oxford University Press, 1982 [1959]), p. 6; Lawson, *East India Company*, p. 129.

180. Blackburn, *Overthrow of Colonial Slavery*, p. 145.

181. Bayly, *Imperial Meridian*, pp. 112–14; P. J. Marshall, "Cornwallis Triumphant: War in India and British Public Opinion," in Lawrence Freedman, Paul Hayes, and Robert O'Neill, eds., *War, Strategy, and International Politics* (New York: Oxford University Press, 1992), p. 64; Teltscher, *India Inscribed*, pp. 229–55.

182. "Review of Bruce's *Travels to Discover the Source of the Nile*," *Analytical Review* 6 (1790): 137; "Review of public affairs," *Critical Review*, n.s., 3 (1791): 584; *Thoughts on Civilization, and the Gradual Abolition of Slavery in Africa and the West Indies*, by a Friend to Commerce and Humanity (n.p., n.d.), p. 3; Jesse Foot, surgeon, *A Defense of the Planters in the West Indies* (London, 1792), p. 90.

183. See Frederick A. Dreyer, "Legitimacy and Usurpation in the Thought of Edmund Burke," *Albion* 12, no. 3 (1980): 262.

184. Marshall, *Writings and Speeches of Edmund Burke*, vol. 7, p. 339.

185. For comparisons of Burke on the French Revolution and on India, see, for example, Hindson and Gray, *Burke's Dramatic Theory of Politics*, p. 167; Janes, "Edmund Burke's Flying Leap from India to France," p. 525.

186. Edmund Burke, *Reflections on the Revolution in France* (Penguin: London, 1968 [1790]), p. 159, comparing the women who stormed Versailles to American savages. See also Linda Zerilli, "Text/Woman as Spectacle," *Eighteenth Century* 33 (1992): 61.

187. For criticisms of Burke, see preface, *The Trial of Warren Hastings printed from the World*, p. xxii.

188. G. M. Ditchfield, "The House of Lords and the Impeachment of Warren Hastings," *Parliamentary History* 13 (1994): 283.

189. Burke, *Writings and Speeches of Edmund Burke*, vol. 7, p. 605.

190. *World*, 4 June 1791.

191. Commons debate, 1787, General Brief Speeches, Impeachment Trial Papers, Bell Library, University of Minnesota, 1786fHa, p. 105.

192. *The Whole Proceedings . . . against John Stockdale*, p. 20.

193. *Oracle*, 7 May 1794.

194. David Turley, *The Culture of English Anti-slavery* (London: Routledge, 1991), pp. 20–22; Wylie Sypher, *Guinea's Captive Kings: British Anti-slavery Literature of the Eighteenth Century* (Chapel Hill: University of North Carolina Press, 1942), p. 203; Moira Ferguson, *Subject to Others: British Women Writers and Colonial Slavery, 1670–1834* (New York: Routledge, 1992), pp. 114, 154; Blackburn, *Overthrow of Colonial Slavery*, p. 48.

195. Blackburn, *Overthrow of Colonial Slavery*, pp. 142–46.

196. William Cowper, *Poems* (London, 1786), vol. 1, p. 121; vol. 2, p. 38; *Works* (1817), vol. 4, p. 293; *Analytical Review* 4 (1789): 282; 5 (1790): 307; motion against empire in United Friars Debating Society, 28 Oct. 1792, Norwich Record Office, COL 9/7; *Cabinet* 2 (1795): 354; 3 (1795): 147.

197. [John Prinsep], *Strictures and Observations on the Mocurrery System of Landed Property in Bengal, originally written for the Morning Chronicle, under the Signature of Gurreeb Doss, with Replies* (London, 1794); *Morning Chronicle*, 18 July 1793; Charles Greville, *British India Analysed* (London, 1793), vol. 1, p. xxii; *A Sketch of the Debate in the House of Commons, on Passing the Bill for the Continuation of the Charter of the East India Company, May 25, 1793* (London, 1793), pp. 40–41; P. J. Marshall, *Problems of Empire: Britain and India 1757–1813* (London: Allen and Unwin, 1968), p. 72; Charles Grant, *Observations on the State of Society among the Asiatic Subjects of Great Britain, particularly with respect to Morals; and on the Means of Improving It* (London, 1797 [written 1792]), p. 104.

198. *Morning Post*, 10 June 1794; for criticisms of his inaction, see *A Letter to Richard Brinsley Sheridan, Esq., on the Proposed Renewal of the Charter of the East India Company. By a Friend to the Freedom of the Press* (London, 1793); *Trial* (1793), p. xxi.

199. *A Letter to the Rt. Hon C. J. Fox on the Subject of his Conduct upon the Charges made by Mr Paul against the Marquis Wellesley* (London, 1806).

200. Edmund Burke, "Conciliation with America," in Harris, *Burke: Pre-revolutionary Writings*, p. 265.

201. McDowell, *Writings and Speeches of Edmund Burke*, vol. 9, pp. 389–671.

202. James Conniff, "Burke and India: The Failure of the Theory of Trusteeship," *Political Research Quarterly* 46 (1993): 309.

203. Thomas Law, *A Sketch of some Late Arrangements, and a view of the rising resources in Bengal* (London, 1792), p. xxiii.

204. Hannah More, "Strictures on Female Education," *Works* (Philadelphia, 1832), p. 347.

205. Mary Wollstonecraft, "A Vindication of the Rights of Men," in Janet Todd and Marilyn Butler, eds., *The Works of Mary Wollstonecraft* (New York: New York University Press, 1989), vol. 5, p. 53.

CHAPTER FIVE: SCANDAL IN AN AGE OF REVOLUTION

1. For these debates, see chapters in Mark Philp, ed., *The French Revolution and British Popular Politics* (Cambridge: Cambridge University Press, 1991); H. T. Dickinson, *Liberty and Property: Political Ideology in Eighteenth-Century Britain* (London: Weidenfeld and Nicolson, 1977), pp. 270–318.

2. Iain McCalman, "Mad Lord George and Madame LaMotte: Riot and Sexuality in the Genesis of Burke's *Reflections on the Revolution in France*," *Journal of British Studies* 35 (1996): 363; Parkyns Macmahon, *Memorial, or Brief for the Comte de Cagliostro* (London, 1786). For earlier rumors about her affairs and political influence, see *Morning Post*, 11, 13 Dec. 1784; *Morning Herald*, 13, 15 Dec. 1784. The *Morning Post* was prosecuted for publishing rumors about the queen; PRO TS 11/46/178. For Lord Gordon's trial, see *The Trial at Large of the Hon. George Gordon commonly called Lord George Gordon . . . on Two Informations, filed ex Officio, by his Majesty's Attorney General, for Libels; one which tended to stir up Mutiny and Dissentions among the condemned Convicts, and those destined to Botany Bay; and the other, against the queen of France, the French Ambassador, the Charge des affaires, and the Ministry of France* (London, 1787) for rumors published in 1786.

3. Sarah Maza, "The Diamond Necklace Affair Revisited (1785–1786): The Case of the Missing Queen," in Lynn Hunt, ed., *Eroticism and the Body Politic* (Baltimore: Johns Hopkins University Press, 1991), pp. 63–89.

4. L. G. Mitchell, *Charles James Fox and the Disintegration of the Whig Party 1782–1794* (Oxford: Oxford University Press, 1971), p. 134; *The Prospect before Us. Being a Series of Papers upon the Great Question which now Agitates the Public Mind* (London, 1788), p. 19; Nathanial William Wraxall, *Historical Memoirs of My Own Time* (London: Kegan Paul, 1904 [1816]), vol. 3, pp. 290, 235, 350; John Brooke, *King George III* (St. Albans: Panther Books, 1974), p. 507.

5. Lucyle Werkmeister, *A Newspaper History of England, 1792–93* (Lincoln: University of Nebraska Press, 1967), p. 181; Conor Cruise O'Brien, *The Great Melody: A Thematic Biography of Edmund Burke* (Chicago: University of Chicago Press, 1992), p. 455.

6. I owe this link to Iain McCalman; see "Mad Lord George," p. 361; Edmund Burke, *Reflections on the Revolution in France* (London: Penguin, 1968 [1790]), p. 179, criticizing British libelers of Marie Antoinette.

7. Burke continued to express suspicion of female influence in private; Edmund Burke to Richard Burke, Jr., 16, 18 Aug. 1791, in Alfred Cobban and Robert A. Smith, eds., *The Correspondence of Edmund Burke* (Chicago: University of Chicago Press, 1967), vol. 6, pp. 340, 361.

8. Burke, *Reflections*, pp. 164–69; Linda M. G. Zerilli, "Text/Woman as Spectacle: Edmund Burke's 'French Revolution,'" *Eighteenth Century* 33 (1992): 65–67; Stephen K. White, *Edmund Burke: Modernity, Politics and Aesthetics* (Thousand Oaks, Calif.: Sage, 1994), p. 46; Frederick A. Dreyer, *Burke's Politics: A Study in Whig Orthodoxy* (Waterloo: Wilfred Laurier University Press, 1979), p. 30; Abraham D.

Kriegel, "Edmund Burke and the Quality of Honor," *Albion* 12 (1980): 340; Paul Hindson and Tim Gray, *Burke's Dramatic Theory of Politics* (Aldershot: Avebury/Gower, 1988), p. 167.

9. Burke, *Reflections*, pp. 113, 120, 125, 326.

10. William Miles, *A letter to Henry Duncombe, Esq., Member for the county of York, on the Subject of the very Extraordinary pamphlet lately addressed by Mr. Burke, to a Noble Lord*, 4th ed. (London, 1796), p. 20; *Monthly Magazine* 1 (1796): 114; [Charles Pigott], *The Jockey Club*, 12th ed. (London, 1792), p. 126; [Charles Pigott], *The Jockey Club*, pt. 3, 3d ed. (London, 1793), p. 102.

11. Joseph Parkes and Herman Merivale, *Memoirs of Sir Philip Francis, KCB with Correspondence and Journals* (London, 1867), vol. 2, p. 282; Vicesimus Knox, *The Spirit of Despotism* (London, 1821 [1795]), p. 51.

12. Hannah More to William Wilberforce, 20 Nov. 1794, Duke University Library, Special Collections.

13. Gregory Claeys, "The French Revolution Debate and British Political Thought," *History of Political Thought* 9 (1990): 59–80.

14. Gary Kelly, *Revolutionary Feminism: The Mind and Career of Mary Wollstonecraft* (New York: St. Martin's Press, 1992), p. 101.

15. Wendy Gunther-Canada, "The Politics of Sense and Sensibility: Mary Wollstonecraft and Catherine Macaulay Graham on Edmund Burke's *Reflections on the Revolution in France*," in Hilda Smith, ed., *Women Writers and the Early Modern British Political Tradition* (Cambridge: Cambridge University Press, 1998), p. 140.

16. Mary Wollstonecraft, "An Historical and Moral View of the Origin and Progress of the French Revolution" (1794), in Janet Todd and Marilyn Butler, eds., *The Works of Mary Wollstonecraft* (New York: New York University Press, 1989), vol. 6, p. 33.

17. [Catherine Macaulay], *Observations on the Reflections of the Right Hon. Edmund Burke on the Revolution in France, in a Letter to Right Hon. the Earl of Stanhope* (London, 1790), p. 54.

18. Catherine Macaulay to Samuel Adams, 31 Mar. 1791 in Macaulay letters, Gilder Lehmann Collection, Pierpont Morgan Library, New York.

19. Mary Wollstonecraft, "A Vindication of the Rights of Men" (London, 1790), in Todd and Butler, *Works*, vol. 5, pp. 40, 43.

20. Mary Wollstonecraft, "A Vindication of the Rights of Women" (London, 1792), in Todd and Butler, *Works* vol. 5, p. 243.

21. Ibid., pp. 125, 218–20.

22. This discussion is indebted to the excellent article by Nicholas Rogers, "Pigott's Private Eye," *Journal of the Canadian Historical Association*, n.s., 4 (1993): 247–63.

23. [Pigott], *The Jockey Club*, pt. 3 (1793), p. 215.

24. [Pigott], *The Jockey Club*, pt. 1 (1792), pp. 36, 120, 62.

25. Lynn Hunt, *The Family Romance of the French Revolution* (Berkeley: University of California Press, 1992), p. 106.

26. Rictor Norton, ed., "*Memoirs* of Antonina [Marie Antoinette], 1791," Homosexuality in Eighteenth-Century England: A Sourcebook, 24 July 2002 http://www.infopt.demon.co.uk/antonina.htm.

27. [Pigott], *Jockey Club*, pt. 3 (1793), p. 72. See also John Thelwall, "Report on the State of Popular Opinion," *Tribune* (1795), in Gregory Claeys, ed., *The Politics of English Jacobinism: Writings of John Thelwall* (University Park: Pennsylvania State University Press, 1995), p. 220.

28. For similar sentiments, see *The Genuine Review of the Political State of an Unhappy Country, as originally written, before it was mutilated by a Right Reverend Prelate* (London, 1787), p. 11; *Morning Post* 13 Dec. 1793; *Cabinet* 1 (1795): 107.

29. [Pigott], *Jockey Club*, pt. 1 (1792), pp. xvii, 2; pt. 3 (1793), p. 54.

30. Richard Godfrey, *Gillray* (London: Tate, 2001), p. 137.

31. [Pigott], *Jockey Club*, pt. 3 (1793), p. 92; [Pigott], *The Female Jockey Club*, 7th ed. (London, 1794), p. 55; Wraxall, *Memorials,* vol. 3, p. 266.

32. [Pigott], *The Jockey Club*, pt. 1 (1792), p. 117.

33. [Pigott], *The Jockey Club*, pt. 2 (London, 1792), p. 32.

34. Mary Hays, *Letters and Essays, Moral and Miscellaneous* (New York: Garland, 1974 [1793]), p. 15.

35. Wollstonecraft, "Vindication of the Rights of Men," in Todd and Butler, *Works,* vol. 5, p. 43; Mary Poovey, *The Proper Lady and the Woman Writer: Ideology as Style in the Works of Mary Wollstonecraft, Mary Shelley, and Jane Austen* (Chicago: University of Chicago Press, 1984), p. 63.

36. For the decline in influence of classical republicanism, see Mark Philp, "English Republicanism in the 1790s," *Journal of Political Philosophy* 6 (1998): 235.

37. Edmund Burke, *Thoughts on the Prospect of a Regicide Peace* (London, 1796), p. 17. This was an unauthorized version of a draft of *Letters on a Regicide Peace;* the authorized version leaves out women; see R. B. Macdowell, ed., *Writings and Speeches of Edmund Burke,* (Oxford: Clarendon Press, 1991), vol. 9, p. 187.

38. John Thelwall, "The Rights of Nature," in Claeys, *The Politics of English Jacobinism,* p. 397.

39. *The Hymen* (London, 1794), pp. 1, 28.

40. *Morning Chronicle,* 27 May 1796.

41. *Argus,* 15 Oct., 3 Nov. 1789; 20, 23 Feb., 23 Dec. 1790.

42. Katherine Binhammer, "The Sex Panic of the 1790s," *Journal of the History of Sexuality* 6 (1996): 424–25. This article contributed greatly to my thoughts on the impact of sex scandals in the 1790s.

43. Robert Haig, *The Gazetteer 1735–97* (Carbondale: Southern Illinois University Press, 1960), p. 199.

44. *The Trial of the Hon. Richard Bingham, for criminal conversation with the Lady Elizabeth Howard* (London, 1794), p. 52; similarly, *The Genuine Trial of John B. Gawler, Esq. for Criminal Conversation with the Rt. Hon. Lady Valentia* (London, 1796), p. 2.

45. *The trial at Large on an Action for Damages . . . by the Rt. Hon. George Fred. Earl of Westmeath, against the Hon. Augustus Cavendish Bradshaw, for Adultery with the Rt. Hon. Mary Anne, Countess of Westmeath* (Dublin and London, 1796), p. 28. The jury was unimpressed by this argument and awarded large damages.

46. For more on gender and plebeian radicalism in the 1790s, see Anna Clark, *The Struggle for the Breeches: Gender and the Making of the British Working Class* (Berkeley: University of California Press, 1995), pp. 141–53.

47. Charles Pigott, *The Rights of Princes, consisting of Extracts from Pigott's Political Dictionary* (London, 1795), p. 8; see also *A Warning to Tyrants, consisting of Extracts from Pigott, Gerald, etc.* (London, 1795). For radical language more generally, see Olivia Smith, *The Politics of Language 1791–1819* (Oxford: Oxford University Press, 1984), pp. 71–72.

48. William Hodgson, *The Commonwealth of Reason* (London, 1795), p. 22.

49. *The Book of Bobs. Being a Serious Caution to the Pensioned Tribe of Albo* (London, 1795?).

50. *The Happy Reign of George the Last. An Address to the Little Tradesmen, and Laboring Poor of England* (London, 1795), p. 2.

51. *The Birthright of Britons* (London, 1792); *The State of the Representation of England and Wales. delivered to the Society, the Friends of the People, associated for the Purpose of obtaining a Parliamentary Reform, on Saturday the 9th of February 1793* (London, 1793).

52. *Proceedings in an Action for Debt between the Rt Hon. Charles James Fox, Plaintiff and John Horne Tooke, Esq., Defendant* (London, 1792); Jon Mee, "The 'Insidious Poison of Secret Influence,'" *Eighteenth-Century Life* 22 (1998): 114–15. For earlier discussions of government payoffs, see James Gillray caricature, "Election Troops bring in their accounts," BMC 7369, in Richard Godfrey, *Gillray* (London: Tate, 2001), p. 75.

53. Rogers, "Pigott's Private Eye," p. 258.

54. Jon Mee, "'Examples of Safe Printing': Censorship and Popular Radical Literature in the 1790s," *Essays and Studies*, n.s., 46 (1993): 84–85.

55. "A True and Particular Account of the Trial of Thomas Paine" (London, 1792 or 3), British Library Collection 628.c26, no. 44.

56. Gregory Claeys, *Thomas Paine: Social and Political Thought* (Boston: Unwin Hyman, 1989), p. 145.

57. Gerald Newman, *The Rise of English Nationalism: A Cultural History 1740–1830* (New York: St. Martin's Press, 1997), p. 235.

58. Diana Donald, *The Age of Caricature: Satirical Prints in the Reign of George III* (New Haven, Conn.: Yale University Press, 1996), pp. 145–59.

59. *The British Constitution invulnerable. Animadversions on a Late Publication, entitled the Jockey Club* (London, 1793?).

60. Dror Wahrman, *Imagining the Middle Class: The Political Representation of Class in Britain, c. 1780–1840* (Cambridge: Cambridge University Press, 1992), pp.

87, 119, 121; James Sack, *From Jacobite to Conservative* (Cambridge: Cambridge University Press, 1993), p. 122.

61. Arthur Young, *Example of France a Warning to Britain* (London, 1793), p. 171; J.A.W. Gunn, "Influence, Parties and the Constitution: Changing Attitudes, 1783–1832," *Historical Journal* 17 (1974): 318.

62. For an excellent analysis of attitudes on the monarchy, both pro and con, see Marilyn Morris, *The British Monarchy and the French Revolution* (New Haven, Conn.: Yale University Press, 1998), pp. 134–57; Linda Colley, "The Apotheosis of George III: Loyalty, Royalty and the British Nation," *Past and Present* 102 (1994): 94–129.

63. Vincent Carretta, *George III and the Satirists from Hogarth to Byron* (Athens: University of Georgia Press, 1990), p. 297.

64. *St. James Chronicle*, 2–5 June 1792, on meeting of "church and king" club at Yarmouth; J. Burton, *Lectures on Female Education and Manners* (Rochester, 1793), vol. 2, p. 137.

65. Haig, *The Gazetteer*, p. 193; for the Prince of Wales accused of allying himself with those sympathetic to revolution, see Young, *Example of France a Warning to Britain*, p. 93.

66. Donald, *The Age of Caricature*, pp. 145–59.

67. Charles Ford, *Hannah More: A Critical Biography* (New York: Peter Lang, 1996), p. 14; William Roberts, *Memoirs of the Life and Correspondence of Mrs. Hannah More* (New York, 1836), vol. 1, p. 287; Thomas Taylor, *Memoir of Mrs. Hannah More* (London, 1838), p. 54.

68. Taylor, *Memoirs*, p. 98; see also Ford, *Hannah More*.

69. Hannah More, "Thoughts on the Importance of Manners of the Great" (1788), *Works of Hannah More* (Philadelphia, 1832), vol. 2, p. 264, and *An Estimate of the Religion of the Fashionable World* (1790), *Works*, vol. 2, pp. 278, 280, 290.

70. Hannah More, "Considerations on Religion and Public Education" (1793), *Works*, vol. 2, p. 309.

71. Hannah More, "The Bad Bargain" (1796), *Works*, vol. 1, p. 46.

72. "Rantipolish" means " wild, disorderly, rakish" (*Oxford English Dictionary*). Hannah More, "Village Politics" (1793), *Works*, vol. 1, pp. 59–61.

73. Hannah More, *Considerations on Religion and Public Education* (1793), ed. Claudia L. Johnson (Los Angeles: Augustan Reprint Society, 1990), p. 13.

74. Anne Stott, "Patriotism and Providence: The Politics of Hannah More," in Kathryn Gleadle and Sarah Richardson, eds., *Women in British Politics, 1760–1860: The Power of the Petticoat* (New York: St. Martin's Press, 2000), p. 44.

75. Patricia Demers, *The World of Hannah More* (Lexington: University Press of Kentucky, 1996), p. 100; Thomas Laqueur, *Religion and Respectability: Sunday Schools and Working-Class Culture 1780–1850* (New Haven, Conn.: Yale University Press, 1976), p. 128.

76. Hannah More, "The History of Mr. Fantom" (1797?), *Works*, vol. 1, p. 122.

77. Susan Pedersen, "Hannah More Meets Simple Simon: Tracts, Chapbooks, and Popular Culture in Late Eighteenth-Century England," *Journal of British Studies* 25 (1986): 84–113.

78. Nicholas Rogers, *Crowds, Culture and Politics in Georgian Britain* (Oxford: Clarendon Press, 1998), p. 194.

79. Kevin Gilmartin, "In the Theater of Counterrevolution: Loyalist Association and Conservative Opinion in the 1790s," *Journal of British Studies* 41 (2002): 291–328.

CHAPTER SIX: FROM PETTICOAT INFLUENCE TO WOMEN'S RIGHTS?

1. Gary Kelly, *Women, Writing, and Revolution, 1790–1827* (Oxford: Clarendon Press, 1993), pp. 25–30.

2. Linda Colley, *Britons: Forging the Nation 1707–1837* (New Haven, Conn.: Yale University Press, 1994), pp. 275–76; for a more detailed historiographical context, see Anna Clark, "Women in Eighteenth-Century Politics: Competing Interpretations," in Barbara Taylor and Sarah Knott, eds., *Women and Enlightenment: A Comparative History* (London: Palgrave, forthcoming).

3. Catherine Macaulay, *Letters on Education* (London, 1790), p. 213.

4. Mary Wollstonecraft, "Vindication of the Rights of Women," in Janet Todd and Marilyn Butler, eds., *The Works of Mary Wollstonecraft* (New York: New York University Press, 1989), vol. 5, pp. 125, 218–20. For a more psychoanalytic insight into Wollstonecraft's apparent hatred for women, see Barbara Taylor, "Misogyny and Feminism: The Case of Mary Wollstonecraft," in Colin Jones and Dror Wahrman, eds., *The Age of Cultural Revolutions: Britain and France 1750–1820* (Berkeley: University of California Press, 2002), p. 214.

5. See her review of Macaulay in *Analytical Review* 8 (1790): 223–54, reprinted in Todd and Butler, *Works*, vol. 7, pp. 309–22.

6. Macaulay, *Letters on Education*, p. 215.

7. Wollstonecraft, "Vindication of the Rights of Women," in Todd and Butler, *Works*, vol. 5, p. 68; similarly, Mary Hays, *Letters and Essays, Moral and Miscellaneous* (New York: Garland, 1794 [1793]), p. 20.

8. For her life, see M. J. Levy, ed., *Perdita: The Memoirs of Mary Robinson* (London: Peter Owen, 1994); for opinions, see [Mary Robinson] Anne Frances Randall, *A Letter to the Women of England on the Injustice of Mental Subordination* (London, 1799), pp. 2, 10, 66, 71, 78.

9. Bridget Hill, "The Links between Mary Wollstonecraft and Catherine Macaulay: New Evidence," *Women's History Review* 4 (1995): 177–92.

10. For this description of her personality, see Kelly, *Revolutionary Feminism*, p. 31.

11. Eleanor Ty, "Introduction" to Mary Hays, *The Victim of Prejudice* (Peterborough, Canada: Broadview Press, 1994); Gina Luria Walker, "'Sewing in the Next

World': Mary Hays as Dissenting Autodidact in the 1780s," *Romanticism on the Net* 25 (2002).

12. Kathryn Gleadle, "British Women and Radical Politics," in Amanda Vickery, ed., *Women, Privilege and Power: British Politics, 1750 to the Present* (Stanford, Calif.: Stanford University Press, 2001), p. 132. For an example of a discussion group that admitted women, see Tuscularum Society minutes, 1793–95, Norfolk Record Office, NNAS Cup. 2.

13. [Mary Hays], "By a Woman," *Monthly Magazine* 2 (1796): 784.

14. Kelly, *Revolutionary Feminism*, p. 173; Mary Hays, *An Appeal to the Men of Great Britain on Behalf of Women* (London, 1798), reprinted in Marie Mulvey Roberts and Tamae Mizuta, eds., *The Radicals: Revolutionary Women* (London: Routledge and Thoemmes Press, 1994), p. 133.

15. Macaulay, *Letters on Education*, pp. 219–20.

16. Hays, *An Appeal*, p. 173.

17. Among many important recent works on Wollstonecraft, see Maria J. Falco, *Feminist Interpretations of Mary Wollstonecraft* (University Park: Pennsylvania State University Press, 1996); and Barbara Taylor, "Religion, Radicalism and Fantasy," *History Workshop Journal* 39 (1995): 102–12.

18. Susan Staves, "'The Liberty of a She-Subject of England': Rights Rhetoric and the Female Thucydides," *Cardozo Studies in Law and Literature* 8, no. 2 (1989): 180; [Mary Hays], *Monthly Magazine* 3 (1797): 193.

19. G. J. Barker-Benfield, "Mary Wollstonecraft: Eighteenth-Century Common-wealthwoman," *Journal of the History of Ideas* 50 (1989): 95–116.

20. Wollstonecraft, "Vindication of the Rights of Women," in Todd and Butler, *Works*, vol. 5, p. 253.

21. Burke, *Correspondence*, vol. 8, quoted in James Sack, *From Jacobite to Conservative: Reaction and Orthodoxy in Britain, c. 1760–1832* (Cambridge: Cambridge University Press, 1993), p. 40.

22. William Roberts, *Memoirs of the Life and Correspondence of Hannah More* (New York, 1836), vol. 1, p. 427.

23. Mary Dawes Blackett, *The Monitress; or, the Œconomy of Female Life* (London, 1791), p. 57.

24. [Laetita Hawkins], *Letters on the Female Mind, its powers and pursuits* (London, 1793), p. 80.

25. Diary of Elizabeth Greenly (Lady Greenly Coffin Brown), 17 Sept. 1792, 19 Feb. 1793, Duke University Library, Special Collections.

26. [Thomas Starling Norgate], "On the Rights of Women," *Cabinet* 1 (1795): 178; 2 (1795): 36–42. Attribution from Penelope J. Corfield and Chris Evans, eds., *Youth and Revolution in the 1790s* (Stroud: Sutton, 1996), p. 190; George Philips, *The Necessity for a Speedy and Effectual Reform in Parliament* (Manchester, 1792), p. 12.

27. *Scots Magazine* 54 (1792): 284; *Analytical Review* 13 (1792): 481–83.

28. *Critical Review*, n.s., 3 (1791): 392.

29. *Monthly Magazine*, n.s., 8 (1792): 198.

30. Thomas Amyot to William Pattison, 18 Feb. 1795, in Corfield and Evans, *Youth and Revolution*, p. 120.

31. *Monthly Magazine* 1 (1795): 181; 2 (1796): 469, 527, 611, 696, 794; 3 (1797): 193; 4 (1797): 274–75. Attributions to Mary Hays from Moira Ferguson, *First Feminists: British Women Writers 1578–1799* (Bloomington: Indiana University Press, 1985), p. 414.

32. Gary Kelly, *The English Jacobin Novel* (Oxford: Clarendon Press, 1976), pp. 17, 30.

33. Claudia Johnson, *Equivocal Beings: Politics, Gender and Sentimentality in the 1790s* (Chicago: University of Chicago Press, 1995), pp. 54, 97.

34. Ty, "Introduction" to Hays, *Victim of Prejudice*, p. v.

35. Sharon M. Stezer, "Romancing the Reign of Terror: Sexual Politics in Mary Robinson's *Natural Daughter*," *Criticism* 39 (1997): 531–55; Anne K. Mellor, "Making an Exhibition of Her Self: Mary 'Perdita' Robinson and Nineteenth-Century Scripts of Female Sexuality," *Nineteenth-Century Contexts* 22 (2000): 271–304; Eleanor Ty, *Empowering the Feminine* (Toronto: University of Toronto Press, 1998), pp. 57–72.

36. William Godwin, *Memoirs of Mary Wollstonecraft* (New York: Haskell House, 1969), p. 101.

37. Ibid., p. 104; Janet Todd, *Mary Wollstonecraft: A Revolutionary Life* (London: Weidenfeld and Nicholson, 2000), p. 417.

38. Wollstonecraft to Amelia Alderson, 11 Apr. 1797, in Ralph M. Wardle, ed., *Collected Letters of Mary Wollstonecraft* (Ithaca, N.Y.: Cornell University Press, 1979), p. 318.

39. Taylor, "Religion, Radicalism and Fantasy," pp. 102–12.

40. Priscilla Wakefield, *Reflections on the present condition of the female sex; with suggestions for its improvement* (London, 1798); Mary Anne Radcliffe, *The Female advocate; or An attempt to recover the rights of women from male usurpation* (London, 1799).

41. Mary Jacobus, "Intimate Connections: Scandalous *Memoirs* and Epistolary Indiscretion," in Elizabeth Eger, Charlotte Grant, and Cliona O'Gallchoir, eds., *Women, Writing and the Public Sphere, 1700–1830* (Cambridge: Cambridge University Press, 2001), p. 281.

42. J. Ann Hone, *For the Cause of Truth: Radicalism in London 1796–1821* (Oxford: Clarendon Press, 1982), p. 47.

43. *Monthly Review* 27 (1798): 321–24, reprinted in Godwin, *Memoirs*, p. 346.

44. *Edinburgh Magazine* 11 (1798): 264.

45. *Analytical Review* 27 (1798): 235–40, reprinted in Godwin, *Memoirs*, p. 337.

46. *Monthly Mirror* 5 (1798):153–54, reprinted in Godwin, *Memoirs*, p. 339.

47. *Monthly Magazine* 5 (1798): 493–94, reprinted in Godwin, *Memoirs*, p. 342.

48. Ty, "Introduction" to Hays, *Victim of Prejudice*, p. 10.

49. *Edinburgh Magazine* 14 (1799): 9.

50. *Gentleman's Magazine*, April 1799, p. 311; the previous page contained a negative review of Mary Hays's *Appeal*. Reprinted at http://www.rc.umd.edu/editions/contemps/robinson/contents.htm. By publishing under an assumed name, Robinson could still earn praise as a lady novelist. "Biographical Sketch of Mrs Robinson," *Monthly Mirror* 7 (1799): 131–36, from Sheffield Hallam University, Corvey Women Writers on the Web, http://www2.shu.ac.uk/corvey/CW3/ContribPage.cfm?Contrib=100.

51. John Henry Colls, *A Poetical Epistle addressed to Miss Wollstonecraft. occasioned by reading her Celebrated Essay on the Rights of Woman, and her Historical and Moral View of the French Revolution* (London, 1795), pp. 18–19; *A Defense of the Character and Conduct of the Late Mary Wollstonecraft Godwin, founded on principles of nature and reason, as applied to the peculiar circumstances of her case, in a series of letters to a lady* (London, 1803), pp. 10, 42, 149; Andrew Elfenbein, *Romantic Genius: The Prehistory of a Homosexual Role* (New York: Columbia University Press, 1999), pp. 126–29; and Andrew Elfenbein, "Mary Wollstonecraft and the Sexuality of Genius," in Claudia Johnson, ed., *The Cambridge Companion to Mary Wollstonecraft* (Cambridge: Cambridge University Press, 2002), pp. 260–80.

52. Mary Wollstonecraft to William Roscoe, 12 Nov. 1792, in Wardle, ed., *Collected Letters of Mary Wollstonecraft*, p. 218.

53. Darlene Levy and Harriet Applewhite, eds., *Women in Revolutionary Paris, 1789–1795* (Urbana: University of Illinois Press, 1979).

54. *Morning Post*, 18 Apr. 1798.

55. This was on 16 April 1798; there were similar debates on 10 April and 11 May 1797 and 23, 26, and 30 April 1798. See Donna T. Andrew, *London Debating Societies* (London: London Record Society, 1994), pp. 357–77.

56. Henry Jephson, *The Platform: Its Rise and Progress* (London, 1892), vol. 1, p. 280; Mary Thale, "London Debating Societies in the 1790s," *Historical Journal* 32 (1989): 84.

57. Sack, *From Jacobite to Conservative*, pp. 40, 87.

58. *Anti-Jacobin Review* 1 (1798): 94–102.

59. *Anti-Jacobin Review* 3 (1799): 146

60. *Anti-Jacobin Review* 3 (1799): 144, 39–42; similar review of her novel *The Natural Daughter* in *British Critic* 16 (1800): 320–21.

61. *Anti-Jacobin Review* 3 (1799): 55.

62. Hannah More, *Strictures on the Modern System of Female Education* (1799), *Works of Hannah More* (Philadelphia, 1832), vol. 1, p. 319; Adam Sibbit, "Thoughts on the frequency of divorces in modern times" (1799), quoted in Katherine Binhammer, "The Sex Panic of the 1790s," *Journal of the History of Sexuality* 6 (1996): 419.

63. *Anti-Jacobin Review* 1 (1798): 94.

64. *British Critic* 12 (1798): 228–33, reprinted in Godwin, *Memoirs*, p. 338.

65. The Rev. Henry Handley Norris, *The Influence of the Female Character upon Society, considered especially with reference to the present crisis, preached in the parish church of St. John, at Hackney* (London, 1801), p. 25.

66. *European Magazine* 33 (1798): 246–51, reprinted in Godwin, *Memoirs*, pp. 340–41.

67. *Anti-Jacobin Review* 3 (1799): 27.

68. Similarly, another poem directly evokes images from Juvenal's Sixth Satire to depict Wollstonecraft and her supporters as lustful women engaged in pagan rites: *Peter not Infallible! or, A Poem, addressed to Peter Pindar, Esq. on reading his Nil Admirari, a late Illiberal Attack on the Bishop of London, together with unmanly abuse of Mrs. Hannah More* (Cambridge, 1800), p. 23. For changes in the gender connotations of Juvenal, see Dror Wahrman, "Gender in Translation: How the English Wrote Their Juvenal, 1644–1815," *Representations* 65 (1999): 1–42.

69. Richard Polwhele, *The Unsexed Females* (1798), Electronic Text Center, University of Virginia Library, from http://etext.lib.virginia.edu/cgib...odeng&data =/lvl/Archive/eng-parsed.

70. "Account of Mrs. Barbauld from the Ladies Magazine," *Edinburgh Magazine* 12 (1798): 194; Grace A. Ellis, *A Memoir of Mrs. Anna Laetitia Barbauld, with many of her letters* (Boston, 1874), vol. 1, p. i.

71. [Elizabeth Hamilton], *Memoirs of the Modern Philosophers* (Bath and London, 1800), vol. 3, p. 310; Kelly, *Women, Writing, and Revolution*, p. 150.

72. Amelia Alderson Opie, *Adeline Mowbray, or the Mother and Daughter* (London: Pandora, 1986 [1802]).

73. Patricia Demers, *The World of Hannah More* (Lexington: University Press of Kentucky, 1996), p. 92.

74. Jane West, *Letters to a Young Man* (London, 1803).

75. *The Scots Magazine* 62 (1800): 165.

76. More, *Strictures on the Modern System of Female Education, Works*, vol. 1, p. 208.

77. Demers, *World of Hannah More*, p. 119.

78. Robert Hole, "Hannah More on Literature and Propaganda," *History* 85 (2000): 631.

79. J. Stonhouse, *Letters to a Young Clergyman, from the late Reverend Mr. Job Orton*, 2d ed. (Shrewsbury, 1800), vol. 1, p. 209. Stonhouse also criticized the poet Mary Scott as "too much of a virago" for criticizing men; J. Stonhouse to Dr. Pulteney, 16 Nov. 1774, Somerset Record Office, DD/X/TCR 2C.

80. Dror Wahrman, "*Percy's* Prologue: From Gender Play to Gender Panic in Eighteenth-Century England," *Past and Present* 159 (1998): 113–25.

81. Norma Clarke, *Dr. Johnson's Women* (London: Hambledon and London, 2000), p. 168.

82. J. Stonhouse to Dr. Pulteney, 16 Nov. 1774, Somerset Record Office, DD/X/TCR 2C.

83. Diary of Elizabeth Greenly Coffin, 14 June 1799, Duke University Library, Special Collections.

84. Hannah More to Messrs. Cadell and Davies, 17 July no year; to unnamed publisher, 30 Oct. 1775; Somerset Record Office, DD/SAS C/2401/11.

85. Clarke, *Dr. Johnson's Women*, pp. 174–76; Robert L. Vales, *Peter Pindar (John Wolcot)* (New York: Twayne, 1973), p. 53.

86. [Charles Pigott], *The Female Jockey Club*, 7th ed. (London, 1794), p. 193.

87. Thomas Taylor, *Memoir of Mrs. Hannah More* (London, 1838), p. 240.

88. More, *Strictures on the Modern System of Female Education, Works*, vol. 1, p. 209.

89. Roberts, *Memoirs*, vol. 1, p. 238.

90. Jane West, *Letters to a Young Lady, in which the duties and characters of women are considered, chiefly with a reference to prevailing opinion*, 2d ed. (London, 1806), vol. 1, p. 18.

91. More, *Strictures on the Modern System of Female Education, Works*, vol. 1, p. 366.

92. For a discussion of women and patriotism in the 1790s, see Anna Clark, "1798 as the Defeat of Feminism: Women, Patriotism and Politics," in Terry Brotherstone, Anna Clark, and Kevin Whelan, eds., *These Fissured Isles: United Rebels, Union and Disunities—Ireland, Scotland and the Making of Modern Britain* (Aberdeen: John Tuckwell, forthcoming). For ladies presenting colors, see *Morning Post*, 11, 19, 21 July, 1, 2 Aug., 1, 7, 24 Sept., 2, 16 Oct. 1798.

93. Jane West, *A Tale of the Times* (1799), quoted in Ty, *Empowering the Feminine*, p. 101.

94. West, *Letters to a Young Lady*, vol. 2, p. 501; vol. 1, p. 59.

95. More, *Strictures on the Modern System of Female Education, Works*, vol. 1, p. 203.

96. Demers, *World of Hannah More*, p. 100; Thomas Laqueur, *Religion and Respectability: Sunday Schools and Working Class Culture 1780–1850* (New Haven, Conn.: Yale University Press, 1976), p. 128.

97. Martha More, *Mendip Annals; or, a Narrative of the Charitable Labours of Hannah and Martha More in their Neighbourhood, being the Journal of Martha More*, ed. Arthur Roberts, 2d ed. (London, 1859), pp. 26, 49; Elizabeth Kowaleski-Wallace, *Their Fathers' Daughters: Hannah More, Maria Edgeworth and Patriarchal Complicity* (New York: Oxford University Press, 1991), p. 73.

98. Hannah More to William Wilberforce, 28 Oct. 1800, Duke University Library, Special Collections.

99. Gerald Newman, *The Rise of English Nationalism: A Cultural History 1740–1830* (New York: St. Martin's Press, 1997), p. 235.

100. More, "A Cure for Melancholy" (n.d), *Works*, vol. 1, p. 169.

101. More, *Mendip Annals*, p. 93.

102. Anne Stott, "Patriotism and Providence: The Politics of Hannah More," in Kathryn Gleadle and Sarah Richardson, eds., *Women in British Politics, 1760–1860: The Power of the Petticoat* (New York: St. Martin's Press, 2000), pp. 39–55.

103. Hannah More, "The History of Mr. Fantom" (1797?), *Works*, vol. 1, p. 122; "The Two Wealthy Farmers" (1796), *Works*, vol. 2, p. 148; Hannah More, *Considerations on Religion and Public Education* (1793), ed. Claudia L. Johnson (Los Ange-

les: Augustan Reprint Society, 1990), p. 13. This pamphlet was published as part of a fund-raising effort by "English Ladies," spearheaded by Frances Crewe, for clergy exiled from France by the Revolution.

104. More, *Mendip Annals*, p. 23.

105. More, *Works*, vol. 1, p. 418.

106. Sack, *From Jacobite to Conservative*, p. 87; see Mark Philp, "English Republicanism in the 1790s," *Journal of Political Philosophy* 6 (1998): 261.

107. Laqueur, *Religion and Respectability*, pp. 75–76.

108. *Anti-Jacobin Review* 2 (1798): 368.

109. *Anti-Jacobin Review* 4 (1799): 195; Charles Daubeny, *A Letter to Mrs. Hannah More, on Some Part of her Late publication, entitled "Strictures on Female Education"* (London, 1799); *A Layman of the Established Church. A Brief Confutation of the Rev. Mr. Daubeny's Strictures on Mr. Richard Baxter . . . and also of his Animadversions, on Mrs. Hannah More* (Shrewsbury, 1801).

110. Demers, *World of Hannah More*, pp. 107–8.

111. More to Wilberforce, July 1794, Duke University Library, Special Collections.

112. More to Wilberforce, 11 Sept. 1799, Duke University Library, Special Collections.

113. Mitzi Myers, "The Cultural Politics of the Blagdon Controversy," in Beth Fowkes Tobin, ed., *History, Gender and Eighteenth-Century Literature* (Athens: University of Georgia Press, 1994), p. 243.

114. *Anti-Jacobin Review* 9 (1802): 236, 393; *Cobbett's Political Register* 2 (1802): 71; Kowaleski-Wallace, *Their Fathers' Daughters*, p. 73.

115. Edward Spencer, *Truths, Respecting Mrs. Hannah More's Meeting Houses, and the Conduct of her Followers, addressed to the Curate of Blagdon* (Bath and London, 1802), p. 56; *The Force of Contrast, or Quotations, accompanied with Remarks, submitted to the consideration of all those who have interested themselves in what is called the Blagdon Controversy* (Bath, 1801); *Elucidations of Character, occasioned by a Letter from the Rev R. Lewis. by Rev John Boak* (Bath, 1802); Rev. John Boak, *Calumny refuted, in reply to several charges advanced by Mr Spencer of Wells, in his pamphlet called Truths, his advertisements and Handbills* (Bath, 1802).

116. More to Wilberforce, 10 Sept. 1802, Duke University Library, Special Collections.

117. Roberts, *Memoirs*, vol. 2, p. 67.

118. Rev. Thomas Drewitt, *Illustrations of Falsehood, in reply to some assertions contained in Mr Spencer's late Publication* (Bath, 1802).

119. Roberts, *Memoirs*, vol. 2, pp. 67–72.

120. Myers, "Cultural Politics of the Blagdon Controversy," pp. 243–44.

121. Stott, "Patriotism and Providence," pp. 39–55; Colley, *Britons*, pp. 275–76.

122. Anna Clark, *The Struggle for the Breeches: Gender and the Making of the British Working Class* (Berkeley: University of California Press, 1995), pp. 36–39; Laqueur, *Religion and Respectability*, p. 242.

123. Wollstonecraft, "Vindication of the Rights of Woman," in Todd and Butler, *Works*, vol. 5, p. 271.

124. *Monthly Magazine* 4 (1797): 415; 5 (1798): 319; 6 (1798): 334; Ruth Watts, *Gender, Power and the Unitarians in England, 1760–1860* (Harlow: Longmans, 1998), p. 72; Catherine Cappe, *Memoirs of the late Mrs. Catherine Cappe, written by herself* (Boston, 1824); and, for Eliza Fletcher, *Autobiography of Mrs. [Eliza] Fletcher, of Edinburgh* (Carlisle, 1874), p. 68; unpublished paper by Jane Rendall, Feminism and Enlightenment seminar, May 2000.

125. Clare Midgeley, *Women against Slavery* (London: Routledge, 1993), p. 48.

126. Gleadle, "British Women and Radical Politics," in Vickery, *Women, Privilege, and Power*, p. 138; Philip Hemery le Breton, ed., *Memoirs, Miscellanies and Letters of the late Lucy Aiken* (London, 1864), p. 137.

127. Margaret S. Carhart, *The Life and Work of Joanna Baillie* (New Haven, Conn.: Yale University Press, 1923), p. 174.

128. Postscript from Margaret Wodrow to Mary Kenrick in John Wodrow to William Kenrick, Feb. 1803, London, Dr. Williams Library, 24.157, f. 237.

129. Norma Clarke, "The Rise and Fall of the British Woman of Letters," in Sarah Knott and Barbara Taylor, eds., *Women and Enlightenment: A Comparative History* (London: Palgrave, forthcoming).

130. Cecilia Brightwell, *Memorials of the Life of Amelia Opie* (Norwich, 1854), p. 126.

131. Ellis, *Memoir of Mrs. Barbauld*, vol. 2, p. 272.

132. Lucy Aikin, *An Epistle on Women* (London, 1810), pp. 4–53.

133. Leonore Davidoff and Catherine Hall, *Family Fortunes: Men and Women of the Middle Classes* (London: Hutchinson, 1987), pp. 1–115.

134. For a conservative linkage of protecting the family with participating in politics, see minutes of the Pitt Club, composed of tradesmen, 1813, and Castle Corporation Minute Book, Norfolk Record Office, MS 502; for liberal articulations of the link between domesticity and politics, see *Oeconomist* 1 (1798): 69, 129–30; this is a different interpretation of middle-class language than that of Dror Wahrman, *Imagining the Middle Class: The Political Representation of Class in Britain, c. 1780–1840* (Cambridge: Cambridge University Press, 1992), p. 398, who argues that until the 1830s, middle-class political and domestic virtues were rarely coupled. The title of the *Oeconomist*, a Newcastle journal, links domestic and political economy; its pages praise domestic virtue and middle-class virtue and explicitly state that to protect a family, a man must be an active citizen.

CHAPTER SEVEN: THE MARY ANNE CLARKE AFFAIR AND THE SYSTEM OF CORRUPTION

1. For a good, detailed account of the Mary Ann Clarke affair, see Peter Spence, *The Birth of Romantic Radicalism: War, Popular Politics and English Radical Reformism, 1800–1815* (Aldershot, Hants: Scolar Press, 1996), pp. 109–35.

2. J. E. Cookson, *The Friends of Peace: Anti-war Liberalism in England, 1793–1815* (Cambridge: Cambridge University Press, 1982), p. 180.

3. John Brewer, *The Sinews of Power: War, Money and the English State 1688–1783* (New York: Knopf, 1989), p. 75.

4. For an interpretation that stresses the success of this consensus, see Linda Colley, *Britons: Forging the Nation 1707–1837* (New Haven, Conn.: Yale University Press, 1992), pp. 97, 310. However, this chapter presents a different perspective.

5. Philip Harling's excellent article, "The Duke of York Affair (1809) and the Complexities of War-Time Patriotism," *Historical Journal* 39 (1996): 963–84, argues that conservatives could use patriotism to criticize royalty. He also explores liberal, critical patriotism in "Leigh Hunt's *Examiner* and the Language of Patriotism," *English Historical Review* 111 (1996): 1159–81. This chapter concurs with Harling's arguments and applies the argument of conditional patriotism to provincial opinion and the East India Company, which have not previously been studied in this context.

6. Cookson, *Friends of Peace*, p. 180; *Cobbett's Political Register* 1 (1802): 683, 791; 11 (1807): 967.

7. M. W. Patterson, *Sir Francis Burdett and His Times (1770–1844)* (London: Macmillan, 1931), p. 187.

8. Philip Harling, *The Waning of "Old Corruption": The Politics of Economical Reform in Britain, 1779–1846* (Oxford: Clarendon Press, 1996), pp. 22–23.

9. Adam Smith, *The Theory of Moral Sentiments*, ed. D. D. Raphael and A. L. MacFie (Oxford: Clarendon Press, 1976), p. 55.

10. J. Burton, *Lectures on Female Education and Manners* (Rochester, 1793), vol. 2, p. 166. For similar sentiments about the superiority of the hardworking middle-class man to the dependent aristocrat, see T. Colfox to William [last name not recorded], 18 Apr. 1818, Dorset Record Office, D/COL B7; and [Elizabeth Hamilton], *Memoirs of the Modern Philosophers* (Bath and London, 1800), vol. 3, p. 245.

11. *A Circumstantial Report of the Evidence and Proceedings upon Charges preferred against HRH the Duke of York* (London, 1809), p. 613.

12. Paul Berry, *By Royal Appointment: A Biography of Mary Ann Clarke, Mistress of the Duke of York* (London: Femina, 1970), pp. 20–45.

13. *The Recollections of Mrs. Mary Anne Clarke: Exhibiting the Secret History of the Court of St. James, and of the Cabinet of Great Britain, for a series of years, and containing anecdotes and biographical sketches of many illustrious personages, communicated to her by H.R.H. the Duke of York* (London, [1811]), vol. 1, p. xxxi, in PRO TS 11/120.

14. *Minutes of Evidence taken before the Committee of the Whole House on the Conduct of HRH the Commander-in-Chief* (London, 1809), p. 242.

15. Pierre F. M'Callum, *The Rival Queens, or which is the Darling? containing the secret history of the origin of the late investigation in answer to Mrs Clarke's "Rival Princes"* (London, 1810) p. 59.

16. Iain McCalman, *Radical Underworld: Prophets, Revolutionaries and Pornographers In London, 1795–1840* (Cambridge: Cambridge University Press, 1988), p. 41.

17. Derek Jarrett, *Britain 1688–1815* (New York: St. Martin's Press, 1965), p. 434; Harling, *Waning*, pp. 63–83.

18. *A Letter to the RT Hon CJ Fox on the Subject of his Conduct upon the Charges made by Mr Paul against the Marquis Wellesley. to which are annexed a faithful copy of the First Letter from the East India Directors to the Marquis, which was sent; and also a faithful copy of the dispatch proposed to be sent to the Marquis from the East India Directors* (London, 1806).

19. Philip Lawson, *The East India Company: A History* (London: Longman, 1993), p. 185. For the debate on Wellesley, see Philip Francis, *Speeches in the House of Commons on the War with the Mahrattas* (London, 1805); John Hudleston, *Substance of a Speech delivered in the House of Commons, on Friday, April 5, 1805, on the motion of Philip Francis* (London, 1805); *A Review of the Affairs of India, from the Year 1798, to the Year 1806*, 2d ed. (London, 1807); Charles Maclean, M.D., *The Affairs of Asia considered in their Effects on the Liberties of Britain, in a series of Letters, addressed to the Marquis Wellesley, late Governor-General of India*, 2d ed. (London, 1806).

20. *Cobbett's Political Register* 11 (1807): 175; Patterson, *Sir Francis Burdett and His Times*, p. 180.

21. *History of the Westminster and Middlesex Elections; in the Month of November 1806* (London, 1807).

22. [J. Paull], *A Second Plain Letter to his Royal Highness, wherein His Plain Duties to himself, his Wife, his Child, and to the Country, are more plainly shewn than in the first; also, that His Royal Highness is an Accomplished Gentleman, a Virtuous Man, a Good Christian, and a Sound Philosopher. with Remarks on the Correspondence upon his Claim for Military Rank and Employment; which likewise prove the Duke of York to be a Great Author, a Good Swimmer, and an Able General* (London, [1806–7]), p. 13.

23. J. Ann Hone, *For the Cause of Truth: Radicalism in London 1796–1821* (Oxford: Clarendon Press, 1982), p. 151.

24. Paul Johnson, "Civilising Mammon: Fraud and Profit in Nineteenth-Century London," in http://www.fathom.com/fks/catalog/feature.jhtml?story_id=121984&featurePageNumber=1, Fathom: the source for online learning.

25. "Andrew Cochrane Johnstone," in Leslie Stephen, ed., *Dictionary of National Biography* (London, 1887), vol. 11, p. 167; *Cobbett's Political Register* 11 (1807): 410.

26. *Cobbett's Political Register* 11 (1807): 15, 962.

27. Spence, *Birth of Romantic Radicalism*, p. 95.

28. *Cobbett's Political Register* 14 (1808): 355.

29. Hone, *For the Cause of Truth*, p. 171.

30. McCalman, *Radical Underworld*, p. 38.

31. [Eaton Stannard Barrett], *The Miss-Led General; a Serio-Comic, Satiric, Mock-heroic, Romance*, 2d ed. (London, 1808). Barrett had profited from an earlier successful satire on the Whigs in the Ministry of All the Talents.

32. McCalman, *Radical Underworld*, p. 38.

33. Spence, *Birth of Romantic Radicalism*, p. 111; Thomas Hague, *A Letter to HRH the Duke of York, or an Exposition of the Circumstances which led to the late Appointment of Sir Hew Dalrymple, and an inquiry into the question, whether he, HRH, as Commander-in-Chief, or his Majesty's ministers, be most responsible to the country* (London, 1808); Thomas Hague, *The Royal Urinead* (London, 1808).

34. Denis Hogan, *An Appeal to the Public and a Farewell Address to the Army* (London 1808), pp. 50–51.

35. Libel trial of Peter Finnerty, 1809, PRO TS11/44/161.

36. McCalman, *Radical Underworld*, p. 40; *Independent Whig*, 12 June 1808. For the prosecution of the *Independent Whig*, see PRO TS 11/40/pt. 1.

37. *Cobbett's Political Register* 11 (1807): 410; 14 (1808): 718.

38. Harling, "Leigh Hunt's *Examiner*," p. 1159.

39. *Examiner* 1 (1808): 674.

40. Spence, *Birth of Romantic Radicalism*, p. 116.

41. Ibid., p. 111.

42. *The trial of Thomas Picton, late governor of Trinidad . . . : for inflicting the torture on Louisa Calderon, by suspending her by the wrist to the ceiling, without any resting place, except a sharp pike for her toe: Tried at Westminster . . . on Monday, Feb. 24, 1806 and found guilty* (London, 1806).

43. Berry, *By Royal Appointment*, pp. 50–76.

44. *Memoirs of Mrs. Mary Ann Clarke, from the age of fifteen years to the present time; including appropriate remarks on her conduct towards the Duke of York* (London, 1809), p. 27; *Sun*, 6 Feb., 4 Apr. 1809.

45. *A Summary Review of the Evidence adduced upon the Charges against His Royal Highness the Duke of York* (London, 1809), p. 23. This pamphlet was reprinted from the *Oracle* newspaper.

46. J. Mason, *Brief Observations on the Present Enquiry into the Conduct of His Royal Highness the Duke of York* (London, 1809), p. 8; for similar argument, see J. Bragge, *An Impartial Examination of the Merits and Demerits of HRH the Duke of York as Commander in Chief* (London, 1811), p. 15.

47. James J. Sack, *From Jacobite to Conservative: Reaction and Orthodoxy in Britain, c. 1760–1832* (Cambridge: Cambridge University Press, 1993), p. 138, quoting *Anti-Jacobin Review* 32 (1809): 322.

48. Spence, *Birth of Romantic Radicalism*, p. 121.

49. *Minutes of Evidence taken before the Committee of the Whole House on the Conduct of HRH the Commander-in-Chief* (London, 1809), p. 122.

50. *Courier*, 21 Feb. 1809; Harling, "Duke of York," p. 985.

51. *Courier*, 15 Feb. 1809.

52. *Courier*, 2 Feb. 1809.

53. *Morning Chronicle*, 22 Mar. 1809.

54. Quoted in Berry, *By Royal Appointment*, pp. 171–73.

55. William Henry Ireland, *The Cyprian of St. Stephen's, or Princely Protection illustrated* (Bath, 1809), p. 23.

56. Arthur Aspinall, *Politics and the Press, c. 1780–1850* (London: Home and Van Thal, 1949), pp. 90, 91, 369; Peter Brett, "Early Nineteenth-Century Reform Newspapers in the Provinces: The Newcastle Chronicle and the Bristol Mercury," in Michael Harris and Tom O'Malley, eds., *Studies in Newspaper and Periodical History* (Westport, Conn.: Greenwood Press, 1995), p. 54.

57. *Sun*, 3 Feb, 1809; Aspinall, *Politics and the Press*, p. 91.

58. *Courier*, 10 Feb. 1809; for examples, *Norfolk Chronicle*, 18 Feb. 1809; *Newcastle Chronicle*, 18 Mar. 1809; *Bury and Norwich Post*, 15 Feb. 1809; *Tyne Mercury*. 14 Feb. 1809.

59. *Courier*, 9 Feb. 1809.

60. *Morning Chronicle*, 7 Feb. 1809; *Independent Whig*, 12 Mar. 1809; *Courier*, 20 Feb. 1809; *Bury and Norwich Post*, 15 Feb. 1809; *Tyne Mercury*, 21 Feb. 1809.

61. *Morning Chronicle*, 13 Feb. 1809.

62. See the very popular play, often performed and reprinted, George Lillo, *The London Merchant, or the History of George Barnwell* (London, 1808 [1731]).

63. [Olivia Wilmot Serres], *Observations and Strictures on the Conduct of Mrs. Clarke, &c &c. by a Lady* (London, 1809), p. 13.

64. *A Circumstantial Report of the Evidence and Proceedings upon Charges preferred against HRH the Duke of York* (London, 1809), p. 601; *Courier*, 15 Feb. 1809, reporting on a sermon.

65. Hugh Kelly, *Memoirs of a Magdalen, or the History of Louisa Mildmay* (London, 1801 [1767]); *Town and Country Magazine* 1–20 (1790–96).

66. *Courier*, 9 Feb. 1809.

67. Pierre F. M'Callum, *The Rival Queens, or which is the Darling? containing the secret history of the origin of the late investigation in answer to Mrs Clarke's "Rival Princes"* (London, 1810), p. 54.

68. Gary Kelly, *The English Jacobin Novel* (Oxford: Clarendon Press, 1976), pp. 17, 30.

69. *Circumstantial Report*, p. vi.

70. *The Horns Exalted over the People; or a New and Complete Book of the Chronicles of the Bishop and his Clarke, containing the Many* AUTHENTIC *and* ECCENTRIC CIRCUMSTANCES *Lately discovered and laid before the Great Council of the United Empire of* GOTHAM; *by the celebrated Mary Ann Clarke, the Royal Concubine, and* ASSISTANTS, *Related in the Oriental Dialect*, 2d ed. (London, 1809), p. 12.

71. Capel Lofft, *On the revival of the cause of Reform in Parliament* (London, 1810 [1809]), p. 10.

72. *Tyne Mercury*, 21 Feb. 1809.

73. *Minutes of Evidence*, p. 255.

74. Ibid., pp. 211, 161.

75. For an illustrated satire on the letters, see *The Magical Note and its Consequences, which set the Country in an Uproar, Displaced a Great Man; and Placed many Little Ones on the Stool of Repentance!!!!!* (London, 1809).

76. *Minutes of Evidence*, p. 385.

77. Ibid., pp. 248–51.

78. Ibid., p. 311.

79. *Circumstantial Report*, p. 8; *Cobbett's Political Register* 15 (1809): 176.

80. *Real John Bull*, 20 Jan. 1822.

81. *Circumstantial Report*, p. 281.

82. *Courier*, 8 Mar. 1809.

83. *Circumstantial Report*, editor's preface, p. v.

84. *Cobbett's Political Register* 15 (1809): 223.

85. Ibid., p. 229.

86. *Minutes of Evidence*, pp. 130, 154.

87. Ibid., p. 147.

88. *Circumstantial Report*, p. 139.

89. *Minutes of Evidence*, p. 107.

90. Ibid., p. 340; *Circumstantial Report*, p. 342.

91. *Courier*, 22 Feb., 8 Mar. 1809; *Morning Chronicle*, 31 Jan. 1809.

92. *Morning Chronicle*, 27 Jan. 1829.

93. *Morning Chronicle*, 20 Feb. 1809.

94. *Bury and Norwich Post*, 19 Apr. 1809.

95. "Paul Pry," *Marmion Travestied; or a Tale of Modern Times* (London: Tegg, 1809), p. 4.

96. *Minutes of Evidence*, pp. 107, 226, 150; *Circumstantial Report*, p. 138.

97. *Circumstantial Report*, p. 408; *Cobbett's Political Register* 15 (1809): 398.

98. *Minutes of Evidence*, pp. 130, 237; *Circumstantial Report*, p. 415.

99. Lawson, *East India Company*, p. 159.

100. *Morning Chronicle*, 3 Apr., 15 Feb. 1809, quoting Charles Grant, the Evangelical EIC official.

101. *Report from the Committee Appointed to inquire into the Existence of any Abuses in the Disposal of the Patronage of the East India Company* (London, 1809), pp. 12, 40.

102. *Examiner* 2 (1809): 224.

103. *Report . . . East India Company*, pp. 78, 167, 116; also *Cobbett's Political Register* 15 (1809): 658.

104. *Report . . . East India Company*, pp. 100, 143.

105. Ibid., pp. 203, 54–55.

106. Ibid., p. 199.

107. For patronage control over Commons seats, see James J. Sack, "The House of Lords and Parliamentary Patronage in Great Britain, 1802–1832," *Historical Journal* 23 (1980): 919.

108. *Report . . . East India Company*, pp. 23–25, 88.

109. Ibid., p. 125; *Cobbett's Political Register* 15 (1809): 576.

110. *Cobbett's Political Register* 15 (1809): 677.

111. *Circumstantial Report*, p. 611.

112. *Tyne Mercury*, 11 Apr. 1809.

113. *Courier,* 22 Mar. 1809.

114. *Circumstantial Report,* p. 309.

115. *Cobbett's Political Register* 15 (1809): 740, 746; John Cannon, *Parliamentary Reform 1640–1832* (Cambridge: Cambridge University Press, 1973), pp. 153–54.

116. Harling, "Duke of York Affair," p. 982; *The Horns Exalted over the People,* pp. 14–15; *Sun,* 16 Mar. 1809.

117. *Morning Chronicle,* 20 Mar. 1809.

118. *Bury and Norwich Post,* 22 Feb. 1809.

119. Spence, *Birth of Romantic Radicalism,* pp. 117–18.

120. *Courier,* 22 Mar. 1809; *Norfolk Chronicle.* 8 Apr. 1809.

121. Eaton Stannard Barrett, *The Setting Sun; or, Devil amongst the Placemen,* by Cervantes Hogg, Esq. (London, 1809), vol. 1, p. 3.

122. *Independent Whig,* 25 June 1809.

123. *Newcastle Chronicle,* 29 Apr. 1809; *Cobbett's Political Register* 15 (1809): 502, 789.

124. Letter from General Heron to Home Office, 15 Mar. 1809, PRO HO 42/96/207.

125. *Cobbett's Political Register* 15 (1809): 794; *Courier,* 30 Mar. 1809.

126. Lofft, *On the revival of the cause of Reform,* p. 8.

127. *Newcastle Chronicle,* 29 Apr. 1809; *Independent Whig,* 9 July 1809; *Norfolk Chronicle,* 15, 22 Apr. 1809.

128. John Pern Tinney, Esq., *A Letter to the Viscount Folkestone, on the Unlawfulness of the Votes of Thanks to Mr. Wardle, and the late Minority* (London, 1809), p. 9.

129. *Circumstantial Report,* pp. 650–62.

130. *Memoirs of Mrs. Mary Ann Clarke,* p. 32.

131. [Serres], *Observations and Strictures on the Conduct of Mrs. Clarke,* pp. 1–5; see also Rev. W. V., *An Address to the Inhabitants of Great Britain, on the Danger of Dissension at the present Alarming crisis* (London, 1809); *Sun,* 3 Apr. 1809; A Citizen, *The Claims of Mr. Wardle to the Thanks of the Country in consequence of his Parliament Conduct on the Occasion of the Charges preferred by him against HRH the Duke of York: considered in a letter addressed to the Mayor of a Respectable Corporation* (London, 1809), p. 7.

132. Harling, "Duke of York," p. 967.

133. *Independent Whig,* 9 Apr. 1809.

134. *Cobbett's Political Register* 15 (1809): 346.

135. *Tyne Mercury,* 7 Mar. 1809; very similar editorial in *Bury and Norwich Post,* 5 Apr. 1809.

136. All copies were burned, except one. *The Recollections of Mrs. Mary Anne Clarke: Exhibiting the Secret History of the Court of St. James, and of the Cabinet of Great Britain, for a series of years, and containing anecdotes and biographical sketches of many illustrious personages, communicated to her by H.R.H. the Duke of York* (London, [1811]), vol. 1, in PRO TS 11/120.

137. Mary Ann Clarke, *The Rival Princes; or, a Faithful Narrative of Facts, relating to Mrs. M. A. Clarke's Political Acquaintance with Colonel Wardle, Major Dodd, &c. &c. &c. who were concerned in the Charges against the Duke of York; together with a variety of Authentic and Important Letters, and curious and interesting anecdotes of several persons of political notoriety* (London, 1810), vol. 1, p. 76.

138. Berry, *By Royal Appointment*, p. 190; A Citizen, *A Second Letter of the Claims of Colonel Wardle to the Thanks of the Country; occasioned by the late trial in Westminster Hall* (London, 1809).

139. *Independent Whig*, 30 July 1809.

140. *Cobbett's Political Register* 15 (1809): 748, 755.

141. *The Plan of Reform proposed by Sir Francis Burdett, with a response by Perceval*, 2d ed. (London, 1809), p. 18.

142. *Speech of the Rt. Hon. William Windham, in the House of Commons, May the 26th, 1809, on Mr. Curwen's Bill, "For better securing the independence and purity of Parliament, by preventing the procuring or obtaining of seats by corrupt practices"* (London, 1810), p. 11.

143. Lofft, *On the revival of the cause of Reform*, p. 8.

144. Harling, *Waning of "Old Corruption,"* p. 119.

145. *The Plan of Reform proposed by Sir Francis Burdett.*

146. Linda Colley argues that the royal jubilee showed that the Clarke affair did not endanger royalty; *Britons*, pp. 217–24. My interpretation is different.

147. *Examiner* 2 (1809): 132.

148. *A letter to Mrs. Clarke, on her Late Connection with the Duke of York, and the Charges preferred against His Royal Highness, by G. L. Wardle, Esq., by A Friend to Church and State* (London, 1809), pp. 23–28.

149. Barrett, *Setting Sun*, p. 65.

150. *The Plan of Reform proposed by Sir Francis Burdett* (London, 1809); *Independent Whig*, 12 Feb., 2 Apr., 23 July 1809; *Cobbett's Political Register* 15 (1809): 425.

151. *Independent Whig*, 21 Jan. 1810. For prosecution, see PRO TS 11/40/pt. 2.

152. Harling, "Leigh Hunt's *Examiner*," p. 1171.

153. Hone, *For the Cause of Truth*, pp. 204, 180.

154. Lawson, *East India Company*, pp. 137–41.

155. Clare Midgeley, "From Supporting Missions to Petitioning Parliament: British Women and the Evangelical Campaign against *Sati* in India, 1813–1830," in Kathryn Gleadle and Sarah Richardson, eds., *Women in British Politics, 1760–1860: The Power of the Petticoat* (New York: St. Martin's Press, 2000), pp. 75–76; Karen Chancey, "The Star in the East: The Controversy over Christian Missions to India, 1805–1813," *Historian* 60 (1998): 507–22; Anthony Webster, "The Political Economy of Trade Liberalization: The East India Company Charter Act of 1813," *Economic History Review* 43 (1990): 404–19. Webster questions whether the government actually responded to pressure from merchants or opened up trade for strategic reasons, but the fact remains that merchants pressured Parliament.

156. Dror Wahrman argues that the activists and politicians appealed to the "middle class" in 1806–7 on grounds of taxation; this chapter demonstrates another angle of middle-class political consciousness and a moment of middle-class agitation; Warhman, *Imagining the Middle Class: The Political Representation of Class in Britain, c. 1780–1840* (Cambridge: Cambridge University Press, 1995), pp. 148–85.

157. Harling, *Waning of "Old Corruption,"* p. 264.

158. For instance, General Sir George Napier could not gain the position he wanted because his interest was with "Bunbury," who had alienated the royal family by calling for reform. He hoped that his counterpart Berkeley's interest would succeed with the duke. Gen. Sir George Napier to Col. Sir John Colborne, KCB 52nd Regiment, 15 Oct. 1820, Duke University Library, Special Collections.

CHAPTER EIGHT: QUEEN CAROLINE AND THE SEXUAL POLITICS OF THE BRITISH CONSTITUTION

1. *Times,* 6 June 1820, quoted in E. A. Smith, *A Queen on Trial: The Affair of Queen Caroline* (Stroud: Allen Sutton, 1994), pp. 29–30.

2. See Anna Clark, *The Struggle for the Breeches*: Gender and the Making of the British Working Class (Berkeley: University of California Press, 1995), pp. 164–74; Anna Clark, "Queen Caroline and the Sexual Politics of Popular Culture in London, 1820," *Representations* 31 (1990): 47–68. Some of the evidence in this chapter first appeared in the *Representations* article. For an excellent recent discussion about class and Caroline, see Nicholas Rogers, *Crowds, Culture and Politics in Georgian Britain* (Oxford: Clarendon Press, 1998), p. 259. For other work on Queen Caroline, see Thomas W. Laqueur, "The Queen Caroline Affair: Politics as Art in the Reign of George IV," *Journal of Modern History* 54 (1982): 417–66; Jonathan Fulcher, "The Loyalist Response to the Queen Caroline Agitations," *Journal of British Studies* 34 (1995): 481–502; Dror Wahrman, "'Middle-Class' Domesticity Goes Public: Gender, Class and Politics from Queen Caroline to Queen Victoria," *Journal of British Studies* 32 (1993): 396–432; Tamara L. Hunt, "Morality and Monarchy in the Queen Caroline Affair," *Albion* 23 (1991): 697–722.

3. E. A. Smith, *George IV* (New Haven, Conn.: Yale University Press, 1999), pp. 21, 30, 62.

4. A Civilian, *Free Thoughts on Seduction, Adultery, and Divorce, with Reflections on the Gallantry of Princes, particularly those of the Blood-Royal of England* (London, 1771).

5. For the following narrative, see Flora Fraser, *The Unruly Queen: The Life of Queen Caroline* (New York: Knopf, 1996); and Thea Holme, *Caroline: A Biography of Caroline of Brunswick* (New York: Atheneum, 1980).

6. Diary of Thomas LeMesurier, 1794, Bandinel Family Papers, Duke University Library, Special Collections, f. 72.

7. [Charlotte Bury], *Diary illustrative of the Times of George the Fourth, interspersed with original letters from the Late Queen Caroline* (London, 1838), vol. 1, p. 37.

8. John Williams [Anthony Pasquin], *A Looking Glass for the Royal Family* (London, 1797), p. 9. This pamphlet refuted these rumors.

9. *A Review, with Suitable Remarks and Reflections, of the Astonishing Misrepresentations and Gross contradictions which have been Circulated in all the Daily Papers relative to a Late Domestic Fracas in a Family of the First Rank; and which has been fortunately succeeded by a Perfect Reconciliation* (London, 1796), p. 45. For the Prince of Wales's defense, see Williams, *A Looking Glass for the Royal Family*; *A Review of the Conduct of the Prince of Wales, from his Entrance into Public Life, till his late Offer to Undertake the Government of Ireland* (London, 1797).

10. *True Briton*, 27, 31 May, 1 June 1796; *Sun*, 28 May 1796.

11. *St. James Chronicle*, 26–28 May 1796.

12. Amelia Murray, *Recollections from 1803–1837*, p. 47, quoted in Holme, *Caroline*, p. 60.

13. Nathaniel Jefferys, *Review of the Conduct of the Prince of Wales*, 2d ed. (London, 1806). The prince paid hacks to write pamphlets against Jefferys; see handwritten note in this British Library copy, 8135.cc.3 (8).

14. *The Royal Wanderer* (London, 1820), p. 509.

15. Bury, *Diary*, vol. 1, p. 33.

16. James J. Sack, *The Grenvillites, 1801–29: Party Politics and Factionalism in the Age of Pitt and Liverpool* (Urbana: University of Illinois Press, 1979), p. 98.

17. British lady's letterbook, 23 Feb. 1807, Duke University Library, Special Collections. This letterbook belonged to a woman well connected at court.

18. *Royal Investigation; or, Authentic Documents containing the Acquittal of HRH the P——ss of W——s.* (London: Hughes, 1807).

19. *An Admonitory Letter to H.R.H. the Prince of Wales on the Subject of the Late Delicate Inquiry* (London, 1806), p. 24.

20. *Cobbett's Political Register* 10 (1806): 261–70.

21. *The Royal Eclipse* (London, 1807), p. 6; See also *A Third Plain Letter to his Royal Highness, upon his plain duties to himself, his Wife, his Child, and to the Country* (London, 1807); Barrister at Law, *A Letter to the Earl of Moira: in which is contained, a Review of the Libelous Pamphlets lately published with Intent to Defame the Character of the Prince of Wales; with Observations upon their Dangerous Tendency and Effects* (London, 1806).

22. Iain McCalman, *Radical Underworld: Prophets, Revolutionaries and Pornographers in London, 1795–1840* (Cambridge: Cambridge University Press, 1988), pp. 41–42; Andrew Barlow, *The Prince and His Pleasures: Satirical Images of George IV and His Circle* (Brighton: Royal Pavilion Libraries and Museums, 1997), p. 12.

23. For the prince's drunkenness, see Bury, *Diary*, vol. 1, p. 59; for indolence, see Smith, *George IV*, p. 172.

24. Fraser, *Unruly Queen*, p. 231.

25. Caroline to George, 1813, letters and papers relating to Queen Caroline, Liverpool Papers, BL Add. Ms. 38,565, f. 14.

26. Peter Spence, *The Birth of Romantic Radicalism: War, Popular Politics and English Radical Reformism, 1800–1815* (Aldershot, Hants: Scolar Press, 1996), p. 185.

27. *Total Acquittal of the Princess of Wales, &c. Substance of the Debate on the Motion of Mr. Cochrane Johnston, in the House of Commons, March 5, 1813, respecting the letter addressed to the Speaker, by her Royal Highness, the Princess of Wales* (London, 1813), p. 57.

28. Charles Dunne, *The Mystery of Royal Separation developed, for the Future Historian of the House of Brunswick* (London, 1814), pp. 19–20.

29. J. Ann Hone, *For the Cause of Truth: Radicalism in London 1796–1821* (Oxford: Clarendon Press, 1982), p. 221; *Address of the Freeholders of Middlesex* (London, 1813), p. 3.

30. Peter Pindar, *The Eldest Chick of the R——l Brood; the Trial of the Dove before Judge Bear; and her Appeal to the Assembly of Birds. Including the Accusations of the Toad and the Viper* (London, 1813?), p. 37.

31. Hannah Colfax née Abbott, 1788–1873, journal of her visit to London, 6 Mar. 1814, Dorset Record Office, D43/F15.

32. Dunne, *Mystery of Royal Separation*, p. 27.

33. *Secret Memoirs of a Prince, or a Peek Behind the Scenes* (London, 1816), p. 59.

34. For Fitzherbert, see *Admonitory Letter*, p. 27; for Lady Hertford and other mistresses, see Barlow, *The Prince and His Pleasures*, p. 52; etching by William Elmes, *Triumph of Love and Folly*, London, 1812, in *Print Room Catalogue* (London, summer 1999), depicting the Lady Hertford, enormous and wearing a coronet, processing to Parliament with the prince, who is drunk.

35. George Cruikshank, "A Leap Year Drawing Room, or the Pleasures of Petticoat Government" (London: Benbow, June 1820), in PRO TS 11/115/82.

36. George Cruikshank, *The Court at Bright a la Chinese!!* (1816), in Barlow, *The Prince and His Pleasures*, p. 19. For Baartman, see Sander L. Gilman, *Difference and Pathology: Stereotypes of Sexuality, Race and Madness* (Ithaca, N.Y.: Cornell University Press, 1985), pp. 85–94.

37. Henry Jephson, *The Platform: its Rise and Progress* (London, 1892), vol. 1, pp. 504–5; James Vernon, *Politics and the People* (Cambridge: Cambridge University Press, 1993), p. 301; Jonathan Fulcher, "The English People and Their Constitution after Waterloo: Parliamentary Reform, 1815–1817," in James Vernon, ed., *Rereading the Constitution* (Cambridge: Cambridge University Press, 1996), pp. 52–82.

38. His name was often spelled "Bergami."

39. *The Attempt to Divorce the Princess of Wales impartially Considered*, 4th ed. (London, 1816); *A Letter to John, Lord Eldon, Lord High Chancellor of Great Britain, on the Rumor of an intended Royal Divorce*, 2d ed. (London, 1816).

40. John Galiffe to John Backhouse, Geneva, 15 Sept. 1820, Backhouse Papers, Duke University Library, Special Collections.

41. Brougham to Lord Hutchinson, 14 June 1819, Liverpool Papers, BL, Add. Ms. 38,565, ff. 20–24.

42. Minute of Cabinet, excerpted in Smith, *Queen on Trial*, p. 10.

43. Lady Charlotte Lindsay, quoted in Smith, *Queen on Trial*, p. 73.

44. Minute of Cabinet, 10 Feb. 1820, Liverpool Papers, BL, Add. Ms. 38,565, f. 29.

45. Smith, *Queen on Trial*, pp. 14–17.

46. Copy of a letter from Geo. Canning to Mr. Bolton of Liverpool, 22 Dec. 1820, Backhouse papers, Duke University Library, Special Collections. For Canning as possible lover, see Fraser, *Unruly Queen*, pp. 123–25.

47. Brougham to Lord H., 3 Apr. 1820, Liverpool Papers, BL, Add. Ms. 28, 284, f. 27.

48. Fraser, *Unruly Queen*, pp. 399–409.

49. Roger Fulford, *The Trial of Queen Caroline* (New York: Stein and Day, 1968), p. 41.

50. Henry Cockburn, *Memorials of his Own Time* (Edinburgh, 1856), p. 374.

51. Anna Maria Larpent, diary, vol. 11, 6 May 1820, Huntington Library.

52. Lady Cowper to Frederick Lamb, 17 Aug. 1820, quoted in Smith, *Queen on Trial*, p. 74.

53. J. C. Hobhouse, diary, 2 Oct. 1820, quoted in Smith, *Queen on Trial*, p. 112.

54. Lady Charlotte Lindsay's Journal of the Queen's Trial 1820, BL, Add. Ms. 37,728, ff. 44–70.

55. Brougham to Hutchisson, 1820, Liverpool Papers, BL, Add. Ms. 38,565, f. 95.

56. William Cobbett to the Queen, 25 June, and Anne Cobbett to James Cobbett, 7 Oct. 1820, quoted in Smith, *Queen on Trial*, pp. 49, 114.

57. Caroline to George IV, 7 Aug. 1820, Liverpool Papers, BL, Add. Ms. 38,565, f. 255.

58. *Black Dwarf* 5 (1820): 173. For other examples of similar language, see Address from 16 Aug. 1820, in *Selections from the Queen's Answers to Various Addresses* (London, 1821), and many examples in Francis Place Collection, British Library, set 18.

59. Lord John Russell, *A Letter to Lord Wilberforce and a Petition to the King, with a Preface* (London, 1820), p. ix.

60. Lady Charlotte Lindsey, quoted in Smith, *Queen on Trial*, pp. 74.

61. Lord Holland to William Wilberforce, Nov. 1820, Wilberforce letters, Duke University Library, Special Collections.

62. Rogers, *Crowds, Culture and Politics*, p. 256.

63. *Black Dwarf* 5 (1820): 173.

64. "Cotton Weavers Broadsheet," PRO HO 40/16/388; clipping from *Englishman*, Sept. 1820, "Answer to the Address from the Weavers of Spitalfields," in Francis Place Collection, British Library, set 18.

65. Report, 17 June 1820, PRO HO 44/2/156.

66. Anonymous letters, 1820, Liverpool Papers, BL, Add. Ms. 38565, ff. 180, 196, 207, 223, 279.

67. McCalman, *Radical Underworld*, pp. 167–74.

68. Hannah More to William Wilberforce, undated, 1820, Wilberforce letters, Duke University Library, Special Collections.

69. James J. Sack, *From Jacobite to Conservative: Reaction and Orthodoxy in Britain, c. 1760–1832* (Cambridge: Cambridge University Press, 1993), p. 142.

70. *John Bull,* 17 Dec. 1820, 18, 4 Feb., 14 Jan. 1821.

71. Diary of Anne Hamond, July 1821, Norfolk Record Office, HMN 5/20/1.

72. As I have written in Clark, *Struggle for the Breeches,* and Clark, "Queen Caroline."

73. Marcus Wood, *Radical Satire and Print Culture 1790–1822* (Oxford: Clarendon Press, 1994), p. 258.

74. George Wells of Weston to Home Office, PRO 40/14/273.

75. *Remarks on the Proceedings against HM the Queen* (London, 1820), p. 20.

76. Henry Crabb Robinson, quoted in Smith, *Queen on Trial,* p. 26.

77. For another example, a pamphlet portrayed Caroline as damaging the "honor of the British empire"; *Gynecocracy; with an Essay on Fornication, Adultery, and Incest; by the Author of Rumours of Treason* (London, 1821), p. 584.

78. *The Palace of John Bull* (London, 1820), p. 4.

79. *The Letters of Patraie Fides, upon the Female Loyalty of 1820* (London, [1820]), pp. 2, 6, 18. See also *The Declaration of the People of England to their Sovereign Lord the King* (London, 1821); *Address to the King. From Inhabitants or Owners of Property,* in Newcastle clippings, British Library, 8135.e.4

80. *Selections from the Queen's Answers to Various Addresses Presented to Her, Together with Her Majesty's Extraordinary Letter to the King; and an Introduction; and Observations illustrative of their tendency,* 3d ed. (London, 1821), p. 1.

81. Hannah More to the Rev. Charles Hoare, 18 Sept. 1820, Huntington Library, manuscript 30617.

82. R. N. Bacon, *Independent Remarks on the Queen's Case by the Editor of the Norwich Mercury* (Norwich, 1820), p. 32.

83. Charles Tennyson, *Observations on the Proceedings against the Queen addressed to his Constituents,* 3d ed. (London, 1821), pp. 12, 27.

84. Lady Cowper's diary, quoted in Smith, *Queen on Trial,* p. 75.

85. *A Report of the Speeches and Proceedings at the Meeting of the County of Northumberland held at Morpeth,* 10 Jan. 1821, revised from *Newcastle Chronicle* of 13 and 20 Jan. 1821, Newcastle clippings, British Library, ff. 28, 15.

86. *An Address to Britons, upon the Triumph of the Queen's Innocence, by the Author of South-American Address* (London, 1821), p. 3.

87. Charles Phillips, Esq., Barrister at Law, *The Queen's Case Stated* 14th ed. (London, 1820), p. 26.

88. *A Word with the People of England, not Forgetting Mr. Wilberforce, and his Parliamentary Friends* (London, 1820); John Evans, *A Sermon preached at the Independent Chapel, Malmsbury, Wiltshire* (London, 1821), pp. 22–23.

89. Tennyson, *Observations,* p. 26.

90. Sack, *From Jacobite to Conservative,* p. 40.

91. Speech of Mr. Wilberforce, 13 Feb. 1821, Newcastle clippings, British Library, 8135.e.4, f. 45.

92. "Copy of an Address to the Queen of England, now signing by the Inhabitants of Taunton, and its Neighbourhood, for the Purpose of being presented to Her Majesty," Somerset Record Office, DD/X/BRO2 f. 31. See also "The Following Address from the Barons and Inhabitants of Sandwich, has been presented to her Majesty the Queen," Kent Record Office, Sa/Zp2.

93. A Presbyterian, *A Vindication of the Ministers of the Church of Scotland, who have prayed for the Queen by Name, notwithstanding the Order in Council on the Subject,* 2d ed. (Edinburgh, 1820), p. 5.

94. William Mackie, comp., and David Stevenson, ed., *The Diary of a Canny Man. 1818–1828. Adam Mackie. Farmer, Merchant, and Innkeeper in Fyvie* (Aberdeen: Aberdeen University Press, 1991), p. 132.

95. J. Brittain, May 1820, PRO HO 44/2/170, quoted in Clark, "Queen Caroline," p. 65.

96. John Mackinnon ms. autobiography, Strathclyde Regional Archives, TD 743/1–3, 1859, f. 75, quoted in Clark, *Struggle for the Breeches,* p. 339 n. 38.

97. See [William Hone], *The Right Divine of Kings to Govern Wrong* (London, 1821).

98. Princess Lieven, quoted in Smith, *Queen on Trial,* p. 40.

99. W. J. Fox, *A Funeral Sermon for Caroline Queen of England, delivered at Parliament-Court Chapel* (London, 1821), p. 5.

100. *Sultan Sham and His Seven Wives. by Hudibras the Younger* (London, 1820). See also *The Queen and the Mogul; a Play, in two acts, adapted for Theatrical Representation, as performed in a Theatre Royal* (London, 1820); *The Queen's Matrimonial Ladder* (London, 1820), p. 17.

101. H. W. Fitz-George, *Memoirs of the Late Mrs. King, (otherwise the Diamond Queen)* (London, [1820]).

102. *Curious in Diplomacy, Dealers in Cat's Meat, and Home-Bread Leaches* (London, 1820), Queen Caroline Collection, British Library 1852.b.9.

103. Edgell Rickword, "William Hone," in *Radical Squibs and Loyal Ripostes* (London, 1971), p. 13.

104. *A Peep at th P*V****N; or, Boiled Mutton with Caper Sauce at the Temple of Joss* (London, 1820), p. 6.

105. *R——L Rumping!! Or, the Courtly Insult to an Illustratious Personage* (London, 1821), probably by John Fairburn.

106. Reports to Home Office, PRO HO 44/2/192; PRO HO 44/2/182; PRO HO 40/14/135.

107. *Tyne Mercury,* after July 1820, in Newcastle clippings, British Library, f. 7; see also cuttings, 17 July, 7 Sept., 18 Oct., 1820, 3 Apr. 1821, Manchester collection of cuttings, Manchester Public Library MPL q. 942.7389.M1, f. 35, 51, 53, 41; letter from D. Grant, Bridgend, Perth, 13 July 1821, Scottish Home Office Papers, Scottish Record Office, RH 2/4, vol. 138, f. 268; J. T. Alston to Home Office, 17 Nov. 1820, PRO HO 102/33/393.

108. Rev. Richard Blacow, *Trial for Libels on her Late Majesty the Queen of England* (London, 1821), p. 12.

109. *Norfolk Chronicle*, 30 Dec. 1820.

110. Rogers, *Crowds, Culture and Politics*, p. 259.

111. Cockburn, *Memorials of his Own Time*, p. 374.

112. J. Webster Wedderburn, *The King's Case Stated; an Appeal to both Houses of Parliament, on the Proceedings Pending Against the Queen* (London, 1820), p. 48.

113. *John Bull*, 31 Dec. 1820, 11 Jan., 4 Feb., 11 Mar. 1821.

114. *The Loyalist Magazine, complete; presented to his Majesty, containing the Principal Facts . . . published during the Rise, Reign, and Fall of the Caroline Contest* (London, 1821), p. 1.

115. *The Declaration of the People of England to their Sovereign Lord the King* (London, 1821), p. 1.

116. [J. Wasborough], *A Second Letter from the King to his People*, 5th ed. (London, 1821). See also *The Loyalist Magazine* (London, 1821), p. 199; *Norfolk Chronicle*, 30 Dec. 1820.

117. Wahrman, "'Middle-Class' Domesticity Goes Public," pp. 404, 407, makes an important point about the triumph of public opinion in the Caroline affair but argues that a middle-class political identity and domesticity were not linked during the Queen Caroline affair; these quotes suggest a modification of his argument may be necessary.

118. *Norfolk Chronicle*, 30 Dec. 1820.

119. *Selections from the Queen's Answers*, p. 46. For further discussion of middle-class public opinion in the Caroline affair, see Dror Wahrman, *Imagining the Middle Class: The Political Representation of Class in Britain, c. 1780–1840* (Cambridge: Cambridge University Press, 1995), pp. 386–87.

120. Tennyson, *Observations*, p. 7.

121. *R——L Rumping!!* p. 3.

122. G.H.R., a Barrister, *Observations on the Queen's Case, and particularly the evidence of Meidge Barbara Kress: in a letter to a friend on the continent* (London, 1821), p. 90. See also Fulcher, "Loyalist Response," p. 491, for an examination of how the Tories tried to link Whigs and radicals in the Caroline affair.

123. Lord John Russell, *A Letter to Lord Wilberforce and a Petition to the King, with a Preface* (London, 1820), p. xv. See also Thomas Sternpost, John Kelson, and others, *A New Version of John Bull's Songbook* (London, 1821).

124. "Parliamentary Reform" Petition from Inhabitants of Newcastle, 26 Jan. 1820, Newcastle clippings, British Library, f. 35.

125. Charles Maclean, M.D., *The Triumph of Public Opinion, being a Standing Lesson to the Throne, the Parliament, and the People, with proposed Articles of Impeachment against the Ministers of the Crown, in the Case of Her Majesty, Caroline, Queen of England* (London, 1820), p. 2.

126. *Black Dwarf*, 19 July 1820.

127. *A Volley at the Peers, both Spiritual and Temporal, or a Veto upon the Votes of Some of Them. by the Right Hon. John MacRainbow* (London, 1820), p. 7.

128. Amos Ogden to Sir Edward Harbourd, 30 Nov. 1820, Norfolk Office, GTN 11/1.

129. *Traveller,* 13 Sept., 9 Nov. 1820, Francis Place Collections, British Library, set 18.

130. For working-class women insulted in elections, see *Coke and Birch, the Paper War, carried on at the Nottingham Election, 1803, containing the whole of the Addresses, Songs, Squibs etc circulated by the Contending Parties* (Nottingham, 1803); *Leeds Intelligencer,* 22 June 1807; Clark, *Struggle for the Breeches,* p. 161.

131. Anne Cobbett diary and *Times,* 20 Sept. 1820, quoted in Smith, *Queen on Trial,* p. 103.

132. London Diary and Commonplace Book, ff. 181–24, Guildhall Library Ms. 3730.

133. *Copy of an Address to the Queen of England, now signing by the Inhabitants of Taunton,* Somerset Record Office, DD/X/BRO2 f. 31

134. Rogers, *Crowds, Politics and Culture,* p. 250.

135. Fulcher, "Loyalist Response," p. 488.

136. *Morning Post,* 4, 7 Sept. 1820, in Francis Place Collection, British Library, set 18, quoted in Clark, "Queen Caroline," p. 60.

137. *The Letters of Patraie Fides.*

138. *Gynecocracy,* p. 10.

139. J. W. Cunningham, *A Letter to S. C. Whitbread, Esq., M.P. for the County of Middlesex, on the Subject of Female Meetings to Address the Queen* (London, 1820), p. 8.

140. Smith, *Queen on Trial,* p. 108.

141. Maria Carter pocket book, Dorset Record Office, D/COL/F40; diary of Fanny Knatchbull, 6 June 1820; also end-of-year summary, Kent Record Office, U951 F 24; diary of Anne Hamond, July 1821, Norfolk Record Office, HMN 5/20/1.

142. Hon. Charlotte Grimston diary, 1820; Lady Louisa Arrowsmith also followed the events closely, diary, 1820; both in Hertfordshire Record Office.

143. Anna Maria Larpent diary, vol. 11, 18 Aug. 1820, f. 108; 3 Aug. 1820, f. 121, Huntington Library.

144. Anne Lister, manuscript diary, 1, 5 Sept. 1820, Halifax, Calderdale Archives, SH 7/ML/E/4.

145. Hannah More to Wilberforce, undated, 1820, Wilberforce Collection, Duke University Library, Special Collections.

146. Hannah More to the Rev. Charles Hoare, 18 Sept. 1820, Huntington Library manuscript 30617; see also *Morning Post,* 4, 7 Sept. 1820, Francis Place Collection, British Library, set 18; for another middle-class woman attacking Caroline, see *An Address to the Peers of England by an Englishwoman* (London, 1820).

147. *An Englishwoman's Letter to Mrs. Hannah More, on the Present Crisis,* 2d ed. (London, 1820); A Widowed Wife [Jane Alice Sargant], *Two Letters to the Queen, and an Address to the Females of Britain,* 9th ed. [Maidenhead, 1820], p. 21.

148. *John Bull,* 17 Dec. 1820, 28 Jan. 1821.

149. *John Bull,* 24 Dec. 1820.

150. *John Bull,* 14 Jan. 1821.

151. K. D. Reynolds, *Aristocratic Women and Political Society in Victorian Britain* (Oxford: Clarendon Press, 1998), p. 133.

152. For an excellent overview of the role of aristocratic women and Caroline, see James N. McCord, "Taming the Female Politician in Early-Nineteenth-Century England: John Bull versus Lady Jersey," *Journal of Women's History* 13 (2002): 31–54.

153. Wood, *Radical Satire and Print Culture,* pp. 369–71.

154. *The New Pilgrim's Progress, or a Journey to Jerusalem,* 2d ed. (London, 1820), in Edgell Rickford, ed., *Radical Squibs and Loyal Ripostes: Satirical Pamphlets of the Regency Period* (Bath: Adams and Dart, 1971), p. 256.

155. *Gynecocracy,* p. 11.

156. Rev. Richard Blacow, *Trial for Libels on her Late Majesty the Queen of England* (London, 1821).

157. *A Peep at the Peers,* quoted in Fraser, *Unruly Queen,* p. 438.

158. John Clayton, *A Discourse on the Death of her Late Majesty the Queen* (London, 1821), p. 20.

159. Smith, *George IV,* p. 129.

160. Marianne Lady Brougham diary, 1819, University College London Library Manuscript Department; G. T. Garratt, *Lord Brougham* (London: Macmillan, 1935), p. 123.

161. Clark, *Struggle for the Breeches,* pp. 164–74.

162. *Norfolk Chronicle,* 23 Dec. 1820.

163. Maria Carter pocket book, Dorset Record Office, D/COL/F40.

164. Evans, *A Sermon preached at the Independent Chapel, Malmsbury,* pp. 17–18.

165. G.H.R., *Observations on the Queen's Case* (London, 1821); Fraser, *Unruly Queen,* p. 438.

166. "Copy of an Address to the Queen of England, now signed by the Inhabitants of Taunton," Somerset Record Office, DD/X/BRO2, f. 31.

167. Smith, *Queen on Trial,* p. 124.

168. Tennyson, *Observations,* p. 26.

169. Lytton Strachey and Roger Fulford, eds., *The Greville Memoirs 1814–1860* (London: Macmillan, 1938), vol. 1, p. 107.

170. The laurel was an emblem for Caroline's supporters; Charles Churchill, city wood broker, diary, vol. 2, 26 Nov. 1820, Guildhall Library, Ms 5762.

171. Hon. Charlotte Grimston diary, 11 Nov. 1820, Hertfordshire Record Office, D/EV/F; Maria Carter diary, 11 Nov. 1820, Dorset Record Office, D/COL/F40.

172. Rogers, *Crowds, Culture and Politics,* p. 264.

173. *Norfolk Chronicle,* 2 Dec. 1820.

174. James J. Sack, "The House of Lords and Parliamentary Patronage in England, 1803–1832," *Historical Journal* 23 (1980): 926.

175. *The Declaration of the People of England to their Sovereign Lord the King* (London, 1821), p. 38.

176. *A Report of the Speeches and Proceedings at the Meeting of the County of Northumberland held at Morpeth, Jan. 10, 1821. revised from Newcastle Chronicle of 13 and 20 Jan.*, BL Newcastle clippings, f. 28.

177. Maclean, *Triumph of Public Opinion*, p. 5.

178. Bishops Hull vestry book, Somerset Record Office, D/P/b.h. 9/1/1.

179. John Hartnall, *A Sermon, delivered in Salem Chapel, Ipswich . . . occasioned by the Death of Caroline, Queen of England* (Ipswich, 1821).

180. W. J. Fox, *A Funeral Sermon for Caroline Queen of England, delivered at Parliament-Court Chapel* (London, 1821).

181. Evans, *A Sermon preached at the Independent Chapel, Malmsbury,* pp. 22–23.

182. Henry Bathurst, *A Sermon to have been Preached before her Majesty the Queen on the Occasion of her Public Thanksgiving at St. Paul's Cathedral* (London, 1820), pp. 11, 15.

183. Wahrman, "'Middle-Class' Domesticity Goes Public," p. 432.

184. Fulcher, "Loyalist Response," p. 488.

185. Hone, *For the Cause of Truth*, p. 318.

186. "The Speech of the Rt. Hon. George Canning, in the House of Commons, 25 April 1822, on Lord John Russell's Motion for a Reform in Parliament," *Pamphleteer* 20 (1822); "The Speech of John George Lambton, Esq. in the House of Commons on Moving for a Committee to Consider the State of the Representation with a Bill for the Reform of Parliament," *Pamphleteer* 20 (1822); *Substance of the Speeches of Lord John Russell on Moving Resolutions on Reform of Parliament on May 9, 1821 and April 25, 1822* (London, 1822); John Cannon, *Parliamentary Reform 1640–1832* (Cambridge: Cambridge University Press, 1973), p. 183.

187. Henry Cockburn, *Considerations on the Situation of the Elective Franchise as it respects Counties in Scotland; stated in a letter addressed to the land-owners of that part of the United Kingdom* (London, 1821).

CHAPTER NINE: SEXUAL SCANDALS AND POLITICS, PAST AND PRESENT

1. *The Whole Proceedings on the Trial of an Information . . . against John Stockdale; for a libel on the House of Commons* (London, 1790).

2. Linda Colley, *Britons: Forging the Nation 1707–1837* (New Haven, Conn.: Yale University Press, 1992), pp. 280–300.

3. James Epstein, *Radical Expression: Political Language, Ritual and Symbol in England, 1790–1850* (New York: Oxford University Press, 1994), pp. 29–53.

4. Dror Wahrman, *Imagining the Middle Class: The Political Representation of Class in Britain, c. 1780–1840* (Cambridge: Cambridge University Press, 1995), for middle-class consciousness.

5. Dror Wahrman, "Middle-Class Domesticity Goes Public: Gender, Class and Politics from Queen Caroline to Queen Victoria," *Journal of British Studies* 32 (1993): 432.

6. Nicholas Rogers, *Crowds, Culture and Politics in Georgian Britain* (Oxford: Clarendon Press, 1998), pp. 84, 142.

7. Amanda Vickery, "Golden Age to Separate Spheres: A Review of the Categories and Chronology of English Women's History," *Historical Journal* 36, no. 2 (1993): 383–414; see also Vickery, *The Gentleman's Daughter: Women's Lives in Georgian England* (New Haven, Conn.: Yale University Press, 1998); Colley, *Britons*; Amanda Foreman, *Georgiana, Duchess of Devonshire* (London: Harper-Collins, 1998). For similar arguments, see Hannah Barker and Elaine Chalus, eds., *Gender in Eighteenth-Century England: Roles, Representations and Responsibilities* (London and New York: Longman, 1997). For views that politics became more hostile to women and more masculinist, see Dror Wahrman, "*Percy's* Prologue: From Gender Play to Gender Panic in Eighteenth-Century England," *Past and Present* 159 (May 1998): 113–60; Kathleen Wilson, *The Sense of the People: Politics, Culture and Imperialism in England, 1715–1785* (Cambridge: Cambridge University Press, 1995), pp. 102–4.

8. Thomas Amyot to [James Bennett], 31 Dec. 1806, Norfolk Record Office, COL/2/112; R. W. Ketton-Cremer, *A Norfolk Gallery* (London: Faber and Faber, 1945–48), pp. 223–30.

9. K. D. Reynolds, *Aristocratic Women and Political Society in Victorian Britain* (Oxford: Oxford University Press, 1998), p. 133. There were, of course, exceptions: see Sarah Richardson, "The Role of Women in Electoral Politics in Yorkshire during the Eighteen Thirties," *Northern History* 32 (1996): 141; Jill Liddington, *Female Fortune: Land, Gender and Authority. The Anne Lister Diaries and Other Writings, 1883–6* (London and New York: Rivers Oram Press, 1998). Anne Lister instructed her tenants how to vote, but she faced insults to her sexuality during the election, since she was seen as a masculine woman and had erotic relationships with other women.

10. John Bowles, Esq., *Thoughts on the late General Election, as demonstrative of the Progress of Jacobinism*, 4th ed. (London, 1803); *Coke and Birch, the Paper War, carried on at the Nottingham Election, 1803, containing the whole of the Addresses, Songs, Squibs etc circulated by the Contending Parties* (Nottingham, 1803).

11. *Leeds Mercury*, 30 May 1807; *Leeds Intelligencer*, 22 June 1807.

12. *Norfolk Chronicle*, 31 July 1802. Amelia Opie's husband rebuked her for speaking at a Norwich election, but her action was not reported in the newspapers, and it is not clear exactly what she did. Cecilia Brightwell, *Memorials of the Life of Amelia Opie* (Norwich, 1854), p. 117.

13. Wahrman, *Imagining the Middle Class*, p. 196.

14. Paul Langford, "Politics and Manners from Sir Robert Walpole to Sir Robert Peel," *Proceedings of the British Academy* 94 (1997): 118. Thanks to Andy Elfenbein for this reference.

15. Gary Dyer, *British Satire and the Politics of Style* (Cambridge: Cambridge University Press, 1997), p. 51. Of course, conservative satirists had imitated Juvenal in earlier eras as well, as in Johnson's *London*. See Niall Rudd, ed. and trans., *Johnson's Juvenal: London and the Vanity of Human Wishes* (Bristol: Bristol Classical Press, 1981).

16. Dyer, *British Satire and the Politics of Style*, p. 13.

17. Anna Clark, *The Struggle for the Breeches: Gender and the Making of the British Working Class* (Berkeley: University of California Press, 1995).

18. For a brilliant exposition of this scandal, see Judith Walkowitz, *City of Dreadful Delight* (Chicago: University of Chicago Press, 1990).

19. Pippa Norris, "The Battle for the Campaign Agenda," in Anthony King, ed., *Britain at the Polls, 1997* (Chatham, N.J.: Chatham House, 1997), reprinted at http://ksghome.harvard.edu/~.pnorris.shorenstein.ksg/articles.htm.

20. For this and other insights into Anita Hill and Clarence Thomas, see Michael May and Elaine May, "Sex, Lies, and Stereotypes: The Politics of the Hill-Thomas Hearings," in William Graebner, ed., *True Stories from the American Past*, 3d ed. (New York: McGraw-Hill, forthcoming). Thanks to Elaine May for sending me this article.

21. Wahneema Lubiano, "Black Ladies, Welfare Queens, and State Minstrels: Ideological War by Narrative Means," and Kimberle Crenshaw, "Whose Story Is It, Anyway? Feminist and Antiracist Appropriations of Anita Hill," both in Toni Morrison, ed., *Race-ing Justice, En-gendering Power: Essays on Anita Hill, Clarence Thomas, and the Construction of Social Reality* (New York: Pantheon, 1992), pp. 323–63, 401–40.

22. David Brock, *Blinded by the Right* (New York: Crown, 2002).

23. Eli Zaretsky, "The Culture Wars of the 1960s and the Assault on the Presidency," in Lauren Berlant and Lisa Duggan, eds., *Our Monica, Ourselves: The Clinton Affair and the National Interest* (New York: New York University Press, 2001), p. 17.

24. Ellen Willis, "'Tis a Pity He's a Whore," in Berlant and Duggan, *Our Monica, Ourselves*, p. 238; see also Janet R. Jakobsen, "'He Has Wronged America and Women': Clinton's Sexual Conservatism," in Berlant and Duggan, *Our Monica, Ourselves*, p. 294.

INDEX

The first full citation of works that are frequently cited in the endnotes is indexed by author's name or, if there is no author, by title.

effeminacy, 11, 15, 32–33, 59, 109, 183, 229n.45; and aristocracy, 117; and Indians, 85–87, 99–101, 108, 111, 254

elections: American, 222; aristocratic influence over, 14–15, 53–56, 68, 71, 76–78, 80, 212, 242n.4; and crown, 53, 121; family compact in, 63, 66–67, 78, 80; Middlesex, 34–36, 58, 210, 212; national, in 1784, 80, 211–12; Newcastle, 61–68, 217–18; and newspapers, 55; Norwich, 80–82, 217; Nottingham, 216–17; 1784, 67–68, 70–81, 96; Westminster, 61, 69–82, 121, 154, 210; women in, 14, 53–55, 63–67, 70–81, 123, 128, 168–69, 214–15; Yorkshire, 217

electorate, 8, 14, 55–56; proposed expansion of, 58, 59, 72, 135, 214, 217, 231n.78, 250n.152; Westminster, 70

Elizabeth II, 62

Ellis, Markman, 260n.93

empire, British, 14, 16–18, 52, 190, 198, 207; critics of, 97, 111; in India, 85–112, 154; and Mughal empire, 86–87, 108; philosophies of, 85–87; and Roman empire, 85–86, 101

Enlightenment, 4, 20, 46; and humanitarianism, 92; attitudes of toward India, 87; attitudes of toward sodomy, 32

entrepreneurs, political, 3, 21, 41–42, 54, 76, 215

Eon, Chevalier d', 43–44

Erskine, Thomas, 108, 110, 120

Essay on Woman, faux, 28, 31; by Wilkes, 20, 25, 30–31, 34, 40–41, 51, 209, 232n.28

eunuchs, 88, 91–92, 95, 255n.29

Evangelicals, 12, 83, 123–25, 141, 143–45, 153, 158–59, 161, 174–75, 189, 202, 214, 218

Evans, John, 292n.88

Faizabad, 89, 91

Faiz-Baksh, 91, 255n.29

family: compact in elections, 63, 66–67, 78, 80; Indian, 112; political image of, 52, 57, 58, 73, 112, 147, 218, 219, 229n.49, 280n.134. See also dynasties

famine, 92

father, 12; citizen as, 10, 43, 130; king as, 6, 24, 38–39, 57, 118, 122, 147–48, 150, 174, 178, 207, 211

favorites, royal, 22, 32, 45, 72, 117

femininity: and corruption, 64; and purity, 83. See also women

feminism, 16, 126–40, 147, 210, 221–23

Fielding, Henry, 14

Filmer, Robert, 6, 38

Fisher, Michael H., Clash of Cultures, 256n.38; "Women and the Feminine," 256n.40

Fitzherbert, Maria, 178, 183, 185

Fletcher, Anthony, 225n.3

Fletcher, Eliza, 146

Fulcher, Jonathan, 288n.2

fops, 33, 43, 78, 116, 240n.162

Foreman, Amanda, 242.n.1

Foreman, Charlotte, 46

Fox, Charles James, 117, 218; and Burke, 109–10, 115; as clown, 105; and coalition with Lord North, 60–61, 67; and East India Bill, 60, 92–94; and elections, 54, 60, 65, 69–82, 121, 128, 210; and French Revolution, 115; and Hastings, 84–85, 94–95, 104–5, 212; later career of, 154; and Libel Act of 1792, 121; as libertine, 53, 73, 78, 214; personality of, 27; political philosophy of, 58, 72; and Prince of Wales, 123; regency crisis and, 114; Whigs and, 57, 71, 76, 78

Fox, W. J., 194, 206

France, 11, 15, 21, 29, 34, 43, 48, 109, 111, 122, 124, 210

franchise. See electorate

Francis, Philip, 249n.135; and Burke, 116; and Hastings's impeachment, 100; and India, 87, 90, 92; as Junius, 38

Fraser, Flora, Unruly Queen, 225n.1

freedom of speech, 30, 34, 204, 221. See also censorship

freemasons, 36, 44

French Revolution, 4, 17, 83, 109, 111–15, 121–25, 131–32, 147, 179; and women, 115, 136, 147

Friends of the People, 121

Gallagher, Catherine, 229n.51

gambling, 31, 43, 56, 70, 73, 113, 120, 123, 140, 174, 178, 210, 213

Gaveston, Piers, 72

general warrant, 29, 34, 40, 213

genius, 47, 126, 131, 135–36, 139, 141, 145–46

George I, 12, 13

George II, 12, 13, 22

George III, 1, 6, 12, 17, 123; and Bute, 21, 25, 211; and Clarke affair, 164; and daughter, 202; domestic virtue of, 150, 174, 193, 206, 207; and East India Bill, 61, 92–94; fatherly image of, 6, 24, 38–39, 57, 118, 122, 147–48, 150, 174, 178, 207, 211; and Hastings, 94; ac-